HANDSOME JOHNNY

ALSO BY LEE SERVER

Ava Gardner: "Love Is Nothing"

Robert Mitchum: "Baby, I Don't Care"

Asian Pop Cinema: Bombay to Tokyo

The Big Book of Noir

Over My Dead Body

Sam Fuller: Film Is a Battleground

Danger Is My Business

Screenwriter: Words Become Pictures

HANDSOME JOHNNY

The Life and Death of Johnny Rosselli:

Gentleman Gangster,

Hollywood Producer, CIA Assassin

LEE SERVER

St. Martin's Press ⚇ New York

www.stmartins.com

Library of Congress Cataloging-in-Publication Data

Names: Server, Lee, author.
Title: Handsome Johnny : the life and death of Johnny Rosselli : gentleman gangster, Hollywood producer, CIA assassin / Lee Server.
Description: First edition. | New York : St. Martin's Press, [2018] | Includes bibliographical references and index.
Identifiers: LCCN 2018026710| ISBN 9780312566685 (hardcover) | ISBN 9781250038258 (ebook)
Subjects: LCSH: Rosselli, Johnny. | Gangsters—United States—Biography. | Criminals—United States—Biography. | Mafia—United States—History—20th century. | Motion picture industry—United States—History—20th century.
Classification: LCC HV6248.R685 S47 2018 | DDC 364.1092 [B]—dc23
LC record available at https://lccn.loc.gov/2018026710

Our books may be purchased in bulk for promotional, educational, or business use. Please contact your local bookseller or the Macmillan Corporate and Premium Sales Department at 1-800-221-7945, extension 5442, or by email at MacmillanSpecialMarkets@macmillan.com.

First Edition: November 2018

10 9 8 7 6 5 4 3 2 1

For Dean

CONTENTS

"Who shot him?"

"Somebody with a gun."

—DASHIELL HAMMETT, *RED HARVEST*

"Remember, children, *crime does not pay*. Not like it used to."

—JOE E. LEWIS, COMEDIAN

HANDSOME JOHNNY

FLORIDA.
THIRTY-THREE YEARS LATER.

"All right if I turn on the tape recorder?"

"Yeah. It's all right."

"Can you tell me what you remember about that day and what you found?"

"Why are you talking to me anyway? Have you gone through the agency handling this?"

"Through the agency. In Miami?"

"This is still an open case."

"Still an open case, yeah. Unsolved."

"Never closed. And federal testimony was sealed. I haven't discussed this case with anybody for some period of time. When was it, seventy-six?"

"Yes, seventy-six."

"I don't want to give you any information that isn't correct. You're welcome to ask."

"Some guys found him . . . some young guys fishing in the bay."

"Yeah."

"*They found an oil drum floating in the water. They said they could see through the holes in the drum what they thought were human remains. . . .*"

"*They saw something. They called it in. I went to the scene. We had the marine patrol boat come tow the drum up to the shore. We asked them to pull the drum up onto the back of their boat. But they weren't going to put the damn thing on their boat. So they towed it to shore and we got a tow truck to take it out.*"

"*You knew right away there was a body inside the oil drum?*"

"*There was a stink coming out of it. We were pretty sure this thing was going to the M.E. office.*"

"*To the medical examiner?*"

"*Yeah.*"

"*You opened the drum there?*"

"*It was opened at the scene. The tow driver helped us open it.*"

"*What did you see inside?*"

"*It was a big blob.*"

"*A blob?*"

"*Exactly.*"

"*It didn't look human?*"

"*Gray-and-white blob. With a powerful smell.*"

"*The body was decomposed?*"

"*It was bloated. It was bloated as it could get inside of this drum. It was filled up with body gas and deterioration being in the water and salt water coming inside.*"

"*The legs were separated . . . chopped off—*"

"*Right. Jammed in there with the body. Along the side.*"

"*Not a pretty sight.*"

"*It was not something you saw every day. Then again . . .*"

"*The oil drum was never meant to be found, right? An anchor or something probably broke off and it floated up.*"

"*Yeah.*"

"Somebody screwed up."

"That's an opinion. My opinion is that it was not meant to come back to the surface."

"How long was it before you got an ID on the body?"

"Couple of days."

"The report says it was tough getting prints from the fingers because they were so deteriorated. All they could print was part of one thumb."

"Yeah?"

"Said he was shot in the gut, and then the bullet was dug out of the flesh. One of the stories in the paper said he was still alive when they put him in the oil drum."

"Well, if I knew about that I probably wouldn't say . . . because it's still an open case. If some guy somewhere wants to confess, the policeman can know if the guy is for real or he's full of it."

"Murders were pretty common in that part of Florida."

"They were shooting up half of Miami back then."

"Cocaine wars."

"Bodies were being found all the time. I think we came close to setting the world record for homicides."

"But when you found out who was in the oil drum it became a big deal."

"They all came down on us. Government. FBI. The press. The Central Intelligence Agency was interested in this guy. Senator Gary Hart runs down here and he wants to know all about it. Of course he was getting ready to run for president."

"Did the government people try to control the investigation?"

"The whole city of Washington and the whole federal law enforcement that got involved with the Rosselli case were all full of shit. I firmly believe that they knew more than they were telling us."

"Many people believe Rosselli's murder was a result of his

testimony at the hearings in Washington—that it was tied to all the talk about the CIA/Castro plot, the Kennedy assassination."

"Johnny Rosselli had been talking way too much. We found out that he had pissed off a lot of people. He lived a charmed life for a long while. But he didn't realize he had gotten old and the charm had worn off."

"He kept saying that nobody was going to bother a retired old man."

"Well. He got that wrong."

1

OUT OF THE PAST

Beverly Hills, California, May 6, 1966

Johnny Rosselli walked down Brighton Way. He was in no hurry, enjoying the warm spring weather and the streets full of pretty girls on their lunch break. Silver-haired and suntanned, groomed to perfection—he was fresh from his weekly visit to Drucker's Barber Shop—in big dark glasses, custom-made suit, alligator shoes. A hard-looking, confident-looking man in late middle age, he appeared very much a part of that opulent neighborhood. Passersby might have taken him for a motion picture producer or a powerful agent, even an old movie star, one of those tough-guy actors from the days of black-and-white.

Nearing the corner of Brighton and Rodeo Drive he paused before crossing, and as he stood there he felt a sensation at his back, a sudden change in the atmosphere, like the chill from a dark cloud crossing the sun.

With a glance over his shoulder he saw two men in black suits coming up the sidewalk, coming up, flanking him at the corner.

One of the men said, "John. We need to talk to you."

He gave no reaction and started across the street. They followed, and on the other side they moved ahead of him and blocked his way.

Staring through big dark lenses, Johnny Rosselli said, "You know how it goes, fellas. If you've got a problem, go talk to my attorney."

The second man said, "You don't want your attorney to know about this."

The first said, "This is different, John. Something new. You need to take a look. . . ."

The second man held out a buff-colored envelope.

Johnny looked at the package but kept his hands at his sides.

"Listen. For your own good. The Bureau knows who you are."

Johnny looked past him, as if no one were there and nothing had been said.

"Do you understand? We know everything."

The first man held out a business card. It read "DuPar's Restaurant," with an address in Thousand Oaks.

"This is a place where we can meet. After you've had a look in the package."

Johnny glanced at the card but did not take it, and he did not take the package, saying, "If you've got a subpoena give it to my attorney. I don't know what you're talking about."

He started walking again.

"Have a nice day, John," said the second man. "We'll be seeing you."

Halfway to the next corner he stopped and looked back. The two FBI agents were gone.

You have a nice day, too.

Vaffanculo.

In the ass.

He entered his place on the eighth floor of the Glen Towers Apartments, a large, modern, sleekly furnished apartment with a sweeping balcony view of western Beverly Hills. Slipped under the door was the envelope one of the men on the street had tried to give him.

He picked it up and dropped it on the glass-topped coffee table in his living room.

He went to the telephone and dialed his attorney's office. He stopped. He put the phone down. He went to the bar and fixed himself a drink, took it to the couch by the coffee table.

He smoked most of a cigarette and then reached for the envelope and unsealed it. He withdrew the contents. There were two pieces of cardboard packing and between the cardboard two black-and-white photographs. He placed them faceup next to each other on the tabletop.

Both were newly made prints but the images themselves were vintage—two figures in the clothing and hairstyles of many years ago. They were formal portraits taken against plain backgrounds in a studio setting. One was of a dark-haired, dark-eyed woman in her thirties, the other a grim-faced schoolboy about ten years of age.

He leaned close to the photographs. He looked at one, and then the other. He had not seen these pictures in a very long time.

My mother.

And me.

He looked into the face of the boy staring out of the picture from long ago. Nearly fifty years had passed since he and that boy had gone their separate ways. Now they shared only a trace of physical resemblance, but once upon a time . . .

He sat in his living room and considered the meaning behind the arrival of these old photos, the two images that connected him to his former self. What purpose did they serve? "We know everything," the agent on the street had said. He turned the claim over in his mind. To a man who held as many secrets as Johnny Rosselli, it was a statement of some concern.

He studied the old photographs on the table, the woeful look on his mother's face, and the boy's grim expression. For a few moments he found himself adrift in sad recollection.

He finished the vodka and lit another cigarette.

Only a handful of people in the world could have connected his present identity to this kid from the distant past and might have been willing to give that information to the law. One of them was going to wish he was dead.

2

It was "Rosselli" with a double *s* and sometimes "Roselli" with just the one.

Somebody at the FBI thought that was a pretty funny thing. When a guy starts to write his name different ways in different years you wonder what is his problem. That was how things got started—you found a loose thread and you pulled on it until something opened up. Here was a little mistake that might lead to a bigger mistake and when you found the big mistake there was a good chance you were going to get your man. Agents started to sniff around. This was in the 1950s, after the Kefauver hearings on organized crime in America. What they learned at the hearings was big shocking stuff. Nobody before then had understood how much of the country was populated by gangsters all working together for the common bad. Johnny Rosselli had been among the many forced to testify. He told the senators his story, about being born in Chicago, losing his parents, and being raised by a kindly old uncle. It was a sad story, with little bits and pieces of the truth thrown in.

Someone at the FBI went to the Bureau of Vital Statistics in Chicago. They looked for the papers on Johnny Rosselli, and they found out something interesting: The document recording Johnny Rosselli's birth had been filed thirty years after the fact; the document itself was a forgery, and there was no other evidence to be found that the person described therein had ever been born—in Chicago or anywhere else.

An investigation into the "facts" of Rosselli's life was begun. In all parts of the country agents gathered evidence, examined files, followed leads, interrogated people from all known periods of the man's life. It went on for years. They found little that wasn't already known, or wasn't what Johnny Rosselli allowed them to find.

He had covered his tracks well—his origins, his early years. The FBI was sure he was not who he said he was. But who *was* he? What was he hiding? For a guy whom everybody in law enforcement knew about for decades—one of Al Capone's boy wonders, the Mob's man in Hollywood, big wheel in Las Vegas, the hundreds of pages of police reports in which he figured, numerous arrests and trials, headlined convictions—he was a mystery.

Agents looked at the file and cursed. It nagged at them. There had to be some good reason he had gone to the trouble of falsifying his birth, covering up his past, when his known record was already so bad. Had he run away from a crime for which he could still be prosecuted? If they could solve the mystery, find out who he was, what he was hiding, they were sure they could nail him good, close the book on another major hoodlum.

One day they lucked out. An old soldier in the LA crime family—and a longtime associate of Johnny's—had become an informant. His handlers in the Bureau kept the informant on a long leash so as not to expose him to his fellow gangsters, but they kept him under observation too. One day they followed him to the airport, saw him greet a stranger from across the country. The agents pulled him in. What was going on at the airport? He wouldn't talk, which made them more interested. They told him the deal again: If he ever held anything back it was over and they would throw him in prison. The mobster tried to figure a way out, but he couldn't. Fuck it, he decided. I'm a rat, I'm dead already. He told the agents he'd been doing a favor for his friend Johnny Rosselli. Rosselli? Keep talking, said the Feds. It was nothing, he said, a little errand. A little cash for the guy's mama. He'd done it before, many times through the years. For Johnny's mother back in Boston. The fella at the airport was Johnny's kid brother.

His mother? the FBI agents said.

Johnny Rosselli had a mother? In Boston? A brother? The agents grinned like cats over a spilled bowl of goldfish.

Armed with the slight but crucial biographical information supplied by their informant, the Bureau refocused its long-running investigation of Rosselli—what it described as an "intensive discreet endeavor to develop the facts," to "uncover some crime committed which would have caused him to change his identity." As long as it was still under the statutes, an old crime was as good as a new one to the Feds. But the goal was not just to convict and punish the man for his individual crimes. The Feds were working to undermine and degrade the whole criminal system—La Cosa Nostra, the Mafia, the Syndicate, the Organization, whatever you called it. To blow it up from the inside. The goal was to get him, and then to "turn" him, to make him talk and to keep him talking.

As the FBI's investigation advanced, moving deep inside Johnny Rosselli's shadow world, on a quest to uncover his hidden past, a strange course of events was set in motion, one that would reach far beyond the investigators' original intent, a Pandora's box opened to unforeseeable consequences, to chaos and scandal, the exposure of dirty secrets and black lies in the corridors of American power, and, in the end, to sudden and ghastly death.

3

His certificate of birth—the real one—is held in the house of records in the Italian provincial capital of Frosinone. The document indicates a male child, last name Sacco, given name Filippo (after his father's father), born on July 4, 1905, to Vincenzo and Maria Antonia Sacco (née DiPasquale), the Comune di Esperia, Provinzia di Frosinone. There is no mention of Chicago.

Esperia rises along the slopes of Monte Cecubo in wooded land in the region known as the Campagna, 110 kilometers southeast of Rome. It is of ancient origin, with scattered remnants of a lost eminence—a medieval castle on the hilltop, a Baroque church, a crumbled monastery—though most of its long history is without distinction. In the early years of the twentieth century it was an isolated and backward settlement. There was no running water, no electricity, no resident doctor; carts and wagons were the only transportation, and workhorses and donkeys plodded the streets, leaving the cobblestones decorated with shit.

In the year of Filippo Sacco's birth much of southern Italy was in the grip of a devastating depression, the result of decades-long cycles of human-made and natural disasters that had left half a nation in misery. It was an era of widespread emigration as millions of southern Italians left their homes, left their country, in search of a better life. The largest number of these traveled to the United States, *l'America*, to the expectant migrants a mythic land of opportunity. And for now America welcomed them, almost without restriction, eager to admit the needed workforce of a booming economy.

In Esperia, in good times, Vincenzo Sacco had made his living as a cobbler, a skilled and respected member of the community.

Now the times were not good, and people had no money to buy new shoes or even to repair their old ones. Vincenzo's father and his brother had both heard the siren call from overseas and gone to find their fortunes in the United States. From their assembly-line jobs in Massachusetts they urged Vincenzo to do the same. It was a troubling thing to leave a wife and a child on the way, but it seemed the best hope for the future, and by the time of Filippo's birth his father was gone, another hopeful pilgrim. He joined his relatives in Boston's large Italian population, found a job assembling shoes at a factory, a paycheck every Friday. He spent little on himself, put a little more away, and sent the rest to his wife and the son he had never seen.

Many of the heads of households who went abroad would send for their family or would return to Italy after two or three years of working and saving. But some did neither, and some were never heard from again, preferring to start their lives over without the responsibilities they had left behind. Years passed, and Vincenzo remained in Boston. Maria and the child lived on the small stipend from America. The boy grew up in cloistered Esperia, on the dirt paths and the cobblestone streets, in the shadow of the ancient knights' castle on the hill.

It would be six years before he sent for them. What frustration and disappointment those years had meant to the mother and child were put away. The future was everything.

They departed Esperia late in the summer, traveling by wagon over the mountain paths to the city of Naples. They joined the crush of passengers at dockside, an apprehensive parade, assessed by a gauntlet of wary soldiers, customs agents, health inspectors, white-uniformed pursers. They boarded the great ocean liner (North German Lloyd's 500-foot *Koenig Albert*, en route from Genoa), hurried through the noise and chaos, the crowded corridors, down to the teeming, dark, foul-smelling quarters they would share with the two thousand passengers in steerage. In the night the ship roared to life, and they moved out across the bay, headed west for America.

On September 10, 1911, the ship entered New York waters, moving north to the federal immigration station at Ellis Island. It was recorded that the number of settlers arriving from Europe that week was so large and the facilities on the island so overwhelmed—immigrants were subject to long waits, invasive health inspections, delousings—that it took three days before the last of the passengers was processed.

Setting off into the roaring center of the modern world, the mother and her boy found their way through glutted Manhattan streets to the station and the train that would take them to Boston. By evening after three weeks of travel from Italy, they reached their destination. Maria saw her husband for the first time in six years, and Filippo saw his father for the first time in his life.

In the 1900s, Boston was a densely populated center of commerce, manufacturing, and education. It was home to every layer of society, regal Brahmins and new-money tycoons at the top, slum-dwelling poor at the bottom. For more than a century it had drawn waves of immigrants from Europe, a new ethnic influx appearing with each generation. The Irish had come in the early 1800s, then the Germans, Poles, Russian Jews. The latest to arrive were the Italians. The southerners who had been coming in great numbers each year since the end of the last century were almost entirely from the peasant class, the *contadini*, uneducated laborers intended for unskilled and low-paid work. They now provided the majority of Boston's pool of manual labor. They repaired roads and bridges, dug tunnels, built buildings, and filled the hundreds of factories and mills in the city and the surrounding towns.

Vincenzo Sacco had been living on North Street in the old red-light district; for his family he found more suitable quarters in East Boston. They traveled on the newly opened subway that ran beneath the harbor, connecting the North End and Boston proper to the annexed East. East Boston was the starting point for successive groups of newcomers to the country, and it claimed one of the two biggest Italian neighborhoods in the city. It was a poor and overpopulated neighborhood; men and families and extended families crowded into broken-down wooden boarding-houses and brick tenements.

On Maverick Street, Vincenzo had rented a small three-room cold-water flat. The windows looked out the back at a spiderweb of clotheslines, an unkempt yard, an outhouse. There was no time for acculturation. The Saccos' new life began with the next sunrise—Vincenzo setting off at dawn for the shoe factory, Maria turning the shabby apartment into a home. On Sundays they went to mass at the small, crowded Roman Catholic church by the square. The six years of waiting were forgiven and forgotten, like a bright morning after a cold, stormy night, the natural order of things quickly restored. Maria Sacco became pregnant; they would have their first American child.

Late in September, Filippo entered the first grade at the Samuel Adams School in East Boston. No consideration was made for immigrant kids who did not speak English. They had to learn as they went, sink or swim. American-born boys taunted them. There were slurs and bullying for the foreigners. "Because of the beatings I received in the first three grades, having a name like Filippo," Johnny remembered, "I used the name of Philip or Phil. I stopped talking Italian because of the beatings." And he learned to fight back. By the time he reached the fourth grade, he would recall, "the tables were turned."

Prejudice was not confined to the school grounds. Nativist animosity simmered in the city of Boston in those years. Italian workers did much to keep the city running, the factories thriving, the roads and bridges open, but the "real" Bostonians disdained them, the Irish cops abused them, called them dirty names. America was a tricky place. It needed its foreigners but it hated them too. The yellow press stirred the public's suspicions with stories of secret societies and subversive politics. Immigrant crimes made for good tabloid headlines. The Italians were thieves, communists, nihilists; they belonged to a murder cult known as the Mafia. Police harassment was constant. The brutal "Red Squads" swept down on protesters and political activists, Italian-American labor groups their special focus. The radicalized immigrants responded with public confrontations and terrorist violence. The conflict would culminate in the controversial 1921 murder trial and eventual execution of Italian immigrants Nicola Sacco (no relation, though Nicola, like Vincenzo, was a shoemaker) and Bartolomeo Vanzetti, a seeming travesty of justice that provoked international attention and outrage.

In East Boston many in the Italian community kept their distance from the often oppressive and dangerous new world. They clung to the comforts and habits of the old. On many streets you were more likely to hear Italian spoken than English. The grocery stores featured the staples and treats of Italy. The men who worked in the factories likely stood at the assembly lines beside fellow immigrants. It was the children most of all who had to confront the challenges of their new home. For boys like Filippo/Phil Sacco, at once eager new Americans and distrusted aliens, life in the United States was like walking a razor's edge, freedom and opportunity on one side, intolerance, humiliation, and violence on the other.

Maria gave birth to her second child in the summer of 1912. A boy, they gave him his father's name. The senior Vincenzo worked hard and they saved, and in time they could afford a little more rent, a larger apartment on a better street. The family continued to grow, a third son—Alberto—two years after the second, then in 1915 a daughter, Concetta, and two years after that another girl, Ida Edith.

Phil left the Samuel Adams School late in 1916 and entered Austin Prevocational in January the following year, starting the seventh grade. He was no star in the classroom, but he learned to read and write, the first in his family to do so. At home, around his mother, he remained a *bambino Italiano*, but at school and in the streets he had become an American kid.

They moved again, leaving behind the overrun immigrant neighborhoods. They rented a house on Belmont Terrace in Somerville, a pleasant, quiet area. It was a happy home: young children, loving mother, a kind father with a steady job and a weekly paycheck.

In 1918 the Great War in Europe, in which the United States had been a participant for almost two years, was coming to an end. In that year there began to appear in many areas of the world a highly contagious and virulent strain of influenza. The exact origin and cause of the virus was never found, though many believed it was a by-product of the war and the impact of new chemical weapons on the soldiers' immune systems, spread by the troops moving back and forth across continents. It would be called the Spanish Flu—a misnomer derived from early reports of the crisis in the Spanish press—and it would become the deadliest medical catastrophe since the Black Death of the fourteenth century.

In the late summer of 1918, a "second wave" mutation of the virus attacked the city of Boston. On August 27 sailors at the Commonwealth Pier were reported sick with flu symptoms. The Chelsea Naval Hospital where the sailors had been treated soon became filled with influenza patients. Within days the patients experienced rapid decline, overcome with pneumonia and fever, a breakdown of the immune system that in almost every case ended in death.

By mid-September the influenza had spread to the city and throughout the state. The Massachusetts authorities had registered one hundred thousand cases by October 1; many more went unreported as all hospitals and medical facilities became dysfunctional, overflowing with the dying and the dead. In Boston and the surrounding area the authorities closed schools, public buildings, theaters, restaurants. Many fled the city, but many more stayed on, hoping to remain safe as the lethal germs swirled around them, and the death toll mounted. People shut themselves up in their homes when they could, the windows closed, rags and towels stuffed under the doors.

Even as the crisis in the city grew worse, Vincenzo Sacco, one of the many workers given no leave to stay home, continued to commute to his job at the shoe factory.

On the morning of October 5 he awoke in pain, running a high temperature. He stayed home in bed, the pain and fever growing worse. Maria covered him in heavy blankets, fed him hot soup. They could not find a doctor who would come to examine him. The hospitals were all in hopeless chaos, bodies filling the corridors, piled up in the alleys. Maria did what she could. She stayed at her husband's bedside for days, without concern for her own safety, the children kept away, Filippo taking care of his young brothers and sisters.

The effects upon contracting the virus were swift and vicious, a kind of superpneumonia that overwhelmed the system, turned the skin black-and-blue and filled the lungs with choking thick mucus. Near the end, a victim lost control of body functions and would cough and vomit with such force that blood ran from the eyes.

Vincenzo Sacco died on October 13. He was thirty-three years old.

———

The flu slowed its fury by November. It vanished in the next year, after having killed an estimated 100 million people around the world. In Boston the aftereffects were devastating, a city of wrecked lives, everywhere the widowed and the orphaned.

He left them only his small savings. By midwinter there was almost nothing left. They could no longer afford to remain in Somerville, and so Maria with her five children went back to East Boston, back to the ghetto. They found inexpensive lodgings at 43 Haines Street. With small kids to care for, Mrs. Sacco could not look for work. They survived on small "relief" payments from the city, and charity offerings from the Church, out of the fund established to help the many families like theirs, with the head of the household killed in the pandemic. They lived on watery soups and scraps of meat sliced to feed six. On cold nights in the unheated apartment they slept together in the kitchen huddled around the burning stove.

Phil stopped going to school. "My mother thought I was attending because I would leave in the morning and not show up until after school hours. I learned later that she had gone to the school to find out if I was there. They told her I was absent . . . Massachusetts was the first state to adopt compulsory education [but] no truant officer ever looked for me nor did anyone inquire as to my whereabouts. I never returned to school." He was thirteen years old.

He wandered the neighborhood looking for work, wanting to bring money and food to his family. "I did almost anything," he'd remember. "Sold newspapers, shined shoes." It was never much, never enough. He hated going home, seeing the misery. He stayed away more and more, wandering the streets. He "helled around" on Maverick Square, he remembered, "where all the wise guys were."

The Maverick Square area was a gathering place for kids, many of them newly orphaned. It was another kind of school, open-air, where you learned everything they never taught in a classroom. On the square he met thieves, dope peddlers, prostitutes (he soon caught his first dose of gonorrhea). He learned all the things some people were willing to do to keep going. Crime was just another way—for some the only way—to stay alive.

Gangsters came around in their sharp clothes with plenty of cash in their pockets. They sometimes put the kids to work running errands or looking out for the cops. They were the local heroes. All the kids on the square wanted to be gangsters when they grew up.

4

In America, on January 16, 1920, the Eighteenth Amendment to the United States Constitution went into effect. In conjunction with the Volstead Act of 1919, the amendment outlawed the creation, transportation, and sale of all intoxicating liquors, including beer and wine, and any other product containing greater than 0.5 percent alcohol.

The ban on alcohol had been decades in the making. Though never a popular movement, in the years before passage it had gathered an unexpected momentum. A sudden confluence of determined and influential enthusiasts—temperance cults, religious leaders, holier-than-thou politicians—were able to force the controversial legislation through Congress.

Prohibition did not stop Americans' desire for alcohol. If anything the ban seemed to increase their thirst. Overnight a new industry was born to meet the frantic demand for the now-illegal product. Bootleggers imported the bottled stuff from Canada, Mexico, and the Caribbean islands. Vintage stocks were stolen whole from padlocked warehouses. Breweries were reconfigured as Mob-protected properties. Licensed stores of medicinal alcohol were obtained, one way or another, from pharmacies and hospitals. Pure alcohol was siphoned from chemical companies and made potable by a network of refiners. Other, less sophisticated concoctions came from basement vats and bathtubs. The liquid gold was peddled in every town and city, on every street corner. It was bought by people who had never touched a drop when it was legal.

The criminal gangs running this underground economy grew big, rich, and powerful beyond anyone's imagining. It was one of the great industrial success stories of the age. Prohibition effectively subverted the "nation of laws." In some parts of the country the level of power the gangs wielded soon made them a virtual shadow government, corrupting and controlling politicians, police, and courts, committing crimes and violent acts without fear of consequence. Previously tame middle-class Americans became lawbreakers, drawn into an underworld culture of speakeasies, gambling, prostitution, and jazz. Gangsters became the iconic antiheroes of the era, their alluring adventures chronicled in pulp stories, Broadway plays, and Hollywood movies. Politicians and do-gooders who had brought about the "noble experiment," as it was often called, could only look upon its consequences with horror and awe. The irony kept on giving: Prohibition would barely make it through the decade, while its spawn—organized crime on a national level—would grow and thrive for the rest of the century and beyond.

5

Maria struggled. It was hard keeping the family going without a husband's help and comfort. Late in the year 1919, she moved the family again. They took a smaller, less expensive apartment at the front of 37 Everett Street. Widowed and alone for a year, she was happy and relieved to discover she had attracted the attention of a widower named Liberato Cianciulli. Liberato lived in a three-story house in the alley behind the Saccos, and had a butcher shop a block away on Cottage Street. Originally from Serino, Italy, he had lived in the United States off and on since the late 1880s, and had become a naturalized American citizen. Maria learned that he was twice a widower, losing his second wife to the Spanish flu in the same deadly month it had taken Vincenzo, and he was the father of five children.

He was fifty-eight, twenty years older than Maria. He was not an attractive man, unhandsome, short, and squat, and his business practices did not make him popular with customers (at election time, Johnny Rosselli recalled, he would crowd the whole shop with posters and banners for whichever candidates paid him two dollars). But with the widow Sacco he was kind and generous, giving her food for her family and helping with other expenses. Now the children always had something to eat, and for that she was very grateful. He called her Maria Antonia to keep from confusing her with his first wife, who had the same first name.

After they had been seeing each other for more than a year Liberato let Mrs. Sacco and her family move into his house on the alley. With Liberato's five children—three young ones and two boys in their twenties—and Maria's five, plus an eighty-year-old man boarding in the attic, it was a crowded home. Phil had to share the bedroom of the second-oldest son, Salvatore, known as "Toody."

Maria became pregnant. She felt shame and told Liberato they had to marry for the sake of the child. Liberato said he would do it, then changed his mind, dragged his heels. One day Phil came home and heard his mother crying out for him. She was in labor, she said, and told him to hurry to the butcher shop and tell Mr. Cianciulli. And he ran as fast as he could and Liberato closed the butcher shop and went to find the midwife. Phil's half sister was born in the bedroom off the kitchen. It was the same room in which Liberato's second wife had died of the influenza and he named the baby Carmela in her memory.

Maria continued to insist that Liberato do the right thing. Another six months went by before he agreed. On February 8, 1922, the couple was married by the East Boston justice of the peace.

Phil became pals with the two oldest Cianciulli boys. Toody and his brother Luigi taught him to play the guitar and mandolin. Toody worked as a milkman for the Hood Milk Company. Six days a week he went off in the middle of the night and worked till late morning, came home, and went back to bed right after dinner. Toody was encouraged to take Phil with him on the job, give him a few quarters to act as his assistant. It would be good to give him some responsibility, maybe he could be a milkman himself in a few years. All winter they would wake at one in the morning, walk in the dark across the empty and bitter-cold streets to the dairy, then drive around East Boston in a horse-drawn wagon delivering the orders. Phil loaded and unloaded the wagon, running bottles up to the stoops and front porches. His pals nicknamed him "Milky."

The relationship between Maria and Liberato was no longer a happy one. Now that he had been forced to marry her he was not as nice as he had once been, and he was not kind to her children, yelling at them and hitting them for the smallest things. One day a neighbor came to talk to her, saying that Liberato was no good. The neighbor said that Maria and Liberato were not married, no matter what words they had spoken and what papers they had signed. She said that Liberato's first wife, who was supposed to be dead, must have experienced a remarkable recovery because she was still alive back in Italy, and that that woman who was alive and Liberato were still husband and wife.

Maria asked her husband about this other woman, this wife: Was she alive or dead? He assured her again she was dead and buried, but Maria would ask many times until he admitted that she was maybe not that dead after all. Liberato told her to speak no more of this—"*Non ti preoccupare, mia donna!*" ("Don't worry, my darling!")—to leave it to him and he would make things right.

One night Phil's stepfather said he needed to talk to him in private. They went in the back of the butcher shop after closing, and Liberato explained that they were having money problems. He was taking care of all of them now, and he had no money. He had some fire insurance, he said, and if they could cash in on that policy then all of their problems would be over. He said, Phil . . . *mio figlio prediletto* . . . my dear boy, you must help me with this for the good of the family. He said they had to have a fire in that place so they could collect on the insurance. So he could have money to take care of them all. He couldn't set the fire himself, he said, because he had to have a damn good alibi when it happened or the insurance guys, those *stronzi*, would suspect something was up and not pay off. If Filippo wanted to be a good kid, make his mama and new papa proud, and help them all he would do this thing he asked.

It was what was known on the street as a "money fire," or a "Jew bankruptcy," and there were characters around you could hire for just such a job—they were called "heaters"—but what was the good of having a stepson if you couldn't use him to save a few bucks when you wanted to burn your house down?

Liberato told him how it would go. "We had a cast-iron stove," Johnny Rosselli recalled, "behind which there was always laundry and diapers hanging on a line. He told me how to start a fire, making it red-hot and make it appear that the rags had dropped onto the stove and accidentally started the fire."

Phil did as his stepfather asked. Some time after the family had gone out and were safely away from the house, he set the fire, stoked it with the drying diapers. He stayed to make sure it kept burning and waited so long that flames rose up and smoke began to surround him. He rushed away, ran from the house. He stood outside in the shadows and watched it burn.

That spring, according to the records of the Immigration Service, Cianciulli, the butcher and bigamist and arsonist, applied for a renewed U.S. passport. On April 22, 1922, with his fire insurance money—he made $800 on the deal—and nothing and no one else, he disappeared.

"Liberato left me and the family," Maria would remember. "He left his children in this country. Neighbors told me he went back to Italy to his wife. I never saw Liberato Cianciulli since that time."

The place on Everett Street was to be foreclosed by the bank. The two families went their separate ways. Maria found some cheap lodging on Bremen Street and went back on public assistance. Cianciulli did not return to America. His children raised themselves and never heard from him again.

Maria no longer held sway over her oldest boy. He came and went as he pleased. He would drop by at odd hours, give her some money, disappear. She would wonder what would happen to him, but with her young children to mind, what could she do? She would sometimes see him with the gangs of kids on Maverick Square, panhandling, making mischief.

There was a local hood who had taken an interest in Phil. Sarro Vaccaro, a twenty-six-year-old from Pennsylvania, who went by the alias Cy Perry. Vaccaro had a long arrest record in a half-dozen states and a scar that ran from his forehead to his chin. Phil was running errands for him, delivering packages. Vaccaro was a narcotics pusher, connected to a small local gang. The bootlegging trade, expanding wildly since Prohibition had taken effect in early 1920, was the province of big, organized racketeers—in Boston, Gaspare Messina, Frankie Wallace, "King" Solomon. Drugs were an insignificant market by comparison to the booze trade. It was mostly left to the small-timers, who served a coterie of addicts, many of them ex-soldiers who picked up the habit recovering from battlefield wounds during the Great War. Illegal booze was a lot smarter business to get into than illegal drugs because everybody liked bootleggers—they were providing a popular national service—and nobody liked dope peddlers, not even the addicts who depended on them.

A man named Fisher, a neighborhood lowlife with a habit, was a regular customer of the peddlers. On September 14, Phil Sacco sold him one-quarter of an ounce of morphine. Fisher came back soon after looking to make another, larger buy, and Philip took him to see Sarro Vaccaro. It was a sting. Fisher had become a rat for the cops. Vaccaro was arrested by Boston police officers. Phil was picked up by three agents of the Narcotics Bureau the same day.

He was booked on a charge of violating Section 332 of the Criminal Code (the Harrison Narcotic Act), specified as "opium trafficking." He was put in the Charles Street Jail, held on a day-to-day basis until the law decided what to do with him. In

October he was transferred as a federal prisoner to the Billerica House of Corrections in Middlesex. A commitment card listed his name as Philip Sacco, aka "Milky"; his address as 8 Seaver Street, Boston; place of birth: Italy; height: five feet seven and a half inches; weight: 126 pounds; hair: brown; eyes: brown (they were in fact flecked with blue and silver, an effect some described as "chrome"); complexion: medium; age: seventeen; no finger-prints were taken.

On October 18 a federal grand jury indicted him on two counts of selling morphine. On October 20 he pled not guilty and was or-dered released on recognizance. The one-hundred-dollar bail was provided by a woman named Mary Ferullo, of East Boston, who put up her apartment house as security. Investigators could find no connection between the accused and the sixty-three-year-old woman, and it was assumed that she had been made to front for other interests who preferred anonymity.

Fisher, the junkie police informant and key witness against Phil Sacco and Sarro Vaccarro, disappeared before the case could come to trial. Authorities suspected foul play. Fisher was never seen again.

6

Tancredi Tortora was a drifter, a day laborer, a crook, and a mur-derer. His parents were southern Italians who had migrated to Marseilles, France, where he was born in 1903. The family moved to the United States in 1920. Tancredi went out on his own soon after. He became a road kid, wandering the Northeast and Mid-west, taking odd jobs as he found them.

In the spring and summer of 1922 he lived in Chicago, Illinois. In April he was operating a soft-drink parlor on Blue Island Ave-nue. When police raided the place on the twenty-ninth of that month they discovered, in addition to the expected fizzy waters and syrups, a quantity of opium, cocaine, morphine, and moonshine whiskey. Tortora was arrested, along with a customer and two women suspected of prostitution.

In August, back on the street, he became caught up in a battle between the gangs of two feuding brothers, Antonio and Charles Charlando. Antonio, aka "Tony Charles," was shot to death in the melee. The police sought several named and unnamed gang members for the murder, including Tancredi Tortora. He claimed to be an innocent bystander, but rather than argue his case he went on the run.

That autumn he was back in the East. In October, on a public street in Boston, he murdered a man named Annibale Stilo. He was caught, arrested, and held in the Charles Street Jail.

It was in the old jailhouse that Tortora saw Philip Sacco for the first time. They never spoke in the prison, but Tancredi had noticed him. The poised young Italian kid stood out among the typical roughnecks and derelicts locked up at Charles Street.

One day, a couple of months later at Christmastime, Tancredi was out on bond, kicking around East Boston, when he ran into his former fellow prisoner on Maverick Square. Phil recognized him too. They greeted each other and stopped to shoot the breeze. They were both looking for work, or whatever. They decided to pair up, make the rounds. They became friends, a team. It was good to have someone to back you up when you were a kid on your own on the streets. They had background and experiences in common. They looked at many things the same way, shared the same sense of humor.

They were together all that winter. Phil brought Tancredi home, introduced him to his mother and family of little brothers and sisters, let him sleep in his bed. The conditions Phil's family lived in were very poor, Tancredi remembered, even poorer than those of his own people. The mother held them together, but by not more than a thread.

The two young friends looked for work in the local underworld. Bootleggers were always hiring for something. Tancredi thought Phil had the makings of a good hustler. He was not the usual street thug. Unlike most of the tough kids roaming around, he was more than a pair of fists. They wandered the city, just living for the day. They worked when they found work. Sometimes they brought money home for the family, and sometimes they didn't. They spent many hours pursuing girls. Not Italian girls so much, that was a hard nut to crack. American girls. They were more *emancipato*, more curious. Phil was very successful in this pursuit. Tancredi said women found Phil very attractive, and he had a way with them. He was gallant, could say the right things. He could pick them up quick. He would drop them just as fast.

In May 1923 Philip got himself in trouble again. He was arrested, charged with burglary and theft of fifty dollars, and thrown in jail. It was true that he had stolen the money, but the victim had made up the circumstances. The man had given Phil the fifty to procure alcohol for him, and Phil had pocketed the money and procured nothing (looked at from a certain angle he was being charged with *not* selling alcohol). On May 4 he was released on three hundred dollars' bail.

With three trials hanging over their heads—Tortora facing a murder rap, and Phil with two charges and the unresolved business of Fisher, the missing police snitch—who might turn up to testify or, more likely, turn up dead, which could be a much worse problem—the friends agreed it was a good time to skip town. Tancredi was an old hand at jumping bail, with bench warrants all over the place, and it had always worked out fine. Eventually the cops got bored and forgot all about you as long as you kept moving. They caught a freight train to New York, Phil leaving Greater

Boston for the first time since the day he arrived from Italy and Ellis Island with his mother. If Maria Sacco—she had resumed her undisputed married name—knew anything about her son's departure or destination, or had concerns for his future, she did not say. She was seldom heard to mention him again, even among her other kids, out of concern for causing him trouble. In those days life was not easy, and you learned to accept and not ask why or you suffered even more. *Occhio che non vede, cuore che non duole.* (What the eye does not see, the heart does not grieve.) He was like her late lamented husband, like her sort-of second husband, and, you could say, like Fisher the police informant: One day he was there and the next he was gone.

7

They stayed with Tancredi's cousin Maria in Brooklyn. They lazed around, rode the subway back and forth to Manhattan, seeing the sights. They chased young females, had a good time. After a few weeks they hit the road again. They wandered to the north. Sometime in the late summer they arrived in Buffalo, New York, the big upstate city on the eastern shore of Lake Erie. Facing Canada, where Prohibition did not exist, the border area was active in the import of illegal alcohol. Somebody gave them a guy to look up, a bootlegger and nightclub operator named Mike Moro who took the two young drifters in, gave them food and lodging. Tancredi mostly "loafed," but Phil worked cleaning tables and pouring drinks in Moro's speakeasy on Eagle Street. Moro liked Phil and might have brought him into the operation, but Moro was away a lot of the time, in Nova Scotia arranging liquor buys and seeing a young girl named Rosen-Crantz. (He later married and divorced her; then she was shot dead, the crime never solved.) Tancredi got restless in Buffalo and wanted to move on. They heard about jobs on the

Pere Marquette Railroad, and they applied for the work and were hired as track hands.

Not wanting the Boston warrants to catch up with them, the two began using aliases. Tancredi became Joe Calcagnio. Phil tried a number of names before he found the one he liked. Somewhere there arose the glamorous notion that his assumed surname had been carefully chosen as a tribute to some great Italian of the past, a Florentine painter of the quattrocento. As he was known to use numerous variants and alternating spellings for a time, it seems doubtful there was a singular inspiration. More likely it came from out of the air, maybe off the side of a truck. In any case, Filippo—Philip—Sacco disappeared, and one day or other John Rosselli was born.

He also changed his nationality. Troublemakers who were not citizens were often deported without waiting for a trial. Especially Italians. There were too damn many of them. From how Phil remembered his place of birth, with the donkeys in the dusty streets and the priests watching your every move, he had no interest in going back to "the old country." He had begun claiming the United States as his birthright while still in Massachusetts. Where in America he was born he had not yet made up his mind. He told Tancredi he came from East Boston and that the record of his birth was destroyed in a fire. At the time of his second arrest he declared he was from New York. On later documents his birthplace was recorded as Newark, New Jersey, then Boston again, and then, for the longest time, Chicago.

The two young men went to work on a maintenance-of-way gang, repairing damage to the tracks and clearing debris on the lines between Buffalo and Detroit. It was backbreaking work, and the wages were low. The gangs were comprised of misfits and foreigners. Bums and dagos, to the foremen in charge. They were shuttled around in work trains and housed by night in makeshift "flops," mostly stripped old railcar bodies. They slept on the floor with the dirt and the rat turds. Johnny's upper body filled out with muscle from the long days wielding a shovel and ax. After a couple of months he and Tancredi decided they'd had enough of the hard work and terrible conditions. They quit and traveled on. In Chicago, Tancredi had another relative, his uncle, Vincent La Morta, who let them stay with him at his place on May Street.

Uncle Vincent was a laborer, a straight citizen who did nothing but work and sleep, and the boys had to behave themselves around the man. They lived on their railroad savings, getting drunk at speaks and, always, looking for girls.

Johnny was awed by the city.

Chicago in 1923: not yet at the peak of its infamy but already unrivaled as a place of violence and corruption. The Eighteenth Amendment to the U.S. Constitution, prohibiting the manufacture, sale, and transportation of alcohol, had been for Chicago a kind of declaration of independence from law and order. The traffic in beer and liquor was immediately taken over by the local vice mongers and bandits, as it was in most other American cities, but nowhere did the rise of criminal enterprise reach the level of industrialization, mixed with anarchy and brutality, found in Chicago. Territories were divided among various rival and allied gangs, and the gangs defended and expanded their piece of the city with crazed enthusiasm.

It was a city increasingly controlled by the mobs, the police and politicians on the take, and everybody else trying to get through the day in one piece. Biggest of the gangsters was Terrible Johnny Torrio, a smart, ambitious strategist who first transformed scattered criminal fiefdoms into a citywide organization. Torrio commanded an army of some eight hundred gunmen, most of them immigrants from Sicily and southern Italy, a great many recruited out of New York.

Among Torrio's imported hoodlums was an associate from one of the Brooklyn gangs, a young Italian American, a pudgy enforcer

by the name of Alphonse Capone, known on the streets as Scarface Al Brown (nicknamed for the angry slash marks on his cheek,
the result of a knife attack by an irate Siciliano who objected to
Capone ass-grabbing his sister). A crude and brutal man but with
a head for business and a rare talent for the illegal, Capone had
distinguished himself within the organization, and in 1923 was
Torrio's valued right hand. Still greater chaos and bloodshed lay
ahead for Chicago, a premature retirement for Torrio, and promotion, power, and worldwide fame for Capone.

Shortly after Christmas, Tancredi was ready to move on. Johnny
was going with him, then he wasn't. Tancredi got tired of waiting—
to stay too long in one place was boring and risky—and he hit the
road. He wasn't sure where he was headed, and didn't care. Johnny
stayed behind in Chicago. He stayed a few weeks. By then his
money was blown, and he needed to look for work and another
place to stay. The icy winds of January made him miserable, and
he thought about going someplace warm. He considered New
Orleans and Florida, and so another future, a different life, would
have lain ahead for him as easily as that. Fate came in a fifteen-cent
telegram.

While he was still in Chicago trying to make up his mind what
to do, he heard at last from his departed friend. Tancredi had ended
up thousands of miles away in Los Angeles, California. He told
Johnny he must come join him. It was beautiful there. It was sunny
and warm like the Mediterranean coast, Tancredi said, and full
of opportunity. Plenty of work to be had for guys like them. He was
in with some Italians who had connections. Tancredi told Johnny
he had to come on out. He had talked him up to some big shots
there, and he could even send him the money for train fare if he
was broke.

Johnny tossed the idea around for a day. For all he knew about

California it could have been in China, but his friend made it seem like paradise, with all the girls in bathing suits and sweet oranges hanging from every tree. It sounded like a good adventure.

He sent a message: Okay, *amico,* send the fare.

On a day early in February, ticket in hand, Johnny boarded the Los Angeles Limited, and the heavy black-and-Pullman-green train pulled out of the station on its journey west. For two days and nights they rolled. Plains, mountains, desert, big railheads and whistle-stops, Council Bluffs, Cheyenne, Salt Lake City, Las Vegas (the boomtown-to-be then a Nevada settlement barely twenty years old and comprising a few saloons, dice joints, and whorehouses). As they crossed the border to California and the desolate floor of the Mojave stretched in all directions, it looked like they had come to the end of the world.

2

ONCE UPON A TIME
IN LOS ANGELES

Los Angeles was the first city of the twentieth century. As a metropolis it was newly born. A generation before it had been a place of unpaved streets and low adobe houses, a down-at-the-heels rancho, one visitor sniffed, "here and there an indolent native hugging the inside of a blanket." Lawlessness and rough justice prevailed, with incidents of lynchings, and racist rioting, like the 1871 massacre of the Chinese on Calle de los Negros ("Nigger Street," the whites called it).

It was a place little known to the rest of the country, difficult and dangerous to reach until the extension of the transcontinental rail line from San Francisco late in 1876. Commerce had been of modest ambition in the area, freshwater sources scarce, and the agricultural possibilities barely exploited: Wine and bee-ranch honey were among the region's few exports.

The new century brought a steady flow of settlers and sojourners, a great surge in Anglo population urged along by railroad promoters, land speculators, and other economically interested parties. The water shortage was relieved by the infamous Owens

Valley Aqueduct (water diverted, that is, stolen, from rural land hundreds of miles away), which supplied enough for two million people. Streets were paved, neighborhoods were developed, multistory office buildings rose. The downtown business district grew as big and busy as any in the country.

Petroleum was discovered to the northeast of downtown—just in time for the invention of the automobile—and by 1900 there were more than five hundred oil wells pumping within the city limits; the nearby ocean ports were expanded to send black gold around the world. A quiet suburb called Hollywood became the iconic capital of a young motion picture industry that had fled the East Coast, bringing international attention and commerce to the city. Los Angeles was the new promised land, and the promises only grew larger and more alluring. In the decade of the 1920s the city's population would increase by 1,300,000, a national record. Los Angeles grew so rapidly, the journalist Carey McWilliams wrote, it was as though it had been "conjured into existence."

It was the new big American city, but it more resembled a frontier boomtown. A city lacking tradition, without roots, the population heavy with strangers. The past it did have—Hispanic—was mostly whitewashed over, and descendants of the earliest settlers disenfranchised, as if they were the last to arrive and not the first. Boardinghouses hung signs in the windows: "No Dogs or Mexicans." The movie business in Los Angeles, being made up almost entirely of uprooted outsiders, New Yorkers, foreigners, theatrical gypsies, became equally suspect in the eyes of the native Angelenos (boardinghouse signs adjusted: "No Dogs or Actors").

Lacking a history, Los Angeles was a place easy to mold, to manipulate, and to corrupt. Beneath the veneer of fresh air and freedom the city was run by darker forces, a shifting mix of rich businessmen, political machine, and racketeers. From time to time little insurgencies arose, and the city fell into the hands of the reformers, but such times seldom lasted for long, and soon enough things went back to normal. In any case, the righteous could be as bad as the outlaws.

For many years the most powerful behind-the-scenes boss of LA was Harry Chandler, a multimillionaire, real estate magnate, owner of the *Los Angeles Times*. Chandler picked political candidates and bought elections, worked to impose laws to serve his investments and ideology, and woe to anyone who crossed him. He used the police department to settle labor disputes and harass his political enemies—which often amounted to the same thing, when special police units were sent after labor organizers and protesting wage slaves.

Chandler was a pious reactionary and an active racist. He did what he could to shape the city—the "White Spot of America"—in his own image. He determined demographics through the marketing of his housing subdivisions to targeted buyers in the Midwest, those who would be philosophically like-minded, Christian, and white.

With the coming of Prohibition, the Jazz Age, the rise of the gangsters, righteous prigs like Harry Chandler began to fall out of step. New alliances were forged. In 1921 the newly elected mayor, George Cryer—whose shifty ethics and quirky populism would keep him in office for the rest of the decade—and his scheming chief of staff, Kent Kane Parrot, turned their backs on the Chandler cabal, going into business with some of the loosely allied big shots of the LA underworld, a mix of bootleggers, bookmakers, pimps, gambling kingpins, including Milton "Farmer" Page; Guy "String Bean" McAfee (late of the city's police department); Zeke Caress, boss of the bookies; the Gans brothers, kings of the one-armed bandit business; Tyrolean vice man Albert Marco (aka Marco Albori); and the de facto leader of the criminal alliance, Charles Crawford.

Crawford—he was called "Good Time Charlie," and "the Gray

Wolf"—was a silver-haired Irish American, a burly man with a girl-ish voice and a frantic Adam's apple, a dancehall keeper who'd become a vice king, formerly of Seattle, Washington, in the bus-tling years of the Klondike gold rush. Moving to Los Angeles a few steps ahead of a crackdown, he brought with him from Seattle some innovative ideas about big-city racketeering and methods of col-laboration between lawbreakers and lawmakers—what came to be known as "the System" or "the Combination."

The way the System worked, a chunk of the profits from vice funded a political machine. In return for money and other stimu-lants the wised-up officials let the racketeers get away with mur-der. It was a cozy mingling of interests, and everyone got what they wanted except the honest public. Politicians visited Crawford's Maple Bar, a saloon and bordello downtown on 5th Street and Maple Avenue, more often than they did City Hall, while Crawford reg-ularly hiked over to Kent Parrot's apartment at the Biltmore Hotel to raise a glass and hand over envelopes stuffed with cash.

The Cryer-Parrot administration was the perfect partner for Crawford and company, and the concept of the Combination, the System, was to thrive in Los Angeles better than anywhere.

The City Hall gang's hold on unlawful enterprise was extensive but not exclusive. Opportunities were simply too large in the cra-zily expanding and corrupt city for any one organization to own it all. Los Angeles drew criminals of every sort—rumrunners, thieves and stickup men, booze makers, dope peddlers, snatch racketeers. The ethnic ghettos hosted crooks of half a dozen languages and various hues. None of these had the favored status with the law enjoyed by the Combination, but they tried their best, and a com-promised police department often made life easier for even the unprotected villains.

Crime rates soared. Liquor, drugs, prostitution, gambling, kid-napping, homicide. Murders often went unsolved in Los Angeles, many never officially reported, let alone investigated. The city boosters lured tourists and promoted homes in the sun while the corpses piled up in the gutter.

Bootlegging was the bulwark in this city of crime—its blue whale. The illegal transport and sale of booze was the fastest-growing industry on the West Coast, as big as the movies. Every year half a million gallons of alcohol were smuggled into Southern California, across the border from Mexico by truck and by sea from Canada and Latin America to the ports and beaches all along the coast. Tens of thousands of gallons more were cooked up in local distilleries, basements, and bathtubs, peddled at a huge profit. Fortunes were being made, and every criminal wanted a piece of the action, even if he had to steal it from another crook.

2

Johnny thought Los Angeles was a fine city. In the middle of winter it was warm and bright nearly every day. In the mornings the crisp fresh tang of the Pacific traveled for miles inland. It was a place so unlike the big cities he had known in the East, dirty, choked, piled up on themselves. Here the hustle of traffic and big business were only a hillside away from green Edens and vast groves of citrus. So much of the city was brand-new, buildings and homes going up everywhere. It was a place that seemed, every day, to hold out the promise of a fresh start and great possibilities ahead.

Johnny and Tancredi Tortora were reunited. His friend had been in Los Angeles for a month or so. He had taken a job as a dishwasher at a club on Figueroa Street. There were moneyed *paisani* who came in there, and Tancredi had gotten friendly with a few of them. He would come out of the kitchen after hours and sit with them and have a glass of wine. He got to know a fellow named Eugenio Tadeo. Tadeo was a young pimp who ran a couple of houses of prostitution and looked like Rudolph Valentino, the love god from Puglia. Tancredi would tell him about some of his adventures back East and would tell him about his *compagno* in adventure, Johnny Rosselli. He said he wished he could get his friend out to California, that he'd like Eugenio to meet him. Tadeo liked to help his fellow countrymen and had plenty of cash from his whores. He offered Tancredi the money for his friend's train fare. Why not?—they could pay him back when they had it.

Johnny shared the room Tancredi rented near the Central Plaza. The plaza was the commercial center of Old Los Angeles, an area of ethnic diversity, Asian and European immigrants, Mexicans (many freshly arrived refugees from the *revolución* across the border). The Italian presence around the plaza was large and well established from early in the century. There were Italian markets and restaurants, tailors, a bakery (the Cosmopolitan), a meeting place and theater (the Italian Hall), and an Italian-language newspaper (*Italo Americano*).

Italians—Sicilians, actually, though few Americans noted any distinction—dominated the organized criminal activity in the neighborhood, the melting pot around the plaza, the one small part of the city where outsider gangs were allowed to thrive, as long as they stayed in place. They were bootleggers, robbers, protection racketeers. Many were mafiosi in exile, with ties by blood or previous association to East Coast or New Orleans "families," often having come out to California to escape the arms of the law someplace else. They were an insular group, often feuding with one another, killing one another. They were seen as peculiar and unpredictable by the establishment gangsters, and were kept to the periphery of the Los Angeles underworld. The police came down hard if the "wops" ever moved above their station.

Johnny found employment at a bootleg joint on West 6th Street. It was managed by a guy named Bert "the Barber" Busterno. The place sold liquor on the ground floor and women upstairs. It was a protected joint, so it ran as openly as if they were peddling coffee and doughnuts. It was a hangout for local tough guys and criminal types. Johnny worked unloading supplies, sweeping the floor, whatever it was. He kept his eyes and ears open while he worked, listened when the crooks talked trade and swapped stories.

Some days they were visited by the actual owner of the place, Albert Marco. Marco was said to have a piece of every whore in the city. He was a close associate of Charlie Crawford's since their Seattle days. When Prohibition began, he'd become a leading distributor of alcohol on the northern coast. Eventually his old friend Crawford lured him to Los Angeles and put him in charge of the liquor and prostitution rackets in the city. In appearance he resembled a wild boar—and he acted like one, too. He had a bad temper and was prone to public outbursts of physical violence, against women as well as men.

After a few weeks at his menial job Johnny—with Tancredi—left to work for another and more simpatico countryman, a neighborhood bootlegger named Antonio D'Acunto.

D'Acunto came from Avellino in the region of Campania (not far from Johnny's place of birth, Esperia), had been in the States since before the turn of the century, lived in Brooklyn, and done time in Sing Sing. In California, before the ban, he had owned a liquor store. After 1920 he started an import-export business, the Golden Bear, dealing in Italian and Californian products—fruit, cheese, olive oil. Though he had been straight for some years, his connections made it easy and tempting for him to put a foot in the prohibited trade, buying wine from Italian grape growers and making his own hard liquor in hidden distilleries.

A tall, distinguished-looking fellow in his late forties, D'Acunto was well-mannered and gracious around women. In the immigrant community he was known as generous and fair and was accorded a great deal of respect regardless of his illegal efforts. He was what they called a "hip pocket 'legger," no competition for the major operators, though he kicked back with tributes to keep the Crawford/Marco people happy. D'Acunto understood that if he kept his profile low he invited less attention and interruption from the big boys. He was content with his small, steady profits.

Johnny and Tancredi did a little of everything for the man. They made deliveries, collected on bills, even now and then lent a hand in production, helping to make the low-grade spirits they sold to D'Acunto's undiscriminating clientele. In backrooms and basements they shifted the bags of raw ingredients, churning the mix, making the fermented mash that became the prized (if barely drinkable) elixir. The basements where this process took place smelled like hell, and there was always fear of fire or an explosion; Johnny preferred to be outside handling the finished product and the money.

Occasionally they had to twist some arms on the job, but D'Acunto didn't like violence as a rule, preferring to depend on the goodwill of his customers, peaceful immigrants who desired some wine at dinner or a shot of whiskey after work. The two young men did carry pistols under their belts, for defensive purposes, as hold-ups and hijackings were increasingly common. Tancredi recalled that the guns were also good for impressing women, at least the sort of women they were trying to impress.

Johnny and his boss became close. D'Acunto treated him with much affection, and Johnny tried to offer the same in return. With D'Acunto's encouragement, Johnny called him Uncle Tony, and people came to think that they really were related. The older man had Johnny to his home many times. Frances Broszner, his common-law wife, was not as well-disposed toward the young hoodlum, could not understand why D'Acunto treated the boy so fondly. Her husband, she said, "was a man of refinement, with a background of gracious living," while she described Rosselli as someone of the street, an "uneducated person . . . coarse in his manners and appearance."

Like Broszner, Johnny could not figure what he did to inspire his employer's interest—maybe he reminded D'Acunto of himself at an earlier time, or of a son he did not have—but he appreciated the attention. He was a young man who understood where he had come from and had begun to give thought to where he might go; he wanted to be more than a hired hand, more than a roughneck. He was open to improvement. The "refined" D'Acunto would help him by example.

In the course of business, and in the pursuit of pleasure after work was done, Johnny came to know Los Angeles. He knew the busy center of big business and the elegant enclaves of the old establishment and the crummy neighborhoods of the immigrants and the poor. He had been to the picture palaces on Hollywood Boulevard and to the fine restaurants in Beverly Hills. He swam in the ocean and walked on the warm sand at Santa Monica and watched from the edge of the continent as the sun burned away beyond the horizon.

Best of all he knew the nighttime world downtown, the city's dark tenderloin of pleasure and vice. It lay just under the skin of the upright offices and government buildings, a wonderland of transgression, from Chinatown opium dens to swank gambling emporiums, brothels, bookie joints, backroom poker games, streetwalkers, hot sheet hotels. And everywhere there were the places to drink, on almost every block—since no one liked to travel far when they were thirsty—speakeasies, club rooms, hole-in-the-wall blind pigs, cigar stores where they sold quick nips for a quarter from a bottle kept under the counter with the French postcards and the pornographic eight-pagers.

They were a community, the bootleggers, the party girls, the pushers, the fences, the Shylocks, the oddsmakers, the thugs. It was a close-knit, friendly enough community—once you were on the inside and accepted and never tried to pull a fast one on your own kind. They lived freely, without the dividing lines drawn by straight society. The prostitutes Johnny and his friend paid to screw on Saturday night might be their dates for an afternoon at the beach on Sunday. One big happy family of outsiders.

The job with D'Acunto went on. Johnny and Tancredi worked, and then they played. It was a good life for young men. Johnny was nineteen. He was making money. He bought his first automobile. He had women, drink, sunshine. It was a good life, though it nagged him sometimes to see what he did not have. At every speak you saw the latest big shots, in their expensive suits, flashing their thick rolls of cash. All around there were fortunes being made.

He had his first encounter with the Los Angeles police. He was visiting a still set up inside a house at South Mariposa, where Uncle Tony's mother-in-law lived in the floors above. The cops swooped down on the building, knocked them around a bit, tore up the still, and dragged them all to the station. The charges were fixed up or maybe the cops couldn't be bothered; either way they all went home by the end of the day.

He was arrested again just after the New Year (1925). Johnny and Tancredi coming out of a nightclub, some joint owned by Albert Marco. Tancredi recalled, "We were young and showing off." Cops in a squad car pulled them over, frisked them, found their guns. The officers asked them if they had permits for those rods. They were locked up for two days. Detectives questioned them. A police report was filed, Johnny's first under his new name. It concluded: "[He] is not a holdup man or a criminal . . . transports a little booze once in a while and carried gun for his protection. . . . Rosselli is in a position to give LAPD good information in the future."

They were released on bond pending a hearing on the gun charge. The case was eventually dropped without explanation. There were months when the courts were so backed up with liquor violations they couldn't be bothered with much else short of murder (and it was said a lot of those cases got brushed aside too).

After more than a year in one place Tancredi was restless. Maybe the run-ins with the police reminded him that he was still wanted for murder somewhere and needed to get out of the bright light in Los Angeles. He hoped his pal would hit the road with him, they could travel up to San Francisco, or maybe cross the border and roam in Mexico for a while.

Johnny was restless in his own way, but he wanted to move up in the world, not just wander it from place to place. He saw possibilities for himself in Los Angeles that Tancredi never did.

It was time to part ways with Uncle Tony, too, whose gentlemanly approach to bootlegging was getting him nowhere. Soon after his friend left town Johnny quit D'Acunto's employ, though the two remained on good terms and Johnny kept a protective eye out for the older man in the years ahead. He went to work for another violator of Prohibition, this one as wild and ambitious as D'Acunto had been modest and small-time.

3

The papers called him the King of the Western Rumrunners, a star among the smugglers by the sea on the California coast, colorful copy with his Stetson hats and pearl-handled revolvers and the bulge of ten or twenty grand in cash in his front pocket. "Rumrunning" was a euphemism from the East. In fact Tony Cornero imported only the finest Scotch and Canadian whisky, gin, and rye, and, come December, cases of Champagne to bring in the New Year. If your tipple was from the Cornero outfit you knew you were getting the very best.

Cornero was an Italian from the Piedmont, in the Alpine foothills. His family were farmers, working land that had been passed down for generations. When Tony was a child his father had wasted their legacy. He preferred games of chance to agriculture, and so the farm and everything else they owned was lost. In 1904, when Tony was four, Papa Cornero packed them up and they joined the exodus to America, all the way to the West Coast, settling in a farming community south of San Francisco. Tony's father drank himself to an early grave. His mother remarried, and Tony's stepdad adopted him, giving the boy U.S. citizenship and a new surname, Strella (though he refused to use it).

Tony had a wild streak. He started doing stickups, spent some years in juvenile prison. When he got out he went into the navy, but life in the service didn't suit him. He was court-martialed and dishonorably discharged six months later. He drove a taxi, did some other odd jobs. At twenty—Prohibition had just begun—he decided to stop wasting his life, to make something of himself. He became a bootlegger.

It turned out that Cornero had a great feel for that line of work, which was then taking form. With his brothers and sisters, a small gang, and some big ideas, he pushed his way into the Los Angeles market. He built his business on speed and efficiency, fair prices, and quality. In the early days of Prohibition on the West Coast, a lot of bad stuff was peddled to a frantic public, quick-mix booze from bordertown distilleries and vermin-riddled basements. Some of it tasted like poison, and some of it was just that. People were really dying for a drink. From the start, Tony Cornero brought in only the good stuff. He made connections with international distributors and created channels between California and Canada and Mexico, where liquor was legal.

The business grew fast. Tony Cornero was clever, and he was afraid of nobody. He became one of the busiest bootleggers in Southern California and the first serious challenger to the rule of the Combination in Los Angeles. The newspapers wrote of Tony Cornero with admiration. He had a rowdy charm in person, a flashy style, and for a professional lawbreaker he was an honest man. He had become a kind of folk hero to those who could appreciate his ornery independence and his high-end product. Not yet thirty, he was a millionaire several times over and lived in a grand house in a neighborhood favored by movie stars. Cornero did not see himself as a crook but as a good businessman who gave the people what they wanted and made a profit from it, a classic American success story.

When he started working for Tony Cornero, Johnny was just another thug for hire, anonymous and expendable. He labored in the warehouses, rode guard on the delivery trucks, and went along when they needed extra help with a recalcitrant customer. He was made a driver on what they called the "midnight run," the late-hour circuit Cornero's big trucks rode to the Pacific shore and back to the city. The trucks went out empty, and they came back packed full with contraband fresh from the sea.

This was the last leg of an elaborate smuggling operation that began a thousand miles away in Canada. A steamship or schooner, several of them secretly owned or co-owned by Cornero, departed Vancouver headed south with a cargo of bottled booze. In the dead of night, in a predetermined position at sea, twenty or more miles off the Southern California coast, the vessel would make an unscheduled stop. In advance, a coded wireless message sent from the captain to Cornero in Los Angeles indicated the place and time of the rendezvous.

The smuggled goods had to be taken from the ship, loaded on the truck, driven back to Los Angeles. Gang members and ship's crew worked together transporting the contraband to land, as many as several thousand burlap-wrapped sacks with eight or ten bottles in each. The work was wet, cold, and dangerous, moving the heavy, fragile packages over the water, from ship to skiff to shore, in the dark. It had to be done without catching the attention of armed federal agents, police, the Coast Guard. The whole process could take hours, and if there were delays, if the water was rough or the mother ship late, it might go on until morning, each ray of dawn light increasing the odds of being discovered.

As soon as a truck was packed full, it set off back to Los Angeles. Hijackers were often staked out along the main routes back to the city. A truck driver had to stay alert for signs of an ambush, a stalled auto or tree limbs in the road. Sometimes the only warning you got was the boom of gunfire. If the hijackers were successful it could be a very expensive night for someone like Tony Cornero, cargo lost (as much as one hundred thousand dollars in liquor at stake), trucks lost (six grand per five-ton vehicle), sometimes personnel lost (worth something or other).

If it wasn't the road pirates lying in wait it was the law. One night Johnny was driving a load from Santa Monica when a sheriff's department patrol caught him. Conviction could mean years in prison. But luck was on his side that night. He was getting pushed around by the arresting officers when their boss weighed in. Frank DeWar was the chief deputy sheriff of LA County. He told the men, "Quit picking on the kid."

DeWar took him aside, talked with him. The chief decided "the kid" was too young to have his life ruined by prison. He walked him along the road, advised him to stay out of trouble, and then told him to start running. In later years DeWar headed the county's Special Anti-Gangster Division and would have been disappointed to know Johnny didn't take his advice.

Johnny made his mark driving for Cornero. A man named Dan Winkler, an underworld denizen in those days, told federal inquisitors many years later that Rosselli was known as "one of the best automobile drivers in the bootlegging industry. He was a daredevil and could make any trip in less time than any other driver . . . and he had a reputation for being very handy with his fists."

His talent was rewarded. Soon, he was brought in from the road and became one of the guys working at Cornero headquarters downtown. At first he worked for Frank Cornero, the boss's brother and business partner. Frank liked him, kept him close. Johnny started joining Frank and other guys in the inner circle late at night when they hung around in the office or in the back room of a nearby speak and would shoot the breeze over beers or a bottle of Scotch.

Tony got to know Johnny, and he liked him, too. The fact that they were all countrymen didn't make any difference. Tony was no flag-waver for the motherland. Try and make a million bucks in Italy, was his feeling. America was the land of opportunity. Johnny agreed. It was just that some of the opportunities could get you shot.

Tony enjoyed Johnny's company. He'd bounce ideas off him. The kid was a born crook, like most of the people Tony Cornero knew, but he had a head on his shoulders, which was rare in that particular vocation. So what if he was only nineteen? Tony was only twenty-five himself.

"This a smart kid," Tony would crack to his brother. "We gotta keep an eye on him."

Johnny became Tony's sort-of secretary and his bodyguard. Wherever Tony went Johnny went with him, Johnny's fingers always close to the revolver in his coat pocket. You couldn't be in a better spot to learn the ropes, meet interesting people. There was more money in it, too, which did not hurt. At Tony's urging he spent some of it on a new wardrobe. The boss didn't want the people around him to look like bums. Johnny went to Cornero's tailor. Linen suits and silk shirts replaced Johnny's workingman's wardrobe. He bought shoes like a pair Tony wore, willow calf brogues as smooth as a girl's ass. He began going to Tony's favored barber, and like Tony went every morning for a hot-towel shave.

At Tony's side, Johnny got a front-row view of the whole grand operation. It was a bootleg empire that reached into three countries. Millions of dollars in revenue. An army's worth of manpower and matériel. Cornero owned trucks, boats, warehouses. He employed more than a hundred people, paid off maybe twice that number. There were big things in the works, including a new base on the Mexican coast, close enough to send a smuggling ship to California and back in a single weekend. There was talk of a move into casinos and gambling boats. Cornero imagined one day having a West Coast operation as lucrative and powerful as the ones the big mobs ran in New York and Chicago.

Johnny was there to see the Corneros' next big thing, a major move into neighboring Orange County. Los Angeles had always been the center of the bootlegging business in Southern California, the big gangs headquartered in the warehouses and warrens downtown and around the train station. The hundreds of thousands of bottles that flowed into Los Angeles from the sea landed at the local harbor at San Pedro or on one of the many beaches along Santa Monica Bay. In recent months those entryways had become less welcoming. The lawlessness and large-scale violations of the Prohibition Act in Los Angeles had pushed Washington and

Sacramento to turn up the heat. Los Angeles County was becoming crowded with federal and state cops, patrolling, investigating, arresting. Unlike the local authorities, who were ambivalent about Prohibition and so often open to negotiation on the subject, the federal enforcers were true believers, and a pain in every bootlegger's ass. The Feds behaved with the righteous fervor of religious crusaders, they were not easy to buy off, and they were provided by Washington with unlimited resources (whatever it took to keep Americans from enjoying a drink).

The county to the south of LA was a place of sleepy beach towns and citrus farms. The big bootleggers had not given the area much attention, and so the federal cops had overlooked it too. Johnny was sent down with Frank Cornero to have a look around. What they found was a place full of influential people—government officials, policemen, and upstanding citizens—with welcoming palms out waiting to be greased.

A plan was conceived, something like Charlie Crawford's "System" in LA, that successful coalition of criminal and government, but here to be spread across a series of small communities. Over a period of several months and after much free spending and many tempting promises, the Cornero gang had put together a promising network of conspirators. The distinguished group would include the justice of the peace at Laguna Beach, the Orange County deputy sheriff, a Santa Ana deputy, the city marshal of Seal Beach, numerous police officers, and several prominent businessmen with useful coastal properties in the area. In return for monetary and certain other rewards the group was pledged to provide safe havens within county lines. The designated smugglers would be free to land their goods, load them, and move on with no interference. As well, the Orange network would be keeping track of federal and state activities in the county, and give warning of any impending threat. Payments were keyed to the amount of contraband landed, much like an import tax, paid on a sliding scale, roughly a dollar per case for higher-ups like judges and sheriffs, down to two bits for minor operatives like patrolmen. This encouraged them to keep things running smoothly, as the more liquor landed, the bigger the kickback.

The enterprise was in operation by summer. It worked like a charm. Under the protective cloak of their partners, the Corneros landed boatload after boatload of illicit goods at various designated spots, in turn delivering piles of cash to some of the county's most important people. The bootleggers sweetened the pot with frequent "wild parties" at the Green Bay Inn in Santa Ana (the proprietor being a member of the network), where top-shelf beverages and low-down ladies were freely available to the conspirators.

In the three years the surfside conspiracy lasted—until its sad collapse beneath a tidal wave of scandal, arrests, and jail sentences—more alcohol would come through the Orange County "free zone" than anywhere on the Pacific Coast.

Even as the Cornero gang was creating its greatest success, back in Los Angeles rival bootleggers were plotting their destruction. This conflict had been coming to a head for months. The competition had grown large. The old criminal alliance that dominated the Los Angeles underworld had seen a decline in its power and profits. The illicit liquor business that once belonged to them exclusively was now shared not only with Tony Cornero but with numerous independent operators, indeed with anybody who could get his hands on a quantity of alcohol. There was just too much business for one gang to control it all. The unsteady circumstances had not been helped by an ongoing rift between the Combination criminals and the Cryer-Parrot administration.

In early '25 the time came to push back. The Combination, including Page, Marco, McAfee, and the rest, began a war to regain their lost power and drive out the encroaching independents.

The war was waged fitfully in the beginning. As winter became spring the dispute grew harder to ignore. There was an increase in the number of hijackings and raids on plants and warehouses that stored what awaited distribution. There were more rats and spies around, and more tip-offs to cops and federal agents.

The Cornero gang was reluctant to fight back, despite growing losses. Tony had too much on his mind, liquor to ship, officials to bribe, and moving ahead with his plan for a new base in Mexico. He was a businessman, not a general.

The press and public also had not shown much interest in the conflict at first, despite the number of corpses and wounded being found on so many mornings. The midwinter killing of a hijacker named William Keefe, also known as George Turner, his bullet-riddled body discovered by police on a bier of shattered sacks of whiskey, encouraged the newspapers to speculate about a "smouldering west coast gang war." But the topic stayed off front pages. It was not until the summer that the battling bootleggers made headlines.

Late in June, Johnny accompanied Tony Cornero to Guaymas, Mexico, to meet with potential suppliers. In their brief absence, hijackers raided several of Cornero's warehouses, all of them freshly stocked with high-priced liquids. No one could say who was behind the raids, but they were pros and working from good-quality information. Cornero continued to restrict himself to a defensive posture, but he was hoping to make it a strong defense. He increased manpower and firepower. He purchased dozens of expensive black-market Thompson submachine guns, rarely seen outside the military—or Chicago—with their heavy rounds deadly enough at close range to slice a man in two. He fortified the warehouses and the vehicles, tried to root out any potential spies or informers. Some nights they ran dummy loads, the trucks carrying only sacks of sand and a contingent of heavily armed gunmen.

One evening along East Perris Road in Long Beach, a Cornero

truck was ambushed. Hooded men with revolvers and shotguns came hurtling from two dark sedans. They swarmed the truck, and were met at once by the roar of automatic weapons, tommy guns lighting up the dark like a bonfire. Overwhelmed, the hijackers fled into the shadows or lay bleeding on the roadside.

One of Cornero's best men, Jimmy Fox, had been wounded in the shootout. His comrades drove him at high speed to Angelus Hospital. As the medical attendants worked to save him, police pushed forward, demanding he tell them what happened. A reporter who was there wrote up the encounter: "The sardonic little gunman laughed bitterly in the face of detectives seeking to track down his assailant. 'I can take care of my own affairs,' Fox said. 'Go peddle your papers.'" The criminal's code: You never squealed. (Unless you did.)

Cornero got Fox whisked out of the hospital before there were any more inquiries and stashed him in a private clinic, where he was mended by specialists (their specialty was keeping their mouths shut).

The critically wounded hijackers had been taken to a hospital in Long Beach. The police questioned them, too, and they were no more cooperative than Fox had been. But their names were revealed for the public record and included: H. C. Munson (real name Harry Schwartz), a man with past connections to the booze trust, and Jack Barrett, the bodyguard of veteran Combination partner Milton "Farmer" Page. The connection to Page—one of the original Los Angeles racketeers and a friend of "Good Time Charlie" Crawford—made it clear who was behind the hijacking attempt.

The battle of Long Beach caused an uproar. To read the newspaper accounts and to hear the chatter, it was as if there had been a foreign invasion. The mention of "machine guns" was the clincher. Here in the land of sunshine and palm trees were the deadly weapons of lawless Chicago, and in the minds of certain Southern

Californians, Chicago was a place as threatening and foreign as Red Russia. Machine guns smelled of anarchy and immigrants to timid Midwestern émigrés.

An irate public was bad for business, could ruin things for everyone. It could not be ignored. Acting District Attorney Buron Fitts called a conference of the county's leading law enforcement officials—with Captain Murray, acting chief of police; Captain Finlayson, chief of detectives; Inspector Davis of the Vice Squad; Sheriff Traeger; and Undersheriff Biscailuz among them—"to devise means of ridding Los Angeles of an impending menace to human life which has developed out of the machine gun battle between enemy rumrunning factions at Long Beach last Monday night."

The gathered lawmen, some of whom had been on the take for years, addressed the subject at hand with straight-faced enthusiasm. They agreed on an immediate and unified course of action: The killers and professional gunmen must go. D.A. Fitts released a fulminating statement:

> The police department . . . vice squad . . . Sheriff's office . . . in conference with this office today . . . are organizing a smash against the killers and gunmen infesting the city of Los Angeles. Those cases involving a violation of the deadly weapon law of California, particularly men who heretofore have been convicted of felonies, and are now found in possession of deadly weapons, will be vigorously prosecuted by this office. The police department and the Sheriff's office are determined to drive these killers and gunmen out. This office will join them in that effort with all its force.
>
> Every official of the police department, the Sheriff's office and the District Attorney's office is sick and tired of these professional killers in their efforts to gain a hold on the city. Human life and property is jeopardized as long as we permit them to remain here. . . . Every one of them is going to

be driven from the city. If they do not leave before the law can get its hands on them then the jails will be fairly filled with the most astounding array of gunmen and dangerous crooks within forty-eight hours that any western city ever has seen.

The cleanup began on schedule. The cops swept through the downtown neighborhoods, raided the hangouts, speakeasies, whorehouses, roominghouses. Anybody with a familiar face, or a shifty-looking one, was taken to jail. If they were found in the presence of alcohol or in the possession of a gun they were charged appropriately, if they were breaking no laws at all then vagrancy was the rap. The paddy wagon ran along 6th Street as regularly as a trolley car.

Johnny was picked up at the Friar's Inn, the downtown cabaret Tony's little sister Catherine managed. Luckily he had left his pistol at home. Cornero was taken into custody in his office at 222 Witmer Street. They were all questioned on the Long Beach incident. All said they knew nothing. Released on bail—Tony's was for a whopping ten grand—they were warned to get out of town within forty-eight hours. This was an idle threat for now, as Cornero's expensive attorneys proved in court. There was such a thing as the law, after all.

The cops conducted another sweep within days of the first, then another, grabbing many of the same people and throwing them in jail. Johnny was picked up twice. He made the local newspapers for the first time—along with several other members of the gang reported arrested—though his name was misspelled as "John Rosselle."

Who could say what was really going on? The police in Los Angeles had seldom done anything just because it was the legal or the right thing to do. Whether they were acting out of concern for the citizenry or taking the opportunity to go after the City Hall gang's rivals, it added up to the same predicament for Cornero and the other independents, under attack from two sides.

The war went on for months. It was stop and go—cooling down for weeks while the participants tried to attend to less-destructive matters, then suddenly erupting in bloodshed—which made it even worse on the nerves. There were gun battles, robberies, property set on fire. People disappeared. Bodies turned up in the sewers and washed ashore from the sea. The old guard took on new personnel, imported thugs and gunmen who worked with a fresh enthusiasm. Bootleggers were kidnapped and tortured for information: One had a finger cut off to make him talk; another was burned with an electric iron held to his bare flesh.

All this while the Los Angeles cops kept up their drive against the Cornero gang and other criminal factions, with more raids, blanket arrests. Having gotten a reputation as lackeys for business and criminal powers, the city police now rebuilt their self-esteem with billy clubs and revolvers. The appointment of James E. Davis as chief of police intensified the change in style. Davis was a big, strutting Texan, a ruthless and some said mentally unstable man, who believed the law was there to serve his purposes and not the other way around. It was Davis who devised the so-called rousting system, his extra-constitutional method of harassing known and suspected bootleggers, pulling scores of men off the streets and out of their homes, throwing them in jail without a charge, interrogating and roughing up some, releasing them a day or two days later, then doing it again, five and six times in a row. As this went on, other police details made illegal break-ins and searches of the prisoners' homes and properties, looking for evidence that would keep them locked up for longer than two days. The crooks claimed the cops also robbed them of their valuables while they were making the search.

"Day by day," Davis told the newspapers, "I am attempting to perfect my defenses, and I have already detailed all the men and equipment that I can spare from other lines of work for this duty. I believe that we have made a great deal of headway and expect to make a great deal more during the coming months."

The problem with giving power to a crazy man was that his solutions could be worse than the problems. Police Chief Davis saw his officers as a military force, supplied them with automatic weapons and shotguns—intended for nothing but killing, for blowing heads off—and demanded the city council supply him with armored trucks with mounted machine guns, just the thing to turn Main Street into a bloody Western Front.

In November a federal grand jury investigating liquor conspiracies in Southern California went into "extraordinary session" on the third floor of the Federal Building in downtown Los Angeles. Various members of the Cornero organization were subpoenaed to testify and U.S. deputies and Internal Revenue Service operatives were sent out to get them. Tony decided it was a good time to take a holiday, and a group of them, Tony and Frank, Johnny, the youngest Cornero brother, Pico, and a few others packed their valises and headed across the border to Mexico.

Miss Mabel Walker Willebrandt, assistant attorney general in charge of the liquor division, told the newspapers the government was about to close in on the Los Angeles liquor barons: *"We have them by the throat,"* she declared with emphasis, *"and we're not going to let go."*

In Ensenada the gang drank and gambled and wenched for some days, then moved along the coast to Rosarito, where they recuperated at a newly opened luxury resort on the beach. They stayed till Christmas, and a good time was had by all.

In the new year—1926—there was another wave of targeted hijackings, and much valuable contraband was lost. The underworld had it that a fellow named Walter Hesketh, alias Eddie Egan, was directing the new attacks. Hesketh was a middling criminal—the papers described him as "a widely known police character"—now rumored to be doing the bidding of Farmer Page and company. There was also a rumor that Hesketh had been put in charge of serving the Combination's "warrant" on Tony Cornero's life.

On a Saturday night near the end of March, Hesketh and a few companions departed a café on West 6th and St. Paul and headed for home. Hesketh was at the curb when a large dark automobile drove by, slowing to a crawl. One, maybe two pistols fired through an open window, then the car roared away. Hesketh took three in the belly. His friends lifted him out of a pool of blood and drove him to General Hospital, where he moaned and tossed in agony for several days. Hesketh said he recognized the man who fired the shots but refused to identify him.

"If I die," he said, "I'm out of luck. If I live, he will be out of luck."

Hesketh was out.

On April 3, hours after the gangster's demise, a warrant was issued for the arrest of Tony and Frank Cornero on a charge of murder. Later that day, in a show of bravado that titillated reporters, the brothers turned themselves in to the detective bureau at Central Station. They were placed under arrest, frisked—Tony, it was noted, had twenty thousand dollars in his pocket—and thrown behind bars.

On April 6 a coroner's inquest was conducted. None of four eyewitnesses was able or willing to identify either Cornero as the shooter. A homicide detective told the jury that the victim did know the identity of his assailant but had "refused to squeal."

The verdict: "Hesketh came to his death by gunshot wound inflicted by person or persons unknown, with homicidal intent."

Tony and Frank were ordered released from jail.

Hesketh's death began a whole season of bad luck for enemies of the Cornero gang. Another hijacker and associate of Hesketh, Eddie "Blondy" Hanson, was visited by some men with revolvers in his room at a boardinghouse on South Hope Street. Hanson died in a hail of gunfire, at least one slug going straight through his brain. The wallpaper behind the bed was so pitted with bullet holes it looked like a polka-dot pattern.

Chicago émigré George Carroll, another reputed road pirate, was shot in the head and his body tossed into a ditch from a speeding vehicle just at the city limit.

It was believed that as many as twenty known hijackers went missing or were found dead in this period of time. The consensus was that they might have all been "out on the road too much."

The wave of hijackings became a trickle.

All the commotion of the past year had taken a toll on the Cornero organization. In need of a fast influx of cash, they quickly made arrangements to import an unusually large shipment from Canada: fifty thousand bottles of high-end whisky. The good stuff had become scarce in the city during the gang war, and Cornero expected to make a killing with a high mark-up on every fluid ounce. In July, freighted with booze, the Panamanian ship *Chasina* sailed out of Vancouver for Southern California.

The hurried caper did not allow for the usual careful planning. There were last-minute problems securing a large deepwater powerboat, and a replacement had to be found. An eighty-foot yacht— the *Donasari*—belonging to the president of the Amex Oil Company was docked for repairs in Wilmington, up the channel from Long Beach. Arrangements were made with the *Donasari's* captain and crew to do some remunerative moonlighting.

It was a rush job all the way, and on July 20, with the many pieces of the operation barely put in place, the *Donasari* sailed out of Wilmington and onto the high seas. The weather was bad, and the belligerent Pacific tossed the big luxury vessel like it was a toy sailboat. No one on board was in any mood for the labor ahead as they neared the big Panamanian freighter rising and plunging in the waves.

It got worse. They had expected to tie up to the *Chasina* and make a direct transfer of the cargo. But the *Chasina*'s captain refused such close contact, certain that the stormy waters would send the yacht crashing into the ship's hull. There was nothing for it but to offload the sacks of bottles from the ship onto two dories and row them back and forth to the yacht across the troubled waters.

The boat made a slow return to land. Every inch of the interior packed with cargo, the gangsters sat on the open deck, drenched in cold sea spray. The shaken captain of the *Donasari* refused to go as far as the rendezvous point and instead took the boat to the nearest harbor at Long Beach. When they arrived in the middle of the night there was nothing to do but leave the fortune in booze on board, go home to dry off, and unload it in the morning.

By that time, alas, the *Donasari* had been reported missing by representatives of Amex Oil. Harbor police found the yacht and discovered its abundant illegal cargo. The captain was tracked down and brought in for questioning by local and federal lawmen. The captain told them the contraband belonged to one Tony Cornero. He was a victim of kidnapping, said the captain, forced by the Cornero gangsters to do their bidding under threat of death. This was not good: If the law ever got any of the gang on a kidnapping rap it could mean twenty years in the big house.

The government had had enough of the rumland czar. The Feds had been following his trail for months. Agents of the Internal Revenue Service uncovered his illegal income and hidden holdings in shipping and trade. Deals were being offered to convicted bootleggers willing to rat him out. There was evidence of violations of the gun laws, and use of a forged gun permit.

Cornero told the gang it was every man for himself now. He

stuffed a bag with cash and caught a night train to Seattle. He chartered an airplane to Vancouver. But the Canadian authorities were also looking for him and he had to keep on the run.

There were rumors he had crossed back into the States and was being hidden by his friend Al Capone in Chicago. Then it was said he had gotten out of the country again and was living somewhere in Germany.

4

With Tony Cornero's disappearance and brother Frank in hiding, the rest of the Cornero gang scattered. Johnny took some cash, and some blonde, and went to Mexico.

He returned to Los Angeles early in 1927, renting a suite of rooms at the Mayfair Hotel on 7th Street. He found a new mistress, a beautiful Indian girl, the manicurist at the hotel barbershop. Making a place for himself as a "sporting man" in the downtown underworld, he ran a race book for big-money gamblers and sponsored elite card games. He managed a few top-dollar call girls servicing select customers and guests at the big hotels. He still moved a little liquor, but never enough to catch the attention of the Prohibition squads. The beat cops were seldom a problem if you were generous. He had a good reputation. An honest crook. He was known by the nicknames "Gentleman John" and "Handsome Johnny."

He employed one assistant, a tough, thickheaded thirty-four-year-old Neapolitan named Salvatore Piscopo, now using the alias Louis Merli. Merli was a criminal since childhood, a gang member and assassin in Italy long before he emigrated to America. He was experienced—if not exactly talented—in nearly every crime in the statutes. He was wanted for murder in New York. In Los Angeles he had been a burglar, a bootlegger, and muscle for hire before coming to work with Johnny Rosselli. He did a little of everything for him.

Merli was without education on either side of the Atlantic and spoke English with a thick immigrant accent of the sort mockingly employed by vaudeville comedians. Wiseguys in speaks would make fun of him, calling him "Organ Grinder" and "Dago Louie." The latter nickname stuck. When someone called him such things within earshot, Merli would do a slow burn, his temper building until it erupted and he beat the piece of *merda* to a pulp.

For Johnny, Merli worked as a collector of debts, a chauffeur, and a general errand boy. He was devoted to his employer. Though Johnny was many years younger, Merli treated him like a respected elder and with a devotion that went above and beyond the salary Johnny paid him. Some people said Johnny had done him some favor, maybe gotten him out of a jam, and Merli owed him big. Johnny would describe Dago Louie as his secretary, but Louis referred to Johnny as his best friend. He asked him to be godfather to his little boy—Louis's pride and joy, even though the child had once led police to a hidden stash of bootleg liquor during a raid on the family home, sending his father to jail for a while.

As Johnny found his place among the high rollers in Los Angeles— as one of the more personable figures in the local criminal milieu— his path would often cross with people from the moving picture community. Movies and vice—gambling, sex, booze, and drugs— were the biggest industries in that city. In a way they served similar purposes. Both sold illusions, escape, an expanded consciousness. They were more entwined and allied than the moviegoing public could imagine, or than the pious executives in charge would ever want known. Even with the occasional headline scandal—a rape, an overdose, a suicide—the outside world had little idea that the movie colony indulged in quite so much shocking and degenerate behavior. With what Johnny knew about the secret lives of Holly-wood people—the alcoholics, drug users, inverts, orgiasts—he could have shut down the whole town in one front-page tell-all, if he didn't like so many of them and believe in the credo "Live and let live," and if the hedonists in the picture business didn't have so much money to spend on their habits.

He drank and dined with them, played cards with them, got them drugs, occasionally fixed a problem or got someone out of trouble. He had a growing fondness for the creative and uncon-ventional characters who made the movies (his fondness for the dazzling creatures known as movie actresses was altogether more intense). On occasion he would visit one of the walled-in picture studios that were scattered about the city and the valley beyond. If he came upon an open set he would stop to watch the actors and crew, losing himself in the visions of make-believe. Some Holly-wood notables Johnny had come to know as personal friends, in-cluding the producer Joe Schenck, the movie star John Gilbert, the actor Jack Pickford (brother of Mary), and the screenwriter Row-land Brown.

After being on the road for two years and more, Johnny's old friend Tancredi Tortora came back to Los Angeles. He had been drifting across his adopted homeland. Christ knew what he'd been up to.

Tancredi went looking for Johnny in their old domain. It was no trouble finding him. Everybody downtown seemed to know Johnny Rosselli.

It was clear when they were reunited which one had made the more productive use of the past few years. Tancredi remained as he had always been, shiftless, a vagabond. Johnny had matured. He was sharper. Nothing seemed to get past him. His appearance evi-denced good fortune and expensive tastes. Gone were the old work clothes and boots, the stubbly face and dirty fingers, replaced with a fine wardrobe, immaculate grooming (movie-star haircut, bronzed skin, manicured nails with the luster of Red Sea pearls). It was hard for Tancredi to see the feral kid he had taken out of Boston, the tough young roustabout he had brought to the West.

The two did not revive their friendship. It seemed that the old rapport had just faded away. If Tancredi was disappointed or upset that Johnny did not find a place for him in his new world, he never said it out loud.

One day Tancredi left town. He felt the call of the road again. Shifting around, he spent time in Chicago, New York, Bayonne, New Jersey, Waterbury, Connecticut. One day in 1934, Tancredi walked into the Waterbury police station and gave himself up for that long-ago murder in Boston. No explanation. He couldn't explain it. He'd been on the lam for a long time, maybe he had just gotten tired. They put him in the penitentiary for fifteen years. When he got out the immigration authorities stuck him on a boat to Italy and told him not to come back. He never saw Johnny Rosselli again.

In September the entire country was in a state of near-hysteria over the coming return match—the Fight of the Century, it was called—between the former heavyweight boxing champ, Jack Dempsey, and Gene Tunney, the man who had taken away his title a year ago. Johnny joined his club-owner friend Joe Santanello and three hundred other Angelenos, including film stars, athletes, gamblers and bootleggers, on the "De Luxe Fight Special," paying $197.92 apiece for round-trip rail service, a ringside seat for the fight, food and drink, and two nights at the forty-story Morrison Hotel on the Loop in Chicago, Illinois, the city of beer and blood.

It was a debauched group that rolled into town and eventually staggered to Soldier Field on the lakefront. The typical roughneck fight crowd was joined for this event by spectators from every walk of life, to the top reaches of high society. The match lived up to the hype, an awesome battle capped by a jaw-dropping controversy. The beloved brute, the iron man Dempsey, had been losing for six rounds to the less popular, more methodical Tunney, the clean-cut champ, the reader of Shakespeare. Then, in the seventh round, the contender erupted, pounding Tunney to the canvas. A hovering Dempsey refused to go to a neutral corner, delaying the referee's count by five or more seconds and allowing Tunney precious extra time to recuperate. He came back strong and defeated Dempsey by a unanimous decision. The crowd boiled over in reaction to the so-called "long count" in the seventh, which grew longer as the arguments about it continued.

After the fight Johnny went with a group to the Metropole Hotel, where a crowded and raucous party was under way in the hotel's ballroom, maybe a thousand people there. The party was courtesy of none other than Al Capone, Chicago's infamous crime lord, who lived in spacious digs on the fourth floor. Showgirls and the smart set, mayors and killers, celebrated together, drinking Champagne and dancing to a "colored" jazz band. Al Jolson—just days away from the premiere of his new film *The Jazz Singer*—got on the bandstand and sang "Toot Toot Tootsie Goodbye."

Johnny ran into his traveling companion, Santanello, who was wavering drunk. He put an arm across Johnny's shoulders, saying, "Come on and meet the Big Fella." And Johnny found himself going along to an adjacent room full of loud people and clouds of cigar smoke. After somebody in a dark suit patted him down, he found himself standing before the most famous gangster in the world.

Meeting Al Capone: For anyone in the rackets it was the equivalent of a papal audience. There he was, the brazen young Italian from Brooklyn whose spectacular career in crime had made him an icon of the age, the living embodiment of malevolent American enterprise, leader of a brilliant and ruthless gang that came to be known as the Chicago Outfit. There he sat, puffy with drink, a large man with big warm eyes, fat purple lips, and three dark pink razor scars on his left side and neck. He looked younger than he did in the newspapers and the newsreels (he was twenty-eight years old). He looked jovial and pleased as he welcomed his guests. They said he'd lost thirty-five grand betting on Dempsey, but his bookies had taken in a million from all the other suckers who'd done the same. Johnny shook the hand of the Big Man, and Capone said something about the good weather in Southern California, it was hard to hear in the noisy room. A line of supplicants advanced, and in another moment someone had taken Johnny's place.

It wasn't much, but it was bound to impress some of the fellows back in Los Angeles.

As it happened he would soon have another encounter with Capone. It was not long after their introduction, and this time on Johnny's own turf.

It was a bumpy autumn for Scarface Al. His reign as the crime boss supreme had lately come under assault. Some of Capone's associates said his love of self-promotion, posing for pictures, giving interviews, kissing babies, had gone too far. At the end of the day they were still criminals. Why rub the law's face in it? There were cops roaming through the halls of the Metropole all the time now, looking for trouble. Capone's businesses were frequently raided, shut down for a couple of days at a time, causing steady financial losses. Every couple of weeks they dragged him in on suspicion, questioned him, sent him home. Capone would stand outside the police station with his attorney and sneer and joke for the crowd, but in fact it hurt his feelings.

The impetus for this new wave of police harassment came from the office of Mayor "Big Bill" Thompson. The wildly corrupt politician, now deluded by ambitions for higher office, had begun to publicly distance himself from his notorious patron. Capone couldn't believe the ingratitude. He moaned to the reporters staked out in the lobby of his hotel: *"I've been spending the best years of my life as a public benefactor!* I've given people the light pleasures, show them a good time. And all I get is abuse—*the existence of a hunted man*. . . . 'Public service' is my motto. . . . But I'm not appreciated. It's no use."

In November, Capone announced he was leaving town for the holidays: "Let the worthy citizens of Chicago get their liquor the best way they can. I'm sick of the job—it's a thankless one and full of grief. I don't know when I'll get back, if ever."

It was expected that Capone was headed for Florida—he'd said as much—but he pulled a fast one at the last minute, slipping around the cops and reporters and in the early morning of December 8, he boarded a train to California instead.

In Los Angeles, Capone, his cousin Charlie "Trigger Happy" Fischetti, and a pair of burly bodyguards took a suite at the Biltmore downtown. The first morning they went over the border to the races at Tijuana. Next day they took a tour of a Hollywood picture studio. Then they went out to look at the ocean, and they ate fresh fish.

Capone had registered under the name "Al Brown," but his actual identity was soon uncovered. A squadron of detectives and uniformed cops arrived at the hotel—an "unwelcoming committee"—to confront the notorious gangster and his entourage. The rumor was that some of the Combination boys had ID'd Capone and demanded the police roust.

Johnny heard the news of Capone's visit and the trouble that followed. He knew a lot of policemen and newsmen and decided he would go over to the Biltmore and see if he could be of any help. He hated to think of Mr. Capone being given a bad impression of the city. When he arrived at the Biltmore, its grand Baroque-Moorish-Renaissance-whatever lobby was jammed with cops and with reporters and photographers waiting for something to happen.

Johnny knew every bellhop at the hotel (the 'hops all worked the "girl racket," getting prostitutes up to the rooms), and he had no trouble reaching Capone's suite.

Big Al was pleased to see a friendly face but was otherwise not in a happy mood. He had been given a hard time all morning, and the Biltmore's manager had just been up to tell them they had to leave the hotel. "I wasn't going to do anything here," Capone said. "I came with my boy friends to see a little of the country. . . . Pretty hard on a fellow like me that didn't mean no harm and only wanted a rest from business.

"We are tourists. And I thought you folks liked tourists."

Capone saw himself as a misunderstood hero, forever doing good things for those who had nothing. Capone declared the big legit businesses were more crooked than the gangs and the government more violent. Washington sent young boys into war overseas—fighting Europe's battles—and got them killed by the thousands. Capone took good care of his guys and never killed anybody who wasn't asking for it. He brought calm to neighborhoods where there had been chaos. The cops should have given him a medal for all the trouble he saved them.

Wanting to make up for his city's rude treatment, Johnny offered Big Al and his pals the use of his own place for the remainder of their stay. Capone appreciated the kindness and happily accepted.

But by the time they had packed up and were ready to go the police were at the door. Detective Ed "Roughhouse" Brown was in charge—Johnny knew of this one and his brutal interrogations—and telling Capone the only place he was going was back where he came from. Capone saw there was no use fighting and agreed to leave. The four out-of-towners were herded into two squad cars and driven away to the Santa Fe Station. Johnny followed along, and at the platform he again apologized for the mistreatment Capone and his entourage had received. Capone took the kind words to heart. He told Johnny to come visit in Chicago, he'd take good care of him. The humbling of the Big Man wasn't over—Capone cried that someone had stolen the two bottles of rye they had taken out for the journey.

The next day the *Times* featured a derisive account of Capone's rapid departure. "'Scarface Al'—Came to Play, Now Look—He's Gone Away!" It was said that the Combination boys shared a good laugh over the story of the visiting crime lord dragged from his hotel room and sent home to Chicago.

It was a mistake to laugh.

5

Johnny could not say how long he had been sick. It had come and gone and come back. He had a chronic cough, recurring infections in his chest. He had pains in the back and in the pit of his stomach.

There were thick strands of blood in his saliva. There were occasions it became hard to catch a breath. He would sit for hours in the steamroom at the Athletic Club on Sunset, inhaling the warm moisture, attempting to chase away what was clogging his lungs. He would feel better some weeks and think he had licked it, then the coughing and the aching came back, worse than before.

The doctor sent him to the hospital. They listened to him breathe, they tested his blood, and they sampled his sputum. He was fluoroscoped and X-rayed. A shadow darkened one lung. The doctor told him he had tuberculosis.

Pulmonary tuberculosis was a contagious bacterial infection. It was spread through infected droplets in a breath, a cough, a sneeze. In its active state the disease attacked the lungs, then went after other organs of the body and, if untreated, likely destroyed them. There

was no certain medical antidote for tuberculosis, only an assortment of supervised "rest cures" and some risky surgical procedures.
In America tuberculosis had been a steadily growing problem since
the end of the previous century. Its sudden spread through the
country was believed to be caused by the unsanitary conditions in
the crowded industrial centers and the ghettos of the immigrants
and the poor.

Where Johnny grew up in Boston, tuberculosis—in general par-
lance "TB" or "consumption"—was commonplace. It was an accepted condition of life in that time. Every apartment house had
its share of residents wasting away in a back bedroom. You could
hear them through the walls at night, coughing themselves to death.
His paternal grandfather—Grandpapa Filippo—had died of the
disease. In Los Angeles tuberculosis reflected the city's recent
booming growth, with the increasing population of outsiders and
transients joined to a lack of public-health care and education.
Some blamed it on poor immigrants. Others said it was spread
by all the "lungers" come from the East to suck up the curative
good air.

The doctors told Johnny he would have to go to a sanatorium, a
medical facility specific to the treatment of tuberculosis. Entering
such a place meant a long-term commitment, anywhere from several months to one or two years or more. He resisted the doctors'
recommendation. He tried to get by with cough medicines and
other store-bought remedies. Early in 1927 the ailment erupted.
He began coughing blood in thick spurts. He was in the hospital
for more than a week. There was no choice now—if, they said, he
wanted to live to be thirty—but to follow the earlier advice of the
physicians.

It was not always easy to find space at one of the sanatoriums.
The number of people needing help was far greater than the number of beds available. To move up on the waiting list you had to
know the right person, or pay off the right person. A place was

found for him at the San Francisco Health Farm (later the Hassler Health Farm), a small facility run by the SF Public Health Services Department, located in a wooded area forty miles from the city.

No one could say how long he might be gone. He closed down his apartment, got rid of his belongings. He got rid of everything. When he left Los Angeles he was as unencumbered as he had been when he arrived three years before.

Intended to both treat and quarantine the patients, tuberculosis hospitals were usually built in rural locations, far from industrial or other polluters, where the infected could benefit from a clean environment while being kept apart from the general population. The San Francisco sanatorium was located in a forest near the small town of Belmont. The wooden hospital buildings rose above lush green hills on an open ridge at the end of a winding road. Aside from patients and employees, snakes, rabbits, and a few mountain lions, there was nothing else anywhere for miles.

The hospital contained facilities for about forty, separated by gender into two main halls (women and men were kept far apart as much as possible). Patients ranged in age from young adults to the elderly, from early-stage cases to those who had been fighting tuberculosis for years. How long patients stayed depended on the state of their disease and speed of recovery, but some of them didn't look like they were ever going anywhere.

Standard treatment for someone with a case of tuberculosis like Johnny's was a regimen of rest, fresh air, and a nutritious diet. Treatment began with a monthlong period of "complete bed rest." The idea was to encourage the growth of fibrosis in the lungs to wall off the tubercule bacilli, and fibrosis grew strongest and fastest with the least amount of activity in the lungs. During the weeks of complete bed rest patients were not permitted to walk, stand, get up to use the bathrooms. No motion at all outside the bed. No talking (except to medical staff). No reading or writing. No music or radio (too exciting). No visitors.

During the period of complete bed rest the only objects to which patients had access were a water cup, a pack of tissues for catching the globs of phlegm and blood that came up when they coughed, and a paper bag for disposing of them. Each morning after breakfast the patients in their beds were wheeled out to a long porch where the air came through large open windows and a retracted roof. At sunset they were wheeled back to the dorms. Doctors made daily rounds. Blood and sputum tests were taken once a week. Temperature and pulse were checked frequently. Dinner was served at six. Lights went out at nine.

After one month, if the patient showed no clear signs of healing, complete bed rest was continued. After three or four months without improvement, more aggressive treatment could be considered. The most common advanced procedure was surgical pneumothorax, the forcible collapsing of the tubercular lung—to compel its inactivity—through the injection of air or gas or oil into the chest. The procedure sometimes required the removal of ribs or the permanent repositioning of certain organs. These operations were imperfect and their aftermath uncertain, sometimes resulting in the death of the patient.

Thirty days Johnny lay in bed, like a corpse in an open coffin.

A second month began. He showed slight but steady signs of improvement. He was allowed "ambulatory privileges." He could get up, go to the toilet, shower. Speech was still discouraged. A shelf of dog-eared books was available to the patients. Reading was something he hadn't done since he was a schoolboy, and not much then. Under the circumstances it had to seem not nearly as bad as he remembered.

One day he received a visitor. That is, he opened his eyes one morning, and a man was sitting near the bed. He was a young Italian. He said his name was Parigi Tortora. He was Tancredi Tortora's brother. Tancredi had told him about Johnny, about their friendship and their many adventures. Parigi had come to Los Angeles. He was hoping to find work in California, maybe open a small business somewhere. He had come to pay his respects to his brother's good friend, but he'd learned that Johnny was sick, in a hospital in the north for no one knew how long. And Parigi decided he would go to visit him there, for his absent brother's sake. He hitchhiked all the way, and it took a long time. Johnny was having a bad week. Parigi understood. He sat there for some hours while Johnny slept. When Johnny awoke in the evening, Tancredi's brother was gone.

A third month passed. A fourth. His infected lungs were healing. It was his sanity that seemed in danger of collapse as almost half a year went by in near-total confinement, surrounded day and night by the sounds of moaning, hacking, vomiting.

Five months. The disease had abated. The doctors told him he could go home.

They warned him that if the TB came back he would have to return to the sanatorium and another course of treatment. And there was always the possibility it could come back and kill him.

In Los Angeles he rented an apartment downtown on West 6th Street. He took things slowly. After some weeks his strength began to return to something like what it had been. He was at loose ends for a while. Then one day he got a message. It was from Al Capone. It said: Come to Chicago.

3

OUR MAN IN HOLLYWOOD

Al Capone spent the first months of 1928 in the sunshine state of Florida. Chicago had become too violent even for Scarface. That was the winter of the Pineapple [hand grenade] Primary, when politicking became synonymous with gunfights, kidnappings, and bombings. Mayor Thompson's machine battled its slightly less corrupt competitors for victory in the next election. Popular public figures were shot dead in the street. Bombs were thrown. Blood spilled all the way to the voting booths. It was the biggest perversion of democracy in the city's—and perhaps the country's—history. The authorities were dying to tie Capone to the murder and mayhem. All said it was a good time to stay where he was and enjoy Florida's balmy weather and the regal comforts of a just-purchased Palm Island villa on Biscayne Bay.

There was still a multimillion-dollar business to run, bootlegging, rackets, unions, vice dens; enemies and upstarts to be killed, politicians to blackmail or bribe. Every week that winter the lieutenants shuttled back and forth from Chicago, meeting and strategizing with the boss at his winter palace, returning with new orders to implement. It had worked out very well. Everything went on as if the big fellow was still at home except that lawmen back home couldn't harass him, and he could do everything in his bathing suit in a chaise longue beside the swimming pool.

It was proof, that sojourn in Miami, that if you could run Chicago from a thousand miles away, you could run some other far-off place as well. Caesar and Napoleon—two fellow *paisani* he had come to admire—ruled whole continents. Why couldn't Al Capone do the same? He was a great believer in manifest destiny, or any other gimmick that could boost his share. In truth the idea had come from Capone's mentor Johnny Torrio: one vast underworld that would reach across from sea to sea, with everyone answering to a single authority. But Torrio had gotten shot up, barely survived, and that was enough, he retired to Italy. With all respects to his good friend, Capone considered himself to be of stronger stuff. Torrio had big ideas, but Capone was the one could make them happen.

The problem for an aspiring Mob emperor in the United States was how much of the country was already claimed by other mobs. The moneymaking centers of the East and Midwest were all sewed up. There was the Purple Gang in Detroit, the Porellos and the Jews of the Syndicate in Cleveland, "Silver Dollar Sam" Carolla and his Black Handers in New Orleans, Maranzano and Masseria, the battling "Mustache Petes" of New York. All with their own dreams and their own armies and their own tommy guns. Even Napoleon would have had a hard time moving in on some of those guys. And without a lot of territory to call your own, you weren't much of an emperor.

2

In Los Angeles, George Cryer neared the end of his third term as mayor. For nearly ten years the alliance of City Hall and the consortium of select racketeers and bootleggers led by Charlie

Crawford had operated with great success, give or take a few bloody gang wars. Criminals and politicians made for a natural partnership anyway, and for certain theirs had done nothing to interrupt the city's prosperity and rise to prominence in the 1920s.

Cryer remained a popular public servant and would have been reelected to another term. But the mayor's enemies were getting louder. Newspapers editorialized about corruption in high office, and rival politicians, including many stained with graft themselves, jeered at Cryer's "bootleg government." The majestic new City Hall building on North Spring Street was compared to New York's Tammany Hall, iconic headquarters of the notorious Boss Tweed. A radio evangelist named Robert Shuler broadcast attacks that were so damning the mayor felt obligated to sue for libel, and lost.

Cryer himself was sick of his administration. He knew how many of the charges of corruption were true. He suffered as well from what he felt were false accusations. Many believed him to be a mere puppet, Kent Parrot the "real" mayor of Los Angeles. Once upon a time Cryer had called himself a reformer, and he might have meant it. He was full of ideas for the greater glory of his city— bringing the coming Olympic Games to Los Angeles just one of them—but they were forever shaded in his mind by the exploits of his crooked partners. In '28, after nine years in office, George Cryer decided he would not run for a fourth term.

Cryer's crooked collaborators pleaded with him to continue, but he refused to change his mind. The mayor and Kent Parrot dissolved their partnership on unfriendly terms. Parrot went on a frantic search for a viable new front man; then, with growing concern for his future—there had been many promises made, now unlikely to be kept—he departed Los Angeles for parts unknown. He never came back.

With Cryer's abdication it was as if a dangerously high platform on which they'd all been standing had suddenly collapsed. One of those quick to come crashing down was vice king Albert Marco,

Charles Crawford's right hand and chief enforcer, arrested for shooting two men during a brawl in a Venice Beach nightspot. Everyone believed Marco would beat the rap, that was how it had always worked, with the police and the courts deep in his pocket— but he was found guilty instead. Given a fourteen-year sentence, he did four in San Quentin and was then deported to Italy.

Late in '28, the boss, Charlie Crawford, was arrested, charged with conspiring to frame a city councilman who refused to take a bribe. The farcical frame-up involved the councilman, a hired temptress, some bootleg hooch, and a pair of red flannel under-pants. The DA's office with the help of the press made a big stink about the city's lord of crime. The year before a case like that against the Gray Wolf of Spring Street would never have gotten to an in-dictment. The charges were dismissed, but the writing was on the wall in big letters. Crawford's power in the city was draining away fast. In another year he would be ancient history. In two years he would be dead, shot to death in his office during an intramural argument.

In '29 the city elected a new mayor. He was Democrat John C. Porter, a teetotaling, Prohibition-supporting, Bible-fondling Iowa transplant, a used-car-parts salesman and formerly a high-ranking member of the Ku Klux Klan. Porter vowed to sweep out the sin and the sinners and make Los Angeles again worthy of sober white Christians.

The new mayor took a hard line on corruption. He created a secret intelligence unit tasked with sweeping out the dirty cops. His appointed chief of police, Roy Steckel, formed a so-called Gangster Squad to put the city's racketeers on the run, with con-stant raids and mass arrests. Steckel led a brutal new drive to arrest and deport Mexican immigrants, declaring that most of the city's problems were caused by the foreign born.

Charlie Crawford's System, corrupters and corrupted working in perfect harmony, stopped working. The old agreements and protections had become null and void. The police and the judges could no longer be trusted to do the wrong thing.

Of course no one expected that the pious new regime was really going to end vice and corruption in Los Angeles, not forever. Not even for very long.

3

Johnny went to Chicago. Summoned to the gangsters' Holy See. The city of corruption and vice. Dirty cops and dirtier politicians. Everywhere speakeasies, whorehouses, gambling joints. There was hardly a straight business left. Big Al was in residence, three floors of the Lexington Hotel on South Michigan, a suite for himself, assorted rooms for bodyguards, a valet, a personal chef, and his latest mistress (a lovely Greek girl who would infect him with the syphilis that later destroyed his brain). The big man welcomed Johnny. He took him out on the town. And there was no town like Capone's Chicago. The nights were the brightest. The best booze, the hottest jazz, the funniest comics, the showgirls all corn-fed Midwest beauties, the six-inch-thick steaks straight from the slaughter. He introduced him to the boys (Johnny already knew them all by reputation: Nitti, McGurn, Campagna, Ricca and the rest). They gathered around, talking and joking, smoking fat cigars and pouring for themselves from bottles of Templeton and Canadian Club. Capone sat squinting and smiling, studying his potential new recruit.

It didn't take much convincing. He trusted his instincts about people. No one had a better eye for criminal talent. His gang of all-stars, from enforcers to accountants to political corruptors, was unparalleled in underworld history. To even be considered for a place in the organization was to have received a great benediction. When the time was right they got down to business. Would Johnny be interested in doing a little work for him out West? A small thing for now. (Some other time for the bigger picture.) He had some investments in Los Angeles, Capone told him. Nothing big. Maybe they would pay off one day. He had an associate there. A business partner of a sort. A Sicilian. Good man, trustworthy. Maybe a little set in his ways. Old-fashioned. Capone was looking to improve communications. To keep this man on his toes. He needed to send this man a go-between. He could send somebody from Chicago, of course, but Capone thought it would be a good idea to have a local boy who knew the territory and would not draw attention from the cops. Someone with a head on his shoulders.

And Johnny said he was happy to do what he could. And the big man was pleased to hear it and filled their glasses with more Iowa rye.

Something like that. The details told only in fragments of recollection scattered through the years to come.

Capone's "Sicilian" was a fellow named Ignazio Dragna. AKA Jack Dragna. He was a longtime member of the Los Angeles Mafia family with a history in the California underworld going back thirty years.

Dragna came from the old town of Corleone in the northwest of the island, sixty kilometers from the sea. As a child he had gone to America with his family, gone back to Sicily, returned to the States a second and final time. In New York's Little Italy he worked as an extortionist and enforcer for a Black Hand gang. When the police came looking to talk to him about the murder of a poultry salesman he hit the road. He ended up in California, was arrested and prosecuted for extortion, did three years in San Quentin. After his release Dragna settled in Los Angeles, went to work in the local Mafia. By the late '20s he was underboss—second in command—to Joseph Ardizzone, the local don.

The Mafia in Southern California was not well known at the time and little valued. As criminals they had never gained the kind of local prominence maintained by the much more powerful and connected City Hall gang or a headline-making independent like Tony Cornero. In the underworld hierarchy they were hobbled by Old World proclivities and prejudices, like their reluctance to work with non-Sicilians, and by many years of internecine clashes and the disruptive tendency to bump off their own leaders. Joseph Ardizzone, the current boss, was a skilled criminal, but he spent more time settling blood feuds than finding new ways to make money. Some mafiosi in Los Angeles made more from their legit businesses like selling and importing fruit and olive oil (Jack Dragna dealt in bananas, grapes, and raisins) than they did from their illegal activities. The big Mob families in the East tended to think of the Los Angeles group as country bumpkins, if they gave them any thought at all.

Dragna was known for his strength of character (at least, on a sliding scale of comparison with his peers), as a man of dignity, notwithstanding his past of theft, intimidation, and throat-cutting. He was said to be a good manager of people, though tight with a buck and often slow to pay his gang their share. He saw himself as a traditional mafioso for whom the oaths and rituals of that secret society—the code of silence, loyalty to the family, obedience to the don, respect for another man's spouse, and so on—were vital, no matter how often he violated them. A "man of honor," as they would say. He was a loving husband and father, and a wise uncle or godfather figure to relatives and those countrymen and neighbors who came to him for help. Away from business he lived a quiet life, without noticeable flaws or vices, excepting an impulse to ingest too much pasta and an interest in women who were not his wife.

Johnny Rosselli had been aware of Dragna in Los Angeles but never had cause to deal with him. The Mafia—the Sicilian Mafia— in LA was an outsider group, and had little interaction with the mainstream underworld. When Johnny met Jack, the Sicilian was in his late thirties but looked older, a short (five feet three and three-quarter inches), burly man with a heavy head, lined face, and dark, soulful eyes. Though his mind was not overly developed, he had a quality of thoughtfulness to him, and he carried about him those qualities of a traditional Sicilian don, caring, warmth, and ferocity.

Johnny and Jack Dragna got along well from the beginning. Dragna would show no resentment or suspicion about their working arrangement. Jack was no pushover, but he was in awe of Capone, and respected the man's advice even if it came by way of a young intermediary. Johnny in turn treated his older associate with deference. Jack was the big boss, that was a given. It was likely a part of the plan, to let Dragna shine and let him grow his reputation, and keep all trace of support by Capone in the shadows. But John's fealty to the man was sincere. And Dragna would return it with a paternal affection and loyalty. It became a deep friendship, and served them well in the many adventures that lay ahead.

With the City Hall gang played out and the law no longer playing favorites, the city's racketeers were were left unprotected. Late in 1928 there was a wave of armed robberies in Los Angeles. Targeted were every variety of underworld venue, speakeasies, gambling clubs, bookie parlors, brothels. The robbers were armed and brutal. Establishments were wrecked, employees beaten, funds scooped up and taken. The gutting went on for weeks. The gamblers and vice chiefs were astonished. Things had run so smoothly for so long that the old-guard racketeers hardly knew how to put up a defense.

It soon became known that the crime wave was connected to a little-known mafioso gangster named Jack Dragna. He and his gang had come out of nowhere and had torn a hole through the underworld establishment.

The old City Hall gangsters were shocked at the sudden, bold move by the Italians. They had always known their place. Was it an invasion from New Orleans or New York, where the "dago" gangs were large and known for their savage ambition? Guy

McAfee, a veteran racket boss and former Los Angeles policeman, ran to his remaining pals on the vice squad, screaming: *"Who the Hell is Jack Dragna?"*

With the racketeers startled into submission, the Dragna gang put the squeeze on. There began a systematic extortion. The racket and vice joints would have to kick back a share of their income every month or suffer more robberies and terror until they did. It was the old Black Hand tactic writ large. If they wanted to be sensible they would accept their new partners; if they wanted war then they would get it. Caught off guard by the unexpected and ferocious assaults, many who were hit capitulated almost at their first lost dollar or blackened eye; others resisted for a while. Capone sent from Chicago a select few seasoned reinforcements to help deal with the resistance, including his cousin and trusted enforcer Charles Fischetti (who in California assumed the alias James Russo). A few heads were bashed, some bellies punctured by lead.

Against those who tried to hold back, the raids were relentless. The old guard had been daydreaming, and the Italians had kicked them in the balls and picked their pockets. Dragna and Johnny (with their silent partner in Chicago ready with advice and more at every stage) were suddenly in charge of a large piece of the action in Los Angeles.

It had happened so quickly and efficiently. It was like the new mob had always been in charge. Dragna's gang grew larger with their widening responsibilities. And it was just the beginning.

Floating casinos in Southern California had been the idea of Tudor Scherer, a gambler and adventurer out of the gold rush days in Nevada. Scherer's notion was to anchor a vessel in international waters beyond the three-mile limit of county rule, where the anti-gambling laws could not be enforced. His anonymous flat-bottomed barge opened for business off the coast of Santa Monica in the summer of 1927, allowing customers to fish for croaker and halibut on deck and play poker and roulette inside. It was followed by a more substantial gambling boat, a converted old schooner named the *Johanna Smith*, which featured dining, music, and dancing in addition to games of chance. Local authorities jumped to find loopholes that would close down the operations. They tried recalculating the distances from shore, calling in the federal authorities, and sheer harassment, but nothing seemed to stick.

As the *Johanna Smith* continued to operate without interference it was inevitable that it would have company. The *Monfalcone* was a five-masted wooden barkentine built for service in World War I, transformed at great expense by a well-heeled syndicate into a flattened barge and "gambler's heaven." It contained a two-hundred-foot gambling salon with forty-one gambling tables and fifty slot machines, a café, a bandstand for seventeen pieces, and a massive hardwood dance floor. The ship employed more than one hundred, including croupiers, cooks, waiters, and armed guards, and even a few people who knew something about handling a ship in the open seas. As many as a thousand "passengers" could come on board in a night, delivered from the Long Beach dock by a fleet of water taxis.

One night the visitors to the *Monfalcone* included half a dozen men armed with pistols and pump guns, led by John Rosselli. They rode over heavy surf, headed to the distant white light in the darkness. From the *Monfalcone's* floating dock they swarmed the gangway. Music wafted up from the ship's innards. Down below hundreds dined, danced, and gambled. Guards on deck called for help. Men ran up from below. One of the ship's owners appeared. Guns were waving on both sides. The owner called for calm. No sense anyone getting their heads blown off. The pirates took the owner below to talk. The passengers went back to rolling dice, chewing their steaks, and dancing the black bottom.

Johnny said, "We're taking over. We're running this thing now."

The *Monfalcone* syndicate agreed to a meeting. Johnny gave back to some of the investors part of what they already owned. It was better to all be friends, he told them, than to have a fight they wouldn't win.

The ship resumed business. Jobs on board—card dealers, bouncers, waiters—were soon mostly filled by members of Dragna's gang. Money washed over the *Monfalcone* like hundred-year waves. People liked illicit gambling as much as they liked illicit booze. Not even the rumor that the ship was now run by "foreign" gangsters could keep the crowds away, pity the fools. The dice tables and roulette wheels were rigged, so if a player was winning too much his luck could be changed on the next throw or spin. If a player did manage to leave with much more than he brought aboard, there was a good chance he'd be robbed of his winnings back on the dock at Long Beach, likely by employees of the ship.

Johnny had a fine time running the floating casino. He would make frequent visits, have a good meal, watch the happy people losing their money. Movie stars and Hollywood big shots were often there, and many beautiful women dressed to the nines. It was a dream of a racket, money pouring in without effort, everything out in the open, and not a thing the cops could do about it, though they still tried.

One night—in late July 1930—Johnny, Jack Dragna, Charlie Fischetti, and John Canzoneri (a cousin of boxer Tony Canzoneri, the world featherweight champion)—were driving to downtown Los Angeles after leaving the ship when a police car moved to stop them. Instinct got the better of the gangsters and they tried to get away, racing through the empty streets. The cop car managed to overtake them and force them off the road. Canzoneri aimed a shotgun at the approaching officers and nearly made an awkward scene much worse, but Jack Dragna took the weapon from him, and the four men surrendered. Cops searched the car and found the shotgun, four pistols, and bags and bags of cash. The cops suspected the quartet of robbery. The gangsters explained they were businessmen, just come back from their place of business with the night's earnings, and the weapons were for protection. They were all arrested. After courtroom appearances and much aggravation, all charges were dropped, but not before the authorities learned who was now running the floating casinos.

Soon other vessels joined the *Monfalcone* and *Johanna Smith*. The aquatic investors in the gambling boats included old names from the bootleg wars, like Tony Cornero, fresh out of prison, who launched the gambling ship *Monte Carlo*, and Milton "Farmer" Page, one of the original partners in the City Hall gang. There was undoubted mistrust among many of these characters, but for a time they tried to behave like good neighbors. The waters off the borderlands between Los Angeles and Orange Counties became known as "Gamblers' Row," and for a time one of the area's most popular attractions.

The *Monfalcone*'s success story came to a sudden end on the night of August 30, 1930, when a leaky oil line in the engine room sparked an explosion that set the ship on fire. Unsecured cans of gasoline were ignited, and in no time the vessel was engulfed in flames, nearly five hundred people on board in a panic to escape. It was a miracle that only a few were injured, and there were no deaths. Some of the rescued passengers were taken aboard one of the other gambling boats nearby and went right back to playing poker and chuck-a-luck.

With the *Monfalcone* burned to the waterline—there were some who suspected arson—Johnny went looking for another ship. He found an aged passenger liner and put together a syndicate of investors for its purchase and extensive, expensive renovations, turning the *Rose Isle* into the most luxurious gambling ship on the West Coast.

Posters and newspaper ads hailed the new vessel: *"Large, magnificent and colorful . . . 3 Separate Decks Full of Thrills . . . Dancing . . . Dinner DeLuxe $1! . . . All Steel . . . FIREPROOF. . . ."*

The *Rose Isle* was another great success for Johnny and Dragna's group. But so many ships dividing up the same pool of suckers began to mean smaller profits. With so much competition at sea some of the casino ships tried to distinguish themselves with additional onboard amusements. Not only was there gambling, music, food, and booze, but certain ships now offered narcotics, "stag shows," and prostitutes. The papers warned the public of the "slimy trail" of criminal connections that enveloped the ships and the risks facing anyone who visited them, from cheating and theft to the clap. There were numerous incidents of violence on board, fights, beatings, attempted murders. The cops began raiding the vessels and to hell with the territorial limits. They swarmed all up and down Gamblers' Row, billy clubs flying, making mass arrests, wrecking card tables and roulette wheels and slots, dragging the expensive gaming equipment out on deck and tossing it all into the ocean.

Johnny and Jack decided the aquatic casino business had run its course; they cashed out, and returned to dry land.

His weak lungs remained a problem, and he suffered from occasional flare-ups of the tuberculosis that still lived within him. The sickness came back in strength twice—paroxysmal coughing and choking, blood in the lungs—sending him for treatment to San Francisco, and another time to a facility in New York.

TB ran in the family. One day he received a message from Boston. Now his younger brother, Vincenzo, had contracted tuberculosis. He was suffering badly. His mother must have been desperate as it was the first time she had reached out to him in California.

Johnny had been resolute in his attempt to leave no trace of his origins. Virtually no one in Los Angeles knew his real name or where he came from. It had become fixed in his mind, like a superstition he didn't dare challenge. The only rational excuse for it—at least to anyone outside Johnny's own head—was the fear of deportation if the law nabbed him for something and discovered he was not a citizen. It was something that often happened to immigrants without paperwork and even to some who had obtained citizenship: After an arrest and punishment the criminal, no matter what papers he carried, would be tossed on the first boat to Naples or Palermo, where Mussolini's thugs would welcome him and lock him up again.

Cautiously, Johnny arranged to have his brother come to California. He also arranged for him to go to the Hassler Health Farm, where Johnny had been treated. Vincent was a gentle, humble person, full of respect for his long-unseen older brother. He and Johnny looked very much alike, though the vitality and aura of success of the one and the humility and pallor of the other made it clear they did not share the same circumstances. When Vincent was discharged six months later, his TB restrained, it was still freezing in the East, and Johnny told him to stay in Los Angeles till the spring. He rented his brother a place in the building where he was then living at 1154 West 7th Street. Johnny had Vincent take the name "Jimmy Rosselli" for the duration. Johnny favored him with attention and affection, regretful for the years he had been out of his family's reach. He took him to expensive restaurants, brought him to his tailor for some nice clothes, introduced him to his barber (Vincenzo Capone, no relation). It was a bittersweet time, a brief experience of family and brotherly love, things Johnny had chosen to live without. When warm weather came back to Boston, he put Vincent on the train with a thick envelope of cash for his mother.

4

In Chicago, on a freezing winter's morning in 1929—February 14, the holiday for lovers—five members of Bugs Moran's North Side gang and two hangers-on (a mechanic and a gangster-loving optician) came to the SMC Cartage garage on North Clark Street. It was later said they were there to make a deal with some renegade Detroit bootleggers for a truckload of stolen booze. Moran himself was due to join them but running late, just blocks away. Around eleven o'clock four men arrived, two dressed in city cop uniforms. They climbed out of a black Cadillac sedan, toting shotguns and Thompson submachine guns, went inside the building, told everyone there that they were the police and to put their hands up. They lined the Moran group side by side against a whitewashed wall, and then the two with the tommy guns began firing. Muzzle flash blazed in the dimly lit garage. The heavy ammo tore through the flesh of the seven like slashing razors. Shredded bodies settled in ghastly formation over pooling blood. Then the two men with shotguns came up for a closer look at the dead and dying, and they blasted the faces off two of them.

Instantly and indelibly dubbed the "St. Valentine's Day Massacre," the execution of the seven Chicago men was a headline story around the world, complete with photos of the blood-and-viscera-spattered crime scene. Just as quickly, responsibility for the carnage pointed to one name. Bugs Moran, who had lost most of the key members of his organization in less than sixty seconds and escaped being the eighth victim by a hairsbreadth, spoke for the majority when he told a reporter: *"Only Al Capone kills like that."*

It was well known that Moran, a longtime nemesis, had been encroaching on Capone territory for months, daring the Big Man to push back. It was not a wise thing for the Irishman to do, but no one had ever accused Bugs Moran of being smart. Retaliation seemed inevitable. Only the brutal efficiency and sickening thoroughness were a surprise. But knowing who did it and proving it in a court of law were not the same thing. The gunmen had disappeared without a trace while Al Capone, on the morning of February 14, was provably far away in Miami, Florida. Not only was he in Miami that day, but at the moment the machine guns were firing in Chicago, he was in the company of three government investigators, answering questions about his income.

There had been big-scale violence in gangland for most of a decade, but something about the spectacle on Clark Street seemed to resonate like nothing before, a last straw for a frazzled public and the frustrated, embarrassed upholders of the law. To let this new outrage go unpunished, with the demonic Capone again triumphant, was to surrender outright to the forces of chaos and evil. The new president of the United States, Herbert Hoover—taking office three weeks after the massacre—personally commanded his Treasury secretary to bring the gangster to justice, to use the full force of the Bureau of Investigation, the Bureau of Prohibition, the Internal Revenue Service, and whatever else it took and—get Al Capone.

In mid-May of that year the Big Fellow journeyed to Atlantic City, New Jersey, to be part of an unprecedented gathering of major criminal gang leaders from all over the country. In addition to Capone and his Chicago colleagues Frank Nitti, Jake Guzik, and Frank Rio, attendees at the so-called Atlantic City Conference included Salvatore Lucania (to be better known later by his assumed moniker, Charlie "Lucky" Luciano), Frank Costello, Meyer Lansky, Ben "Bugsy" Siegel, Dutch Schultz (born Arthur Simon Flegenheimer), Gaetano Lucchese, Vito Genovese, Carlo Gambino, Louis "Lepke" Buchalter, Abner "Longy" Zwillman (all from the New York/New

Jersey region), Morris Dalitz of Cleveland, Detroit's Purple Gang bosses William and Abraham Bernstein, Charles "King" Solomon of Boston, Giovanni Lazia from the Pendergast Machine in Kansas City, Philadelphians Max "Boo Boo" Hoff and Harry "Nig" Rosen, Santo Trafficante (senior) out of Tampa, Florida, representatives from New Orleans, Providence—and on and on. Playing host was Atlantic City vice lord/Republican strategist Enoch "Nucky" Johnson.

Also in attendance at Atlantic City was a figure of great importance in the life of Al Capone, his mentor Johnny Torrio, who had come back from years of self-imposed exile (having been shot up in Chicago), fleeing Italy and Mussolini (who'd gone to war on gangsters) and resettling in New York. He was revered not just by Capone but by many of the top young mobsters, who admired him for his brains, his innovations, and his accomplishments. Torrio had become an adviser to what could be called the progressive wing of big-time crime in New York. His ideas about a united criminal consortium and a move into legitimate businesses were favored by Lansky, Luciano, Abner Zwillman, and other "young Turks" of the East Coast as well as by Capone in the Midwest. A multigang affiliation—the Combined or Big Seven Group—had been introduced in the greater New York area. Now, in Atlantic City, the springtime summit had been in large part about implementing an audaciously larger alliance, a crime syndicate that would crisscross the entire United States.

Conspicuous by their absence in Atlantic City were senior Mafia bosses Joe Masseria and the "Castellammarese" (after their birthplace, Castellammare del Golfo) Salvatore Maranzano of New York, Joseph Ardizzone of Los Angeles, and others of the traditional wing. To the young Turks, those old Sicilian gang leaders—the so-called Mustache Petes—were mired in the past. They wasted time with rituals and blood feuds, outworn proscriptions, and ethnic prejudices. The veteran capos were reluctant to do business with non-Italians, and not much more comfortable with non-Sicilians. By contrast, those commingling at the conference included Jews, Germans, Russians, an Englishman, and at least one Swedish-Irish-American.

The gangsters met in pairs and quartets and larger forums, old pals some of them and some old enemies trying to get along. They ate and drank, smoked cigars, told dirty jokes, posed for pictures on the boardwalk; they walked on the sand beach and at the water's edge, in the South Jersey humidity, sweaty heads in wilting wide-brim fedoras, barefoot below their rolled-up suit pants, carrying a shiny wingtip in each hand. They were like the execs at any corporate convention, bragging of their latest triumphs, trading tales of woe, and cursing the government, ruminating on where they were and where they were going. The Roaring Twenties would be over in little more than six months. The long era of national prosperity might be ending as well: In March there was an economic tremor, a "mini-crash" that warned some of worse to come.

The most pertinent concern of the men gathered by the sea was the future of Prohibition, the righteous legislation that had launched their kingdoms of crime. Many felt sure the ban would not be around much longer, despite the recent election of a "dry" president. After nearly a decade the public had gotten weary of the commotion, the violent headlines, terror in the streets; they wanted things the way they had once been, a pleasant weekend visit to the beer garden or a couple shots of Old Overholt at the corner saloon after work, without all the fuss and all the machine guns.

The end of Prohibition? And then what? the worried bootleggers asked. No one wanted to give up what they had gained. To go back to haunting the ghettos and sticking up pushcarts. The forward-thinking gangsters told them it didn't have to be that way. Fuck Prohibition. It was a new day. This future was an underworld conglomerate: the gangs across the country working together, keeping their individual territories but pooling their powers. Adhering to a set of general principles and mutually beneficial efforts. Fixing prices and eliminating competition, decreasing rivalries and internecine wars, avoiding public relations travesties like that St. Valentine's bloodbath (Capone's headline-making activities were as aggravating to many gang leaders as they were to the White House). A steady move into upper-world business—sports, manufacturing, entertainment, the unions—the lords of criminal enterprise no longer to be separated from the legit.

The gangsters liked what they heard. Expansion, more money, more power for everyone, the prospect of a national crime syndicate. They came away from Atlantic City with raised expectations for the future (and a box of saltwater taffy each, courtesy of Nucky Johnson).

Al Capone and his bodyguards were headed for home when their car broke down near Philadelphia. They decided to go on to Chicago by train. With time to spare they took in an early talkie (*The Voice of the City*, a crime drama starring Willard Mack). Coming out of the movie house they were stopped by policemen. They were searched, arrested, booked on weapons-possession charges. Capone spent the night in jail, and by the next afternoon he was convicted and sentenced to one year in prison, as easy as that (the judges in Chicago called in sick—with shame—that day).

The Big Fellow got out of Eastern State Penitentiary in March 1930. One year later he was indicted for federal income tax evasion. Everyone in the world knew that Al Capone was a free-spending millionaire. At his trial the prosecutors attempted to prove it. They presented to the jury a mountain of paper illustrating untaxed income, check stubs, invoices, deeds, a ledger seized by a minister in an anti-vice raid, as well as inculpatory testimony of shop clerks, cashiers, realtors, hotel operators, and a few brave business associates. It wasn't the terrifying portrait of the gangster life seen in a photo of the St. Valentine's Day Massacre, but in the end it got the job done. On October 17, 1931, Capone was found guilty of five felony counts and two misdemeanors. A week later the judge hit him with the stiffest penalty for a tax rap in history: a fifty-thousand-dollar fine and eleven years in a federal prison.

Nine months after the Atlantic City conference ended, the feud that had been simmering between rival New York Mafia bosses Joe Masseria and Salvatore Maranzano erupted in a full-scale gang war. For more than a year the so-called Castellammarese War would rage—shootouts, raids, assassinations, dozens of men killed on both sides. It was everything Lucky Luciano and the "progressives" had wanted to avoid.

Determined to end it, Lucky and several other Masseria lieutenants sold the man out, crossed over to Maranzano's side, and on April 15, 1931, dispatched a team of five killers to murder Joe the Boss while he was playing cards at an Italian restaurant on Coney Island.

The war ended there, but other matters remained unsettled. Those who wished to move forward found that the old ways still prevailed, and worse. With victory Maranzano awarded himself a title. He was now to be known as *capo di tutti capi*—"boss of bosses." Lucky Luciano, Maranzano's new second in command, saw his dream of a national crime conglomerate going poof before this vainglory. And Maranzano, not liking to have one of his people unhappy, paid Vincent "Mad Dog" Coll twenty-five grand to kill him. Lucky struck first. On September 10 a hit team—this one all Jewish, assembled by Meyer Lansky—rushed Maranzano in his office, stabbing and shooting him to death. And for safety's sake five Maranzano loyalists were clipped the same day. Romantics called it "the Night of the Sicilian Vespers."

According to legend, the next several months saw the elimination of other gang leaders of the old school, though latter-day researchers dispute the so-called "purge." Either way the story may

have served the same purpose, to change the mind of anyone an-
tagonistic to the aims of the rising national crime syndicate.

In Los Angeles, for many years now, the feral and prideful Joseph
Ardizzone had been the boss of the local Mafia Family. An unex-
ceptional leader, he had gone unnoticed by the powerful families
in the East. In recent months he had been content to spend much
time at his place in the countryside, for all the world as though he
were back in the sleepy Sicilian valley of his birth, letting those
under him do the work and bring in the money. During the Cas-
tellmmarese War in the East he had voiced his support for Maranzano. Perhaps someone back there paid attention. Early in
1931 he was driving in his car with a friend when gunmen ambushed them. His friend was killed, and Ardizzone was badly
wounded. In the hospital he let it be known that he was thinking
of retiring.

On October 15 he was still thinking. He drove away from his
home in Sunland, going to pick up his cousin at a ranch in Etiwanda.
He was never seen again. Some believed it was the long reach of
the new Syndicate, getting rid of another old-school boss. Others,
more familiar with circumstances in California, wondered if a
supposed Syndicate killing spree made a good cover for someone
who wanted to be rid of Ardizzone for his own reasons.

The leader of the Mafia in Los Angeles was now Jack Dragna.

5

Johnny Rosselli had found himself a unique position in the criminal underworld. As Jack Dragna's adviser and partner, and the West
Coast "secret agent" of Al Capone and the Chicago mob, he was a
trusted ally of two big-city American gang leaders (the papers re-

ferred to Dragna as "the Al Capone of Los Angeles"). Working with their two outfits he had access to power, money, muscle, and information, but without the responsibilities and risky exposure of the bosses. A member of the gangs and yet not a member. It suited him. He was a lone wolf by nature. He had no ambition to become a boss himself; the job as he'd observed it simply didn't appeal, playing the grumpy father figure to a bunch of lethal children. He preferred the role he had carved out for himself, strategist, problem solver, and he wanted to keep at least an illusion of independence.

This insider-outsider status with the mobs allowed him to easily maintain his separate, relatively legit identity in straight society. Most of the people who knew him only from entertainment or business circles had no idea the extent of his underworld connections. To them he was a well-heeled sporting gentleman. A high-end bookmaker and owner of a piece of an offshore gambling boat. An adventurer. A little disreputable, maybe a little dangerous, but like a Damon Runyon hero, not a public enemy.

His circle of Hollywood friendships continued to grow. One acquaintance introduced him to another, he was invited to parties, to gala movie premieres, attended the shows at the popular clubs, sometimes with a female star on his arm. He was attractive and good company, a tough guy no doubt, but a gent, rough edged yet cordial and generous. He knew the biggest movie stars on a first-name basis—even Charlie Chaplin, an amiable tennis partner (as long as you brought along a beautiful woman or two). Hollywood high society was unusually fluid, a wealthy elite but hardly blue-bloods, many of the most important people in town coming from the most beggarly beginnings. He had no trouble moving among them. He had even made friends with the most elite group of all, the men who owned and operated the big studios. The moguls and top executives were some of the town's biggest gamblers, and thus natural acquaintances of a top bookie like Johnny, who offered the excitement of a no-limit book (insuring himself against big losses by laying off the bets with a large city bookmaking syndicate), and judicious tips on "sure things."

He had pals throughout the Hollywood social and business worlds, men like restaurateur Frank Kerwin, from whom he bought a large stake in the New Yorker Club on Hollywood Boulevard (known as an underworld hangout, it soon closed due to pressure from the police), and many contacts in the media—columnists, reporters, publicity agents. He was always ready to do a favor for one of them if they got into some trouble, and expected he could rely on them for the same if ever the need arose. Among his closest friends was one of the most vital figures in the local press, William "Billy" Wilkerson, a former bootlegger, now a publisher and entrepreneur, owner of the trade journal *The Hollywood Reporter* and top local restaurants and nightspots including the Vendome and the Café Trocadero. At the Vendome on Sunset one day, Wilkerson recalled, he was trying to collect funds to purchase an automobile for some nuns who had an orphanage outside Los Angeles, when Johnny Rosselli called him to his table, introduced himself, offered a large donation, and a friendship bloomed.

Johnny followed the action wherever it went. With the December '29 opening of the Agua Caliente Racetrack and Casino in Tijuana (owned by three Americans and a secret fourth partner in the Mexican government), weekend trips across the border became essential for Hollywood high rollers. The track, and its adjunct resort hotel and casino, swarmed with executives, producers, movie stars, agents, wives, and concubines. Liquor flowed openly in Mexico, and the races were great entertainment, anarchic, with much mayhem, jockeys sometimes flailing each other bloody with their whips like charioteers in *Ben Hur.*

Johnny was a regular visitor, often driving down with his writer-director friend Rowland Brown (whose screen story, filmed as *Doorway to Hell*, and his directorial debut, *Quick Millions*, were among the first in the sensational new wave of "talkie" gangster movies), usually accompanied by two or three young starlets. On one occasion he joined a group flown down by private plane as guests of Joseph Schenck, the president of United Artists, one of the track's investors, and an old pal of Johnny's. The rich gringos took in the races, gambled, boozed, threw bacchanals, and otherwise struggled to have a good time until Sunday's return homeward.

It was on one of these social circuits that Johnny met Harry Cohn.

Harry Cohn was the West Coast production head and co-owner—with his New York–based partners, his brother Jack Cohn, and Joe Brandt—of Columbia Pictures. Like Universal and United Artists, Columbia was one of the "minor-majors" in the Hollywood studio hierarchy, without the stature and resources of M-G-M, Paramount, Fox, and Warner Bros. at the top, but considerably better off than the numerous small, fly-by-night outfits at the bottom. It had started out very small in 1919 as CBC (Cohn-Brandt-Cohn) Film Sales. They made low-grade, unglamorous movies, and industry wise guys referred to CBC as "Corned-Beef-and-Cabbage." In the sound era, renamed Columbia (with a prideful American Goddess the studio's logo), based on Sunset and Gower, the studio thrived under Cohn's strong-willed creative guidance with a steady supply of modest-budget audience pleasers, and the occasional larger-budgeted production comparable in quality to the better work of any studio in town.

Harry Cohn, the man Johnny Rosselli would come to consider his closest friend, was one of the most widely and deeply hated men in Hollywood. He was hated not for any of the usual reasons, the cheating, exploiting, and backstabbing of the everyday ruthless tycoon—in fact he was generally considered to be honest and fair in his business dealings—but rather almost entirely because of his belligerent, crass personality. Cohn on the job exhibited a rare, staggering vulgarity and a mean-spiritedness toward employees that could make grown men weep. Examples of his cruelty and gross insults were countless, such as his telling one producer that the only reason for his employment was for Cohn "to piss on him," and publicly inquiring of an actress whether her reputed talent for performing fellatio was accurate. "The meanest man I ever met," said the writer Budd Schulberg, speaking for many. Those who said he acted like a dictator meant it quite literally: He was for a time an admirer of Italy's Benito Mussolini, going to Rome to meet him and later having an exact copy of Il Duce's office re-created on Gower Street. A verbal assault by Cohn could feel to the recipient like physical violence, like a whipping or a beating with a baseball bat. Adding to the terror was his appearance, the glaring eyes, hatchet-like beak, and cruel mouth, the overall look of a dyspeptic, obscenity-spouting vulture.

He was a born filmmaker, and thrived on the nuts and bolts of story construction, casting, editing, the nurturing of talent before and behind the camera, and there were some in the picture business he treated well and who saw a good side to Harry Cohn, who had evidence of his charm, loyalty, square shooting, but they were greatly outnumbered by the many who knew him as a sadistic son of a bitch.

Cohn's background as a first-generation American Jew from a poor immigrant family was similar to that of many of the other studio owners who had "invented Hollywood." The moguls were tough men, from tough schools of hard knocks, former scrap dealers, peddlers, sideshow operators. Cohn had once earned a living as a pool hall and bowling alley hustler, and as half of a low-rung vaudeville act. But whereas most of the Hollywood founding fathers tried to paint over their low-born origins with gradual assumptions of gentility and public displays of high-mindedness, Cohn wore his as a badge of honor, relished his reputation as a foul mouthed, uneducated bully—a gangster.*

Those who might seek an explanation for his antisocial behavior in the then-new science of psychiatric analysis would have found a potential jackpot in the turbulent mind of Harry Cohn. The movie mogul lived with a traumatizing secret: He had been born in an outhouse, a fetid backyard toilet where his eight-and-a-half-months pregnant mother had gone to defecate and had uncontrollably released him into a pit of excrement. His life was saved only by the arrival of neighbors who'd heard the screams of the hysterical Mrs. Cohn. In time, his Russian-born mother, whom Harry worshipped and yet fought with like a rabid dog, would use the incident as her trump card in angry disputes, screaming at him, *"You were born in a shithouse and I should have left you there!"*

As an adult—so he would confess to a physician on one night of duress later in life—any pleasure the Columbia Pictures king might have derived from his rise to the top was greatly diminished by thoughts of this unclean beginning, by recurring feelings of self-loathing and exposure. Cohn spent his life trusting few people, suspicious of most. He obsessed over personal cleanliness, spending hours a day taking showers and washing his hands, and lived—he confided to the doctor—"in constant fear that someone will know my secret."

With his aversion to respectability—so-called decent people made him uneasy—Harry Cohn was naturally drawn to a man like Johnny Rosselli, a mysterious, potentially dangerous character who seemed to reside outside the bonds of conventional society. From the start they got along very well. Johnny placed Harry's many bets,

---

* One cinematic portrayal of Cohn's persona may be seen in "Mr. Potter," the villain of *It's a Wonderful Life*, whose screenwriter, Albert Hackett, told me he had based the character on Harry.

gave him advice, amused him, and consoled him. The mystery man soon became the powerful Hollywood figure's closest, most trusted friend. In Johnny's company Harry could drop the ogre persona and be funny, relaxed, even sentimental. They became like brothers, and certainly closer than Harry and his real brother, Jack, who communicated with each other only by telephone in coast-to-coast disputes.

Harry and Johnny went out on the town together on many nights, sometimes with women, sometimes not. They dined together. They went to catch the shows at the top nightclubs. They went to the Tuesday boxing matches at the Olympic Auditorium. They went to the races in Mexico, and—when it opened in '33—to the Santa Anita track in Arcadia. Harry would have Johnny to his home to play tennis on his private court, and they would go out to Cohn's place in Palm Springs, play golf and cards with the other Hollywood weekenders. In Los Angeles they would often end up at the Clover Club, an "open" illegal casino on the Sunset Strip, with its swank supper club in the front and gambling den in the back, featuring roulette, dice games, and no-limit chemin-de-fer. Cohn would gamble for many hours, along with movie mogul peers—David O. Selznick, B. P. Schulberg, Joe Schenck—degenerate gamblers all. Johnny would stand behind Harry, patting his shoulder encouragingly, as the Columbia boss played and usually lost a fortune.

Cohn would invite Johnny to come to the studio, for lunch in his private dining room or for cocktails in his office, talk about the ponies, women, and the movies. The guards at the gate were instructed to allow Mr. Rosselli entrance at any time. People on the lot became used to seeing the boss in the company of the tough-looking, elegantly dressed Italian gentleman. On many evenings Cohn would have Johnny join him in his screening room to view the "rushes"—that day's unedited footage from the movies in production. Cohn solicited Johnny's reaction to what he saw, especially if it was an underworld picture.

Marc Lawrence was a talented young actor working steadily in supporting parts at Columbia Pictures. His real name was Maxie Goldsmith, a Jew from the Bronx with family roots in the Yiddish theater. In Hollywood his saturnine looks and snarling delivery got him typecast as various Italianate hoodlums. Lawrence, like many who worked at Columbia, knew that Harry Cohn was pals with Johnny Rosselli and that Johnny Rosselli was some sort of "big goddamn mobster." One time Rosselli and Cohn were together in the projection room watching the rushes of a crime movie, Lawrence would recount. "It was a scene I was in, and Rosselli said to Harry—Harry's wife told me the story—he whispered to Harry, 'You know, that kid up there . . . he's pretty good . . . acts like the real thing. He could be in the mob . . .' And after that Harry Cohn loved me! He loved tough guys. All that gangster shit."

One day Marc Lawrence was at the studio, just starting work on another gangster movie, when he got a summons from the boss. Cohn said he was going to be tied up in a meeting all evening, and could Marc go in his place to the fights with his pal Johnny? Lawrence knew better than to turn Harry down for anything, and agreed to the request. The actor made to leave but Cohn spoke again. "'Listen, you're doing this new picture,' he says. I was playing some kind of gangster, threatening some guy's wife and kids, the same old shit. Who the fuck knows what they called it? [The film in question was likely *I Promise to Pay*.] He says, 'When you're with Johnny I want you to watch him. Study him. The way he talks, the eyes, everything. That's how you want to do it in the picture.' He wanted me to study this guy and then imitate him for the camera. He wanted me to act like Johnny Rosselli in this fucking

movie. I tell him, 'Okay, Harry. Sure, that's a great idea!' So that
night I go to the fights with Rosselli. And I'm *studying him*, like
Harry said. He talks. He watches the fight. He eats a hot dog. And
he's great. Good conversation. He pays for everything. He laughs
at my jokes. What the fuck was I going to do with any of this? I'm
playing a vicious gangster, and this guy's a sweetheart. I didn't know
what to say to Harry next day, so I avoided him for as long as I
could."

Johnny and Harry's friendship grew deeper through the decade.
When Cohn was considering a—potentially expensive—dissolution
of his marriage to his first wife, Ruth, he asked Johnny to play
divorce detective and find some "dirt" on her. Johnny looked into
it, then reported to Harry that his spouse was not playing around.
Cohn asked Johnny if he couldn't "set her up" with some fake evidence of marital infidelity. Possibly drug her and photograph her
in bed with another man. Johnny laughed and told him it was a
crummy idea and that it would probably land them both in jail.
After Cohn had separated from his wife, Johnny found him an
apartment in the same luxury building on Sunset Boulevard where
he then resided; for a time the two men lived within fifty yards of
each other.

When gambling was outlawed in Mexico by the puritanical
President Lázaro Cárdenas, the Agua Caliente Casino and Racetrack were shut down by the government. Two years later, putting
dinero before ideals, a rep from the capital offered one of the
original gringo investors—Gene Normile—the chance to reopen
the track for a short season for a fee of one hundred thousand dollars (the official rationale was to pay off track workers' back wages).
Johnny was offered a one-quarter interest in the enterprise. It was
more than he could cover at that moment. He went to Harry Cohn
for a loan of the money, and Cohn gave it to him without a second

thought. At the end of the season Johnny handed Harry a check
for the amount plus another two grand for interest. Cohn tore it
up and told him to write it again minus the interest. Johnny did so.
He took the two thousand dollars he got back and bought himself
and Harry a pair of matching gold rings with star rubies. They both
wore them for years, until the time came when the two men were
no longer friends.

6

His position with Al Capone and the Chicago outfit was an evolv-
ing one; which is to say it was whatever Capone and the boys said
it was. As Chicago's representative on the West Coast, Johnny was
there to keep an eye on their investments, while alerting them to
new opportunities as they appeared. Regarding Chicago's dealings
with Jack Dragna, he served as a covert channel of information in
one direction and influence in the other. As the friendship with
Jack deepened to a fraternal bond, the element of subterfuge faded
and Johnny became protective of the older man's interests. Dragna
anyway was pulling in so much money now that he didn't ask questions.

When high-ranking visitors from Illinois and sometimes elsewhere (Very Important Gangsters, you could call them) came to
Los Angeles, on business or on vacation, Johnny would play the host
and facilitator, a kind of honorary consul, making sure they got what
they wanted from the visit and nobody got into any trouble. Sometimes he would be required to help resolve a dispute, to chastise
an individual who'd gotten on the wrong side of somebody back in
Chicago and had fled to LA. He preferred not to take part in the
messier sort of claim resolution, and when civilized threats failed
to solve a problem he would have Jack Dragna dispatch one of his
reliable killers to conclude the matter.

On several occasions he accompanied a Chicago emissary—it is believed to have been Murray Humphreys, Capone's Richelieu—to the neighboring state of Nevada. In 1931 Nevada was considering a change in the gaming laws to allow open, legal gambling. Proponents in the government believed it would bring needed cash flow to the state's coffers, emptied by the Depression, while certain others favoring the change hoped to profit from the thousands of newly employed laborers working at a huge dam project southeast of Las Vegas and needing someplace to spend their pay. There remained many legislators who were on the fence about the gambling bill, and potential investors in Chicago tried to influence the decision, hence the repeated visits by Johnny and Murray Humphreys. Among Nevada insiders at the time it was a common belief that the out-of-towners had handed out cash payments to those whose votes could be bought. An attorney and close friend of Humphreys's named Irv Owens stated it bluntly to the historian Gus Russo: "Humphreys and Johnny Rosselli bribed the Nevada legislature into legalizing gambling."

The state assembly passed the bill and on March 19, 1931, it was signed into law by the governor. In Vegas, Reno, and elsewhere, the old illegal poker and dice rooms threw open their doors to the light, while eager entrepreneurs broke ground for big-time casinos and gambling resorts. Among those who moved to Nevada at this time were several familiar names from the Los Angeles rackets and the floating casinos of the Pacific, Tony Cornero and Guy McAfee among them. Chicago would quietly invest in several of the new Nevada ventures, more evidence of Al Capone's growing interest in the West.

Early in '31 Johnny got a message from Illinois asking him to help out a "friend" visiting from the East Coast. The friend was Abner Zwillman—"Longy" he was called for his great height, from the

Yiddish *der langer,* the long one—the bootleg and vice king of New Jersey. A tough Jew out of Newark's Third Ward ghetto, Zwillman handled as much as 50 percent of the illicit liquor imports in the Northeast, and controlled most of his state's gambling, slot machines, numbers rackets, cigarette vending, and assorted speakeasies and restaurants. A very powerful and dangerous gangster, he was known for a harsh temper and a tendency toward brutal violence when angered. He was also considered one of the smartest minds in crime, had been one of the chief architects of the Big Seven group, progenitor of the nascent national crime syndicate. But Zwillman's presence in California had nothing to do with any of that, unless you were talking about a crime of the heart.

He told Johnny he came highly recommended as a person one could trust, which he was surprised to hear as everyone else in Los Angeles seemed to be a backstabbing shit. Zwillman said he was looking for a person to keep an eye on someone for him while he was out of town. It was a young lady. An actress. She needed a bodyguard. But not just that. Someone to keep her occupied and away from other people. People trying to influence her. She was a very special sort of young woman, said Longy. To hear him tell it you could live a million years and not meet another like her, not even in Newark. Her name was Jean Harlow.

That Jean Harlow, the Blonde Bombshell, snowy-haired teenager plucked out of bit parts in two-reelers to play the female lead in Howard Hughes's World War I epic, *Hell's Angels.* On screen as a two-strip Technicolor vixen she looked sensational, and with Hughes's hype machine she'd become the most desired woman in America. Zwillman had met her through her stepfather, an oily con man named Marino Bello, while she was on a cross-country personal appearance tour and he had been obsessed with her ever since. Now he'd been gone from home too long and needed to get back to business in Jersey. Miss Harlow unfortunately would have to stay in California.

Zwillman took Johnny to meet her. She was all he had said, and he hadn't told the half of it: a glowing vision of fresh-faced youth and red-hot sex. She dazzled the eye wherever you looked, doll-like features, fairest skin, lucent white-gold hair, a lush, curvy body that quivered and flared at her slightest breath. He bowed to Zwillman's good taste, but didn't think much of his common sense, leaving someone like this alone for even an hour.

Longy left town, and Johnny played bodyguard/escort for the young actress as he had promised the smitten Jersey gangster he would. Harlow seemed not very put out by Zwillman's sudden retreat. She was a live-for-today sort of gal. Johnny took her to dinner, the movies. She was bright, funny, fabulous company. "The Baby," as she was known to friends and family—her real name being Harlean Carpenter—had lived a quixotic life, a story no Hollywood scriptwriter would ever dare pitch. She'd nearly died from scarlet fever, been taken away from her beloved father and family fortune by an impulsive mother, married a rich wastrel, lived as a hard-drinking Beverly Hills socialite, gotten divorced, and signed a five-year contract with a movie studio, all by the time she was seventeen. Now, nearing her twentieth birthday, she was a star, a sex symbol, and didn't give a damn about any of it. "I know I'm the worst actress that was ever in pictures," she'd say, laughing at herself. She much preferred a carefree day at the beach, or a long afternoon of cocktails, to the furtherance of her career. It was her wildly self-absorbed mother who'd wanted to be famous ("Jean Harlow" was actually *her* name), pushing the girl into show business and living through her success. Mama, Marino, and Baby shared a house in Beverly Hills, the rent paid by Longy Zwillman.

Johnny and Jean got along great. Very soon Longy's name stopped coming up in the conversation. Johnny had no doubt what Zwillman would do to him if he found out he'd tried anything with the girl. But it was worth it. Thirty, forty years later he was still telling people she was the most exciting woman he'd ever known.

"Oh, *Jean Harlow*, her *hair*, her *face*, he thought everything about her was the greatest," said his longtime friend Betsy Duncan. "She had the best breasts he'd ever seen."

"He was crazy about her," said Tony Martin, the singer–movie actor and a friend. "I don't think Johnny'd ever been that crazy for one girl. Of course, everyone who met Jean fell in love with her."

The affair lasted a couple of months. Zwillman finally got back to Los Angeles, eager to resume his place in Harlow's life. If Johnny and Jean found ways to see each other after that, it was with great care. Longy continued to call on him for advice, picking his brain about her associates in the movie business. Zwillman was fighting with Howard Hughes, who had Harlow under a long-term, low-paying contract, and was lending her out to other studios for large fees and keeping the profit for himself. Zwillman, meanwhile, was supplementing her salary with a weekly cash infusion. Hughes was so far refusing to renegotiate her contract, or to sell it outright, even at a considerable financial gain. Longy was considering having him killed.

For her part, Harlow had become embarrassed by her amoral screen image. She complained that all her roles since *Hell's Angels*—in *The Secret Six, Iron Man, The Public Enemy*—were vamps, molls, and sluts. Where was a nice, decent character for a change? "I'll either be a good girl," she said, "or I'll step out of pictures."

It was Johnny who came to her rescue. He talked to Harry Cohn, who agreed to let Longy cover what the studio would pay to Hughes for a loan-out (and a bit more to Harry as an incentive), and an "appropriate" role was found for Harlow at Columbia. It was a newspaper comedy, very au courant in the summer of 1931, set to star Loretta Young and Robert Williams. The Baby was given the part of a wealthy society debutante who marries a roughneck reporter only to lose him in the end to his working-girl true love. Not quite the lead but a nice part with—relative—"class." Cohn assigned his top director, Frank Capra, and at the urging of Jean's boosters changed the title (and with that, the focus of attention) from *Gallagher* (the name of Loretta Young's character) to *Platinum Blonde*. The finished film was pretty good, but despite Capra's skilled direction, Harlow's acting remained less than inspired. Her voice still mingled Kansas City twang with finishing school elocution lessons. The camera, anyway, loved her, or perhaps lusted after her would be a more appropriate term, framing her ripe bosom and her overripe buttocks with lingering fascination.

Even under the watchful eyes of Zwillman, Johnny, and her family, Jean managed to find other influences. In particular there was a Metro-Goldwyn-Mayer executive by the name of Paul Bern, a producer-supervisor at the studio, the right hand man to Metro's production executive and "boy genius" Irving Thalberg. Bern had borrowed her from Hughes's Caddo Company for an M-G-M gangster picture, *The Secret Six*. They formed a warm professional friendship, Bern becoming a steadfast supporter, a believer in her ultimate talent, so he said, to her delight.

Bern began escorting her to industry events and other formal outings, where New Jersey gangsters would not be welcome. An agitated Zwillman, on the East Coast again, asked Johnny to find out about this producer she said was just a friend. Johnny, nursing his own crush on the Baby, agreed to look into it, and called on his contacts at Metro to ask around about Paul Bern. He told Longy what he learned: Bern was known at the studio as a "pansy" and a "eunuch" in private but who liked being seen in public as a ladies' man and was always in the company of beautiful women. Zwillman—and Johnny—breathed a little easier.

But Paul Bern's interest in Harlow appeared to increase. He

pushed to bring her back to M-G-M, and paid Hughes what it took to get her for another film. He tended to her at the studio, made sure everyone treated her with care. Her performance in the picture *Beast of the City* would be her best to date. Harlow was delighted—not for her success as much as for evading another humiliating effort and more bad reviews. She now saw Paul Bern as her savior. Bern pushed M-G-M to buy her contract from Howard Hughes. It was just then, with the U.S. economy devastated by the Depression, that Hughes's cash cow, the Hughes Tool Company, had taken a nosedive. He made a sudden decision to get rid of his Hollywood assets. Hughes negotiated a deal with M-G-M for Harlow's contract (he would pocket thirty grand for her release). The actress went to work for the studio in the spring of '32.

Longy Zwillman was stuck in the East, managing a crisis in his bootleg business. Aviation hero Charles Lindbergh's baby had been kidnapped from his New Jersey home, and for two months the state was on lockdown, cops roaming every road, making it difficult to impossible for Zwillman's hundreds of liquor trucks to move. Product piled up, orders went unfulfilled, customers became terribly thirsty. Longy longed for Harlow, his only comfort a few tendrils of her pubic hair tucked into his gold pocket watch. The situation became so desperate that the bootlegger made a public offer of one hundred thousand dollars for anybody who could find Lindy's missing child. By the time Longy could get back to California, Jean Harlow and Paul Bern were engaged to be married.

Johnny tried to take the turn of events without tears. She was a fantastic girl, but a will-o'-the-wisp: You couldn't expect to hold her. And after all, he'd been poaching on someone else's territory from the start. Zwillman, though, was furious. He had not only lost his lovely mistress, but a dream of happy ever after with a platinum-blonde star, and an imagined future for himself as a Hollywood producer.

Zwillman went to her. According to Harlow biographer David Stenn, their meeting was heated and ugly.

"*Have you laid him?*" Longy said with anger.

"No, I haven't," said Jean. "He's a *gentleman!*"

Zwillman told Harlow what Johnny told him—her fiancé was a homosexual. Harlow told Zwillman to go to hell.

On July 2, 1932, Paul Bern and Jean Harlow were married. On September 5 of that year Bern's naked body was found on the floor of his home, crumpled before a full-length mirror, a gun in his hand and a bullet in his head.

The death would be ruled a suicide. A note was (supposedly) found (supposedly) confirming Bern's state of mind (distraught) and motive (impotence). But many thought its meaning was open to interpretation, and some called it a forgery. M-G-M personnel, including Louis B. Mayer, Irving Thalberg, the head of publicity, the head of security, and a studio photographer, had come to the house before the police were called, and for several hours they examined the scene, tampering with evidence as they saw fit. The studio people had concocted from the scene a storyline for the sake of the dead man's wife, a plot to protect their rising new star—this was gossip that lingered in the movie colony for a long time to come.

And so: Paul Bern had killed himself, due to personal sexual difficulties and self-loathing. Not exactly a sweet-smelling story, but it at least affirmed that death was by his own hand. However, alternative versions remained in the air. That Jean Harlow had shot her husband to death in a drunken row. Or that her shady stepfather Marino had done it. Or Bern's mysterious, mentally deranged first wife. Each motive, each suspect, would have its share of adherents.

One other theory lingered, never officially investigated, but said to have been privately claimed by the ostensible guilty party himself: Paul Bern's death was a professional killing arranged by Abner "Longy" Zwillman. A spurned lover had taken his revenge.

Johnny remained a friend to Jean. Zwillman, though, gave up his pursuit of the actress soon after Bern's death and returned to the East Coast for good. Curiously, Harlow would become close friends with another Eastern gangster soon to make his presence felt in California, Bugsy Siegel. At M-G-M Jean Harlow would be revealed as a brilliant comic actress, becoming one of the great and beloved stars of the era. On June 7, 1937, she died of kidney failure. She was twenty-six years old.

Around the time Jean Harlow was working on the lot at Columbia, Harry Cohn came to Johnny Rosselli with a problem of his own. Columbia Pictures' three owners—Harry, his brother, Jack, and Joe Brandt—had not enjoyed a smooth partnership. Brandt, the oldest of the three, had grown sick and tired of the Cohn brothers' constant cross-country bickering and in mid-'31 he decided to give up his piece of the studio he had helped to build. He offered to sell his one-third share to whichever of the Cohn brothers was the first to hand over five hundred thousand dollars cash (current equivalent eight million dollars).

Jack Cohn, based in New York and with close ties to the Eastern money men, was expected to have the upper hand. But it was the depths of the Depression in America, with several of the Hollywood studios in receivership, and banks were reluctant to invest. Harry's approach to A. P. Giannini at the Bank of America in California proved equally futile.

The clock ticked on Brandt's offer. Harry feared that one of Jack's financial connections could still come through at any moment, or some other interested investor might turn up, and his chance of being the uncontested boss of Columbia would be gone for good.

He pleaded his case to Johnny. The money, he said, could be paid back with interest within a year. Johnny said he would see what he could do. He talked with Longy Zwillman. Two days later, without further discussion, half a million dollars was delivered to Harry Cohn. Brandt was paid for his share of the studio, and Cohn became Columbia Pictures' chief executive as well as its head of production, his dream come true. In all future business decisions his brother Jack could just shut the hell up. Johnny, for his part in setting up the deal, pocketed fifty Gs.

There was a fly in the ointment, however. Having concluded the transfer of assets with Brandt, Cohn was expecting to give Zwillman his personal note for the money loaned plus appropriate interest at the time of repayment. Instead Zwillman said he had a different idea. The half-million worth of Columbia stock (even if legally kept in Cohn's name) would be his property. He would not collect interest on the cash but dividends on the stocks, which he would sell to Harry at a time of his own choosing. Zwillman left no room for argument. In effect the gangster king of New Jersey was now the owner of one-third of Columbia Pictures.

What happened after that, whether Zwillman cashed in and relinquished his claim on the stocks, or if he held on to the investment, is uncertain. It would be whispered in Hollywood for decades, the details subject to the vagaries and variations of secret histories, that a portion of Harry Cohn's majority share in Columbia Pictures belonged to some faction of organized crime, with Cohn fronting for the hidden investor(s) and personally dispensing the dividends in cash. At the time of his death in 1958, Harry Cohn's probate was taken over by a mob lawyer, Sidney Korshak, the notorious legal adviser to the Chicago Outfit, and a longtime associate of Longy Zwillman. Korshak was frequently called upon to settle financial situations best not dealt with in open court, or in the light of day. The disposition of Harry Cohn's estate was curious to say the least, and remained a subject of much gossip among Hollywood insiders.

Longy Zwillman died exactly one year to the day after Harry Cohn, on February 27, 1959. He was found hanging from a plastic cord in his West Orange, New Jersey, home. His body was bruised and there was evidence of his having been bound and tortured. The police and the coroner seemed to find these things irrelevant. It was ruled that he died by his own hand. Let us call it an assisted suicide. Assigned to the disposal of Zwillman's financial affairs was the same man who'd done the job for the Columbia boss: Sidney Korshak of Chicago and Beverly Hills.

7

With the Great Depression continuing its plaguelike sweep over the country, Americans were desperate for solutions, pushovers for change. Through the first years of the crisis President Herbert Hoover had kept a steady hand on the ship of state. Too steady, rigidly running it into a hole and then digging deeper. In the November '32 election the people gave the job to Franklin Delano Roosevelt, the New York patrician who promised new ideas, economic recovery, aid to the poor and the desperate, and an end to Prohibition, which he declared would restore four hundred million dollars (in taxes) to the nation's empty coffers.

On February 20, 1933, the U.S. Congress ratified the Twenty-First Amendment, which repealed the Eighteenth. It would take until December to complete the legal process and adopt the repeal as law, but people began drinking openly almost at once. Prohibition was dead.

In Los Angeles the public had grown tired of the smug former Klansman John C. Porter. In two terms as mayor he had shown himself less interested in helping the city to prosper or be rid of corruption than in chasing vagrants and maintaining his own racial and ethnic prejudices. (Asked by an African American why he could not appoint a man of his color to the police commission, Porter responded: "I cannot appoint a Negro as I could not appoint a Catholic or a Jew . . . And anyway, you people did not support me in the election.")

The new mayor was Frank L. Shaw, a county supervisor and former grocer ("the grocery boy made good," said a detractor), a hearty, roly-poly figure with a Hitler mustache. Shaw had run on a campaign promise to "clean up Los Angeles," and once he got his hands on City Hall there was no doubt the sort of cleanup he had in mind.

His first and most rewarding appointment upon taking office was his brother, Joseph, another bluff Irish American, late of the U.S. Navy. Brother Joe's catch-all position as the mayor's secretary put him in charge of graft, kickbacks, bribes, and all other emoluments, of which there were to be a great many during the Shaw administration. It was soon said around town that everything in City Hall was for sale including the furniture and the toilet paper, as long as you paid cash. A schedule of under-the-table fees was established for any and all hirings and promotions in the city government, including those in the police and fire departments. "Sailor Joe," as he was known, even sold the answers to the civil service exams.

To those on the other side of the law—to say "the wrong side of the law" would be a distinction without a difference in the Shaw years—the administration was equally open for business. Brothels, casinos, bookie joints never needed to fear the police closing them down if their account with the mayor's office was kept up to date, in the form of weekly rake-offs delivered right to Joe Shaw's desk. For the city's big-time, big-money gangsters, the Shaws were ready to roll out the red carpet, offering the sort of sweetheart deals given to a city's most important patrons.

Johnny Rosselli watched the turn of events at City Hall with great interest. Lines of communication were soon established. The mayor's brother was always open to a night on the town. And another after that. Johnny was very generous with Sailor Joe. He sent him cases of his favorite booze. He found him a new girlfriend. He and Joe Shaw became best friends. They became business partners, conspiring on a variety of moneymaking ideas, Johnny doing most of the thinking, Joe the drinking. Joe Shaw hated the old Crawford bunch and didn't trust them. A new mayor needed a new mob. Things went so well with Johnny on board, that Joe Shaw shifted most of his responsibility for dealing with his underworld partners to his new friend. Johnny knew the territory, could handle those people better. After all, it was more agreeable to do business with one man who was as good company as Johnny Rosselli, and could get his hands on Bushmills aqua vitae besides, than to be collecting envelopes all week from a couple of dozen dirty racketeers.

And so Johnny took charge of the Shaws' graft machine, overseeing the administration's interaction with the Los Angeles underworld, communications, collection, enforcement. Johnny's more thorough knowledge of criminal activity in the city meant that many more miscreants could be found and invited to pay up. Johnny, Jack Dragna, and Chicago got their share of everything, which left more than enough to please the brothers at City Hall.

It was, in essence, the return of the System, the commingling of criminals and elected officials that had once worked so well for the likes of Cryer and Parrot, Charles Crawford, and the rest of them, before it had come apart at the close of the 1920s. The old California racketeers had lost their place. Now they would be the ones in the back of the line, picking up scraps. The leadership of the Los Angeles underworld had changed hands, and with barely a nosebleed. Now the Italians were going to run it all.

It was ten years since Johnny had first come to Los Angeles, a young drifter from Boston, with a few dollars and zero prospects. He was an outsider then, with a distant view of the powerful men who ruled the city. How much had changed. Those powerful men were finished. Parrot and Cryer long gone. Crawford murdered. Albert Marco jailed, then thrown out of the country for good. The City Hall gang a memory. Only the System itself had survived, up and running. Under new management.

4

BLEEDING THE DREAM MERCHANTS

On May 4, 1932, Al Capone boarded the Dixie Flyer, bound for the U.S. Penitentiary in Atlanta, Georgia. He was going away for a long time. For more than a year there was speculation concerning the future of the Chicago organization he was leaving behind, many thinking that without Capone's dynamic leadership the gang was destined to wither away. Capone had enjoyed hogging the spotlight—he would now suffer the consequences—and as a result few outsiders saw that behind him was a highly structured operation and a carefully selected inner circle that shared much of the credit for the Capone success story.

Few people had heard of the man finally chosen to take the Big Fellow's place of command: Francesco "Frank" Nitto, so little known to the public that the papers had spelled his family name as "Nitti" and the misnomer stuck, becoming his alias. (To avoid confusion we will use his better-known handle throughout.) A former Capone bodyguard, Nitti was executive boss of bootlegging, short, drab looking, a low-key personality, but a brutal disciplinarian, skilled administrator, and a key strategist in the Mob's rise to the top. Like Capone—and others high in the Outfit hierarchy, his older brother Ralph Capone, Jake Guzik, and soon, Murray Humphreys—Nitti was sent off to prison for income tax evasion, a more reasonable sentence than Al's, returning to the city just in time for his promotion.

Nitti's *lack* of spotlight was in fact perfect for the post-Capone era. No more showy headlines, street fighting, and everyone thinking with their trigger fingers. Some controversy lingered around the appointment. Meyer Lansky and Lucky Luciano in New York pushed for the Outfit man they knew best, Syndicate liaison Paul "the Waiter" Ricca, who was in fact Nitti's protégé and hardly likely to supersede him. Frank Nitti's rep was strengthened greatly in December '32 when he survived an unprovoked shooting—three bullets to the back and neck—by a Chicago policeman acting under orders from the newly elected mayor, Anton "Tony" Cermak. If Cermak was ready to go that far to see the new boss eliminated, the underworld big shots figured, then Frank must be doing something right. That ill-considered maneuver on the mayor's part left Nitti virtually "untouchable" by Chicago law to the end of Cermak's reign (which came just a few months later on March 20, 1933, in Miami, when Cermak died from wounds—plus aggravated colitis—sustained during an assassination attempt on President Roosevelt).

Nitti faced a great challenge as the Outfit's leader. Prohibition had been a divine gift to the American underworld. Without it most of the major gangsters would still be running backroom poker games or holding up lunch wagons. Now the era of Prohibition was at its end. To sustain the levels of wealth and corrupting power the Chicago mob had achieved in the past decade, let alone expand on them, they would need to establish large and reliable new sources of income. Various possibilities for expansion had already been under discussion before Capone's departure: gambling and casinos, off-track betting, new territories (Florida, California), the national unions, and the entertainment industry. Nitti was looking for big scores, bigger than bootlegging.

Nitti, like Capone, was particularly interested in the possibilities offered by the city of Los Angeles. A major new metropolis, a dishonest mayor, corrupt cops, money galore, and the home of the motion picture business. The circumstances of the picture industry were ideal for a big knockover: a globally successful business run by a handful of owners (most of them vulnerably foreign-born), the major assets all contained within one twenty-square-mile grid, with wholly owned supply chains—production, distribution, exhibition—simple, vulnerable pipelines that could be manipulated and squeezed at any point—and a workforce almost entirely controlled by unions. Added to all that was the low-hanging fruit, the rich and famous of filmdom with secrets to hide—rapes, drug use, pederasty, vehicular homicide—ripe for exploitation. With Johnny Rosselli, their eyes and ears in Hollywood, the Outfit already had a network of alliances in the city, with the local Mafia, the movie studios, and City Hall. Hollywood was a money tree just waiting to be shaken down.

2

Los Angeles had always been a tough town for unions. From the moment the Chamber of Commerce opened for business in 1888, with a mandate for low wages and open shops, the autocrat class had sought to stop any and all attempts to organize labor in the city. Agitators, picketers, and the like were dealt with harshly, by the owners' private security forces and by the police, which often amounted to the same thing. There were stories of union recruiters tortured and dumped in the desert. The *Los Angeles Times* editor Harrison Otis even refused to accept advertising from businesses that were considered "pro-worker."

But as the city grew so did the labor movement, and by the 1900s unions had fought their way into many industries, and workers proved they could fight as hard as management's vicious goon squads. A strike at the *Times* in 1910 climaxed with the bombing of the newspaper's headquarters and the death of twenty-one souls.

The movie business arrived in Los Angeles just about the time the *Times* was blowing up. In those first, unconstrained years, production companies were closer to drifting carnivals than to serious businesses. One of the attractions of Southern California for the moviemakers coming from the East had been a certain open-mindedness about things like labor laws and humane treatment of workers. Employees would be worked until they dropped, six and seven days a week, for low wages and no overtime, no benefits or job security, forced to compete for each day's work at a morning cattle call known as the "shape up." The abuses made inevitable the allure of unions to fight for workers' rights, and by the 1920s a high percentage of movie people had signed on with one or another of these organizations. In November '26, after much squabbling and ultimatums, labor and management finally worked out terms of employment both sides thought they could live with, what was called the Studio Basic Agreement (SBA), guaranteeing standardized wages, increased job security, and a selection of improved conditions. However, disputes were far from over, between the two sides, or between union factions that vied for jurisdiction among the employees.

The financial chaos that came with the Great Depression brought labor relations in Hollywood to a new crisis point. In March 1933, facing a combination of declining ticket sales, overwrought banks calling in their loans, and a general air of imminent doom, the studio bosses made a collective announcement: immediate pay cuts for all employees, 25 percent for those making under fifty dollars a week, 50 percent for those making over that.

Discontent followed. Few believed the studios were offering a fair deal—motion picture executives belonged to the highest-paid job category in America, and on the same day the cuts were announced, M-G-M's Louis B. Mayer hired his son-in-law David Selznick at a salary of four thousand dollars per week (current equivalent seventy-one thousand dollars). The freelancers had no choice but to accept the pay cuts or be fired, but those in the unions were protected by contract, and the strongest of the unions in Hollywood, IATSE (the International Alliance of Theatrical Stage Employees), or IA, representing craft workers in movie studios, laboratories, and theaters (everyone from sound editors to electricians, prop builders to projectionists), rejected the pay cuts outright.

The moguls, paternalistic, hard-nosed, and thin-skinned, took any opposition as a personal betrayal. The IA jumped to the top of their enemies list. The local union leaders made it easier for them, inciting workers' resentment of the studio heads with anti-Semitic pep talks. The studio bosses eagerly awaited a chance for revenge.

It came that summer. In July a dispute between Columbia Pictures and the sound-recording engineers escalated ("sound" work had come too late for the original SBA). On July 24 the IA issued an ultimatum regarding wage scales for the engineers. The studio reps ignored it, and on the twenty-fourth all IA locals did a walkout on eleven motion picture companies.

The studios risked a disastrous loss of revenue if the strike caused a lengthy slowdown in production, but the moguls in their anger were ready to risk it. The union side had its own vulnerability. The grim economics of the day left many workers with fears of the future, nerves frayed, not up for a hard fight. Management tasted blood. They launched a tough strategic response, hitting from several directions, undermining the union at every turn. Hundreds of strikers were wooed back to work with individual contracts. "Backroom deals" were given to rival craft unions like the IBEW (International Brotherhood of Electrical Workers). The ever-helpful *Los Angeles Times* pitched in with interim scab labor. And when IA pickets appeared at the studio gateways they were met with force—gangs of unknown thugs wielding blackjacks and baseball bats, strikebreakers. This brutal anti-strike force was working under the direction of Johnny Rosselli.

Johnny had kept a close eye on the union-management standoff. In conference with Chicago a plan had been conceived. Soon after the strike was called, Johnny went to see an old acquaintance, Pat Casey, the chief labor negotiator for the studios. Casey was a sturdy, red-faced New York Irishman who had worked as a troubleshooter for Loew's/M-G-M New York boss Nicholas Schenck before taking on the unions for the Association of Motion Picture Producers (AMPP), an offshoot of the MPPDA (the Motion Picture Producers and Distributors of America). He was an affable wheedler on the outside, but underneath it was all steel and cold blood, fortified with potcheen. Johnny understood that Casey wasn't interested in any protracted negotiations with the IA this time. Indeed, he didn't seem interested in negotiating with them at all.

The two men discussed how they might work together. The way Johnny remembered it some years later—before a U.S. Senate Special Committee—it was just a case of him giving some good people some gentle advice. "The . . . studios were in difficulty. The unions were trying to get on to this, I don't know whether it was for higher wages or recognition or what it was. I have forgotten just what it was at the time."

There was what Johnny demurely called "a little rough play around. . . . And the studios naturally didn't want it. They didn't want their workers hurt. They needed some cameramen to go back to work, and they had been threatened through some people. They had asked if I could help. I said, 'The only way to help is to fight fire with fire.'"

Casey liked the sound of it. What did he want in return for this assistance?

Johnny said, "I don't want anything. . . . You just pay the men that I will go out and hire to protect these people going to work in the studios, and later on . . ."

Well . . . later on they would think of something.

He said, "You couldn't give me a hundred thousand to do this thing, but I will do it for nothing. I will help you all I can."

Such altruism was enough to make Pat Casey open a new bottle.

In two days Johnny had a dozen or so Dragna hoods at hand. They rode around in a convoy of dark sedans, pulling up to the studio lots, clearing the entranceways of the picketing workers, letting the nonstrikers and scab hires get through and getting in the faces of those who didn't like it. Fights broke out, and some people got bloodied. The hoods made free use of fists and clubs. Johnny Rosselli's "security" men kept the gates open for business.

"Within a week," he'd recall, "it was all over."

Production had gone on nearly without interruption. With a well-calculated and ruthless series of maneuvers the studios outsmarted, defeated, and humiliated what had been the most powerful labor force in the movie business. In calling the strike the union had made procedural violations of the SBA that rendered the hard-won contract invalid for everyone. Three-fourths of the local IA membership would end up jumping ship, joining other organizations or going freelance. In Hollywood, in one week's time, IATSE had gone from power broker to pariah.

A very pleased Pat Casey again asked Johnny what he wanted for his services.

Johnny said, "I would like to get a job."

He suggested a loosely defined position, a sort of consultant's role.

Casey warmed to the idea. Johnny had showed he could handle a situation and not lose his head about it. The studios had always employed a certain number of "gray area" specialists—problem solvers, influence peddlers, leg breakers. And so Johnny went on staff with the AMPP, with the title of assistant for labor relations, given a place down the hall from Casey in the Hollywood & Western Building, owned by M-G-M's Louis Mayer and Irving Thalberg, home to the association as well as to the movies' censor board, and to the offices of central casting.

He sent word of the appointment to Chicago. Beneath his black mustache, Frank Nitti smiled.

There was an expression in Italian: *Un lupo a sorvegliare le pecore.*

A wolf guards the sheep.

3

In a place and time—Hollywood of the 1920s and 1930s—crowded with extravagant characters, there were very few quite as tenaciously extravagant as the movie actress and Ziegfeld Follies dancer Lina Basquette. From the time she was a child, and for all the headlong years to follow, she seemed to live in a whirlwind of equal parts passion, scandal, and disaster. The ordinary seemed always to elude her, just as the wild and the strange could find her every time. It was only typical that Lina's most notable on-screen appearance was in an astonishing oddity, Cecil B. DeMille's *The Godless Girl*, the story of a high school advocate for atheism at war with a Christian cult, during the filming of which an all-too-real fire burned off her hair and eyebrows and nearly killed her. Typical, too, that her most ardent admirer was Adolf Hitler, who wrote her feverish and near-obscene fan letters.

"Lina," said Marge Champion, her half sister—who would herself become a glorious performer in M-G-M musicals and the model for Disney's *Snow White*—"was the original 'flapper.' She was vivid, unorthodox, extremely liberated. She really was one of the guiding lights of what they called the Jazz Age."

An intense-looking, sensuous brunette beauty, she had been married four times by the age of twenty-four (widowed twice). The first was to the much-older Sam Warner of the Warner brothers, who died suddenly on the eve of the premiere of his own pet project, *The Jazz Singer.* A nasty battle with the Warner family lost her custody of her baby daughter. Her fourth marriage was to a sharp-witted, tough-guy ex-boxer and legendary trainer named Teddy Hayes, known to some as "the man who taught Jack Dempsey how to fight." Hayes had angrily split up with Dempsey a few years back and at the time of his marriage to Lina was a man of many interests, fingers in an assortment of murky pies, from Tammany Hall politics in New York to nightclubs in gangland Chicago.

The Hayes-Basquette relationship, like so many of Lina's, was *un amour fou* all the way—boiling down in her own words to "violent fighting, followed by violent sex, followed by violent fighting, followed by violent sex." It did not help the marriage any to find out that Teddy was a bigamist, with a first wife living in Red Bank, New Jersey. Lina, hurt and humiliated, had run out on him, while Teddy fought with increasing force to win her back. Basquette then instigated an affair with Teddy's despised former employer and ex-friend, the former world heavyweight champion himself, Jack Dempsey. In quick time the affair grew serious, Dempsey falling head over heels, asking Lina to make him her next husband.

Hayes was furious and overcome. He begged Lina to take him back. He told her he would straighten out all that business with the other wife and everything would be fine again. Lina wouldn't listen. What was he going to do?

One day Lina got a phone call at her Hollywood home. The

deep-voiced caller said he was a friend of her husband. What friend? Johnny. Johnny Rosselli, he told her. Do I know you? Lina said. He was calling because he didn't like the way she'd been treating his pal Teddy. He told her Teddy was a wreck. She needed to do the right thing by him. Lina told him it was none of his business, thank you. The conversation became unfriendly. Lina told him she was hanging up and not to call her again and to go to hell. Johnny said there was no telling what Teddy might do feeling like he did. How would she like it if something bad happened . . . if Teddy were to hurt himself . . . or if somebody else got hurt . . . like her friend Jack Dempsey, for instance?

Sometime after the conversation ended, more irritated than alarmed, Lina called the former world champ at his training camp in Reno, Nevada. She told Jack her husband had been pestering her, now setting his friends to make disturbing threats. She asked him if he knew anybody by the name of Johnny Rosselli.

A long silence followed.

"Are you there?" said Lena. "Did you hear me?"

Jack Dempsey said, "Don't you have anything to do with him, Lina. What did he say to you?"

"It wasn't . . . anything."

"Lina," said Dempsey, *"Johnny Rosselli is a Capone hit man. He's a dangerous guy. You keep away from him."*

The idea of Teddy sending a "dangerous" emissary to plead his case somehow made her husband more appealing. The two were eventually reconciled. She got around to asking Teddy about the man who'd made that threatening phone call on his behalf. Oh, Johnny? Forget about it, said Teddy. He was a great guy, and the thing was, Teddy had been jealous and out of his mind wanting her back. He begged John to make the call, and make it good. Capone hit man? Dempsey was punchy! In the weeks ahead, Teddy would speak often and admiringly of his "guinea pal," and Lina grew eager to meet the man who scared Jack Dempsey and held such

appeal for her husband. One day Teddy told her Johnny was coming for dinner.

He arrived, accompanied by a young blonde in a very short skirt
(she wore orange rouge on her kneecaps and no underpants, recalled the observant hostess). From prejudicial assumptions Lina
had expected Rosselli to be an unsightly bruiser. She was surprised
and impressed. "He was nothing like I had imagined." The "guinea"
was handsome and dressed with "exceptionally good taste. . . ." He
was "magnetic . . . [his] unsmiling chrome-colored eyes bored into
mine. . . . His eyes, half closed, unblinking, were the coldest I had
ever seen. For a moment I couldn't form a single syllable. . . . The
lining of my stomach tightened."

Lina had to work hard to control her interest in her husband's
friend. They got through dinner, and then Johnny went off with
the blonde-without-panties, and that seemed to be that. A couple
of months went by, time for lots more of Lina's usual melodrama:
another split and reunion with Hayes, a bizarre encounter with
Howard Hughes, an attempted suicide with a straight razor, and a
bad case of choledocholithiasis (gallstones in the bile duct). She was
in the hospital at the start of a long stay, and one morning looked
up to see Johnny Rosselli in her room. He was alone, bearing flowers. He was solicitous, charming. He didn't stay long, but he came
the next day and every day she was in the hospital. The room filled
up with his flowers.

"Somewhere," Lina wrote, "the warning bells were ringing loud
and clear."

She came out of the hospital. Teddy had by now straightened
out that matter of his lingering first marriage. She was barely home
when he rushed her out of town. They drove across the border to
Nuevo Laredo and got married—remarried, whatever. They re-
crossed the border, drove on to New Mexico, to Jemez Springs,
in Pueblo Indian country, a couple of hours west of Santa Fe.
There was a property Hayes wanted to see, a large hacienda-style

ranch tucked away in the foothills. Maybe he'd buy it for them, he told her.

When they got back to Los Angeles, they moved into a rented bungalow at Toluca Lake. Johnny found the place for them. He and Teddy were doing a lot of business together, and Johnny was a frequent visitor to the house. The attraction between Johnny and Lina was still there, but with her marriage renewed, and his partnership with her husband continuing, they held themselves back.

Regarding that partnership, Lina was never exactly sure what the two men did together. They would often be gone all night working on some deal, or one or both might go out of town for days. When she'd ask where he'd been, Teddy would only say it was "business" and to stay out of it. When her husband did tell her something it was almost always queer and out-of-nowhere, like the time Teddy announced that he and Johnny were taking a stud horse to Oregon to sire a string of polo ponies. Sometimes it was just easier not to ask.

She soon had other things to preoccupy her. She was going to have a child.

Her sister Marge, now a very pretty fourteen-year-old, began staying at the house to help out. "I was visiting her a lot," Marge Champion remembered. "Ted would go out of town and she would have me come over. She was living in a little house they rented and she was quite pregnant. I barely knew what that meant because my parents never opened their mouths about such things. I had a lot of misconceived ideas."

Marge already dreamed of a career in dance and the musical theater and one day had told her sister how she wished she could go to a certain musical performance in Hollywood on the following Sunday. "It was not a professional thing, kind of an amateur showcase, and I had met the singer in school and was excited to go see her. Lina decided I *should* go and that *Johnny Rosselli* could take me. I knew this man was a friend of hers and she thought very highly of him. I didn't know very much about him. He was a mysterious character as far as I was concerned. She talked to him about going out with me, arranged the whole thing. Didn't think anything of it."

Johnny picked her up at the curb outside her parents' house. "He had a very nice car. He was very well-dressed. I remember he smelled of some very masculine cologne. I didn't know him very well at all and I hardly knew what to say. He seemed so much older. He was probably not that old at all. But I was a very young girl!"

They went to the showcase in Hollywood. "I thought the girl singer was wonderful. And he thought she didn't look so hot."

After the show they went back to the car, and Johnny suggested they go for a drive.

"He said, 'Where do you want to go? We can do anything you want?'

"I told him, 'I guess I should go home. My parents don't like me to be out late.'

"Johnny said, 'Let's go over to my place. Come on, I've got a present for you.'

"I didn't know what to think about that. Before I could say anything he started the car and we were off. He drove us over to where he lived. It was an apartment on Orange Drive, I think it was, near Sunset. We got there and parked outside.

"He said, 'Won't you come upstairs? I'll give you the present I've got for you. I brought it back from Mexico.'

"I didn't know why, but I didn't think that was a good idea. Maybe I'd heard someone talk about men bringing girls up 'to look at their etchings.' I said, 'No, I better wait here.' He said, 'Are you sure?' I said, "Yeah. I have a class in the morning. Maybe I'll come some time with *my sister.*'

"He stood looking at me and then he shrugged and turned and went upstairs. He came back down with a package in his hand. He handed it to me in the car. I opened it up. It was a large bottle of very expensive French perfume. *Joy* perfume, which was the big new thing back then. And I thanked him. He said, 'Okay, kid,' and started the car. Then he took me home and I thanked him some more and then he drove away into the night.

"Looking back years later it did seem like a peculiar kind of thing, going out on the town with this man at the age I was, and the sort of character he was . . . but I'm sure my sister just wanted me to have a good time."

Lina gave birth in May '34, a boy: Edward Alvin Hayes. Lina and Teddy asked Johnny to be the child's godfather. And the Church did certify it as so.

Lina was not impressed with Teddy's parenting skills. After the initial pride and joy he seemed barely to notice the newborn in the house. Johnny, by contrast, she recalled, was attentive and affectionate toward the boy whenever he came to visit. The "hard-as-nails" gangster would "crumble and soften any time he was around little Eddie."

Later in the year they all went by car to New Mexico—Lina, the baby, the maid, sister Marge to help care for Edward, and, following behind in a second vehicle, Teddy and Johnny. They were headed for the Mexican-style ranch Lina and Teddy had visited on their honeymoon, a rambling, picturesque compound in the sparsely inhabited foothills. Teddy had bought the place without telling her, he said. He'd wanted it to be a surprise.

"It was a beautiful place," Marge Champion remembered. "A beautiful house. I had my own lovely room. But we were pretty much cut off from the world. I didn't have any idea what we were all doing there." Johnny and Teddy spent most of each day talking business behind closed doors. Lina rode horses, hiked, practiced ballet. The attraction between Lina and Johnny continued, if anything increasing with their round-the-clock proximity, living under one roof.

After a week Johnny left for Hollywood.

A couple of days passed, and the ranch had unexpected visitors—at least Lina hadn't expected them.

Big black sedans drove onto the compound filled with men in big black suits. Lina and Marge were told to stay inside while Teddy went to greet them and directed them to the guesthouse. He was gone for most of the day. Lina was dumbfounded. When Teddy came back he was shaken up, refused to explain anything, told her to mind her own business. The black-suited strangers kept to themselves, but you could hear them late into the night, drunken loud voices, raucous laughter. Lina demanded to know what was going on. Teddy gave in at last. Those men . . . those gentlemen were from Chicago. They were the actual owners of the ranch. Teddy was a front, they'd had him buy it for them. Her "heavenly home," as Lina had called it, was a gangsters' hideout.

"They had a terrible argument," said sister Marge. "And she came to my room and said, 'Pack up, we're leaving!' So we got in the car and drove to Albuquerque, two hours over a very bumpy road, in the dark, and I had the baby in my arms all the way."

Lina phoned Johnny in California.

"Johnny, I've *had* it. Find me a place to live."

She moved into a house just below the Hollywood sign on a lovers' lane known as "Condom Cove." Johnny came over for dinner. They had the house to themselves, and that night they did what they decided they had wanted to do from the beginning. "Pent-up passion for each other released," Lina recalled the moment, in Technicolor, "and surfeited with satisfying regularity."

They saw each other as often as they could, discreetly as they could, mostly in the daytime, at a secluded hillside bungalow Johnny had borrowed for the purpose. Lina was, by her own admission, a highly sexual creature and the two spent most of their hours together in very close contact. When they got bored with the bedroom they went out to the small swimming pool surrounded by eucalyptus trees, and they swam and sunbathed in the nude. "It was a blue heaven," said the Godless Girl, "an idyll. . . ."

Johnny pushed her to get a divorce. He didn't like Teddy still being a part of this thing. It made him feel bad. They talked about going to Reno for her to get a "quickie" split—it took a mere six weeks in the state of Nevada. They'd bring Eddie with them. She would be free, no more need to hide from anybody.

Lina would listen to him, in the bungalow's darkened bedroom. She would think it could happen, just like he said. And then, later, she'd come down to earth. Thinking with her head this time. One day she would notice he was carrying a gun in his jacket, or on another she would wonder what sort of "business" he had been taking care of the night before. Teddy's antics, his secret deals and his gangster pals, were bad enough. Rosselli was a genuine criminal. She had lost her daughter (and her movie career) to the machinations of the Warner family and their lawyers, who had done their best to prove she was not a fit mother. She couldn't let anything like that happen with her second child. How would she fare in a divorce court—or in tabloid headlines—when lawyers showcased her as a gangster's moll?

It went on for a while. Wonderful afternoons. Things said, and left unsaid.

And then it was over.

4

George E. Browne was the sort of man who, if he got caught out in the rain, would think he had peed himself. He was a burly, uncomplicated fellow, a heavy drinker who was said to consume a hundred bottles of beer a day. He enjoyed carrying a revolver in his pocket and drawing it at unexpected moments, one time firing at the stage lights from his seat inside a theater, and another time accidentally shooting off one of his own toes. He was an unlikely master criminal, or master of anything. That he became an important part of one of the greatest felony swindles of the century was just a case of happenstance or good—followed by very bad—luck.

For most of his life Browne had been working in Chicago theaters as a stagehand, shifting props and scenery flats. At union meetings he could yell pretty good, and he had ended up getting a position on the staff of the stagehands' IA local. Browne found that union staff work was a lot easier than moving furniture, and there was money to be had beyond the piddling salary if you figured out how to get it. He moved up to become a business manager by threatening his rival for the job with a steel pipe.

Browne made a surprisingly good show of himself as a union officer, breaking heads and risking his life to defend his workers' rights, getting shot during one violent encounter. In those rough-and-tumble days of the union, brawn was often more impressive to the rank and file than brains. He found enough support to run in the national elections and served a term as the IA's national vice president. A try for the presidency was less successful. And then everything went to hell. The Depression had all but destroyed the live theater business in Chicago, and Browne's career and his moneymaking capacities bottomed out. He drifted into low-level rackets and misused his union credentials to extort from strip joints and burlesque theaters. His life was in need of a kick start, and he soon stumbled upon it in the gross form of a footloose criminal acquaintance named Willie Bioff.

If the ancients had worshipped a god of scumbags, he might have looked something like Willie Bioff. Russian-born, a bully, thief, and rapist since adolescence, a teenage pimp, forcing young girls into prostitution at knifepoint, later running a protection racket at the Fulton Market, extorting kosher chicken salesmen under threat of arson, a sometime thug-for-hire with both Al Capone and Frank Nitti, though neither gangster wanted much to do with him. Squat and thick, a face like a sneering blobfish, he was an ugly little man inside and out.

With Browne's IA ID card, and Bioff's vile audacity, the pair began a shakedown tour of Chicago's theaters. Browne was the reasonable one, the "good cop" who warned of possible walkouts. Bioff favored hardball tactics, threatening theater owners with the release of stink bombs and hungry sewer rats in crowded auditoriums. They worked their hustle all the way up to the grand Balaban and Katz chain, right to A. J. Balaban himself, demanding twenty thousand dollars, claiming it was for raises and other legit workers' needs, though as Bioff would one day admit, "We didn't care whether wages were reduced or raised. We were only interested in getting the dough, and we didn't care how we did it." To their surprise, Balaban didn't care either. If the money could guarantee him peace in his theaters it made no difference to him who got it.

One day, coming away with a five-figure check in hand, the two chiselers decided to celebrate and went to a joint on East Superior called the Club 100, a nightclub with a gambling den. Drunk and full of themselves the two discussed their caper at such loud volume that others in the place became interested. The club was Mobbed up, managed by Al Capone's cousin Nick Circella, alias Nick Dean. Only a fool shouted his secrets in such a place. Playing point man, Circella cozied up to the loudmouthed pair, pursuing the story of their sudden wealth. He had it all in no time, and then he told it all to Frank Nitti.

They grabbed George Browne and took him to Nitti's place. Nitti growled at him. Shaking down businessmen? Who the fuck did he think he was, running a scam like that without permission? He told Browne he would have to kick back a 50 percent share of the Balaban payment and the same from any future contributions he received. It might have stopped there, but George Browne had gotten scared and wanted to explain himself, make it clear he was no upstart crook for them to worry about. It was just that things were tough in his line of work. Normally he was a legit guy. You could ask people about him. He'd been a pretty big man at his union. You know the IATSE, Mr. Nitti? The what now? Nitti refocused. What are you talking about, fella? Browne repeated himself, elaborated. It was a surprising story, if true. This unimpressive lunk had not only gotten an executive position with the Chicago office of the IA, but in '32 he'd made a bid for the presidency of the union. He had lost, but he had done pretty well to hear him tell it. See what I'm saying, Mr. Nitti? I ain't no grifter. I just had a lot of bad luck lately.

Frank Nitti knew about the IA. They ran the hard labor for nearly every theater in the United States, carpenters, stagehands, and the projectionists in the picture houses. In Hollywood they had for many years been the dominant representatives of the laborers who worked in the movie studios, with the power to shut down that whole industry. Of course they had lost much of that power after a failed strike against the studios, that loss thanks in large part to the efficient strikebreaking work of Outfit associate Johnny Rosselli. As a consequence of that defeat the IA in the movie capital had been ruined, reduced to a fraction of its old membership. That defeat was still having repercussions. The reigning president of the "International" had been given much of the blame for mismanagement of the Hollywood strike and was considered a likely loser in his upcoming bid for reelection. The position was wide open.

Nitti summoned George Browne for another meeting. This time he quizzed him about that run for the presidency. How had he put that together? Where did he get his support? Where did they go against him in the election? Browne said he'd done pretty well in the sticks but he couldn't get enough votes in the big cities and urban centers, New York, Cleveland, St. Louis, New Jersey. Nitti said that was interesting. Those were almost all places where he or his associates had a lot of influence. Wasn't it too bad they didn't all know each other back then?

"George," Nitti said at last, "let me ask you something. How would you like to run for president again? And this time, how would you like to win?"

5

Johnny made the most of his position as Pat Casey's assistant, gathering data from the inner workings of that industry association. The files contained contracts, confidential reports, random indicators of labor and management strengths, weaknesses, fears. The secretaries were useful, too, full of raw gossip, and Johnny happily cultivated friendships with many of them.

With no labor unrest at hand, Pat Casey would occasionally ask him for help with other matters that could benefit from his special skills. One such assignment came down from a higher-up at Metro, likely Louis B. Mayer, or Eddie Mannix, his roughneck general manager. It involved a potentially ruinous threat to one of the studio's biggest female stars. Some transient salesman possessed what were said to be pornographic photographs of the actress. Rumors of a sordid past had trailed the woman for some time, and the sample pictorial offered in proof was apparently compelling. Paying blackmail was considered a chump's game—blackmailers tended to come back for a second dip, and another after that—but the studio brass just wanted the threat to go away now, by any means necessary. Johnny met with the man somewhere, threatened to kill him or—depending on the version of the tale—worse; in any event the blackmailer disappeared. The star's reputation remained unsullied, and she went on to win an Academy Award.

Another group located in the Hollywood & Western Building was the Production Code Administration, the movies' homegrown censors. Its newly appointed head was a man named Joseph I. Breen, who worked down the hall from where Johnny Rosselli had his office.

There had always been a board of censors in corporate Hollywood, but they had recently assumed a much more repressive place in the moviemaking process. The Hollywood films of the early sound era had become naturalistic in their style and content—earthy, bawdy, real—reflecting Depression hard times while making a sensationalist appeal to a scrimping public. This in turn led the movie business to be attacked by censorious civic bluenoses and religious spoilsports like the Roman Catholic Church's Legion of Decency. Trying to forestall further rebukes or government-imposed standards, the MPPDA had opted for greater self-censorship in the form of a more severe and more closely monitored Production Code. To keep Hollywood films "decent," the industry appointed Breen, an Irish-American former journalist, public relations man, and a judicious Catholic ideologue. Breen and his staff would spend the next two decades scrutinizing screenplays and rough-cut previews for signs of turpitude, evidence of sacrilege, anti-Americanism, visible nipples, and other cinematic transgressions. The moralist and censor was an unlikely pal for Johnny Rosselli, and yet a friendship between them blossomed.

Fifteen years older, Breen fashioned himself a father figure to Johnny, parental and priestly. They would sit together at lunch or in Breen's office and talk theology, morality, the perfidy of producers. Breen was concerned over the young man's lapsed religious status and sought to bring him back into the fold. He had Johnny to his home, introducing him to his wife, Mary, and their six children. Johnny became a frequent visitor, a regular at Sunday dinners. He became very close with Breen's son Joe Jr.; they were like brothers, many said, and they would stay devoted friends for life.

As with many of Johnny's upper-world friendships, his with the movies' chief censor was built on compartmentalization and deceit. Ironies abounded: The moralist bedeviled by the amorality of Hollywood, the movies and the people who made them, unknowingly confiding his feelings to one of the leading architects of the city's corruption; the man who had done much to chase the gangster movie off the silver screen for its evil influence offering friendship and paternal guidance to an unregenerate gangster and associate of the Capone Mob.

In Chicago, Nitti and the Outfit brass were shaping plans for a move on the IA. The run-in with George Browne had been the unexpected catalyst, but the dream of taking over one of the internationals was an old one among the Windy City strategists. Short of the federal government or a major religion, there were few organizations in America that controlled so much power and influence as a big union. If the IA was not the largest or the richest of them, it remained a powerful entity nationwide, a critical force in the entertainment industry, and generated millions of dollars. The IA leadership had access to all its national business, from contracts to work stoppages and strikes to the monthly fees paid by all members. Criminal control of the IA offered a multitude of opportunities—theft, skimming, shakedowns, gouging, money laundering. But what seemed to excite Frank Nitti most of all was the IA's association with the movies. The sheer glamour of robbing Hollywood had the mobster enthralled.

Nitti had Johnny Rosselli come to Chicago from Los Angeles

to give a kind of tutorial on the movie business. With key members of the Outfit gathered around, he explained the way things worked in the picture business, the studio system, the major and minor studios and the personalities who ran them, the production centers in Hollywood versus the financial and marketing divisions in New York, the relationship with labor and the unions, the unions' and guilds' strengths and weaknesses (including the present weakened state of the IA, to which Johnny and the Outfit had contributed). He described the unbroken line from production to exhibition, overheads, assets and liabilities, profits and losses. He told them how much an average movie cost, how much it could make, and how much of the take went into the pockets of the studio heads. He revealed the moguls' fears, their vulnerabilities, where they could be hit, and for how much.

When he was done, there was applause and grumbles of commendation.

The number crunchers played with the facts and figures Johnny had presented, divided everything by the rate of extortion, and came up with a rough idea of the potential yield: a million dollars per year [current value seventeen million], every year.

The number cracked like thunder, and the gangsters smiled like bright stars in the blackest night.

The IA's biennial convention opened for business in Louisville, Kentucky, on June 3, 1934. It was an unconventional convention to say the least. On arrival the Mob's candidate was isolated in his hotel room and guarded like a prized trial witness. One man attempting to make contact with him was given a severe beating by Outfit thug Frank Diamond; turned out the man was an old friend of George Browne's just coming to wish him luck. The press and all outsiders were banned from the convention hall. At the entranceways were beefy hoodlums wearing sidearms. Inside, keeping sharp eyes on the proceedings, were most of the top names in the national syndicate, Lucky Luciano, Meyer Lansky, Bugsy Siegel, Longy Zwillman, and a good portion of the Chicago Outfit. The floor manager was Louis "Lepke" Buchalter, the leader of Murder Inc. The mobsters moved among the rank and file, making sure everyone knew what to do with their vote. When the convention concluded on June 4, the new president of the International Alliance of Theatrical Stage Employees was George E. Browne.

Frank Nitti, Frank Rio, Paul Ricca, and the rest of the Chicago Mob contingent, with Browne, Bioff, and Circella, gathered to celebrate the election results.

Nitti explained how things would proceed. Nick Circella and Willie Bioff would both be named personal representatives of the president. Bioff, Browne, and Circella would next go to New York to take charge of the IA executive office at 1450 Broadway to introduce themselves around and to meet with Hollywood's visiting top mediator, Pat Casey. In New York there was also an expense fund of thirty grand or so in the IA coffers that Nitti wanted secured and brought back to him in Chicago. Then Bioff would be going out to Los Angeles to run union matters there, under the (secret) supervision of Johnny Rosselli.

The gang leader emphasized again the importance of getting Casey and the producers to restore the jurisdiction of the IATSE on the West Coast, and getting all those lost members back into the fold. Mobsters, led by Johnny, had helped destroy the IA in Hollywood, and now they were going to make it strong again. "Now get yourselves organized," said Frank Nitti, "and start getting some dough."

It was made clear that Circella would be keeping a close eye on Bioff and Browne in New York, so the tetchy Bioff wasted no time undermining his authority. On the morning of a scheduled meeting with Casey, a hungover Circella overslept. Bioff and

Browne went without him. It was a brief, friendly meeting with Casey, some talk about conditions on the West Coast and the need to return the IA to its prestrike status. Casey agreed there was room to negotiate on the matter, and they left it there for now.

When Circella found out from Bioff what happened, he berated him. He'd been warned they might try something, maybe to hit up Casey for a private kickback. With Johnny Rosselli working for Casey *and* the Outfit, a delicate balance had to be maintained, and not fucked up at the two hustlers' first opportunity.

Circella didn't even want to hear what had been said at the meeting. "You're coming with me," he told Bioff.

They took a short cab ride north to 57th Street and 6th and entered the Medical Arts Building at 57 West. An elevator took them to a sanitarium floor high in the eighteen-story structure, where Circella led Bioff down the corridor and into a patient's room. In the bed was a man in his thirties, skin burnished with suntan, an oxygen mask hanging around his neck, a cashmere robe draped over his shoulders. He was sitting up, playing solitaire.

Nick Circella said, "Hello, Johnny."

He looked to Willie Bioff.

"I want you to meet Johnny Rosselli," he said.

The man in the bed greeted him. He was gracious and apologetic, Bioff remembered. He was in the hospital with a bit of lung trouble, he said, sorry to bring them out of their way. He asked Bioff to excuse him for a minute. "I have got something to discuss with Nick, and I want to talk Italian to him, so please forgive me."

"It's okay, Johnny," Bioff said. "I'm used to these things."

Johnny and Nick spoke to each other. Then Johnny shifted in the bed to face Bioff.

He said, "Now, Bill, tell me, is it correct that you said [such and such] to Pat Casey this morning?"

Bioff started. It was almost word for word what he'd said.

Yeah, he told Johnny, he'd said something like that.

And then Johnny said, "Casey said [such and such] in return?" Was that right?

Bioff said that was about right, more or less.

But what he meant was it was exactly right, like it was coming from a transcript of the private conversation. The point was clear, Johnny, in his hospital bed there, with his oxygen mask and his suntan, already knew every word of the meeting.

"Yes, Johnny," Bioff said finally, "That is the exact conversation that took place."

Johnny looked at Nick Circella and smiled. Nick smiled back.

Johnny begged Bioff's pardon again, and he and Nick talked briefly in the language of their fathers. Then Nick said to Bioff, "See, Willie, I am only trying to show you there is nothing you can do or say to any producer or head of any of these producing companies that we won't know. Johnny is our man. He handles the West Coast. He is on Pat Casey's payroll. If there is anything that goes on on the West Coast with any producing company, we will know. You understand? Anything you say to Casey comes back to us. Any deals you try to make with one of the studios, we will know about it."

Willie Bioff said he understood. He didn't say whether he liked it, and nobody asked.

It would take half a year for the mob's infiltration of the entertainment workers' union to go from nominal authority to full control. They had to move around the map, one city after another, closing out local administrators and establishing the rule of the "International." Union officers in each city were fired and replaced by an assortment of criminal minions and Outfit relatives, a portion of all salaries kicked back to Chicago. Mob accountants were put in charge of the books. Mob lawyers handled legal affairs. It was not always easy, as the locals in many cities were already run by criminals, by local mobs and in-house dictators who weren't looking for new leadership. Some people always had to do things the hard way, and in the course of the takeover some of those people ended up unwell. Tommy Maloy, the powerful president of the IA Projectionists' Local 110, and himself a murderous crook, was not cooperative with the Outfit plan to replace him, and one morning a sedan pulled up alongside his Packard on Lakeshore Drive in Chicago and somebody sprayed him with machine-gun fire, erasing the Irishman's face. George Browne attended Maloy's funeral, then took over the Projectionists' 110, noting for the record, "I am pleased that this organization has settled down to a proper business management."

Despite Pat Casey's assurances that a new offer for the IA was in the works, the studios stalled. Johnny Rosselli advised Frank Nitti that he could find no reason for the delay, as the studios had supposedly favored Casey's recommendations (many of which had been whispered in his ear by Johnny himself). Nitti had known the plan would not happen overnight but finally decided they had waited long enough. While the IA had little power left on the production end of the movie business in Hollywood, everywhere else, across the country on the exhibition end, it had plenty. On November 30, the union called a wildcat strike by projectionists in the Midwest, New York, and San Francisco. In some theaters the projectionists ran the movie upside down, or took a middle reel and opened the picture with it, or put a newsreel in the middle of a movie in progress. Hundreds of others just switched the lights out and left the theaters in the dark. The projectionists went missing from their jobs the next day and picketers appeared at many theaters.

The message was received. An emergency meeting was held between George Browne and representatives of the major movie

companies. The negotiations were brief and the concessions immediate. The IA would go back to its pre-1933 jurisdiction in Hollywood, with the guarantee of a closed shop for the categories of
employment IA would represent (carpenters, prop men, electricians, assistant-level camera crews, laboratory technicians, grips).
Signs were to be posted at all major studios in Los Angeles to the
effect that affected personnel had to join or rejoin the IA to continue their employment. It worked. Within weeks the IA's membership among West Coast studio workers would go from a few
hundred to more than ten thousand. It was the biggest, swiftest
reversal of fortune in Hollywood labor history.

The studios were no pushovers. They did not make such a major
concession without thinking there was something in it for them. It
was a bad time for big businesses to leave themselves vulnerable
to union problems. The FDR administration had become an aggressive champion of prolabor reforms and union expansion. Powerful international labor organizations like the American Federation
of Labor (AFL) and the brand-new Committee for Industrial
Organization (CIO) were seen by the ownership class as aggressive, radical opponents, marauders about to sweep down and sign
up every industrial worker in the country. By making a quick deal
with the IA, the movie companies could keep their workforce out
of the hands of these more threatening representatives. And in return they were granting the IA little more than the recognition
they had already given them once before.

At first all the union leaders seemed to want was their place
back at the table and to look good to their members. It was a good
deal, Pat Casey said (as Johnny Rosselli had said to him). By giving
nearly all their business to Browne's IA (there were still a number
of smaller labor groups and creative guilds to contend with), the
studios were giving themselves a layer of protection against more
threatening forces (the CIO, the White House, the reds), and em-
powering what would essentially be a company union.

A few months later they would have a clearer idea of what it meant to be in business with Bioff and Browne.

The leading movie studios and the Hollywood unions had their annual contracts meeting in New York. For the first time in years the IA would be the largest of the West Coast labor groups in attendance. George and Willie were coming to make sure they got everything that had been promised by the studios in the December poststrike agreement. And maybe a bit more than that.

Two days before the first scheduled meeting, Willie Bioff made an unscheduled visit to the offices of Nicholas Schenck on Broadway. Schenck was the fifty-four-year-old Russian-born movie pioneer, the chief executive of Loew's Inc. and Metro-Goldwyn-Mayer, chairman of the Producers Association, and effective patriarch and grand poobah of the American picture industry. He was a tough, serious businessman who reflected no sign of the glamour and gaiety of the movies themselves, and few people who dealt with him were not intimidated, including M-G-M's West Coast autocrat Louis B. Mayer. Bioff seemed oblivious to any of that, demanding that they speak then and there, and Schenck warily agreed.

Bioff began with a rant about his workers never getting all that the studios owed them. The companies, Bioff told Schenck, had benefited by many millions of dollars, and now the IA wanted some of that money back. He went on in righteously indignant mode for a few minutes before he got to the punch line.

"I told him," Bioff would recall, "to get together with the heads of the different companies and get a couple million dollars together. . . . I told him that was it. He had better get together with the heads of those other companies and before we got into a meeting we had better have an understanding."

Schenck looked confused and asked him to repeat what he had said.

Bioff shouted it: "*I said, 'We want two million dollars from you and your pals here. Or else!'*"

Schenck threw his hands in the air and, in Bioff's description, began to rave: "Are you insane? Where did you get this idea? Two million dollars!" (Current equivalent $34,160,000.)

Bioff calmly repeated the demand. "I told him," Bioff recalled, "if they did not get together we would close every theater in the country, every circuit in the country."

Nick Schenck stood angry and dumbfounded. Bioff told him to get with his colleagues, sort it out, and have his answer before the big gathering two days hence. Then Bioff twisted his warthog body in the direction of the door and walked out.

On April 16 the negotiators arrived at 1600 Broadway, the various union leaders and the representatives from the movie studios, with Schenck of M-G-M, Sidney Kent, the president of Twentieth Century–Fox, and Maj. Albert Warner of Warner Bros. presiding. Schenck went looking for George Browne and angrily waylaid him outside Pat Casey's offices. Schenck asked if he knew what his man Bioff had done.

"He wants two million dollars from us!"

Browne shrugged. "Yes?"

Schenck said, "The meetings are going on and we don't know what is going to happen. He demands we will either get two million for him or we will have terrible trouble."

Browne replied, "That is not in my department, you will have to talk to him about it. I am just going to be meeting about hours and wages. Any business you have with Bioff will be okay with me."

Schenck became more agitated. The man was mad, he said. He was insane. He could not give up such money like that, they didn't know where they would get it, it would ruin them.

Browne was impassive. "That's your business and his. You talk to him about it."

The studio chiefs and the union leaders began gathering in the conference room. Browne huddled with Bioff to tell him about the conversation he'd had with Schenck.

When the meeting broke for lunch, Bioff took Nick Schenck and Sidney Kent into a small side office.

Bioff said, "Now look, I thought the matter over since I was talking to you. I asked for two million dollars. Well, I guess that is too much all at one time. I want a million dollars, and that is about the best I will do, and I don't want to talk about it. You make your mind up that is what I want."

Schenck said, "No, we will not do it."

They argued back and forth for eight or ten minutes. Bioff's temper flared by the end. "You'll do it!" he snarled. "We'll close all the theatres and you'll take millions of dollars of losses. We showed you what we did in Chicago and those other places. You can't afford to take that loss, so you are going to pay and like it."

On the last day of the meetings Bioff again took Schenck and Sidney Kent into another small office at Casey's suite.

Bioff said, "Well, what about it?"

Schenck said he would not do it.

Bioff said, "Well, I thought the matter over and I have got a different way that I want it. I want fifty thousand dollars a year from each large company, twenty-five grand from each small one."

Schenck started to complain. Bioff cut him off. He said, "Now listen, before the day is over you will let me know one way or the other, because the next day I will not talk to you anymore about it, the meetings will be finished the minute we get out of here and if you say you won't do it I will close the theatres at the end of the day. So all I want from you is an answer, not an argument."

Schenck and Kent stood frozen in place.

"That's all right, that's all right," said Bioff. "Then I am finished."

He started to walk out, and the two movie executives stirred at last.

Schenck said, "All right now. If we have to do it we have to do it. We can't afford to have our business destroyed so we will have to pay."

Bioff said, "I want my money in cash. And I want it tomorrow."

Schenck told him it might be impossible for them to get it that fast.

Bioff said, "Well, I'll call you tomorrow and you let me know, but I want to get away from you and I want that money."

Schenck conferred with the other studio reps. There was outrage all around. But what to do? Refuse them? Even with recent rising profits the studios could not afford weeks of disrupted production, whether or not there was a legal victory at the end of the fight. Call the cops? By the time the police or the FBI did something, said Albert Warner, much damage could be done. And with the administration in Washington supporting the unions over management at every turn, who could say the authorities might not side with the extortionists? They went back and forth. At least, it was said, the payments would guarantee a period of peace with the union.

In the end they decided to cooperate with the crooks. There was too much at risk. For now it was better to pay the money than to call Bioff's bluff. Take the loss and see how it went. Each of the major studios—Metro, Fox, Warners, Paramount, Universal, and United Artists—would pay fifty thousand dollars for the year, and two so-called minor studios, RKO and Columbia, would each pay twenty-five thousand. The reps were left to schedule their individual payouts to Bioff over the next couple of days.

Willie insisted the grand movie executives deliver the money— cash only—in person. The debasement tickled him.

Schenck and Sidney Kent arranged to make their payments together. They went to Bioff and Browne's hotel, the Waldorf-Astoria, found the room.

As Schenck recalled the scene, Bioff opened the door. The two movie execs entered the room. Someone was using the toilet, they could hear, finished, flushed. George Browne came out and greeted the two execs. Schenck took out his package, opened it, and said, *"Count it."*

Bioff took it and put it on one of the twin beds and said to Browne, "Count it," and waited and then said, "Is it correct, fifty thousand?"

"Yes. Fifty thousand."

Then Sidney Kent, of Twentieth Century–Fox, put his package on the bed, and Bioff picked it up and handed it to Browne and said, "Count it."

There were twenty-five Gs in Kent's package. The executive apologized. It was all he could arrange to get on such short notice. He would be able to have it in a matter of days. Was that all right? He could get it to him in Los Angeles.

"In person," Bioff said.

Nick Schenck couldn't hear anymore. He took out a cigarette and went over to the window. He tried to lose himself in the clouds above Park Avenue.

In January '36 the IA held an executive meeting in Miami. There were more gangsters than executives in attendance. The union people were gathered at the Fleetwood Hotel on West Avenue, but most of the important talk was done at Frank Nitti's vacation place at the beach. Bioff joined Nitti and Rosselli in a discussion of the state of things in Hollywood. Nitti was very pleased. The extortion of the studios plus the vast increase in membership dues and fees had already brought in more than a million dollars. And they were just getting started. They discussed the upcoming plans for Los

Angeles, where Bioff would join Johnny and take charge of the IA local.

Nitti told Bioff he was to put Johnny on the union's payroll. A nice weekly stipend. Bioff objected. He did not want to give away another fucking buck to these guys. They were already taking 70 percent of everything. But what he said was, it was a bad idea, it was too risky. As Johnny was already on Pat Casey's payroll, Bioff said, "his name would stick out like a sore thumb, not being affiliated with our organization . . . it just would not look well."

Nitti told him it would have to be done through a "dummy" name, somebody who would kick back his pay to Rosselli (after deducting for taxes and a little tip for his troubles).

Johnny said nothing, just listened.

"There's no way I can put him on the payroll at this time," said Bioff. "What payroll do you suggest?"

"I don't care what payroll you put him on," Nitti said with sudden force. "I want you to put him on. That is your problem."

A dinner was held at Al Capone's mansion on Palm Island. Ralph Capone hosted for his absent brother, with Nitti and the other big shots from Chicago there, along with Johnny Rosselli, Bioff, Browne, and Circella.

Glasses were raised and good wishes sent to the Big Fellow, locked away now at the brutal federal pen on Alcatraz Island. "The Rock" was intended for violent, incorrigible prisoners, but Capone had been deliberately transferred there by the government for extrajudicial punishment. His health was declining on the island, from harsh prison conditions, cold weather, and from the advancing effects of neurosyphilis.

For dinner they ate Florida pompano—it was Al's favorite.

Johnny Rosselli and George Browne took the train from Miami to Los Angeles. Willie Bioff, already treating himself like a Hollywood mogul before setting foot in the place, traveled by luxury cruise ship through the Panama Canal. While they awaited Bioff's triumphant arrival, Johnny played host to Browne, taking him around town, showing him the hot spots, arranging for him to take a VIP tour of one of the movie studios. He introduced him to producers, directors, a few movie stars.

Johnny and George met Willie Bioff when his cruise ship docked at Long Beach. In Los Angeles they got right to work. Willie made his first appearance at the IA local hall on Santa Monica Boulevard. He arrived in time to interrupt an officers' meeting. Bioff, the personal representative of the union president, handled this first piece of business in the movie capital with the finesse of a three-fingered pickpocket. He declared the "International" was now in charge of all Los Angeles business, fired the local officers, and announced an immediate 2 percent surcharge on all member earnings, an ostensible "strike insurance" to cover lost wages in the event of a walkout. But of course the money served no such noble purpose and was delivered to Chicago just as soon as it was collected.

5

In the late spring Johnny got word from Boston that his brother Vincent was very sick. He had caught pneumonia and everyone feared the worst. Johnny had not been home since he had gone on the lam as a teenager. He took an airplane to Boston, one of the new DC-3s, eighteen hours coast to coast. He stared out at the sky, the clouds, trying not to think of the past. Thinking of the past. "I went immediately to the hospital in Brookline," he would remember. "My brother was in an oxygen tent. He was holding the cross with Jesus in his hand. When he saw me he pleaded with me not to let him die.

"He died in my arms just ten minutes later."

Johnny made all the arrangements. He paid for Vincent's funeral and his grave and for perpetual care of the grave.

He rode in the black limousine with his mother and siblings. It had been so long since they had seen him that when his sisters stared at their brother Phil it was as if at a stranger. They had no strong memories of him now, only bits and pieces of information, half-heard legends they had to swear never to repeat.

He gave his mother a large sum of money. Then he went away. He would not see her again for thirty years.

Johnny had to stop in Chicago on his way back to California. In the city he took care of some business he had put off for a while. One of the boys got him together with somebody who knew his way around certain kinds of official paperwork and how to make something fake look like something real. Soon there was a file with names, dates, addresses, appropriate witness signatures, notarization stamps, and whatever else was required, and then these documents—left with a well-placed associate—were quietly inserted into files of the Bureau of Vital Statistics and the Health Department.

He was now "officially" John Rosselli, birthplace Chicago, Illinois, United States of America. Another loss in the family. Filippo Sacco was dead.

5

THE BIG SQUAWK

What is it they say? If you want a job done, give it to the busy man. As a new year—1937—began, Johnny Rosselli was hard at work on multiple fronts. He was the underworld's liaison with Los Angeles mayor Frank Shaw and his bagman brother, Joe; West Coast ambassador for the Chicago Outfit; a labor negotiator for the motion picture industry; secret administrator to a motion picture union; business partner with the boss of the Los Angeles Mafia; a partner in the local racing wire and a co-owner of the Agua Caliente track in Mexico (set to reopen in June). In addition to these efforts he maintained an equally daunting social life, which was often business by another name. There were morning rounds of golf at one or another elite country club, afternoons attending the races at Santa Anita or (from '38) Hollywood Park. In the evenings he went to the top restaurants and nightclubs. On weekends he might go out of town to Palm Springs or Del Mar or Tijuana, the guest of movieland notables.

Of course, Johnny always found time in his schedule for women. In matters of romance he strove more for variety than depth of interest. Fledgling actresses and silver-screen hopefuls, young and beautiful, were his characteristic companions. In Hollywood, young women wanting to get into the movies were treated as currency, traded, exploited by any man with a little access to the dream factories. Johnny was not above wooing attractive aspirants with his industry connections, though unlike the average Hollywood wolf he might actually follow through on a promise, arranging more than a few studio introductions and screen tests. The ladies came and went, though some remained friends for many years and might turn to him for help or advice in times of need.

On occasion a relationship fell outside the usual pattern. In 1937 he was introduced to a young woman named Marajen Stevick. She was the daughter of David W. Stevick, a man of wealth, the owner of an influential Midwest newspaper, the *Champaign News-Gazette*, in Champaign, Illinois. That winter Marajen had come to California for a sojourn with her mother, escaping the cold weather, hoping to mingle with movie stars and have some fun. She was a tall, semiattractive blonde, high spirited, had lots of money at her disposal, and liked to spend it as frivolously as possible. She was a real-life version of those unpredictable heiresses in the era's screwball comedies (*Bringing Up Baby, My Man Godfrey*, and the like), eager to defy convention in favor of adventure and romance.

Billy Wilkerson, owner of *The Hollywood Reporter*, introduced Marajen to Johnny Rosselli. "He's a good friend and a bad boy," said Billy. That caught her attention. She was drawn to the sort of man of whom her grim, traditionalist father would never approve. They went out one evening. Then another. Marajen was smitten, eager to be a part of Johnny's colorful life. There was talk of her investing in one or another of Johnny's business schemes. Maybe in several of Johnny's business schemes. One impulsive afternoon, in high screwball style, Marajen rented a private plane and the two of them flew down to Mexico, and somewhere over the border they got married.

The brief ceremony was followed with a couple of robust nights in a Pacific resort hotel room. Then, with the honeymoon satisfactorily concluded, they had the marriage annulled and returned to Los Angeles. It was Marajen's formula for enjoying an erotic holiday without disobeying her parent's edict against sex before marriage.

Johnny's and Marajen's eccentric romance continued for a time after the annulment, but ended when Marajen's father—alarmed by reports of his daughter's wayward behavior out West—summoned her home to Champaign. Mr. Stevick committed her to the care of a psychiatric facility where she would undergo a series of therapeutic electroshock treatments (something that never happened to the madcap leading ladies in the movies).

Al Capone had been rotting in Alcatraz since 1934. His wife, Mae, made trips to visit him, a long journey from Chicago to the West Coast, and on one occasion she had come by way of Los Angeles. Mrs. Capone was a sweet, simple Irish Catholic woman, devoted to Al. Johnny looked after her in LA and then became her escort for the long ride north. In San Francisco, Johnny met a man who served as chaplain at both the San Francisco General Hospital and at Alcatraz (the prison's first), a Jesuit priest and scholar named Joseph Mahoney Clark. Capone had suffered badly on the Rock, and Father Clark had comforted him, said mass for him, and gotten him medical attention, for which Mae Capone was tearfully grateful. They went to dinner in the city, Johnny, Mrs. Capone, and Father Clark.

Evidence of the priest's sympathy, insight, and intelligence left Johnny deeply moved. He hoped they could talk again. Clark offered his friendship, and the two remained in touch, exchanging letters and meeting for long conversations any time their paths crossed. Johnny had been raised a Roman Catholic, and in some small room at the back of his mind he remained one, but it had been a long time since he'd considered himself worthy of the Church's consolation. In Father Joe, Johnny found someone with whom he could speak of things—matters of conscience, matters of the soul, fears, regrets—things he had left unexamined, and certainly never expressed out loud. In the years ahead Johnny would use the priest as a conduit for charitable acts and financial aid to Jesuit schools, neighborhood programs, and individuals. Clark's friendship remained of very great value to Johnny for the rest of his life.

In '37 he moved into the newly built Sunset Plaza Apartments on the Sunset Strip.

In the early thirties he had followed the social drift out of downtown Los Angeles, settling in the area to be known as West Hollywood, a couple of square miles between Hollywood and Beverly Hills. This was unincorporated land, under the jurisdiction of Los Angeles County. The Strip, running along Sunset Boulevard at the base of the Hollywood Hills, was home to chic restaurants and watering holes, glamorous hotels, high-end gambling emporiums (most notably the renowned Clover Club), a "classy" brothel (the House of Francis), and Schwab's, a pharmacy/lunch counter popular with starlets (by legend the site of Lana Turner's "discovery"), where Johnny became a regular customer for late-morning coffee and eggs ("The sweetest guy you'd ever want to meet," said the owner Leon Schwab to biographers Charles Rappleye and Ed Becker). The Strip was looked after by the perpetually corruptible sheriff's department, which maintained an equitable balance between law and order and vice and dissipation. It was a colorful, lively neighborhood, and conveniently located, midway to anywhere. Johnny found it most congenial and would live thereabouts for many years.

For a time he had an apartment at the high-rise Colonial House on Havenhurst, then moved around the block to Crescent Heights, taking a "villa" at the Garden of Allah, a former private estate now cluttered with twenty-five rental bungalows, favored by transient creative types doing time with the movie studios, many of them New York writers of a dipsomaniac bent.

The Plaza, his latest home, was part of an elegant complex containing eighteen deluxe units designed by Paul R. Williams in haute-Georgian-revival style. There was a swimming pool, tennis courts, an underground parking lot and dormitory for servants, and elaborate landscaping throughout. Fresh linens were hand-delivered every day. The residences were in one three-story and two two-story groupings, built with privacy and the California sunlight in mind, more like individual houses than apartments. The horizontal architectural plan was considered so innovative that the complex was featured in many professional magazines. The interiors were furnished and decorated by the design specialists at Bullock's on Wilshire Boulevard. Rent at the Sunset Plaza began at two hundred dollars a month and climbed, when an average monthly rental in Los Angeles was thirty dollars.

Many of his neighbors were from the Hollywood elite, the actor Ralph Bellamy, Katharine Hepburn, Warners ingenue Anita Louise, friend Harry Cohn when the Columbia mogul separated from his wife, and the irrepressible bandleader Tommy Dorsey (who brought unwelcome publicity to the Plaza after a drunken brawl on the terrace with movie star Jon Hall, attacking the actor with a switchblade knife and slicing open his nose).

In late spring another well-known figure moved into the complex, the writer Edgar Rice Burroughs, creator of Tarzan, the Ape Man, who arrived with a new bride and two stepchildren. Rosselli and Burroughs became acquainted and soon established a good neighborly friendship. The gregarious author would invite him over for cocktails and conversation. A writer could never meet too many exotic characters, and Burroughs enjoyed getting to know a genuine Hollywood gangster, even if Johnny claimed to be a respectable businessman. Burroughs was recovering from a rough year, a messy divorce, and an even messier Tarzan movie he'd coproduced, the picture having gone bust on location in Guatemala with everyone involved owed money except Jiggs, the chimpanzee, who'd been paid in advance. Burroughs entertained with such stories and Johnny presumably shared a few of his tales from the urban jungle. Edgar excelled at making cocktails and was even more adept at consuming them.*

"*Ebby* [E. R. Burroughs] liked Rosselli very much," his stepson, Lee Dearholt Chase, remembered. "We all did. He was nice to everybody. He got along with everyone and was always very polite and considerate. I don't think he would have actually admitted it but everyone seemed to have known what he was. You couldn't miss it. The way he talked, the way he dressed. He was just like someone you saw in the movies, an Edward G. Robinson or Humphrey Bogart character. Always well-dressed, very dapper looking, but in a rough sort of way, wearing a black shirt with a white tie, that kind of thing. No one would ever mistake him for a banker!

"He often had this fellow with him, a henchman, a bodyguard—whatever you want to call him [this was likely Dago Louie Merli]. They came and went in a big black Packard, or a Cadillac it might have been. He always seemed very busy, coming and going. But if

---

* Burroughs was among the contributors to the 1935 author/mixologist collection titled *So Red the Nose, or: Breath in the Afternoon*, along with Ernest Hemingway, Erskine Caldwell, and the great travel writer and cannibal William Seabrook. It is speculative, but Burroughs might well have served Rosselli his personal "Tarzan Cocktail." The recipe is as follows: 1 ounce Bacardi rum; 1 teaspoon Cointreau; juice of ½ lime; shake well with shaved ice.

he saw you he'd stop and smile and ask how you were doing. His bodyguard, however, never spoke, just stared like he thought he might have to shoot you. But I was only a little boy!

"Mr. Rosselli was always giving out presents. He'd bring presents for us kids, for my mother. He brought my mother a box of beautiful silk handkerchiefs. I remember one time he found out I was having a birthday party. He sent his bodyguard out to get me a gift. He gave me a big Charlie McCarthy doll . . . the eyes opened and closed and the mouth moved. It was almost as big as I was."

The Burroughs family moved on, but the author did not forget his Sunset Plaza neighbor. Living in Hawaii during World War II, he would write a novel, *Tarzan and the Foreign Legion*, the final book of the celebrated series, this one a timely tale of a downed U.S. bomber crew escaping the Japanese army with the help of the loincloth-clad hero (now a colonel in the RAF—out of uniform, natch). Among the cast of characters was a Johnny Rosselli caricature Burroughs called "Tony Rosetti," a barely literate young mobster ("Rosetti doesn't speak American—just Chicagoese"), a product of the Prohibition mean streets, his father "killed in Cicero in a gang war when he was a kid," his mother a gangland moll. Whether or not Johnny ever knew of Burroughs's literary tribute is unclear.

He found another friend—if you defined the word loosely enough and with some irony—in lethal, unpredictable Ben "Bugsy" Siegel. Since childhood a partner in crime with Meyer Lansky and Charlie "Lucky" Luciano, Siegel was a founding father of the national crime syndicate and Murder Incorporated. He was a very effective gangster, smart, merciless, charming, psychotic. Hands on. He was one of the few top Mob leaders who still killed his opponents personally, for the sheer joy of it.

By '37 Siegel had abandoned New York for Los Angeles. His hometown had become afflicted by a crusading special prosecutor named Thomas E. Dewey, who had vowed to take down the crime lords of Manhattan—an admiring press called him "the Gangbuster"—and had been doing a pretty good job of it. He'd achieved national hero status with his successful prosecution of Luciano on sixty-two counts of white slavery (compulsory prostitution), and a court sentence of thirty to fifty years behind bars. Since July 2, 1936, Luciano had been cooling his heels upstate in frigid Dannemora prison, near the Canadian border. The Dewey offensive was a good excuse for Siegel's move to California. No one could blame a man for fleeing an unscrupulous, headline-chasing prosecutor (it was believed—in gangland anyway—that Dewey had coerced witnesses to lie in the Luciano prosecution). But Bugsy's motive for the move ran deeper than a getaway: He was point man for a potential big incursion from the East.

Little happened anywhere in the American underworld that escaped the notice of Meyer Lansky. The "Little Man" had watched with interest how the Chicago Outfit, with their secret agent Johnny Rosselli, made a clandestine grab of Los Angeles. The quiet alliance with Jack Dragna, followed by Dragna's gang thriving as never before. The takeover of the movie union and the shakedown of the Hollywood studios. Lansky didn't know everything about Chicago's interests in Los Angeles, but he knew enough to be intrigued and likely envious. Anyway, it was a violation of the Commission rules to move into new territory without prior agreement. That had to be answered, one way or another. Or maybe Meyer thought two wrongs could make some money. With Dewey breathing down their necks in Manhattan, threatening to close the whole city to them, it was smart to consider an escape route and maybe a new home base, and Rosselli and the Outfit had done a good job revealing the possibilities on the West Coast. Lansky and Luciano (from Dannemora) agreed, the time had come to establish a beach-head in California.*

Siegel arrived with a safe-conduct pass from Lucky to Jack Dragna. The Mafia boss was instructed to play ball with Benny. Dragna was understandably annoyed: *"Why they send this fucking Jew to my town?"* Johnny counseled him to ride it out. New York was in a bad mood. It was a humiliating moment for them, the chairman of the Commission put away for life on a pimping rap.

Siegel skipped around Hollywood like a brat let loose in a toy store, grabbing anything that caught his eye. He cut himself in on bookmaking, prostitution, drugs run from Mexico. Through his old pal, the movie actor George Raft—one-time hoofer at Manhattan's Mobbed-up El Fey Club—he befriended other stars and producers, hitting up many of them for "friendly" loans of five and ten grand or more, none ever to be paid back. He bought a piece of the Tijuana racetrack where Johnny was a partner, and for a time he got control of the screen extras' union (a scaled-down version of the Outfit's takeover of the IA). It was almost as if he was following in the footsteps of Johnny Rosselli and Jack Dragna (and their Chicago partners), emulating their path to success in Los Angeles. It wasn't just business practice the newcomer seemed to copy. To some Bugsy appeared to be stepping into Johnny's shoes. Any way one saw it, they seemed to have much in common. They were two clever men, alluring, attractive characters with a dangerous edge, sharp-looking lotharios with movie-star style (to that notion Siegel added a *folie de grandeur*—he gave thought to *becoming* a movie star, arranging for his own screen test). Johnny saw

---

* Luciano later claimed that Bugsy and Meyer, the two longtime friends, had had a private falling-out, the details of which were not shared, but the rift was somehow irreparable and may have been a factor in Siegel's relocation . . . and perhaps explained Lansky's later reluctance to save Siegel's life (how few friendships are forever, alas!).

any such comparison as far from complimentary. Bugsy was a smiling cobra. When dealing with Johnny and Jack, he played nice and respectful, but it rang false, had a hidden bite, and neither man trusted him. Anyway, he was a pain in the ass.

Worse was his imported muscle, a onetime boxer and Mob enforcer named Mickey Cohen. Sent to Los Angeles to do Bugsy's bidding, the loutish, impetuous Cohen preferred to do a few things for himself first. He went on a spree, knocking over numerous bookie joints, including one run by Dago Louie Merli. At the Dago's place he got away with thirty grand and an old stickpin Merli declared was a family heirloom. Jack Dragna was outraged. Ordinarily he would have sent somebody to teach Cohen a painful lesson, but Cohen was Ben Siegel's man, and Siegel was the Syndicate's man. Dragna did not want a war with the East Coast powers, or a messy outbreak of violence in his hometown. Johnny went to talk with Bugsy. Siegel had a bemused talk with Mickey Cohen. Cohen refused to give back the money. He'd stolen it fair and square, he said. He did agree to return Dago Louie's heirloom. He had "too much class to keep it," he said.

Following Johnny's advice, Jack Dragna suffered their presence for now, but he looked forward to the time he could offer an appropriate response.

2

With the Los Angeles mayor's laissez-faire approach to crime, and efficient management by the Rosselli-Dragna team, racketeering in the city had grown beyond even Roaring Twenties/Prohibition numbers. There were two hundred gambling rooms and casinos in operation, one thousand whorehouses, and more than two thousand bookies and betting parlors.

The biggest moneymaker, and organized crime's single best provider since the illegal booze business, was the racing wire, the bookmaker's lifeline, the networking device that had galvanized off-track betting. The coded racing wire system was created at the turn of the century by a man named John Payne. Leasing facilities first to Western Union, and then AT&T, Payne gathered fresh information from various tracks, last-minute odds, track conditions, scratches, and almost instant race results, and delivered it to his subscribers. Once sampled, the service became an immediate necessity for every bookie, not only for their own calculations but to deflect the advantage of crafty customers who could have access to that same late track information and use it against them. The business ran on a fine line of legality: Off-track betting was against the law in America, but the use of electric communications for "interstate transmission of sporting news" was not. Clearly the wire was in aid of illegal gambling, but without direct involvement in the crime, and with a legit owner "fronting" in each city where the service opened, it seemed that little could be done to stop it.

The most successful of the race wire operators was a veteran newspaper man named Moses Annenberg. The Prussian-born Annenberg had been Hearst's circulation manager in Chicago, ruthless and brutal at the job, ordering other papers' newsboys beaten up and newsstands bombed when it helped to sell more of his boss's rags. He saw the enormous potential in the racing wire, both in the Chicago area and beyond—he named his company the Nationwide News Service. In order to do business in Chicago, and to destroy rival wire services, Annenberg entered into a devil's bargain with Al Capone, who owned many of the racing books and muscled kickbacks from most of the others. Annenberg provided the service, Capone and his men provided the subscribers.

The Great Depression had been a godsend for horse racing. The United States had closed all tracks in the first two decades of the twentieth century, as they were considered crooked, cruel to animals, and encouraged unlicensed gambling. In the economic crisis after '29, the states' need for taxable cash led to a complete reversal of perspective, and soon racetracks began opening from coast to coast, now considered reformed with incorruptible pari-mutuel betting systems and every dollar won taxed by the state government. With so much action in play across the country the number of bookmaking operations grew like the summer grass. They all required a wire service, almost every one paying large annual fees for the Nationwide News feed. The subscription base grew so big it required the leasing of sixteen thousand miles of telegraph wire.

Nationwide's West Coast headquarters was in Los Angeles at the Bank of America Building on 6th and Spring. The legit face of the business was Gene Normile, sportsman, former manager of Jack Dempsey, and the man in charge of the revived Agua Caliente Racetrack in Tijuana, Mexico. All things "illegit" were the responsibility of Johnny Rosselli. Johnny liked to refer to Normile as his partner, but Normile later testified more than once that Rosselli and his associates had muscled in on his franchise, demanding 50 percent of everything for their services, or else.

Johnny, some years later, would give a relaxed accounting of his Nationwide days to the Kefauver crime committee's chief counsel, Rudolph Halley, presenting himself as an affable subordinate.

MR. ROSSELLI: Los Angeles had several hundred what you would call open books. You could walk in from the street into a cigar stand and make a bet. They needed this type of [wire] service in order for them to function in their business. So occasionally someone would open and I was known in and about Los Angeles, and I would refer them to Normile's office at the Nationwide News.

MR. HALLEY: And what was your influence over these bookmakers?

MR. ROSSELLI: None at all.

MR. HALLEY: He had no trouble selling wire service?

MR. ROSSELLI: Yes, he would, I guess; maybe. Some could get along without him and others could not.

MR. HALLEY: Now, Mr. Rosselli, who could get along without it if they could get it? You know very well the wire service was something that every bookie wanted and really couldn't live without. If he couldn't get it he had to steal it.

MR. ROSSELLI: True enough. So they would be stealing it. So I would probably talk somebody into not stealing it.

MR. HALLEY: How did you persuade people to not steal it?

MR. ROSSELLI: Just by discussing it with them.

In truth, persuasion, discussion, did not always work, and there were times when the resolution of a dispute required other means.

George "Les" Bruneman was a veteran Los Angeles gangster, club owner, and big-time bookmaker, a former member of the late Charlie Crawford's syndicate. He had been on the scene in the Southern California underworld for as long as anyone could recall, the son of a Polk Gulch butcher come down from San Francisco years back with his friend Eddie Nealis (now co-owner of the elite Clover Club on the Sunset Strip). He was among the many who'd switched his focus from bootlegging to gambling at the end of Prohibition. Bruneman's main claim to infamy was his involvement in the 1930 kidnapping of the underworld accountant Zeke Caress. Bruneman had been roped into cashing Caress's ransom checks and was caught in the kidnap car after the snatchers had shot and crippled a Long Beach policeman. An initial conviction was overturned, and "defense attorney to the stars" Jerry Giesler got Bruneman acquitted in a retrial. In '37 he was running a string of nightspots and bookie joints, in Hollywood and in the small beach towns south of Santa Monica. He was doing all right, though he always dreamed of a return to his Roaring Twenties glory days.

Les Bruneman had taken the fall of the original City Hall gang very hard, and he nursed a grudge against the Italians who had moved into their place of power. It was beneath him to steal the wire service, but he was damned if he'd keep handing his dough to those spaghetti slurpers.

Johnny repeatedly requested the money Bruneman owed, but the debt remained unpaid. Some Dragna heavies showed up at one of Bruneman's books and wrecked it. Bruneman still didn't back down. He spread it around that the dispute was over Rosselli cheating him and other bookmakers, misusing the wire service, and "past-posting" track information.

The feud reached a time where Bruneman sent word to Chicago acquaintance Bob McLaughlin (of the Checker Cab wars) that he was looking to hire some gunmen to come to Los Angeles and "handle" Johnny Rosselli. Bruneman thought that in the Windy City he could not only get some first-class killers but could keep it a secret by hiring from outside Rosselli's sphere of influence, ignorant of his close connection to Chicago and the Capone gang (testament to Johnny's discretion in LA). Bruneman's inquiry was passed to the Outfit, which relayed it back to their man on the West Coast.

Johnny shared the information with Jack Dragna. The two men agreed: Enough was enough with this *schifoso*.

The hit on Bruneman was assigned to Frank Bompensiero, a favored soldier of Dragna's based now in San Diego, and to Leo Moceri ("Leo the Lip," for his outsize embouchure), an enthusiastic killer-for-hire who'd come to California to get away from a murder investigation in Toledo, Ohio. They tracked Bruneman to the Surf Club, his place on the gambling strip by the waterfront in Redondo Beach. The joint was crowded, and they decided to wait till he showed himself outside. Sometime later the bald, bespectacled Bruneman exited the club with a young blonde (Patricia Eatone by name), and they strolled north along El Paseo. Moceri and Bompensiero followed, and then, with Moceri keeping watch behind him, Bompensiero rushed up to Bruneman, firing at his back. The gambler sensed the attack, broke away from the woman as the gun sounded. Just one bullet caught him. He stayed on his feet, lurching across the street. The woman screamed, and Bompensiero balked. He spun around and he and Moceri ran to the getaway car while Bruneman disappeared into the lobby of the Fox Theater on the corner. Somebody called for the cops.

Detectives rode with Les Bruneman in the ambulance.

"You know what this is all about?" said one of them. "Somebody muscling in or the Syndicate sore at you?"

"It's all a mystery to me, boys," said Bruneman, adhering to the criminal code.

"Talk and take yourself off the spot."

"I don't know anything."

Bruneman recovered at Queen of Angels Hospital, watched around the clock by armed bodyguards and nurses, one of the latter becoming his new girlfriend.

District Attorney Buron Fitts, the chief law officer of Los Angeles County, announced an investigation. The erratic Fitts needed to make a good show, having been trailed just then by an investigator from the office of the vigilant State Attorney General Ulysses Webb. He wasn't likely to disrupt the corruption at City Hall, but he had to cover his ass, and harassing racketeers always made good copy. Fitts called eight men for questioning, described as "captains of the Los Angeles underworld": Guy McAfee, Tudor Scherer, Chuck Addison, Farmer Page, Ross Page, Eddie Nealis, Jack Dragna, and Johnny Rosselli.

"We want to find out what any of them may know about the

shooting of Les Bruneman," said Fitts, "reputed to have been the result of a gang war over gambling interests."

Always the same: A couple of guys trying to settle a little disagreement with each other, and the law made it into a war. Fitts vowed to "get to the bottom of the gambling situation in the county," and to call before a grand jury the mayors and chiefs of police of forty-three incorporated communities "to give an accounting of gambling conditions and to be assured that the grand jury, the Sheriff, and the District Attorney mean business."

With so much heat on, it was more than two months before Bompensiero and Moceri found another opportunity to kill Les Bruneman.

One night in late October, following a tipoff, they caught up with him in Hollywood. He was finishing some business at a "queer bar" he owned called the Club Montmartre (the basement housed a racing book, a classy room with plush leather chairs for the customers). Coming out onto a crowded Hollywood Boulevard, Bruneman got into his car with a woman—Alice Ingram, his golden-haired nurse from Queen of Angels—and drove away. Bompensiero, Moceri, and their driver followed him eastward. Bruneman at last pulled in to the Roost Café on West Temple Street, a locals' dive where they expected to meet up with Ingram's sister and her boyfriend.

Bruneman paused on the way to his table, dropped a large bill on the bar, and said, "Give everybody a drink."

It was his valedictory.

A couple of minutes later Bompensiero and Moceri came up on the Roost's wood-plank porch.

Bompensiero said, "Leo, this time you take him and I'll cover you."

A woman putting a coin in the jukebox saw the two men outside and opened the door to admit them. Moceri pushed her out of his way, crossed the room, holding out two heavy .45 automatics.

Moceri would remember: *"I walk right up to his table and start pumping lead. . . . Believe me, that sonovabitch's going to be dead for sure this time."*

In the small room the noise of the .45s was like cannon fire. The wave of point-blank shots knocked Bruneman up out of his chair and threw him to the floor. A half-dozen bullets went through his head and chest and out the other side. He was gone to his reward long before the noise stopped. The Bruneman nurse-girlfriend caught a slug in the leg and was screaming like a siren.

Moceri spun and headed for the door. He expected to see Bompensiero watching his back (as he told his friend Jimmy Fratianno). "I turn around and I see this *football player . . . coming at me.* Bomp's nowhere in sight."

The football player—a twenty-one-year-old waiter at the club named Frank Greuzard—had impulsively followed the gunman out to the porch. Moceri shot him dead. He ran to the car, where he was appalled to find Bompensiero already seated beside the driver.

A messy piece of work, with a messy aftermath. The killing of the criminal Bruneman was one thing, but the cold-blooded murder of an innocent young man made it so much worse. The public could identify with that. It could have been them, their kid. The newspapers pumped up the angst, ascribing the killings to ruthless rival mobsters and declaring the start of a new blood feud. The *Daily News* headlined: *Eastern Gun Gang Threatens Reign of Terror in L.A.*

The police brought Johnny in for questioning. His alibi was unbreakable and he went home an hour later, but still, the attention was not good for business. He was depending on the Shaw machine to take the heat off. And in an ordinary week, and even with the additional public relations burden of an innocent bystander's death, the dirty local law enforcement—dedicated to staying out of the way of sanctioned underworld activity—would have gotten the word, handled it properly: a perfunctory investigation of the crimes, an absence of arrests, and the citizens' outrage left to fade. But the Bruneman-Greuzard murder case did not go away so easily. This was thanks in large part to the efforts of a certain crusading citizen and purveyor of cheap three-course meals by the name of Clifford Clinton.

Clinton was a cafeteria magnate, owner of a string of popular low-cost restaurants. The establishments were unique, built with the cash-strapped Depression public in mind and Christian spirit on open display. His eateries were sprinkled with neon crosses, tiny chapels, and at one a diorama of the Garden of Gethsemane for postprandial meditation. Legendarily charitable, Clinton gave away thousands of meals to the poor and indigent (and to an occasional disgruntled customer as well, due to his famous guarantee, "Dine Free Unless Delighted"). With success had come self-importance and a desire to give more to society than a cheap meatloaf-and-two-veg. Wishing to test the waters of public service, Clinton used his connections to secure a place on the 1937 county grand jury.

The grand jury in Los Angeles was a notoriously shady enterprise, weighted with appointees loyal to Frank and Joe Shaw or to various of their crooked partners. It was guaranteed that any accused connected to the Shaw network was unlikely to be prosecuted (as the foreman instructed the '36 jury, *Be a mill and grind up what they bring you"*). From the moment his appointment began, Clinton was a problem for this dubious gathering, questioning their questionable decisions and their sympathetic attitude toward racketeers. His suspicions raised, Clinton launched his own fact-gathering apparatus called CIVIC (Citizens Independent Vice

Investigating Committee). CIVIC produced a shocking report on the city's corrupt cosmos, the thriving rackets, gambling joints, sex emporiums, and so on. The Shaw people were irate, but dealing with Clinton was a delicate matter as news reports of his work were turning him into a public hero (one paper called him "the White Knight in rimless glasses").

Now, with the Bruneman shooting, Clinton stepped up, putting himself in charge of a special session investigation, and sending out subpoenas to dozens of witnesses and to about half the gangsters in Los Angeles. The writs were hardly out the door when, on the night before Halloween—Devil's Night—a pipe bomb exploded inside Clifford Clinton's mansion at 5470 Los Feliz Boulevard. The bomb blew up part of the basement and sprinkled the kitchen all over the lawn, but the restaurateur and his family escaped injury.

A frazzled Clinton told a reporter from the *Daily News,* "The same bunch did this bombing that did the Bruneman killing. . . . They think I possibly know more than I do about [the] murder."

If they thought Clinton knew something it was because it seemed very much as if he did. Clinton and his investigators—now aided by FBI agents sent from Washington—had been looking in all the right directions. Johnny Rosselli was mentioned by name in more than one news report referring to "captains of the underworld" and "rival mobsters." Any legitimate, reinvigorated investigation was bound to follow the same trail. Strong suspicions, an arrest and trial, no matter where it all wound up, would mean the end of Johnny Rosselli's legit connections and would screw up any Outfit plans for Hollywood. Jack Dragna had sent Moceri and Bompensiero into hiding out of town, and now, as the situation was becoming more unpredictable, Dragna and Johnny were considering a similar long vacation for themselves—when the plot took another unexpected whirl.

The facts concerning the intentions of Harry Raymond, former vice cop and, briefly, San Diego's chief of police, are inconclusive. An equivocal character, Raymond was either a blackmailer trying to sell evidence of the collusion between the mayor's office, the police, and the underworld, or an intrepid investigator for Clifford Clinton's CIVIC who knew too much, or both. Any way it went, Raymond had sniffed out some facts that certain people didn't think he should be smelling. It was not so difficult to prove that the local government was corrupt; the hard part was staying alive after you proved it. On January 14, 1938, around ten in the morning, Harry Raymond went into the garage of his Boyle Heights home and got behind the wheel of his automobile. As he started it up an ignition-wired dynamite bomb exploded. The car and garage were blown apart. Harry Raymond was broken and burned, and a whirlwind of shrapnel ripped his skin raw.

Somehow he survived.

In the hospital a reporter got to him.

"Who do you think did this?" said the newsman.

Raymond, in agony, clutching a pistol under his bedsheet, no signatory to the underworld's code of silence, and not much caring whether he was right or wrong, gasped: *Earle Kynette."*

Kynette: A captain in the Los Angeles Police Department, described as "a doughy-faced . . . psychopath," ran the mayor's Special Intelligence Unit, the eighteen-man "Spy Squad" dedicated to keeping track of the mayor's and the police department's enemies and political troublemakers. He was also an occasional enforcer for organized crime.

"City Hall sent him," said Raymond, through his pain and shredded flesh.

An investigation found plenty of evidence against Kynette. With federal authorities watching his every move, and the public following the case in alarm, District Attorney Fitts—who had himself been charged with crimes of bribery and perjury in the past—

could not afford to look like he was being soft on a dirty cop. Kynette was indicted for attempted murder.

The trial provided a shocking exposure of the iniquitous Shaw administration. One after another the witnesses revealed the administrative blight. Even the boldly assertive Police Chief Davis was reduced to a confused and shamefaced testimony, leaving himself open to further scrutiny. Kynette refused to take the stand, or even to pay attention to the trial, and sat through it all pointedly reading a copy of the U.S. Constitution as if it were the racing form.

The jury found him guilty, and the judge gave him two to life in San Quentin. (He would do seven years.)

The mayor's office became like the deck of a sinking ship. Clifford Clinton began broadcasting a radio program three times a day devoted to Frank Shaw's ouster. A recall election was authorized, and on September 16, 1938, Mayor Shaw lost his job to the Clinton-sponsored reform candidate Fletcher Bowron—the judge in the Earle Kynette trial, no less. It was the first time in American history that a major city mayor had been recalled from office.

Joe Shaw—the ex-mayor's brother and Johnny Rosselli's good buddy—was indicted on sixty-three counts of civil service fraud. The verdict was guilty. Sailor Joe got five to seventy years.

Police Chief James "Two Gun" Davis was dismissed along with dozens of high-ranking officers. Bowron went through the force with a scythe, cutting the Intelligence Unit, the Spy Squad, and all the other private enforcement wings created for the feculent Shaw regime.

The new mayor promised a better, cleaner city, a new era of municipal ethics, an end to graft, influence peddling, vice rings, and the other hallmarks of the prior administration. Remarkably, he seemed to mean what he said.

———

And so it was that the second coming of the System did perish, and with it the hopes and dreams of the many who made a dishonest buck in the city of Los Angeles.

As for Les Bruneman, whose feud with Johnny Rosselli and whose execution was the catalyst for the tumultuous sequence of events that followed, his name had gone off the front pages after the Raymond bombing, but not far enough. It was in everyone's interest to close the case as soon as possible. The cops combed Los Angeles looking for suspects, with a preference for the kind without complicating "connections" or the hope of a good lawyer. They pulled in every old lag in town for rough questioning. The eyewitnesses to the shooting were made to study lineups and squint at random mug shots looking for a familiar face. Eventually, one woman from the bar said she recognized a twelve-year-old photo of an ex-con named Pete Pianezzi as the man she had seen kill Bruneman and Greuzard at the Roost Café. The suspect was thought to be drifting around Northern California, and it took a while to find him. The DA's office paid no attention to his alibi, rushed him to trial. Two witnesses claimed that Pianezzi was the shooter (one of them later recanted), while nearly two dozen variously testified in his favor, some to say he was not the man they saw at the Roost and the rest swearing he had been in their sight all that night at a club eight miles from the scene of the crime. The jury went with the minority opinion and found Pianezzi twice guilty of murder in the first degree. The judge sentenced him to imprisonment in the state prison at Folsom for the term of his natural life.

It was said that Jack Dragna would on occasion express his regret over this miscarriage of justice—though of course never to anyone who could do anything about it.

3

Willie Bioff in Hollywood was happy as a pig in slop. With his cut of the money squeezed from the producers and the union, he was rolling in dough. And as the top dog in the Hollywood unions he wielded more power than he had ever dreamed of in the halcyon days bullying kosher chicken dealers. He threw his weight around at every opportunity, and took an obnoxious delight in humbling all those who had to deal with him, the powerful and the helpless alike. He made scenes, and he made enemies. It was not the safest way to run a racket like this. On the other hand, Bioff was a success at implementing the Outfit's plans. The producers had coughed up half a million in a year in straight kickbacks, while the increased dues and special fees collected from the members amounted to twice that. Bioff revised the IA charter to include new categories of worker, undermining the small independent unions while gaining more members for IA to gouge. He was bringing in a fortune for the Outfit shareholders, and Chicago did not want to mess with success.

In April the situation with the independent Hollywood craft unions took an unexpected turn. Afraid of losing any more authority to the rising dominance of the IA, and disdainful of hooking up with the unsavory Browne and Bioff, the independents—a dozen or so groups including the painters, grips, makeup people, hairdressers—came together to form a new organization they called the Federated Motion Picture Crafts (FMPC), with roughly six thousand members. Led by Charles Lessing and the firebrand Herb Sorrell of the Studio Painters Union, the FMPC made an immediate demand on the producers for a 20 percent pay hike. They were immediately refused. Further attempts to negotiate went nowhere. The studios had no interest in bolstering another big union. On April 30 the FMPC called a strike. As many of the striking craftspeople were specialists and not easy to replace, all first-unit production at the studios came to a standstill.

Willie Bioff had refused the FMPC's request that the IA honor their walkout, and with the strike on he did his best to impede their progress. As ordered by Frank Nitti in Chicago and Johnny Rosselli in Los Angeles, the plan was for Bioff to show the studios he was on their side and to help defeat the rival union. He strategized with the producers, offering advice and manpower, and he spread negative rumors, telling reporters the renegade FMPC were "communistic troublemakers" and getting their orders direct from Red Russia. On the fourth full day of the strike Bioff started a "membership drive" at the IA union hall. Anyone who came through the door could sign up and be sent to the studios to work.

This was all Herb Sorrell—an ex-boxer, fearless and belligerent by nature—was willing to take. He gathered up a "wrecking crew" of about thirty of his toughest FMPC laborers (scene painters, grips, and the odd hairdresser) and raided the IA union hall at 6472 Santa Monica. All wore plain white armbands to identify one another in the melee to come. They crashed through the office doors without warning, swarming over anyone inside—a large group of new hires had just gathered—overturning furniture, hurling chairs through the glass windows. The *Times* report would call them "terrorists," using "gangster tactics" to have their way. The attackers tossed IA men across the room like a bucket brigade shifting water, throwing them down a full flight of stairs to the front landing. There was blood in the air, and the howls of the victims with bruises and broken bones. It was fast and vicious. The FMPC gang was gone before police could respond.

With Willie Bioff out of town reporting to Frank Nitti in Chicago, Johnny Rosselli stepped into the fray. He arrived at the union hall to find the place in shambles, the wounded being taken to the hospital, and the remaining IA staff in distress. He summoned Dago Louie and six or eight armed men to watch over the place and sent another contingent of thugs to guard the executive office in the Taft Building.

He conferred by long-distance phone with Nitti and Charlie Fischetti, after which Chicago flew a platoon of hoodlums west to help in the dispute. By the end of the week it was all-out civil war, with pitched battles on the picket lines. Johnny, in the backseat of a sedan, directed the goon squads like a general, moving his troops from one studio battlefield to the next. During a clash at the United Artists lot at Formosa and Santa Monica, witnesses reported hand-to-hand fighting and men lying bloody in the street. Herb Sorrell, much experienced with labor violence, said, "It was the roughest strike I ever participated in." He claimed that several men were killed during the course of it, though no loss of life was reported in the press.

It was too much for the majority of the strikers, who had only been looking for a small raise in salary. Solidarity collapsed, many went over to the IA, and in the end only Sorrell's steadfast Painters Union made a good deal, though nothing compared to what the IA got out of the strike. Signing up the FMPC refugees swelled the IA's ranks, bringing in more dues and surcharges (most of it, of course, going to the boys in Chicago), while the IA's management's strong, if secretive, support of the studios made Willie Bioff a hero in the moguls' eyes. They now were willing to see his ongoing extortion as just the price of doing business. If they were indeed helping to create a "company union," then the cost of it was a bargain. Instead of having to meet the needs of thousands of whining laborers, you simply paid off a handful of thieving union executives. With Bioff on the pad the studios would expect no further trouble from the IA membership, salaries would be kept down, and any troublemakers would be made to disappear. That was the kind of union an industry could enjoy doing business with.

Bioff basked in the afterglow of the FMPC's downfall. The fact that most of his actions had been directed offstage by Frank Nitti and Johnny Rosselli seemed to elude him. He was the fair-haired boy, and he took every advantage it gave him. In the months following the strike, he solicited around thirty thousand dollars in cash and stocks from Louis B. Mayer at Metro. Bioff was said to have signed on to help Mayer with his pet project, the attempted undoing of the Screen Actors Guild, with the writers' and directors' guilds to follow. In this dream of Mayer's, the ornery artist guild members would end up with no choice but to join the more cooperative IA and take orders from his new pal Willie Bioff. It would be an extraordinary coup: the entire employee structure in Hollywood controlled by a single corrupt union in collusion with the moguls themselves. In addition to Mayer's private donations, Bioff also received a large block of stock shares from his friends at Twentieth Century–Fox, and similar considerations from the other studios. Bioff kept very quiet about such things, concerned that his mobster overseers would find out. Frank Nitti had warned him against exactly this sort of private deal making. But in Bioff's head it was only his due: It was the mob that was stealing from him.

Bioff's closest associate among the producer class was the reliably unprincipled Joseph Schenck. No doubt Schenck had his own reasons for cultivating a friendship with Bioff, and they were not likely to include Willie's endearing personality. There came a time when Bioff decided to join the ranks of the landed gentry and buy himself an upscale farm property. He made Schenck his personal Realtor, and Schenck obliged, finding him a grand estate in Hidden Valley (it belonged to former Fox chief Winfield Sheehan) worth three million dollars, but Joe said he could get it reduced to 10 percent of that amount. Bioff said it was a little too high-hat for his taste, but they continued to discuss the matter, and Joe offered more suggestions and connections until Willie did see a place he wanted, for the price he wanted. He then went to Schenck for help with another problem. Since Bioff planned to buy the property with ill-gotten gains for which he had paid no taxes, he needed a legitimate source to account for the money or risk the serious attention of the Treasury Department. Tax-evasion charges, as Al Capone and many others could attest, were the Feds' favorite way of bringing down big money and white-collar criminals. For something like this it might have made sense for Willie to turn to one of his Chicago associates for help; they were masters in the art of money laundering. But Bioff did not want any of the boys getting curious about his finances or finding out about his secret deal making.

So Bioff asked Joe Schenck if they might make some arrangement—Bioff would give him the money and then take it back as a loan, so he could show the government, if he was investigated, that the money had been borrowed from Mr. Joseph Schenck.

Schenck, without giving it much thought (which was his style), said, "I think I can arrange that for you. When you are ready for it let me know. It won't take me very long to handle this."

But when Willie thought it over he decided it wouldn't look so good for a union leader's name to appear on an industry leader's books taking one hundred grand from him. Joe Schenck said, No problem. He said, "I will have my nephew, Arthur Stebbins, make the loan to you. I will make arrangements with the bank that Arthur will be able to get $100,000 from them." (Arthur "Artie" Stebbins of Stebbins and Company was a well-known insurance agent who handled most of the biggest policies in Hollywood, thanks to the influence of Uncles Joe and Nick Schenck.)

And so Willie delivered the money in cash to Joe, and Joe's nephew then gave Willie a check, which meant giving back to Willie his own money. It worked out great.

As Willie Bioff's power increased, so did his self-esteem, and his indignation. He hated the Mob for taking so much of the loot he earned, giving him orders, like he was still a punk selling protection to Fulton Street butchers. He nursed a particular resentment toward Johnny Rosselli, that slick Hollywood playboy always breathing down his neck, keeping an eye on him like a store detective trailing a shoplifter. When Johnny got credited for his part in handling the FMPC strike, Willie was furious. And it burned him that Johnny got a weekly kickback from the IA—$194 (current equivalent $2,600) for doing nothing; now he wanted another $100 a week to go to his "chauffeur," Louie Merli. Bioff balked at anything Johnny told him to do, and at any show of his influence.

One day he received a call from Harry Cohn. Harry told him he had two refugee cameramen he wanted to put to work without their having the proper union credentials. Harry then added that "it was okay with J.R."

Bioff said, "Will you repeat that, Mr. Cohn?"

Cohn said, "It is okay with J.R."

Bioff said, "Well, since it is okay with J.R., you cannot have them. J.R. ain't running this. I am running this out here."

Johnny came to see him. According to Willie: "I told him, I says, 'Johnny, I won't stand for you peddling me to anyone. The best thing you can do for yourself is to take care of your business and I will take care of mine, because you might find you will be embarrassed one of these days, that things like that come up where your name is used ain't going to get you anywhere."

Johnny ignored him. The guy was making them money, let him blow off some steam if it made him feel bigger. But Bioff wouldn't leave it alone. "When something would show up I seen Rosselli's hand in I would call up and make a complaint," said Bioff. "I complained about the Columbia setup with Johnny's connection with Cohn, about the cameramen. I says I cannot carry on having someone around there peddling me, but if they want me to be in the capacity I am in that they are going to have to curb Rosselli."

He went to Frank Nitti. "Am I running this thing or is Rosselli?"

"*We're* running it," Nitti replied. "And Johnny speaks for us."

It happened that Harry Cohn at Columbia Pictures never paid the original twenty-five thousand dollars Bioff had demanded from the smaller studios. His good friend Johnny Rosselli had stepped in to approve the delay, claiming the studio was experiencing economic hardship. Johnny knew better than to give Cohn a permanent pass on the money, but they were friends, and maybe running even temporary interference was another favor he could cash in sometime. Not that Cohn seemed to think he needed much help. In Harry's account he had from the beginning refused to "join the team." Bioff had assigned Leo Spitz, head of RKO, to bring the news to the Columbia boss.

Spitz said, "Your share will be $25,000."

Cohn said, "For what?"

"To avoid labor difficulties," Spitz said. "To keep the theatres open."

"I own no theatres," Cohn said. "Why should I pay?"

Now a second year's twenty-five grand was due, and it was clear that Cohn thought he was getting away with it. Maybe he believed his friendship with Johnny Rosselli would keep him safe. Maybe— if the story of a secret shareholder was true—he was counting on a powerful partner named Longy Zwillman. Or maybe he just had bigger balls than the other moguls. When high-ranking Outfit man Louis Campagna was visiting Los Angeles, Bioff explained the situation to him and was given a go-ahead to get what they were owed. Protocol would have indicated Willie confer with Johnny, give him time to save face, before taking action against Cohn. But Bioff's whole idea was to put egg on Rosselli's face. In November, without warning, while Harry Cohn was on vacation in Palm Springs, Bioff called a wildcat strike at Columbia. He ordered hundreds of craft people to walk off their jobs. All activity on the lot was halted.

When Johnny heard from Harry what was happening he phoned Bioff. Willie refused to take his calls. Johnny drove down to the IA headquarters in Hollywood and stormed into the office. Bioff was alone, seated facing the door, with a large-caliber pistol on his desk. He seemed to be waiting for just this moment.

"What's the idea, Willie?" Johnny said.

"Well," said Bioff, "I think I know what you want."

Johnny demanded an explanation for the move on Columbia. It wasn't any of his business, Bioff told him. Cohn owed them money, and Chicago said to get it.

It was a terrible thing to do, Johnny said, "knowing of my relations with Cohn—to put me in that kind of spot, to call a strike on Columbia without telling me about it."

"That was my orders," said Bioff. "And if you can straighten it out with Chicago it's okay with me."

"To hell with you," Johnny said. "And Chicago."

That night Bioff had unexpected visitors. Standing in the doorway of his opulent home was Johnny Rosselli, side by side with Jack Dragna, the head of the Los Angeles Mafia. Jack was getting older, plumper, but he still had about him the aura of an experienced killer. At any age or weight he looked like nothing you wanted to see standing in your doorway after dark. Johnny told Willie he needed to talk to him. They were going for a little ride. Wasn't that how they put it in the gangster pictures? They went to Johnny's car, Dragna got in the back, Bioff given the front passenger seat. Hit men called that the hot seat. They drove in darkness in the Hollywood Hills, Dragna breathing heavily somewhere behind Bioff's neck. The drive was long enough to give Willie time to think about what he'd done, and what he was going to do next.

When they came out of the hills they were on Sunset Boulevard, and they drove on to the Strip and to Johnny's residence at the Sunset Plaza. Waiting for them in Johnny's apartment was Harry Cohn.

Bioff went over to the Columbia boss.

He said: "The strike is off. You can thank Johnny. Nobody but Johnny could have done this for you."

Two weeks passed. Bioff decided just to stay away from Harry Cohn. But then Outfit heavy Louis Campagna called Bioff and wanted to know what had gone on with that Columbia problem. They were still waiting about that, Bioff told him.

Campagna said, "Make that collection."

Willie apprised Johnny of the conversation. His tone was more polite now. He didn't want another nighttime visit from Jack Dragna. It was Chicago talking, not him, saying they had to get that money.

Johnny said, "It looks like I can't get it either. Cohn crossed me. Go ahead, strike him again. It's okay with me."

Bioff wasn't expecting that. Maybe Johnny was making a joke. What the fuck? They needed to get that money, not put together another strike. But Johnny had no more to say on the matter, offered no help, just dropped the problem back in Bioff's lap, and left him to answer to Chicago. He'd screwed him good.

Cohn never did pay. "Not a dime," said Harry.

Willie was flying too high. His wings were beginning to melt.

A majority of the IA members had submitted to Bioff's bullying rule, satisfied to be getting full-time employment or afraid of losing it. Some took the position that if Bioff was a son of a bitch he was *their* son of a bitch, and just the sort of thug they needed to fight the producers (in fact Bioff had won many concessions for the IA workers even after he had begun his secret alliance with the studio heads). But there had arisen a defiant minority, unhappy with the evident corruption: the abrupt closing of the IA Local, the dubious 2 percent surcharge, the tactics used against the striking FMPC. Who was this man Bioff? Where did he come from and how did he get here? The dissidents funded a secret investigation of the labor leader. SAG (the Screen Actors Guild) did the same. Private detectives began digging up evidence of Bioff's long criminal history. Union members had attorney Carey McWilliams take the findings to State Assembly Speaker William Jones in Sacramento. A committee was formed to investigate the complaints of fraud and racketeering, and hearings were to begin on November 12, 1937. A writ was issued for Willie Bioff to appear before the committee on the thirteenth.

Bioff was enraged. How did this happen? Who had betrayed him? He became convinced that the rat was Louis B. Mayer. Mayer had good connections in the state government. Wasn't he the big shot who'd gotten California governor Merriam into office? Bioff demanded a face-to-face with the M-G-M boss. Mayer reluctantly agreed. On November 11 they had a meeting at Joe Schenck's house, with Bioff, Mayer, Joe Schenck, and his brother Nicholas in attendance.

Bioff began "abusing" Mayer, according to Nick Schenck. Mayer was shaken. He said to Bioff: "I had nothing to do with this whatsoever, and I want you to know it. If I did I would say so, but I had nothing to do with it. That is not the way I would ever go about anything."

"You're a liar!" said Bioff, jabbing his finger in the M-G-M executive's face. "Look, Mayer, there is no room for the two of us in this world and I am going to be the one here."

Nick Schenck and his brother looked on as the Lion of Culver City cringed and backed away. Nick Schenck described LB as "absolutely white and trembling." Schenck had no great love for Mayer, and so he watched the ugly scene and did nothing. Maybe even enjoyed it.

Mayer made a call to attorney Col. William H. Neblett, whose law office had close ties with Assembly Speaker Jones, the man in charge of the hearings. Bioff was asked to listen in on another receiver. Mayer nervously chatted with Neblett—who had an inside track on doings in Sacramento—about how the investigation got started and how he—Louis—was in no way involved. Mayer acted it up big for Bioff's ears, doing a regular Luise Rainer on the telephone, but the performance was strictly from Monogram.

"Well," said Bioff at the end, "never mind . . . but I still don't believe you."

Two days later. The state committee members were assembled and ready to begin their questioning of Willie Bioff. Instead came word from above: The members were dismissed, the hearing adjourned. No explanation was given. Only much later did one become likely, when it was discovered that Willie Bioff's headquarters had delivered a retainer to the law offices of Louis B. Mayer's pal Colonel Neblett—who was State Assembly Speaker Jones's professional associate—in the amount of five thousand dollars (current equivalent eighty-three thousand dollars). As soon as the check was in Neblett's hand, Speaker Jones seemed to lose all interest in Willie Bioff.

Willie's escape from scrutiny did not last long. A Sacramento district attorney investigating corruption in California politics discovered the five Gs that had been paid to Colonel Neblett just before Bioff was to testify. Neblett evaded prosecution, but was forced to give up a planned run for governor and resigned from the bar rather than be disbarred.

Willie Bioff was forced to answer questions at last. He did his best to stymie any search for truth, ascribing all accusations against him to communist propaganda. But it was getting late for bullshit. The exposure kept growing, complaints coming in from all directions. The movie star Robert Montgomery, in his role as president of the Screen Actors Guild, gave testimony regarding Bioff's attempts to undermine SAG independence and place it under IA's control.

Now entered the scene a man named Westbrook Pegler, a widely syndicated (six million readers) Chicago-based columnist, an ultraconservative, resolute Roosevelt-hater, racist, anti-Semite, and dedicated adversary of "goose-stepping" labor unions. Poking around the Hollywood IA story, Pegler uncovered a hidden treasure from Willie Bioff's past. In Chicago years ago Bioff had been working as a pimp (the lower form of pimp known as a "steerer") for the brothel keeper Jake Zuta, and was arrested and convicted on a pandering charge. He was due to serve time in jail but had one way or another managed not to serve a day of it. An embarrassed Illinois state's attorney sought his extradition from California. Bioff fought it, but in the end he would be sent back to Chicago and forced to do five months in the city jail. Pegler also exposed the criminal past of Nick Circella (the columnist's muckraking would win him a Pulitzer Prize). This was getting too close to home for the Outfit, and they forced Circella to abandon his position at the IA and to disappear.

By this time the federal government had become involved. A squad of Treasury agents arrived in Hollywood, forensic accountants who began looking at the Bioff matter. After some digging around they found something curious: a loan of one hundred thousand dollars to Willie Bioff from the nephew of Joseph and Nicholas Schenck. (Some sources say the activist/labor lawyer/writer Carey McWilliams tipped the IRS to the check.) Why was union boss Willie Bioff getting a very large, unsecured loan from a man who had close ties to Hollywood studio management and was a blood relative of two moguls? Wasn't Bioff an adversary to such people?

While Willie did jail time on the old pimping conviction, the investigators in Los Angeles went on digging. The nephew who made the loan led them to his uncle Joseph Schenck. That stalwart and profligate film tycoon was called in to explain his relationship to Bioff and his connection to that one hundred grand. Schenck was nervous, unprepared, and contradictory. His story became less believable and more incriminating each time he tried to defend it. The agents smelled blood, dug deeper. They found more evidence of financial improprieties. Schenck had long skated on the edge of things. He was a libertine, high-stakes gambler, pal of gangsters.

He was also a flagrant tax cheat and scofflaw. The agents broke him with ease. He was indicted on multiple counts of tax evasion and perjury, found guilty, and sentenced to three years in prison.

Schenck was debauched, but he was no tough guy. The minute the gate slammed shut behind him at the Danbury Federal Correction Institution he began bleating to be let out. He met with U.S. Attorneys Matt Correa and Boris Kostelanetz.

"Gentlemen," Schenck said, "I'll talk."

He had a good story to tell: Bioff and Browne, dirty deals, cash payoffs, threats, all of it, except anything to do with Chicago and the Capone gang (he was profligate and desperate, but he wasn't crazy).

With Schenck's confessions in hand to guide them, the U.S. attorneys called a federal grand jury hearing in New York. This was not a state-run inquiry. This was big-time. A federal investigation— deep pockets, nationwide reach, all the resources the investigators might need to get what they wanted. They cast a wide net, summoning anyone with a link to Schenck, Bioff, the IA in Hollywood. Assorted moguls and financial executives were forced to answer questions, a rare humiliation. As a member of Pat Casey's staff, Johnny Rosselli was also caught in the drag. Johnny bet that the Feds didn't know of his secret connections to IA at this stage of the investigation. Risking perjury charges, he crafted his testimony to put himself far from the center of Willie Bioff's criminal schemes. He'd met the man for the first time a year or two ago in front of the Brown Derby Restaurant in Hollywood, introduced to him by George Browne, and that was the first time and one of the only times he had ever seen him. He knew nothing about any unusual payments, demands, or threats. No, he had never been employed by any union or union organization; no, he had never received any money from Bioff or Browne or any person who worked for a union.

As Johnny heard the attorneys' questions, their informed context, it became evident to him that they knew much more of the story than he'd anticipated. Someone was talking. The law was aware that Bioff and Browne had been pulling a shakedown on the studios. But did they know the rest? Had they discovered the real power behind the enterprise?

His first move was to reach Willie Bioff and warn him to watch his step and keep his mouth shut. From New York he called Bioff in California.

He said, "You just listen and try to understand what I'm trying to tell you. . . . There is going to be a lot of trouble . . . people you have done business with have squawked. Do you understand what I am saying?"

Bioff said yes.

"Conduct yourself accordingly. I will be seeing you shortly."

It was too risky to say more on the telephone. They would go over his story in person in Los Angeles. But the law moved too fast. Three days later, on May 23, 1941, Willie Bioff and George Browne were indicted on charges of racketeering and income tax evasion.

4

Things had gone so well for so long. It did not seem fair the way it all turned to shit so quickly. The Bruneman problem had led to unexpected chaos and exposure, the busybody Clifford Clinton, the investigations, recall elections, Johnny's name in the papers. The collapse of the Shaw regime ended the partnership with City Hall and with it a golden time of unrestrained vice and enormous profit. The brilliantly initiated Hollywood studio/union shakedown was now imperiled before the looting had barely begun. No one could be sure what the government would uncover. And more: another cash cow in jeopardy, the rake-off from the mobsters' unofficial partnership with Moses Annenberg in the Nationwide racing wire, control of which was lost after Annenberg was indicted for tax evasion (he'd foolishly made enemies in the Roosevelt White House). Annenberg pled guilty and was sentenced to three years in prison and a fine of eight million dollars, what was then the largest tax fine in history. The hardship of incarceration would kill him.*

Annenberg's racing wires and related publications were taken over by a tough old newspaper vet named James Ragen, who outright refused to continue the mobster alliance. The mob did not like to take no for an answer, but the energy required to address the problem would be more than anybody expected, and they soon had other things distracting them.

It was at this of all times, amid professional disappointments, commotion, and trouble, that Johnny Rosselli's private life had entered a contrasting state of something close to bliss. He had fallen in love.

Her name—her Hollywood name—was June Lang. She was a movie actress, a silver-screen blonde beauty, just twenty-one years old when the affair began late in 1938.

Born Winifred June Vlasek in Minneapolis, Minnesota, of Polish-German descent, she'd been a strikingly pretty child with a natural talent to perform, singing and dancing in public from the age of four. Her parents believed she had star quality, and they'd

---

* It was believed that Moses had plea-bargained a deal to keep his son, Walter, from being prosecuted. Allowed to walk for his share of the crimes, the junior Annenberg went on to grow the father's publishing empire and through his wealth, powerful Republican friendships, and judicious philanthropy, was able to attain great social standing and erase any lingering stigma from his and his father's close connections with the Capone gang. In 1969 he was appointed U.S. ambassador to Great Britain by President Richard Nixon; Sunnylands, Annenberg's modernist estate in Rancho Mirage, California, would be visited by notables including Queen Elizabeth II, the Shah of Iran, and at least eight U.S. presidents.

all moved to Hollywood, hoping to put her in the movies. By the age of fourteen she looked several years older and so alluring that she stood out even in a part of the world lousy with young beauties. Her break came as a swimsuited extra in a picture at Fox called *She Wanted a Millionaire* (it is star Spencer Tracy's least-remembered credit). She caught the eye of the Fox production chief Winfield Sheehan. Whether he spotted a promising talent or just a girl he wanted to know better, he put her under contract at Fox and appointed himself her patron, which meant that anybody else should keep his hands off.

She was given assorted small parts in Fox features (*The Man Who Dared; I Loved You Wednesday; Chandu the Magician*), billed as June Vlasek; then Sheehan decided that "Vlasek" was not marquee-worthy and she became June Lang.

Fox had been floundering, and soon merged with the upstart Twentieth Century Pictures, formed in 1933 by Darryl F. Zanuck and Joseph Schenck. Twentieth wanted little from Fox besides the studio's acreage west of Beverly Hills and their national chain of movie theaters. "There was a big shakeup," June Lang would recall to interviewer Colin Briggs. "Mr. Sheehan resigned. Darryl Zanuck inherited his job and my option was not renewed in 1935."

But then six months later they signed her up again and paid her more than she would have gotten on her old deal. The studio began the usual buildup, column mentions, cheesecake poses, photos in the movie mags. An organization of sculptors proclaimed her "The American Venus." Articles appeared under her byline telling readers how to keep a perfect figure.*

She appeared in four or five films a year, working her way up

---

* "Lie flat on your back and be sure the floor isn't padded! Roll back and forth on your hips, from one side to the other. You won't get sea-sick. Roll thirty times, twice a day.... One should be stimulated but not all tired out.... And I always recommend a light girdle."

the cast lists from featured player to lead. She was Shirley Temple's schoolteacher in *Captain January*, Shirley Temple's mother in *Wee Willie Winkie*, supported Laurel and Hardy in *Bonnie Scotland*, and all of the Dionne quintuplets in *The Country Doctor*. Whatever the studio wanted. She played small-town innocents, Arabian Nights princesses, tough girl reporters, a Western Front angel of mercy.

"She was terrific," remembered Tony Martin, her love interest in the Eddie Cantor vehicle *Ali Baba Goes to Town*. "Talented. A gorgeous girl, lots of fun. We had a great time on the picture. . . . I don't know why she didn't go on to bigger things. Whether being John's girl hurt her chances I don't know. I don't think it helped."

They began seeing each other some months following her 1938 divorce from Victor Orsatti, the high-powered talent agent. Orsatti, with his brothers, represented many of the biggest names in Hollywood, and the wedding in the spring of '37 had been one of the most star-attended events of the year. The wedding was a hit, but the marriage flopped. The couple separated before the end of the year. Where she met John Rosselli, or who introduced them, are facts lost to history. Reporters took note of her new beau but made no mention of any of his criminal connections, though one Los Angeles daily described him as a "mystery man" who had been "questioned in the investigation of the murder of Les Bruneman" (but they were quick to clarify that "he was unable to throw any light on the slaying"). The gossip columnists referred to him as a well-known businessman or investor. Hollywood columnists were not so much journalists as industry publicists and seldom stirred up trouble without permission from above.

They made a perfectly glamorous couple, the dapper tough guy and the stunning blonde movie star, doing the high-profile rounds, seen at the top restaurants and nightspots, klieg-lit movie premieres. She was very much his type, a performer, young and beautiful. And maybe he was hers: Johnny and her ex-husband were both red-blooded Italians with mysterious pasts (the Orsattis were bootleggers before they were ten-percenters, and it was said that brother Frank served as Louis Mayer's personal pimp). Johnny and June saw each other steadily through '39 and into the next year. For Johnny it became the most deeply felt relationship of his life.

They were both then in the throes of occupational stress. After Lang's contract with Fox was not renewed, her career began a rapid descent: film work offered by the lowlier studios (Hal Roach, Universal, Republic) and then by the subterranean (Monogram, PRC). Johnny's fortunes suffered a similar decline. Many of the rackets and capers from which he had drawn fees and profit shares had come undone in rapid succession, and both his legit and illegit activities were in such disarray that he had felt forced to take work as an agent on commission for a businessman friend named Herman Spitzel, the owner of a Los Angeles insurance agency.

Perhaps the shared state of aggravation had brought them so close, each providing the other a refuge from the outside world. Or something. It was a kind of relationship with which Johnny had little experience. He'd known a lot of women through the years, and he had always known when to move along. What had gotten into him? he'd wonder to friends. *"Mooning around like fucking Andy Hardy."*

One weekend at the end of March they packed some things and drove out to Palm Springs, then traveled on south and east into the desert. They drove to Yuma, Arizona, the old frontier town that was now known for fast-track weddings (Arizona law required no state residency, no blood tests, and had no ban on first cousins getting married). At 5:00 a.m. on April 1, 1940, they hauled a justice of the peace out of bed. He said the words, took the cash, and Johnny and June were husband and wife. For a week they honeymooned in Arizona and Nevada, traveling alkali-dusted highways, eyeing the Grand Canyon and the Boulder Dam, spending nights in vintage hotels and slipshod motor courts, long hours on well-worn beds.

Back in California, the newlyweds moved into a rental at the Wilshire Palms Apartments in Beverly Hills. It was a luxury residence with all the trimmings, but June started pushing him to look for a house. She wanted a nice place out in the Valley, something with room for kids one day, and for her mother sooner than that. Newlywed bliss came and went. June told people they no longer got along as they once did. There were arguments. He grew distant. He went away on business trips, but seldom made it clear where he went or on what sort of business. June began to sense that her second marriage was no less a mistake than her first. They lasted a year and a few months, after which June moved out. She found a lawyer. She filed for divorce—requested on the grounds of extreme cruelty—in January '42. An interlocutory decree was issued on February 20, a final decree granted on March 1, 1943.

By the time June left him, Johnny had so much going wrong he couldn't think about the ruin of his marriage. Later years, any regrets stayed buried, and when he mentioned it at all, it was to shrug off the whole sentimental experience. *"Who the fuck falls in love with broads?"* he said to his friend Jimmy Fratianno. *"You fuck them and pass them on to someone else.*

"I was once married to a fucking actress. You remember June Lang, don't you? She was a nice kid, but *love* . . . ?"

5

The Bioff-Browne trial was scheduled to begin in October 1941. The Outfit's legal adviser, the brilliant, amoral Sidney Korshak, had crafted a defense: There was no embezzlement; the money from the Hollywood studios was a private slush fund donated to help promote favorable legislation from Washington lawmakers, with

Willie Bioff just a hired liaison, collecting the payments for Joe Schenck. Pin any wrongdoing on Schenck, the fucker who squealed. It *might* work, said Korshak.

There was also some talk about stopping the whole mess before it went any farther, getting rid of Bioff and Browne. Or Schenck. Or all three. Some felt that clipping Bioff and Browne would be unfair—weren't they our guys, did the job they were told—more or less—and hadn't they earned some support? Paul Ricca had a private talk with Bioff and suggested that Willie and his partner could drop out of sight—hole up at a ranch the Outfit owned down in Mexico or someplace. Bioff didn't think much of the ranch idea—Willie Bioff a schnorrer in a sombrero!—or being forever on the run; he wanted to clear his reputation, believed they could beat the rap in court.

At the trial the prosecution's VIP witnesses included Louis B. Mayer, Nicholas Schenck, and Harry Warner, grave, serious men, each recounting a version of Bioff's gross, menacing demands for money. The "blame Joe Schenck" defense was negated before it began. The verdict: guilty. The sentence: ten years for Bioff, eight for Browne. There was no chance to run, the judge ordering them into custody at once.

The missing Nick Circella was tracked down by the Feds and arrested on December 1, 1941. He pled guilty, hoping this would mean a lesser sentence, but the judge gave him a full-count eight years. All three of the former IA officers were soon calling the Leavenworth Penitentiary home.

The Outfit exhaled. No one was happy about the way the Hollywood business had come apart. But with the convictions of Bioff-Browne-Circella, they could now assume the government was finished with the case and the heat was off.

By the time the Bioff-Browne trial had ended in December '41, the attack at Pearl Harbor had occurred and America was at war. Rage and bloodthirst swept the nation, millions eager to fight the Axis enemy, the recruitment centers of the armed forces overwhelmed with volunteers.

There were some elements of society less likely to see the appeal of military service—gangsters by and large preferred silk suits to khakis and looked ahead to a profitable exploitation of the home front. In this regard, as in many others, Johnny Rosselli appeared an outlier. However much his life's work undermined the idea, he saw himself as a steadfast American. He was shocked by the attack in Hawaii, the assault on his country, the murder of his countrymen, and in the feverish first weeks of war he became filled with an emotional patriotism and an urgent desire to serve. Not very long after December 7, he went to the local enlistment office and offered himself to the army. At thirty-six he was several years past the ideal range for enlisted men, and with a medical history that included recurring attacks of tuberculosis, bronchial problems, and multiple hospitalizations over the past fifteen years, he was easily rejected for service.

In Los Angeles the city's reform movement continued along its righteous path. The rackets were reduced to penny-ante stakes. Johnny was now making most of his money from legitimate enterprises. For the Herman Spitzel Insurance Agency he'd been selling expensive policies to many of his wealthy Hollywood acquaintances. It was easy enough—he was not a bad salesman— but dull. When Spitzel was drafted, Johnny agreed to visit the West 5th Street headquarters now and then and keep an eye on things. Appropriating the man's executive office as his own, he often used the place for non-insurance-related meetings, and sometimes Jack Dragna would drop by with a bottle of brandy, and they would get drunk and shoot the breeze. (Johnny wasn't the only unorthodox employee at the Spitzel HQ. The office manager was a Russian named Isadore Ruman. According to FBI reports, Ruman was under observation by federal agents, suspected of being a Soviet agent, part of the ring run by Boris Morros, who was a Soviet spy and a Paramount Pictures music director.)

He tried other legit tasks to make ends meet. For a time he worked as a freelance broker for Dupont, attempting to sell raw film stock to the film studios for a commission. But the major studios had long-term contracts with their suppliers, mostly with Eastman, and not even Harry Cohn would bite. He found interest in the cut-rate celluloid from some Poverty Row outfits like Monogram and the independent producer Arnold Pressburger, but they hardly seemed worth the effort.

Not exactly the glamorous gangster life. Maybe those days were over. He had been at it an awfully long time now. On Broadway that season his writer pal Rowland Brown (a recent Academy Award nominee for *Angels with Dirty Faces*, starring Jimmy Cagney) had staged his new play, *Johnny 2×4*, set in the Prohibition-era Roaring Twenties, featuring a character he'd based on Rosselli: a gentleman bootlegger, a spats-wearing symbol of the picturesque past. It was enough to make a man feel old.

There was one bright spot, a new steady girlfriend. Her name was Bernice Frank, but sometimes called herself Beatrice Frank, and for now used a stage name, Ann Corcoran (middle name plus mother's surname). She was, yes, an aspiring performer. Young and beautiful, yes and yes. It seemed to some to be "serious"—the Hollywood gossip columnist Louella Parsons wrote that Corcoran and "June Lang's ex . . . expected to wed."

Even with the new romance, he felt at loose ends. The war went on without him. But the longing to be a part of it did not go away. By the end of '42 he again tried to enlist. Whether he had found some means of influencing the process, or if, after a year of fighting, the military's need for troop replacements had caused a drop in standards, his second attempt was successful.

On December 4 he was taken into service at Fort MacArthur in San Pedro, then moved to the army training center at Camp Cooke, 150 miles north of Los Angeles.

He adapted to the austere barracks life without complaint. Weekend passes helped relieve the need for fancier food and female company. But the rigors of basic training—as predicted—proved too much for his battered lungs. After three weeks of exercise and road marches he collapsed, unable to catch his breath. He was diagnosed with bronchitis, and spent two weeks at the camp infirmary. The army doctors told him to quit smoking and sent him back to active duty. In the first week of February '43, he went with his regiment—the Eighty-First Armored—by train across country to Fort McPherson, outside Atlanta, Georgia. There they awaited transfer to Europe, and war.

As Pvt. John Rosselli was being readied for combat with the Germans, federal attorneys Correa and Kostelanetz were in New York gathering the forces for a battle with organized crime.

The prosecutors of Bioff and Browne had always suspected that a union hack and a small-time grifter could not have pulled off such a substantial criminal enterprise without some much more experienced power behind them. Thorough investigators were bound to notice the reported peculiarities of George Browne's successful IA presidential campaign and the presence of well-known gangsters from the East and Midwest; Nick Circella's many years of close contact with elements in the Capone organization; and, once you started looking, other bits and pieces linking the Outfit to the union and the criminal Hollywood operation. In the trial itself there had been one quiet bombshell, a passing reference by witness Harry Warner of Warner Bros. One holiday season, said Warner, Bioff came to him demanding an extra twenty grand from the brothers, explaining it was a mandatory Christmas gift for *"the boys in Chicago."*

Taking down members of the Capone gang on a federal rap was a thrilling notion for the prosecutors. But suspecting something and proving it were very different things. The witnesses could only provide secondhand testimony. None had admitted any direct contact with mobsters. Everything had gone through the IA bosses, and they weren't talking. Not yet.

Correa and Kostelanetz pursued the three prisoners through the first year of their imprisonment, offering reduced sentences, protection, anything they could think of to get them to tell their story in court. Bioff and Browne sat tight, believing the Outfit would find some way—payoffs, threats, political influence, something—to get them sprung. But Nick Circella was still unsettled by what he now saw as his foolish surrender, followed by a judicial double cross, a sentence without mercy. What the hell was that? When you saved the government the cost of a trial they were supposed to throw you a bone. The prosecutors worked on his anger, turned it against his comrades. He was encouraged to think about the coming eight years he was going to spend doing hard time while all his pals in Chicago would be back home living it up, blowing all that dough he'd helped them steal. They screwed you good, didn't they? the federal attorneys said. Talk and you walk, they told him. They kept at it, week after week, until Circella could think of nothing but the injustice that had been done to him by everybody. He agreed to a meeting. He wasn't ready to say much, just testing the waters. Let them do the talking, tell him what they had to offer. Where was the harm?

———

Nick Circella had a mistress by the name of Estelle Carey. Nick was married, but Estelle had been the number-one woman in his life for quite a while. She was an Irish looker, a sometime model, occasional prostitute, and by night the most popular dice girl at the Colony Club (and the best cheat, able to substitute a pair of loaded dice in the blink of a sucker's eye). She had been with Nick on the lam until he was captured by the police, and now she was lying low in the city, considering her prospects, while Nick was locked up in prison.

Carey lived in a third-floor apartment at 512 West Addison on Chicago's North Side. The afternoon of February 2, 1943, around one o'clock, she received a visitor. Police believed the visitor was known to her. The evidence indicated she had allowed the person inside, they'd sat together at the kitchen table, drunk cups of hot cocoa. As the medical examiner reconstructed it, some short time after the visitor had finished his cocoa he bashed Estelle Carey in the face with a blackjack, breaking her nose and knocking her teeth out, then stabbed her in the belly and crotch with a broken bottle, causing blood to spray over the room, then doused her with lighter fluid and set her on fire. Neighbors reported smelling smoke, and firemen came, breaking into the flame-filled apartment to find Carey's burning corpse, her legs gone to ashes.

Rumors and theories regarding the brutal killing went around the city. It was a robbery. She was killed by an angry ex-suitor. A jealous woman rival. To Nick Circella, however, only one possibility rang true: Her murder was a message from his pals in Chicago. Keep your mouth shut.

Prosecutor Boris Kostelanetz assigned U.S. marshals to guard George Browne's wife. Willie Bioff's spouse had disappeared by then, gone into hiding.

Browne and Circella kept a mortified silence in response to the Carey killing, but Bioff—always the truculent contrarian—was

loudmouthed and outraged. "We sit around in jail for those bastards," he bellowed, "and they go killing our families! To hell with
them!"

Kostelanetz confronted him. *Now* was he willing to talk?

Bioff said: *"Whatcha wanna know, Boris?"*

Bioff told his tale to the grand jury, the truth now, naming every
name, detailing every dirty deed. His story was then confirmed by
George Browne, who'd thrown in with his persuasive pal one more
time. Neither demanded anything for talking beyond a guarantee
of safety for their families.

Johnny Rosselli was summoned to appear before the grand jury
in March, as the proceedings were coming to a close. He came up
to New York direct from the army base in Atlanta and appeared in
the courtroom in his private's uniform. The questions were mainly
based around Bioff's damning testimony, though he was also asked
about his relationship to other persons, from Harry Cohn to Al Capone. Johnny's response to every question was the same, claiming
his Fifth Amendment right against self-incrimination. He was the
final witness and treated almost as an afterthought. The prosecutors were eager to get to trial after Bioff and Browne's comprehensive confessions.

In Chicago the Outfit hierarchy had a good idea what was coming
for them. At a midnight meeting they considered their options. Was
there someone they could still buy off? Kill? Should they run
away—turn fugitive? Did anybody know what that hideout in New
Mexico or someplace was like? The atmosphere was heated, short
fuses all around. Paul Ricca lost his temper and began to berate
Nitti for the situation they were in. This whole fucking thing was
his fault, Ricca said.

"My fault?" said Nitti. "You were on this from the fucking beginning! We all wanted that money."

Louis Campagna and Phil D'Andrea—two more veteran Outfitters from the Capone era and likely to be part of the government's roundup—chimed in, backing Ricca's view of the situation.

Nitti did not look well. His health had been in decline for several years, ulcers, heart trouble, depression. His first wife had died unexpectedly in 1940. He married again, but the loss had left him damaged. He was fifty-seven but looked years older. Talk like this was not what he needed to hear.

Paul Ricca, Nitti's second in command and heir apparent, had taken on many of the responsibilities of a boss in that same time. He liked it, had his own ideas for running the organization, and looked forward to being in charge for real when Frank stepped aside. Going to the pen for many years was not part of his plan for the future.

"Bioff was your guy," he told Nitti. "This whole thing was your idea, Frank. You got to take responsibility. . . ."

On March 17, 1943, U.S. Attorney General Francis Biddle directed Matt Correa to institute prosecution under Sections 420a–420e, Title 18, USC, of the following persons:

Frank Nitto, alias Frank Nitti

Louis Campagna, alias Little New York, alias Louis Cook,
    alias Lefty Louie

Paul de Lucia, alias Paul Ricca

Phil D'Andrea

Francis Maritote, alias Frank Diamond

Charles Gioe, alias Charlie Joy

Ralph Pierce

Louis Kaufman

John Rosselli

Johnny was preparing to return to the base in Georgia when he got the news. They came for him in his hotel room at the Waldorf-Astoria. He was arrested and arraigned, bail set at one hundred thousand dollars. He was taken to a cell in the Lower Manhattan detention center known as the Tombs.

March 19 was a Friday, cold and wet in Cook County, Illinois. Clouds gathered, low and gray, three in the afternoon dark as twilight. A slow-moving freight train backed over tracks on an Illinois Central branch line in North Riverside. As the freight crawled along, caboose first, a member of the crew—switchman Lowell Barnett—standing on the forward platform, noticed a figure up ahead, a man in an open overcoat wobbling drunkenly along the train's path. He held what looked like a revolver in his hand, waving it in the air. The man lurched from the tracks to the dead grass and weeds of the fenced-in siding, and then the gun went off and went off again, and the man stumbled and fell to the ground. Barnett signaled the engineer to stop. The switchman and the conductor got off the train and the two started toward the fallen figure. They went close, then no closer. They saw the body stir. His eyes came open, and he pushed himself upright against the fence.

"Well," said the switchman to the conductor, "if he tried to kill himself, he didn't do a good job."

Then Frank Nitti raised the .32 Colt in his hand, pressed it to his skull, and pulled the trigger.

6

CRIME DON'T PAY

The trial began in New York before the Hon. John Bright on October 5, 1943. The press fed nationwide interest in the biggest extortion case in American history. It was a story to steal thunder from war: Hollywood, gangsters, a million-dollar sting, a crime boss's suicide. The session began with a decision to cease prosecution of the late Frank Nitti, whose case had now gone to a higher court. The clerk then called the names of all eight remaining defendants—Ricca, D'Andrea, Campagna, Gioe, Pierce, Maritote, Rosselli, Kaufman—and each found his place inside the rail by the cluster of high-priced legal advisers. On the government side, Matt Correa having gone into the army, Boris Kostelanetz was designated special assistant attorney general to direct the prosecution.

Johnny Rosselli's initial appearance was thought by some to give him an unfair advantage over his coconspirators. Still a member of the U.S. military, transferred since May to the command at Fort Jay, Governors Island, he began the morning of the trial with reveille, then, with permission, made his way to the courthouse in Manhattan. While the other defendants were dressed in suits and ties, Johnny wore his army uniform. Was it possible that a jury might look more sympathetically at a defendant who was clearly in the service of his country in its time of need? Kostelanetz thought so and demanded Rosselli be made to wear civilian clothes. Johnny's skilled defense attorney, brought east from Los Angeles, Otto Christensen—a protégé of the legendary Clarence Darrow, and a recent successful defender of accused murderer Bugsy Siegel— protested. "There is a grave question as to whether he would not be violating the Articles of War," said Christensen, gravely. "I think unofficially he has been advised that if he does appear in civilian clothes it would be a violation of the regulations—"

"Unofficially?" Kostelanetz scoffed.

Christensen said, "We can take the matter up with the author- ities. We can even call the assistant secretary of war and determine the situation."

Judge Bright agreed to have the army clarify its position. The assistant secretary being busy with World War II, some other authority was found: Rosselli was not to be tried in uniform.

"Then of course," said Christensen, "he can appear in civilian clothes—*as soon as they arrive.*"

No need, said Kostelanetz; he'd already obtained a suit for the defendant to wear in court.

Christensen countered: "I do not know how anybody here would know his *size!*"

The judge had had enough. He ordered Rosselli into plain clothes by morning.

Opening statements began with the government. Prosecutor Kostelanetz explained for the jury what he called the heart of the indictment: "That Nitti and Campagna and de Lucia and D'Andrea and Gioe and Pierce and Maritote, this Chicago group, and John Rosselli, of California, conspired to dominate and control and direct the affairs of the IATSE. . . . it is charged that through this domination these defendants conspired to have the victims pay over one million dollars for protection and to dissuade the defendants from injuring the business of the victims by the misuse of power."

Kostelanetz proceeded to give a detailed history of the business of moviemaking in California, the twenty-plus-year relationship between Hollywood and the unions, the shifting fortunes of IATSE, and how it was infiltrated by criminal elements through a corrupted election and the eventual conspiracy by the defendants to "racketeer" the motion picture industry by threat and force. Each of the defense attorneys then had their turn, promoting their clients' varying claims of innocence, including, most provocatively, the assertion that extortion in this case was in fact bribery, and the conspiracy committed not by the gentlemen on trial but by renegade union officials and a cabal of greedy movie executives intent on undermining their workers while stealing shareholders' profits to pay for it.

Johnny's man, Otto Christensen, sought to further separate his client from any wrongdoing. "Mere association and mere relationship is not proof of conspiracy," he declared. "There must be intentional participation in the transaction with a view to the furtherance of the common design. Now we say that the evidence will show that Mr. Rosselli had no knowledge either of a conspiracy on the part of the producers to bribe labor leaders or on the part of labor leaders to be the recipients of bribes or to extort money, and that he received no proceeds of any money, whether bribery or extortion. There will be no competent evidence at all except from a polluted source, and I do not even think there will be that."

The government called its first witness, Morris—"William"—"Willie"—Bioff, come to court direct from the Federal House of Detention on West Street. He was as well their star witness, carrying on his thick shoulders the largest share of the incriminating evidence (he and George Browne had been in Prosecutor Kostelanetz's office nearly every day for more than a year preparing for this appearance). Bioff, as a convicted criminal at hand to rat on his associates, was precisely the "polluted source" to whom Christensen had referred, and his credibility as a witness—no one was even hoping for likability—was crucial to the prosecution's case. Kostelanetz's questions led him through the facts of his life, a motherless immigrant boy from Russia, at age ten alone on the merciless streets of Chicago, odd jobs in pool halls and whorehouses, then hoodlum, union thug, pimp, con man, on to his scammer's partnership with Browne, the fateful visit to the One Hundred Club and the alliance with the boys in Chicago. Everything he'd said previously, everything he'd denied at his own trial, he now admitted had been a "lie, lie, lie." He was an open book, gave no excuses. "I am just a low, uncouth person," Bioff said. "Oh yes, I am a very despicable man."

It was a clever strategy by the prosecution, a man's admission of his own awful character as proof of his honesty. Wouldn't a jury more likely believe in the testimony of a man so—belatedly—open, so free from guile?

Bioff provided an unprecedented view of a national organized criminal cartel at work, a matter-of-fact accounting of Mob interconnectedness across the United States. "I remember distinctly," Bioff told the courtroom, "Nitti said, 'We will take care of Jersey and New York; we will take care of Jersey through Longy Zwillman.' That was his contact in Jersey. He would take care of New York through Lucky Luciano—Charlie Lucky Luciano—and Louis Buchalter; he would take care of Cleveland through Al Paliese, he would take care of St. Louis through Johnnie Dougherty. And Kansas City . . . he would see to it that the boys of them cities would contact the delegates and the heads of the unions and have them vote for Browne."

Bioff's command of narrative detail, however much rehearsed, was most impressive. He could account for every day of illicit dealings, each studio payoff (re Warner Bros.: *"I received money from Major Albert Warner. I received money from a Mr. Carlisle, their auditor or bookkeeper. I received money from Albert Warner's secretary, a young lady. I received money from H. M. Warner. I received money from a brother-in-law of Warner's, who was the theater manager out on the West Coast . . . Halprin I think it is . . ."*), every extorted dollar dispersed (for example: *"Of that particular $75,000, I got $12,500 out of it, Browne got $12,500 out of it, and Paul [Ricca] $50,000"*). He went on like that for ten days. No one escaped the witness's comprehensive recollection, the tenacious indictment, like a gross spider slowly capturing each defendant in its viscid web.

One morning the questions were all about John Rosselli. Bioff recalled his first meeting with the man from California, the affably threatening encounter in a New York hospital room (*"Circella says to me, 'This is our man, Johnny,' meaning the Chicago boys' man, their representative . . ."*), Rosselli's influence with the studio's union negotiator, Pat Casey (*"He was on Pat Casey's payroll . . . with Rosselli there we would have every break . . . Johnny would see to it that Casey went along with us . . ."*), the convoluted arrangements for getting John his secret IA salary (the "laundered" weekly check for $194 sent off from New York to a front man in Chicago, who cashed it, deducted for tax and effort, and posted $150 to a third party in Los Angeles, who delivered it back to Willie Bioff at his office, who handed it to Rosselli), the disagreement over the strike at Columbia, and Johnny and Jack Dragna taking Bioff for a drive in the night, the surrender to Harry Cohn—everything.

In the cross-examination, Christensen challenged few of

the witness's facts. He seemed more concerned with exposing Bioff's dislike for his client and use of what he called "vile language" (*"Q: Did you then say: 'Rosselli is a pimping bootleg bastard and I will run him out of town'? A: No, sir."*) than with Johnny's innocence.

When Bioff at last stepped down, George Browne took his place on the witness stand. He mostly repeated and confirmed his partner's recollection of events, though in a manner more reserved, redolent of dread. Before the dead-eyed glare of the defendants, he looked the way he must have felt: like a man turning his prison term into a death sentence.

Browne was followed by a medley of motion picture executives, including Nicholas Schenck of Loew's/M-G-M, Harry Warner and Albert Warner of Warner Bros. (only brother Jack was absent), Harry Cohn of Columbia, and—after he was finally persuaded to come out of hiding in Mexico—Joseph Schenck of Fox. Those who had testified in the Bioff-Browne trial, and helped put B&B behind bars, again told their tales of thievery and threat. This time they were all perforce on the same side, the execs backing up Willie and George's updated version of the facts. With the prosecutor's careful guidance, the witnesses portrayed themselves in the best possible light, as honest victims, even heroes. Of course they cooperated with the extortionists. They had no choice. They'd had to protect their businesses. So many people depended on them. What would happen to all the workers, not to mention the poor stockholders, if the movie companies came under attack, were shut down, made bankrupt? Some among the execs claimed that their lives had been in danger, that they might have suffered a terrible fate if they failed to cooperate. Harry Warner, the Warner Bros. president, revealed that he'd carried a gun for a long time after his dealings with Bioff began, and had employed studio guards to accompany him when he went out in public.

The attorneys for the accused not surprisingly wished to put these witnesses in a different—less heroic—light. They pursued an alternative version of events. Far from being victims of a shakedown, weren't the producers themselves in a conspiracy with Bioff and Browne? Weren't the payments to Bioff and Browne in fact bribes for their collaboration with the studios and their betrayal of the union? How much money did the studios save by giving under-the-table cash to Bioff and Browne instead of paying raises and settling strikes for the benefit of the union workers? Exactly whose money was it that these executives were doling out by the tens of thousands? And why was it—if they were being extorted—robbed—not one of them called the police for help?

"There was a district attorney in Los Angeles, was there not?" lead defense counsel James Murray asked Harry Warner. "There was an F.B.I. there, wasn't there? Did you go to the county prosecutor?"

"I didn't go to any law-abiding agency."

"You didn't go to the United States Attorney either, did you?"

"No, sir."

"You had little faith, did you, in the law enforcement agencies of the United States? Is that right?"

"No, sir."

"But you went on worrying about what Bioff might do to you without ever appealing to them for protection; is that right?"

"That is right. I took my own precautions. I created my own protection."

"What did you have? What did you do, employ a couple of Keystone Kops?"

"Yes, sir. . . ."

"Didn't you know," said the defense counsel to M-G-M's Nick Schenck, "just at that time that a number of racketeers connected with unions who had demanded money from employers had been sent to jail by Thomas E. Dewey?"

"That would not change it at all," said Schenck.

"I asked if you knew it," said James Murray.

"Possibly," said Schenck. "I read the papers."

"Did you know it at that time when Bioff and Browne were demanding money from you?"

"I was not thinking of anything except what effect it would have on us if we didn't pay it."

"Wasn't it before April of 1936 that you heard what Dewey was doing to those racketeers?"

"I certainly don't know," said Schenck, "and neither would you know it if you didn't look it up."

"Whose money was this that was paid to Bioff and Browne? Was it yours?"

"No."

"It was the stockholders', wasn't it?"

"Yes."

"How many stockholders at that time?"

"How many did we have? In Loew's about 18,000."

"There were between eighteen and twenty thousand stockholders were there?"

"Yes, and I saved possibly six or seven or eight million dollars by doing it, I myself."

"At any rate it was not your money that was going into the pockets of Bioff and Browne, was it?"

"No, sir."

"It was the stockholders', wasn't it?"

"Correct, sir."

"And you knew, didn't you, that on the books of your company were being entered fake entries for the purpose of deceiving the United States Government as to the disposition of that money? Is that right?"

"No, sir. All I knew is that we had to pay it, and I knew as far as I am concerned it was done for the company's sake, to save them, and whatever way it was done it was done. I can't tell you how."

Albert Warner, the Warner Bros. co-founder and treasurer, was similarly adamant—and vague. The defense asked, did he not realize that some simple act of his could have produced "overwhelming evidence charging [Bioff] with extortion, right here in New York County? Didn't you know that?"

"The damage would have been done. I have told you that twelve times now."

"You mean," said Murray, "that justice is so slow-footed that in a period of two weeks from the time you first saw Bioff until the next time you saw him, Assistant District Attorney Dewey's office, the F.B.I., the Federal Government and the Police Department could not protect you, is that what you mean?"

"That," said Warner, "was my feeling."

The attorney wondered if he had at no time considered, for instance, using a recording device to gain evidence of Bioff's threats. "Did you ever hear of the use of a Dictaphone?"

"I have heard of a Dictaphone," said Warner. "I know what it is."

"You could have procured evidence for the authorities that would have resulted in his conviction for extortion . . . if he were in fact extorting money from you . . . you knew that, didn't you?"

"I don't know," said Warner.

"Didn't you know, Mr. Warner, that you could have purred to Bioff like a kitten, disarmed him of suspicions, and then when he came back for the money that the money could have been marked, did you know that? Was there anything that prevented you from marking money and having the bills there when you handed them to Bioff?"

"I don't know."

"Well, you have seen some of your moving pictures, haven't you, that Warner Bros. put out?"

"Yes, sir."

"You have looked at them, haven't you?"

"Yes, sir."

"Have you seen any of Warner Bros. pictures where marked money was passed?"

"Oh, I imagine we must have made them."

"Yes."

"I cannot recall the name of the picture."

"Do you remember *Scarface*, one of Warner Bros.' pictures?" asked the attorney.

"I think you are wrong."

"You did not have *Scarface*?"

"I doubt it very much," said Albert Warner. "Try again. *Little Caesar.* I will help you out. *Little Caesar. Public Enemy.* I am for anything saving time, sir."

"All right. I ask you what happens in *Little Caesar*—"

"I was hoping you would."

"—far as the law is concerned?"

"Crime . . . don't pay?"

Harry Cohn stood apart from the other moguls called to the stand. The Columbia boss was the only one of them who had ever met any of the men on trial. More than that, of course—by his own description, Cohn and John Rosselli had been close friends through the period of the crimes charged. He was as well the only one of the studio heads who had refused to comply with Bioff's demands. The fact that he suffered no consequences for his defiance might have undermined the government's portrayal of those accused as threatening extortionists. If Cohn had so easily opted out, perhaps the threat was not all that the victims and the prosecution claimed. But his admitted friendship with the defendant weakened such a conclusion. In the end his testimony served mostly to confirm Rosselli's intricate involvement—however hostile—with Willie Bioff.

Week after week they marched to the stand: union men, tax men, bankers, bookkeepers, eyewitnesses to this or that, two-fisted Herb Sorrell, publisher-nightclub proprietor Billy Wilkerson, seething Westbrook Pegler (slayer of labor unions). On November 24, counsel for Ralph Pierce moved to have the indictment against his client dismissed. The Capone gunman and gambling boss was no less a criminal than the rest, but the prosecutors had been unable to connect him to anything within the time frame of the indictment. The motion was granted and all charges against Pierce were dropped. Attorneys for the other defendants immediately attempted the same ploy for their clients but without success.

In December the trial entered a third month. When freezing weather arrived, Johnny Rosselli's lungs seized up. He was taken to Station Hospital at Fort Wadsworth on Staten Island. Confined to a hospital bed, he signed a form allowing the trial to proceed in his absence. Paul Ricca and Frank Diamond decided they too would rather be in bed and submitted their own sick notes and waivers, which left the gangster population in the courtroom reduced by half.

The defendants, exercising their constitutional right, had chosen not to testify. In mid-December the last of eighty-one witnesses was excused, and the attorneys began their closing arguments. The prosecution offered a blunt regurgitation of mostly Bioff's testimony along with a criminal résumé for each of the defendants (a tactic of dubious legality as the crimes mentioned had little relevance to the case, and nearly all the noted arrests that went to trial resulted in not-guilty verdicts). The defense attorneys were more nuanced. With derision they described for the jury the curiosity of an extortion case that seemed to have resulted—per government witness Nick Schenck—in more profit than loss for the extorted. They painted the wealthy Hollywood executives who were the proclaimed victims of the plot as ruthlessly practical businessmen, cowardly opportunists, and outright lawbreakers. They scorned a prosecution that depended for its evidence on the word of a self-confessed liar and convicted felon. "Bioff, the repulsive and unbelievable," said counsel Murray in summation, "the diabolical . . . pathological . . . that *thing*. . . ."

On the morning of December 22, the jury was charged by Judge Bright, then retired to begin deliberations. At 10:05 that evening a verdict was returned.

2

Federal District Court case #114–101, *US v. Campagna et al.*, revealed in a public forum the state of organized crime in America. In the autumn and winter of 1943 it was a revelation of some historical significance, but—like the more limited earlier disclosures of Abe Reles, Dixie Davis, and a handful of others—it would go unrecognized as such.

The public knew little about the growth and diversification in the underworld since the repeal of Prohibition. The gilded age of the big-shot mobster had supposedly ended with Al Capone's train ride to the big house. Headlined special-edition stories—the takedown of Lucky Luciano, the hunt for Louis "Lepke" Buchalter of Murder Incorporated—were localized, concerned traditional gangland crimes, robbery, homicide, vice. The idea of a national crime syndicate, a multifarious cooperative of outlaw kingdoms, reaching from coast to coast, penetrating major American institutions, was considered the stuff of pulp fantasy.

The trial of Johnny Rosselli and associates, and the courtroom testimony of Willie Bioff and dozens of other witnesses, exposed the startling reality. The meticulous recounting of the Chicago Outfit's takeover of an international labor union, the details of the corrupt election of George Browne involving the cooperation of various underworld powers, the threats and actions against a major industry that were carried out on a national scale, the continual appearances in the narrative of gang leaders from assorted cities and regions and the numerous references to collaborative Mob operations that crisscrossed the map—amounted to clear evidence of a vast and thriving criminal alliance. *"An underworld empire,"* Boris Kostelanetz described it to the jury.

It was a discovery that should have inspired a shock to the system in the government and the agencies of law enforcement, and no little interest from the press and public. Perhaps the headline nature of the trial itself—Hollywood versus the Mob, the first mass prosecution of a modern underworld gang—had eaten up all the attention, or maybe the overwhelming news of the war (the Allied bombing of Berlin, the march to Rome, the Tehran conference, fighting in the Pacific at a brutal peak, with massive loss of life). Whatever the reason, Kostelanetz's announcement went completely overlooked. It would take seven more years, and the findings of the U.S. Senate Special Committee to Investigate Crime in Interstate Commerce (the so-called Kefauver Committee) before there was open recognition of a national organized crime syndicate, and nearly a decade after that, the more knowing McClellan Committee, the travesty of the Apalachin Mafia summit, and the belated assault by the FBI, before anybody at the national level was ready to do anything about it.

3

Three days before Christmas.

10:05 p.m.

The jury came back to the courtroom.

"Ladies and gentlemen," said the clerk, "have you agreed upon the verdict?"

"We have," said the forelady.

"How do you say?"

"We find the defendants guilty as charged."

"You say you find all these defendants guilty, and so say you all?

"We do."

Judge Bright gave leave to the defendants, letting them return to their homes for the holidays, extending the bail of each until December 30. The press hyped the government's victory. Encouraged by the prosecution, the newspapers led readers to believe that the entire Al Capone gang had been defeated, fully and fatally, and while this was not the case, there had never been so many top gangsters put away at one time. The public felt good about the lawmen, and the lawmen felt good about themselves.

On the thirtieth the defense attorneys moved to set aside the verdict, and moved for an arrest of judgment and for a new trial. All motions were denied. On the thirty-first, the sentences were delivered. Louis Campagna, Paul de Lucia, Phil D'Andrea, Francis Maritote, Charles Gioe, John Rosselli, sentenced to ten years' confinement and fined ten thousand dollars. Louis Kaufman sentenced to seven years and fined ten thousand.

On the last day of 1943 Johnny and his colleagues were remanded to the Tombs lockup (only Kaufman was permitted to make bail—twenty-five thousand dollars—and allowed to live at home in New Jersey during the appeal process). There they were to spend the rest of the New York winter while the legal team tried to undo the court's decision. The attorneys' efforts were unsuccessful.

On March 4 the convicted murderer Louis "Lepke" Buchalter was given a seat in the electric chair just up the river in Sing Sing. He had been a great help to the boys in stealing the IATSE election. Now he was the first significant American crime boss ever to be executed. It was a bad month for bad guys. On March 25, Johnny—with Campagna, Ricca, D'Andrea, and Gioe—was taken from the jail at White Street, put in a prison van, and transported to the U.S. Penitentiary in Atlanta, Georgia.*

Under the provisions of the U.S. Army regulations, Section AR 615–366, concerning the conviction of a crime by a civil court, Johnny Rosselli's military service was concluded, Fort McPherson, Georgia, issuing an official discharge described as "other than honorable."

The Atlanta pen was a turn-of-the-century colossus, a massive main structure of funerary red brick at the southeast edge of the city. It had been an impressive and pridefully modern facility when it opened in 1902, a pet project of President William McKinley, but it had gradually gone downhill in one way and another and was now a notorious hellhole, unhealthy, overcrowded, infested with rats. But disciplined. It was run by Warden Joseph W. Sanford, a penal professional who'd come up through the ranks and had whipped Atlanta into shape with his fierce but—said his distant

---

* Maritote's and Kaufman's attorneys had managed to put their clients on a different schedule from the other convicts; Maritote would pursue additional appeals of his conviction, a delay that only caused him to do an extra year of time, as Kostelanetz gloated, "for free."

overseers—fair command. He was a star to the Bureau of Prisons, whose director recalled him as "aggressive, likeable, ruthless in dealing with those who crossed him."

A decade before, Atlanta had provided accommodations for Al Capone. In those days a VIP prisoner could buy himself special privileges, and Capone was able to enjoy bottles of rye whiskey, Italian food items, and fancy bedding. But those days were no more. Warden Sanford ran a tight operation. He also ran a racist operation. He was a devout white supremacist and a steadfast member of the Ku Klux Klan. A promoter of the organization, he even encouraged appropriate prisoners to join and offered to put in a good word for them with the local Grand Dragon. He was a busy man, of course, but he managed to find time to hate Jews, Catholics, Hispanics, and those of Mediterranean descent nearly as much as he did blacks. When Sanford learned that the government was sending a collection of "wop" gangsters his way he could not have been more thrilled.

The Chicago bosses came on strong in their new home. They were used to getting things their own way, and not even a ten-year prison sentence was going to change their attitudes overnight. Paul Ricca was in a particularly bad mood. It weighed on him that he had not gotten to take his place as the leader of the Outfit after Nitti's suicide. He'd approved giving the position to Tony Accardo while he was gone, but he had to consider that ten years away would be too long a "vacation" to ever get the job back.

Warden Sanford worried about his Italians. A little bird told him that some of them were "throwing their weight around," and some of his native-born prisoners were intimidated. Intimidation, Warden Sanford believed, was his job alone and not to be shared. One day Paul Ricca complained about the prison food aggravating his diabetes and demanded a special diet. An infirmary orderly requested a urine sample for testing, and Phil D'Andrea—the ex-bodyguard once known as "Capone's Constant Companion"—collared the orderly and threatened to have him hurt if Ricca's test didn't "show a little sugar in it." Warden Sanford heard about the threat and decided to pay D'Andrea a visit. Many a prison chief would have let his deputy handle an issue like this, but Sanford liked to let the prisoners know they could share their problems with him personally. Flanked by two armed guards, the warden sucker-punched the Outfit leader to the ground, grappled with him on the floor of the cell, then beat him till he was bloody and barely conscious. Both D'Andrea and Ricca were charged with "conniving" and placed in punitive segregation for seven days.

Johnny wanted to avoid any disputes of that sort if he could help it. There was hard time and there was hard time. Why make things any worse? You had to be stronger than the situation in which you found yourself. The man who kept his cool could get through anything. Do one day at a time and let everything else go fuck itself.

Either way, life went on. Days crawled into weeks. Constrained, slow moving, never pleasant. Cold cell. Bad food. Reading books and magazines from the library. Writing letters. Church services on Sunday. Rales in his lungs. Rats.

The world, far away, kept turning. News filtered through the bars. The war moved toward its furious climax. German cities crumbling under Allied bombs. On June 6, 1944, the Allied invasion of Normandy. In the Pacific, the Japanese in retreat. Tales of blood and pain and death. He learned that Jack Dragna's eighteen-year-old son had been among the first U.S. troops engaged in the Battle of Luzon, and lost an eye to an enemy hand grenade. The worst news was connected to old friend Dago Louie; his beloved son (Johnny was the kid's godfather), a pilot, had been killed in combat.

The war made strange bedfellows. Lucky Luciano, in prison since 1936 on a compulsory prostitution conviction, had made a deal with the government: receiving commutation of his sentence in exchange for helping to prevent enemy sabotage on the New York docks, and for facilitating antifascist contacts (that is, mafiosi) in Sicily; he was later released from prison and deported.

Another day there was this: Esperia, the quiet, isolated Italian village where Johnny—where Filippo Sacco—was born, had become a part of the conflict. In the wake of the Allied victory at Monte Cassino, units of the French Expeditionary Force, mostly Moroccan colonial infantry, were given leave by their general to pillage the surrounding communities without fear of punishment. The African soldiers stormed over the undefended towns and villages, for two days defiling and murdering at will. In Esperia some seven hundred girls and women or half the entire female population, including children, were raped by the Moroccans, and many of the rape victims were murdered or died by their own hand. Hundreds of Esperian men were also killed while attempting to protect their families and neighbors.

In the penitentiary Warden Sanford organized a fund-raising drive for the American Red Cross. Prisoners were paid a few cents an hour for the work they did in the prison factories, money they used to buy cigarettes and candy bars. Sanford seized these small savings for his charity. Atlanta's own literary queen, Margaret Mitchell, the author of *Gone with the Wind*, made a special appearance to acknowledge the prisoners' generous contributions. The warden was always ready to help the war effort: On another occasion he volunteered some prisoners to test a new antimalaria medicine for the army.

While Johnny did his best to cope with the stress and anxiety, the boys from Chicago wallowed in it. The miserable conditions, the malevolent warden, and for Paul Ricca the loss of power and control, were unendurable. Over and over they sent the message to Chicago: Keep on it, find a way, get us out of here. They wanted to be sprung, of course, some technicality, early parole, find something. But for right now just get us out of fucking Atlanta.

The Outfit's political fixer and brain trust, Murray Humphreys, the wily Welshman, one of Al Capone's earliest and sharpest recruits, took charge. Money was gathered for the work ahead (including, it was said, a large donation from some fearful moguls in Hollywood who'd helped put the boys away). A group of select, well-connected attorneys was put on the case. Their straightforward requests for transfers having been turned down, they explored less conventional methods of getting it done. There were private meetings on the subject with assorted and influential officials in Washington, including, it was said, the new U.S. attorney general, Tom Clark.

In Atlanta, Warden Sanford had made efforts to keep his gangster clique separated from one another. Johnny had little to no contact with Ricca, D'Andrea, and the rest of them. One day while he was working as a prison file clerk, he happened to see the new transfer list. The names of his colleagues were on the list. They were being moved out of Atlanta. Johnny knew nothing about it, and heard nothing more when the July transfer date came and went.

It was a while before he knew what was going on. The boys had gotten their transfers. They'd been moved to Leavenworth Penitentiary in Leavenworth, Kansas. It had a better reputation than Atlanta, and it was five hours closer to their associates and family members in Chicago. Johnny was told to sit tight. His transfer was coming. They were not so inconsiderate as to just abandon him, but the boys came first. He spent two and a half more months in place before the arrangements were worked out; then, on September 29, he was sent five hundred miles north to the federal pen at Terre Haute, Indiana.

After eighteen months at the joint in Georgia, Terre Haute was like a luxury resort. Just five years old, it was built by President Roosevelt's Public Works Administration, created as a showplace for modern, enlightened ideas about incarceration and rehabilitation. The prison building had no outer wall around it, there was decent accommodation and food, facilities for physical and mental health care, and a schoolroom. The convicts were allowed to converse at mealtime and to keep a greater-than-normal variety of personal possessions in the cells. Their delicate sensibilities were safeguarded where possible, the word "convict" itself frowned upon in favor of the less judgmental "inmate."

As an aid to the rehabilitative process, the governors of the forward-thinking Terre Haute pen believed in the new sciences of the mind, and requested that every prisoner submit to a psychiatric examination. Johnny was interviewed at some length by a visiting clinician who then composed a detailed profile (unearthed by Rappleye and Becker). "Beneath the surface," the psychiatrist concluded, "one detects systematized paranoid ideas with a coloring of hysteria. . . . A moderately severe paranoid personality."

Only eight and a half years to go.

4

On April 12, 1945, Franklin Delano Roosevelt died in office after more than twelve years as president. He was succeeded by the vice president, Harry S. Truman, who had been at the job for less than three months. With Roosevelt's failing health in mind before the last election, the choice of running mate had been a grave concern, and it came about that the "too progressive" incumbent VP, Henry Wallace, was eased from his job in favor of the more mainstream senator from Missouri. FDR barely knew Truman and had met with him only three or four times before he cold-handed him the keys to the White House.

In contrast to the patrician, privileged Roosevelt, Truman started out in life an ordinary Midwest farmboy with few prospects. As a young man trying to find a place in the world, and after dropping out of law school and failing to make it as a haberdasher, he'd fallen under the influence of the Kansas City political boss Thomas Pendergast. From his headquarters in a small brick building beside the Monroe Hotel on Main Street, Pendergast ran the state to his specifications, handpicking political candidates, corrupting cops, fixing elections, meting out favors, threats, violence. Truman had been one of those chosen to enjoy Pendergast's benefaction when he entered the field of public service in 1922, running for a job as county commissioner, and twelve years later, when he went after a seat in the U.S. Senate, the boss of Kansas City was still his most powerful ally.

Pendergast chose as Truman's campaign manager a whip-smart St. Louis attorney named Paul Dillon, who would do whatever it took to send Harry to Washington. Along the way to victory Dillon and Truman became great friends, as they remained in 1945 when Truman became president of the United States. When Murray Humphreys and the Outfit went looking for an open-minded lawyer with good connections in the federal government, they could have done no better than to bring a blank check to the law office of Paul Dillon.

For more than two years the attorney worked the case. Dillon's White House hall pass got him in to see anybody in the capital (*"I'm Paul Dillon, a friend of the President,"* was his standard salutation). The gangsters' advocate waged a hard-sell campaign for his clients' freedom, roaming the corridors of power in search of soft targets. Dillon made a particularly close friend out of a certain T. Webber Wilson, the dissolute chairman of the parole board. Exactly who else was seen, what was said, what was promised or paid, remain matters of speculation. Results were what mattered, and these were to be startlingly apparent.

A new year began. In January 1947 a story reached the inmates of the Terre Haute prison. Al Capone, the legendary king of crime, the face of the Roaring Twenties, and Johnny Rosselli's esteemed patron, had been living in quiet retirement at his home on Palm Island, Florida. His years in stir, most spent in dreaded Alcatraz Federal Penitentiary, had been very hard. The government handlers had done all they could to make an example of him. Illness and maltreatment stripped him of his health and his sanity. Weak and defenseless, he became a frequent victim of fellow prisoners, the aggrieved, the envious, the insane. One man had tried to poison him, and another had stabbed him in the back with scissors while he was mopping the barbershop floor. He spent most of the last year of his incarceration in a prison hospital, treated for the advancing effects of venereal disease, though the various abuses he'd received added much to his declining condition. Released in November 1939, he settled in his Florida mansion, where, increasingly enfeebled and partially paralyzed, he lived with his wife, his son, his sister-in-law, two servants, and an elderly fox terrier. On good days he was said to have had the mental faculties of a five-year-old child. The glory days were forgotten like an old dream. By his brother Ralph's account, Al had stashed more than one hundred million dollars cash in safety deposit boxes around the Midwest. With his memory shot, the former gangster could no longer remember where they were—they tried hypnosis, everything, to jar his memory—but the money was never recovered. In January '47 he experienced a brain hemorrhage, and soon after developed bronchial pneumonia. On the twenty-fifth, a Saturday evening, he died on Palm Island. Al Capone was forty-eight years old.

———

As the date of the Outfit prisoners' initial eligibility for parole got near, their legal team worked around the clock in preparation. Before a parole hearing could be considered, the way had to be cleared of any technical impediments, matters hanging over the prisoners' heads such as unpaid taxes and fines. There were as well impending criminal charges for mail fraud that prosecutors had been holding on to for a rainy day. Inexplicably, the indictments were dropped.

On July 4—it was Johnny's forty-second birthday—he appeared at a meeting with parole officials inside the Terre Haute pen. In attendance were Judge Fred Rogers of the U.S. Board of Parole, Mr. Nelson, the prison parole adviser, and a stenographer to take notes. It was a pro forma gathering and over in no time.

In anticipation of the coming parole hearings, a chorus of politicians, prosecutors, and police and prison officials stepped up to decry any thoughts of the mobsters being set free. Judge John Bright advised the Bureau of Prisons to "inflict full sentences," while prosecutor Boris Kostelanetz reminded everyone of the group's past and potential danger: "[They are] successors to the power of Al Capone . . . vicious criminals who will stop at nothing."

The admonitions, too, were pro forma. The legal system had done its job, the "untouchable" Capone gang was locked away. It was silly to fear the Feds would ever set loose this notorious bunch so soon after their conviction. They had been behind bars for three years, and it was more than likely they would be there another seven.

On August 11 the U.S. Board of Parole convened in Washington. It was exactly the first day of eligibility for early release of Louis Campagna, Philip D'Andrea, Paul Ricca, and John Rosselli. To those who knew how parole hearings worked, the processing of these particular prisoners seemed exceedingly rushed. The formal requests for parole were barely a week old. The usual recommendation

letters and progress reports by regional parole offices, prison officials, and other relevant sources had not been solicited, and any
investigation of the candidates by the board members had been
cursory at best. The session was brief, to the point. The three board
members, Judge T. Webber Wilson, Fred Rogers, and Boleslau
Monkiewicz (after his delayed arrival), voted unanimously in favor
of parole.

Less than seventy-two hours later, Webber resigned from his
position as board chairman, got out of town, and never came back.

5

Johnny Rosselli exited the Terre Haute Penitentiary, a free man for
the first time in nearly four years.

Federal agents watched from nearby. At the prison gates he was
met by someone the G-men identified as Jack Kearns, from Chicago, Illinois. "Doc" Kearns was an old friend, a former boxing
manager and promoter (in more recent times indicted for violations of the Securities Exchange Act with his partner, Princess
Zulieka, the astrologist, but that's another story). Johnny got into
Kearns's car, and they drove three hours north to Chicago. Kearns
checked him into a hotel, gave him his plane ticket for a next-day
TWA flight to Los Angeles. He slept on a proper bed for the first
time in a long time.

In LA he took a room for a brief stay at the Alexandria Hotel
on Spring Street before moving to a bachelor apartment (Apt. 5)
at 627 South Catalina, secured in advance of his arrival by his
friend from the Spitzel agency, I. A. Ruman (the suspected Soviet
spy). He would eventually migrate back to his preferred neighborhood west of Hollywood, settling in an apartment (a modest one-
bedroom overlooking the swimming pool of the two-story U-shaped
building) on Crescent Heights, off the Sunset Strip.

He celebrated his homecoming with a visit to Jerry Rothschild's in Beverly Hills, getting measured for some suits and shirts, then upstairs to the salon for a haircut, shave, the works; in the evening, dinner at Perino's, martinis, steak Diane, and a warm welcome from Alex, the proprietor.

With his parole supervisor's permission he drove up to Santa Barbara and checked himself into the Sansum Clinic for a week of restorative therapy. He returned to Los Angeles feeling nearly human.

The rules governing a paroled con were endless and exacting. Get caught violating any of them and you went right back to prison. You were required to report to the parole officer weekly. You were required to find legitimate full-time employment. You were subject to questioning, to searches at your home or job without warrant or prior notice. You were required to notify the parole office in advance of any move or change of residence or employment, and you were not to travel more than fifty miles from your home without approval. You were not to be in the company of known lawbreakers present or past, or at the scene of criminal conduct. Any and all laws of the land were to be obeyed; even a traffic violation could put you behind bars. The conditions remained in effect through the full term of sentence, in Johnny Rosselli's case until the year 1954.

He gave the appearance of being a compliant parolee, of obeying the rules and following instructions. He reported to the parole office on schedule. He engaged in gainful employment. He never crossed a red light or drove a mile above the speed limit. His parole officer, Cal Meador, and his parole adviser, Father Joe Thompson, a Roman Catholic priest, gave him high marks for accountability and positive disposition. Many of his friends in the straight life were pleased to believe he had truly turned over a new leaf, even if it was for no more noble reason than to stay out of jail.

But the acquiescent ex-con bit was a con job. He was doing what he had to do to maintain his freedom. He was not reformed, merely discreet. Maybe not even that discreet. Peculiarly, he had taken as his lawyer a man named Frank DeSimone, who shared an office on South Spring Street with Otto Christensen, Johnny's defense counsel in the Hollywood extortion trial. DeSimone was an experienced criminal attorney, a USC Law School grad, class of '33. He was also a gangster. In fact, a prince of the realm, the son of Rosario DeSimone, a leader of the Los Angeles Mafia in the 1920s.* It was waving a big red flag for Johnny to use an insider like DeSimone as his new attorney while trying to play the repentant on parole. It was lawful, but why encourage the extra scrutiny? Anyway, the authorities seemed not to have noticed or shown any interest. It's possible that the parole board was not aware of DeSimone's lineage.

Johnny resumed his role as adviser to Jack Dragna, and not a moment too soon as far as Jack was concerned. The tranquil Los Angeles underworld had lately caught fire. In the years Johnny had been away, Dragna and Bugsy Siegel had continued their wary affiliation, more or less splitting the LA rackets between them. But Bugsy had been distracted by Las Vegas, the rising gambling mecca in the Nevada desert, muscling in on a project of Johnny's entrepreneur friend Billy Wilkerson, the resplendent gaming resort they named the Flamingo. Siegel's squandering of millions of Syndicate dollars combined with his wayward chutzpah earned him a death sentence at the Commission conclave in Havana, Cuba. Permission for the hit to occur in Los Angeles was courteously requested of Jack Dragna as ranking regional boss. Jack not only gave his permission, he agreed to take care of the whole matter for them. He

---

* Frank was also the uncle of future top mobster Thomas "Two Gun Tommy" DeSimone, said to be the basis for the character played by Joe Pesci in the film *Goodfellas*.

had actually come to have a lot of respect for Bugsy, allowed that he had a lot of brains, some good ideas. But Jack's resentment of Siegel's move on Los Angeles had never gone away. It was like they said in the old cowboy pictures: "This town ain't big enough for the both of us—*you Jew motherfucker.*"

On the night of June 20, 1947, Bugsy was sitting in the living room of his girlfriend Virginia Hill's rented house on Linden Drive in Beverly Hills. Someone outside in the darkness with a .30-caliber M1 fired nine shots through a window. Siegel was hit twice in the head, the impact of the bullet at the bridge of the nose blowing his left eye out of the socket and across the room.*

With the interloper from the East finally gone after all these years, Jack Dragna felt a great relief. Now he could go back to running Los Angeles without interference, or so he assumed. But it was only a couple of months after Bugsy's eye-popping demise, and already there was a new problem at hand, as Jack explained to Johnny when he returned home from prison in August. Siegel's un-couth bulldog Mickey Cohen had quickly decided he was taking his leader's place in the Hollywood hierarchy, and maybe taking more than that. Cohen claimed his ascendence was sanctioned by the Syndicate back East, but the way events played out did not tend to confirm this. Whatever the reality, Cohen's colorful, cock-sure, attention-whore personality, contrasted with the glowering, publicity-shy Dragna, made it seem like Mick was already running everything in LA. When you were the only gangster getting your picture in the paper—in loud ties and colossal Borsalinos, yet—people were quick to accept you as the man, king of the rackets.

---

* In spite of accumulated evidence, other theories have been suggested as the motive for Bugsy's murder, including revenge for his mistreatment of Virginia Hill, and an argument with one or another member of the Chicago Outfit, but the idea that somebody in the organized crime world, outside the Commission itself, would risk ordering the killing of a high-value Syndicate member is very unlikely.

Johnny and Jack analyzed the situation. It wasn't going to be easy controlling Mickey. But nothing to do with Mickey was ever easy. Cohen had put together a good, tough gang, a mixture of fearless Jews and ferocious Italians (many of the latter imports from Cleveland, Ohio, his old stomping ground). He had paid off a lot of lawmen, and generously, and it was believed he had something going with LA County Sheriff Biscailuz. Jack and Johnny decided it was best to proceed with caution. Poke around the edges at first, chip off some of that strength. They had an idea to make nice to some of Cohen's Italians, try and lure some of Mickey's *paisani* over to Dragna's team.

In September, Johnny went to Dago Louie Merli's place to meet one of Cohen's associates. Aladena "Jimmy" Fratianno was a Napoli-born, Cleveland-bred professional criminal. "Jimmy the Weasel," they called him—behind his back—a nickname he'd gotten for his appearance and shifty style as a kid. Fratianno was smarter than the average thug, with a sharp mind and good insights about people, but he hadn't made much use of these traits up to now. Thirty-three in 1947, he'd spent most of his adult years in the Ohio Penitentiary for aggravated assault. When he got out he emigrated to Los Angeles for a fresh start. He was a jack-of-all-trades, could steal, extort, make book, kill somebody, whatever was required or paid the rent. Fratianno ran a bookie joint out of the Chase Hotel on the beach in Santa Monica, in Mickey Cohen territory, and he'd become friendly with Mickey and many of his inner circle, as well as a few guys on the other side, like Dago Louie Merli.

When Merli asked him to drop by the house, where he could meet Johnny Rosselli, who was just out of the joint, Fratianno was thrilled. For years he'd heard people talk about Johnny Rosselli, Al Capone's man in Hollywood, lover of beautiful movie stars. In the Ohio pen, Thomas "Yonnie" Licavoli of the Purple Gang—doing a life sentence for murder—had sung Johnny's praises as a man, said Jimmy could have no better friend if he ever got to the

West Coast. Louie Merli agreed. "I know-a Johnny half-a my life," he told Fratianno. "He's-a been like a brother to me."

They met that day at Merli's. Jimmy was not disappointed. The veteran gangster looked like something you'd see in the movies, the clothes, the style, like Cary Grant or Alan Ladd. He was soft-spoken, cool. He was tough but gracious. No showing off. He treated Jimmy like they were equal caliber. They talked and drank, got along well. Fratianno felt like half-a-fag staring at Johnny's perfect teeth and expensive clothes. He only grew more impressed as the evening went on, as Johnny shared some of his experiences, or listened sympathetically to the stories Jimmy told. This was a fuck-ing gentleman, a man of distinction. Jimmy felt in comparison like what he was: "a hustler in search of an identity" (per his biogra-pher, Ovid Demaris). By the end of the get-together he knew he'd found what he'd been missing in his life, a role model, a *hero*. He vowed that the first thing he'd do when he got home that night was burn his shitty-looking wardrobe.

It didn't take much convincing to get Fratianno to switch sides. He agreed to stay friendly with Mickey Cohen, in effect to spy on him for Jack and Johnny. Let them know if Mickey was doing any-thing of interest. Cohen had a big mouth, and it wouldn't be hard to hear him when he talked. At the same time Jimmy could keep an eye on Cohen's gang, see who else over there might want to make a change. It was risky business. If Mickey found out, he might shoot Fratianno on the spot. Jimmy understood. In this business you had to accept certain risks. It was a dice roll either way. Plenty of people never took chances and still ended up dead. His philos-ophy was summed up in his standard response to bad news, no matter how bloody: *"What are you gonna do?"* he would say. *"It's just one o' them things."*

5

Included with the attorney's formal request for a prisoner's parole was a so-called "parole plan," offered for approval, an account of prerelease arrangements made for living quarters, work, respectable sponsors, intended as evidence of the convict's good intentions when/if he got out.

Employment-wise, the Chicago contingent listed a variety of sham no-show jobs: Paul Ricca was going to be a farmer, Charles Gioe a salesman for the Consolidated Wire Company, and Phil D'Andrea a vegetable inspector for Krispy Klean Vegetables.

Johnny Rosselli's gig seemed on the whole more promising. The parole plan described a job waiting for him with Mr. Bryan Foy, Vice President in Charge of Production, Eagle-Lion Films, Los Angeles, California.

Good old reliable Joe Schenck had arranged it. The irrepressible producer and exec who had helped to put so many people in jail believed that bygones were bygones and shouldn't get in the way of an old friendship. The studio to which Johnny was pledged, Eagle-Lion, was a newly formed production and distribution entity, an upgrading of Wall Streeter/railroad industrialist Robert R. Young's Producers Releasing Corporation (PRC), with investment by the prestigious UK film company owned by J. Arthur Rank.

PRC had been one of the lowlights of Poverty Row, supplying the nation's fleapits with scruffy Westerns (*Three in the Saddle*), threadbare horrors (*Devil Bat's Daughter*), rock-bottom crime dramas (*Detour*), and raggedy-ass what-do-you-call-'ems (*Secrets of a Co-Ed, How Doooo You Do!, White Pongo, Nabonga*—some of PRC's titles looked as if they weren't even spelled right), with a roster of favored players that included an ex-burlesque stripper, a doped-up Bela Lugosi, and a man in a gorilla costume. Rank produced commercial films of a major studio standard along with the occasional breakout hit and distinguished Academy Award–winner (*Henry V, Great Expectations, Odd Man Out*). But British movies had a hard time getting into the vast American market, where, despite a common language, they tended to be treated as no less esoteric than pictures from Italy or France. Rank hoped that with Eagle-Lion they'd have a proprietary source for good medium-budget fare in Hollywood and a reliable U.S. channel for the company's UK productions. Robert R. Young hoped that with twelve million dollars of his own money spent on improvements and quality projects, and with a steady influx of Rank imports, Eagle-Lion would be able to compete with the major studios and kiss off the days of *White Pongo* and stars on the nod.

Appointed president of Eagle-Lion was Arthur Krim, an esteemed, New York–based entertainment lawyer. To take charge of the studio in Hollywood (PRC's facilities, the former Grand National Pictures studio at 7324 Santa Monica Boulevard), Young and Krim tried to lure away one or another of the big-name executives working for the majors, but a start-up linked to the down-market PRC sounded like a career risk. The job was eventually taken, at a salary of four thousand dollars a week, by a seasoned if plebeian picture maker named Bryan Foy. Known to everyone as "Brynie," Foy had been born into show business, in the 1900s he was the oldest sibling in a famous traveling vaudeville act, "the Seven Little Foys" (Bryan, Charlie, Richard, Irving, Eddie Jr., Mary, and Madeline), led by their song-and-dance-man father, Eddie Foy Sr. In his twenties Brynie'd gotten into the movies, directing short subjects and writing for Buster Keaton. Improbably he became a part of motion picture history, in early 1928 producing and directing the first all-talking feature film, *The Lights of New York*, a crudely made but in certain ways arresting movie about mobsters, speakeasies, and bootleg booze that let screen audiences hear the sounds of the roaring big city and actors speaking the tough argot of the underworld.

Through the '30s and '40s Foy worked at several major studios, with some years in between as an independent producer of exploitation pictures, taking on such shocking, Code-busting subjects as eugenic sterilization (*Tomorrow's Children*), teen pregnancy (*What Price Innocence?*), and nudism (*Elysia, Valley of the Nude**). He was best known for his years as head of the Warner Bros. low-budget B-picture unit, where he produced more than one hundred movies in six years and was referred to as "the Keeper of the Bs." A glance at Foy's résumé might indicate he was better suited to working at PRC than at the aspirational Eagle-Lion, but there was no doubt he could get a picture made, and on a budget.

Foy welcomed Johnny Rosselli to the studio with open arms. The two had known each other socially for many years, and Foy personally had no concerns about Johnny's shady past. Having grown up in a seedy world of itinerant entertainers, gamblers, frisky chorus girls, and gunslingers (his father was a pal of Doc Holliday and Wyatt Earp), Foy saw gangsters as just another part of the passing parade. How open-minded people like R. R. Young and Arthur Krim were was another matter, but for now Brynie'd been given his head to run things at the studio, and the corporate people in New York had plenty of their own problems to distract them. Anyway, there was nothing to worry about as Johnny Rosselli was a *reformed* gangster.

Officially employed as an assistant purchasing agent, at a salary of sixty-five dollars a week, in reality he became a kind of producer-in-training. He accompanied Foy to story conferences, production meetings, business lunches, to view rushes and screen tests. Foy would solicit his thoughts and opinions on pictures, casting choices. It became much like the relationship Johnny had enjoyed with Harry Cohn at Columbia back in the day. (At one time Harry had

---

* "The first authentic feature filmed in an American nudist colony! Children under sixteen not admitted unless accompanied by a parent."

wanted to make him a producer at Columbia, but Johnny had laughed it off, telling Cohn that the proposed weekly salary was what he spent on tips for waitresses.)

"Foy knew everything you could ever know about making movies. I think he'd done every job in the business at some time," recalled the actor Paul Picerni, who would work in several of the movies Foy produced. "I don't know if Johnny knew anything about the business but he was an interesting guy for sure.

"They were funny together, they bounced off each other. Brynie was this fast-talking Irishman, kind of highstrung guy, slippery. Johnny was smooth, Italian, very soft-spoken, handsome devil. Always smiling, easygoing but tough underneath. Brynie was not a tough guy. Maybe he wanted to be a tough guy.

"They were both really crazy about dames. They were always looking out for women, offer them screen tests, parts in a picture. And there were the hookers. There were always hookers visiting. Brynie would give them bit parts. You watch some of the pictures I did for him—*House of Wax*, other ones—you'll see them in little bits."

With Foy approving Johnny, no one at the studio questioned his presence. Strangers might not be so accepting. One day Brynie was visited in his office by Harry Anslinger, the commissioner of the Federal Bureau of Narcotics, and George White, one of his agents. (Small world: White had dealt with Rosselli associates Meyer Lansky and Lucky Luciano when Luciano agreed to help the U.S. government during the war.) Anslinger, a hardheaded, self-promoting antidrug zealot, had come to demand Foy produce a motion picture in tribute to the FBN, as had been done in the past for the FBI, the Treasury Department, and the Texas Rangers. Johnny—whose first conviction was for drug trafficking—was relieved to see Brynie blow him off.

Eagle-Lion had been in business for little more than a year when Johnny Rosselli got there in the summer of '47, and already the

enterprise was on rough ground. The country had entered a period of decline as a result of the weakening peacetime economy.
In the movie business the boom that had existed during the war—
there was hardly a picture released that didn't make money—had
finally gone bust. With the number of customers decreasing, the
big studios tightened their grip on the marketplace. The chance of
a newcomer like Eagle-Lion breaking through became even more
unlikely. It did not help any that their initial slate of releases comprised mostly tired comedies and romances with performers past
their prime. If audiences wanted to see traditional fare like that,
they went to the big-studio versions with the expensive production
values and the big-name stars. That first year nearly every one of
Eagle-Lion's movies had flopped.

With Robert R. Young having dropped millions on worthless
product and overhead, and the interest on loans come due, he was
forced to adjust the studio's goals downward. Instead of expanding as an integral entity, controlling production and distribution,
Eagle-Lion would have to depend on subcontracted work, using a
hodgepodge of independent producers to make the movies and to
share the costs and profits. It was a business model that had worked
well for United Artists, but UA's producing partners had included
Samuel Goldwyn, David O. Selznick, and Walt Disney. Eagle-
Lion's prospective partners were workaday names like Edward
Small, Ben Stoloff—and Bryan Foy.

For Johnny the studio's tribulations became an unexpected
opportunity. "Mr. Foy thought that I had the ability to become a
producer," he'd recall. "'You and my brother, Charlie,' Foy said,
'can possibly finance [a picture], and if you haven't the money, I will
lend you some, or whatever you can do.'" Johnny asked him, "How
much money would it take?" Foy said, "It wouldn't take too much.
We can get it and organize a firm."

So that was what they did. They put together a production company, to be fronted by a veteran movie exec named Robert T.

Kane, with ownership shared by Johnny, Bryan Foy, and his brother Charlie (now a local restaurateur). No papers regarding the exact details of his participation seem to have survived—if the details were ever committed to paper—but an FBI report based on their investigation found that Johnny had put at least $90,000 of his own money into the first production, which would have a budget of approximately $250,000, and court papers in a 1948 district court case recorded a "14/64 interest of 50%" in two produced films.

Johnny the producer began looking for something to produce. Eagle-Lion's shaky circumstances meant only a certain kind of picture would be feasible. No stars, no costly adapted material. Nothing the big studios could do better. They had to depend on original stories. And sensation. A true story was best (and free), something "torn from the headlines," as it was put in the coming attractions.

"I was in the process of getting a story down," Johnny remembered, "when [there was] a prison break in Colorado. . . ." On December 30, 1947, a dozen prisoners—convicted robbers and murderers—escaped from the Colorado State Prison in Canon City, Colorado, for three days terrorizing the community until police finally recaptured or killed them. The last escapee to be caught, a convicted murderer named Sherbondy, in an unexpectedly generous act, had given himself up when one of his hostages required emergency medical treatment. The press called the Canon City incident the most spectacular prison break in years.

"Mr. Foy and I . . . developed an idea to do this picture," Johnny would recall. "We put a writer to work on it." They gave the project a title. First: *Blood on the Snow*. Then: *Canon City*. Everything moved very quickly and efficiently, Bryan Foy's sure hand at low-cost moviemaking proving invaluable. Assigned to write the script and to direct was Crane Wilbur, a former actor who, in 1914, had starred with Pearl White in *The Perils of Pauline*, and in recent years had been stuck making cheap two-reelers. It didn't sound a promising choice, but Crane was a longtime colleague of Bryan

Foy, who knew him as a good, fast writer and flexible, risk-taking director (in '34 Wilbur and Foy had made *Tomorrow's Children*, the exploitation shocker about state-imposed sterilization). The creative team would be mostly made up of people who had already done work for Eagle-Lion. The director of photography was a studio contractee named John Alton. Alton had long been in demand for lower-budget movies because he was fast and cheap; good was not a primary concern for those jobs, and it was as yet not widely understood that he was also a cinematographic genius. The cast would be comprised of newcomers (wayward movie star Lawrence Tierney's brother, Scott Brady, in the lead), and assorted minor names and character actors (Jeff Corey, Whit Bissell, Stanley Clements).

Canon City would be a model of the new subset of "authentic" crime movies, merging the dark melodrama (what the illuminati in France were calling "film noir") with the trappings of documentary. Inspired by the famed *March of Time* newsreels (and anticipating Italian neorealism), the films mixed factual stories and authentic backgrounds with actors and dramatic technique, movies such as *House on 92nd Street, Boomerang, The Naked City.* "There was a lot of talk among movie people about these films, and this man Louis de Rochemont who produced most of them," said Arnold Laven, *Canon City*'s script supervisor. "They were a whole new approach, using stories from the news, location shooting, in some scenes using local people instead of actors. It was a very exciting approach and this was the way we were making films at Eagle-Lion."* Much of *Canon City* would be shot at the actual locations in Colorado State Prison and the surrounding area, and

---

* *T-Men* was the first Eagle-Lion film in the de Rochemont style, and no doubt an influence on the others to come. Of course, nothing new under the sun: Bryan Foy had made his nudist colony movie as a "semidocumentary" back in 1933.

arrangements were made to film the warden, Roy Best, and real-life inmates and guards who had been present at the time of the breakout.

Everything was in place. They were ready to make a movie. In less than six months, Johnny had gone from prisoner to parolee to "assistant purchasing agent" to Hollywood producer. It was an impressive trajectory by any standard.

Officially welcoming him to the filmmaking fraternity, his bene-factor (and fellow ex-convict) Joseph Schenck invited him to dinner at the old Russian's mansion in Holmby Hills. That night Schenck introduced Johnny to a sweet and almost uncontrollably sexy young woman, an aspiring actress named Marilyn Monroe. She was evidently living with him. Joe had kept starlets as mistresses from the time Johnny first met him in the 1920s, probably hundreds of them by now. He would find them, adore them for a season, try to help them with their careers, then take them to the window like a cupped butterfly and let them fly away. Schenck was sure the Monroe girl had star quality but Darryl Zanuck at Fox had disagreed, and now he was looking for someone with more sense to give her the break she deserved. Perhaps, he suggested, there was something at Eagle-Lion? Johnny had to explain that the only female part in his prison movie was an old lady who hits a convict in the head with a hammer. Schenck was sure Johnny could think of something for the girl and encouraged him to have a meeting with her. Joe had always had a generous nature and liked to share the good things in life with his friends, especially when they were things he was ready to get rid of. Johnny told people he and Mari-lyn became very close for a while in that time before all the world knew her.

Filming began in Colorado in early March 1948, in and around the city, and inside the prison, where the surviving members of the prison break were still in solitary confinement for doing the things the moviemakers now hoped to re-create. "We left Los Angeles, it was warm and sunny," remembered Arnold Laven. "We arrived in Canon City and the temperature was below zero. We started shooting immediately. It was a very misty night, not good for the camera. But John Alton loved it. He was remarkable. He did the lighting himself. He was fast as can be. He always got what was needed with very little light. He made the most difficult things look easy. We shot for several days at the prison. It was supposed to be one of the toughest prisons in the country. It was not a pleasant place at all. We were working very close to the actual prisoners and a lot of them were not happy people. The men behind bars. Some of them were like animals. If you got close to them they'd scream and spit at you. The warden spoke some lines in the picture. With his dogs. The warden was not the nicest character. He used to flog prisoners with a leather strap, which I believe was against the law. I didn't think his dogs were nice either."

Shooting was completed in early April, and the finished film was ready for release in July, just six months after the actual events the story depicted. Opening with an introductory assurance that the events were to be portrayed "exactly as they occurred and were photographed where they happened," the film began in documentary style with travelogue images and the authoritative voice of a narrator. As the camera arrived at the entrance to the state prison, the narrator described a grim place "of grey stone walls, of watchtowers, of armed guards . . . a home for those who like to have their own way too much, and have taken forbidden steps to achieve their aims." Warden Best then appeared for an interview in his ten-gallon Stetson, after which the camera roamed the prison interior, past endless cell blocks, the factories and workrooms, pausing to meet some "average" prisoners (a fourteen-year-old killer, an elderly man behind bars since 1896), and at last merged reality with fiction as the actors from Hollywood appeared on screen, already plotting their escape. For the rest it was a relentless and relatively accurate telling of the recent events, the breakout, the struggle to escape in blizzard conditions, various shootouts and violent encounters with civilians and police, and the ultimate killing or recapture of the twelve escapees (nine prisoners survived), all of it having occurred in just sixty-one hours in reality and in eighty-two minutes on the screen.

The movie would have its world premiere in Canon City on July 3, 1948. A chartered aircraft flew the Hollywood contingent— including Bryan Foy and star Scott Brady (but not Johnny Rosselli)— to Denver's Stapleton Airport, where they were met on the tarmac by Warden Best, who posed for photos with Brady and a quartet of young females wearing promotional sashes and tight-fitting prison uniforms. The premiere occurred simultaneously at the Rex and Skyline Theaters downtown and at the prison chapel inside the penitentiary. Invited guests at the prison screening included eight of the nine surviving convicts who had made the actual escape, the warden permitting them to leave the solitary block (known as Little Siberia) for the first time in six months. The ninth man, Schwartzmiller (played by Jeff Corey in the film), was not allowed to attend because he had been caught digging an escape tunnel three days earlier. The prisoners who did see the movie were said to have laughed uproariously each time a "screw" (guard) was shown being beaten or shot.

Johnny had started looking for a second project before the first had gone into production. The plan was to follow the pattern of *Canon City*, a storyline derived from an actual headlined crime case of recent vintage, to be shot on authentic settings as much as possible, with a cast of good but little known (and inexpensive) actors. He began going through newspapers and magazines in search of a filmable story. In midwinter he left Los Angeles for a week in Palm

Springs, his car filled with reading material. He told a friend there that he had a pile of "stories about G-men" and "wanted to make a G-Man picture" (a metamoment for the FBI agents when they heard about it).

He soon found a subject for filming—a police case it was, with some federal involvement—that was quickly agreed on by the producing team. It concerned a two-year crime and murder spree that had taken place in Los Angeles County in 1945 and '46. A man, subsequently identified as William Erwin Walker, burglarized numerous stores, factories, and a military armory, stealing tools, electronic and scientific devices, handguns, ammunition, and seven Thompson submachine guns. An expert in electronics, he built a workshop in his garage, where he put the stolen tools and electronics to use on experimental projects of his own invention. He attempted to fence some stolen motion picture equipment to a sound engineer, but the engineer called the police, who were waiting for Walker when he arrived. There was a shootout, two officers were seriously wounded, and Walker was hit twice. He escaped by entering a storm drain. He continued to burglarize stores and factories for select items until one night, leaving the scene of his crime, he was stopped by a policeman. The two exchanged shots. Firing a tommy gun, Walker shot the policeman nine times, killing him. A tip-off brought cops to the killer's home. There was another shootout, and Walker was wounded and captured. In custody he coldly admitted to all of his crimes. Investigators found that Walker had been in combat in the Pacific and had held himself responsible for the death of a fellow soldier. The traumatic event appeared to trigger a negative personality change, severe antisocial behavior, paranoia, and the eventual plunge into crime and cold-blooded murder. He was found guilty of his crimes and sentenced to death in the gas chamber, but after being diagnosed as insane he was instead transferred to the confines of a state hospital. In Walker's confessions he claimed that his robberies were committed to fund his invention of a ray gun that would turn military weapons to dust and put an end to war.

The project was called *The L.A. Investigator*, then *29 Clues*, and finally: *He Walked by Night*. Crane Wilbur went to work on an adaptation, gathering unreported details of the case through interviews with the police and eyewitnesses. When Crane left to direct *Canon City*, the script was handed over to another Hollywood veteran, John Higgins, who had written Eagle-Lion's *T-Men*. Chosen to direct (for a salary of five thousand dollars) was Alfred Werker, a hardworking journeyman since the early '20s, with the occasional above-average credit (*Advice to the Lovelorn*, *The Adventures of Sherlock Holmes*, *Shock*). He'd made one other film for Eagle-Lion, the odd, entertaining crime fantasy called *Repeat Performance*. That film featured the debut appearance of a young actor named Richard Basehart, and Werker recommended him for the role that was based on William Walker (in the script given the name David Kent, then Roy Martin). Carried over from the cast of *Canon City* were Scott Brady as the pursuing police sergeant and Whit Bissell as the electronics fence. Roy Roberts took the role of paternalistic Captain Breen, the name an in-joke reference to two old friends of Johnny Rosselli, the long-serving Hollywood censor/scold Joe Breen Sr., and his son Joe Jr., who had come back from service in the war with a Silver Star for bravery and serious wounds to his head, and had now joined Eagle-Lion in the story department. When the screenplay was completed, Bryan Foy cleverly assigned Joe Jr. to take it to his father for Production Code approval. The elder Breen demanded only that they remove from the script all mention or depiction of machine guns.

Filming began in late April at assorted locations in and around Los Angeles (including downtown LA, Glendale, and Montebello) and ended in late May. As on *Canon City*, the cinematographer was the brilliant, resourceful John Alton, shooting with great flair and speed. To maintain authenticity in the scenes of police activity the LAPD loaned the production a technical adviser, Sgt. Marty Wynn, who had been a part of the Walker manhunt. Wynn's guidance gave the film a natural quality, showing the way things were really done, the way the cops talked, reacted, sloughing away the Hollywood clichés. Somewhere down in the cast list was a twenty-eight-year-old actor named Jack Webb, playing forensics analyst Lee Whitey in what would be his first credited feature film role. Webb became intrigued by the idea of the story having come direct from the city police files, and by the realistic depiction of police procedure and the presentation of cops not as Hollywood heroes but as dutiful public servants. With *He Walked by Night* as his clear inspiration, and with advice from Sergeant Wynn, Webb would create and star in a highly successful and influential television series about workaday policemen and using factual crime stories. That program, *Dragnet*, with Webb playing the taciturn Sgt. Joe Friday, became a virtual hymn to the Los Angeles Police Department, happily endorsed and promoted by the LA force, including most notably the police chief William Parker. The series would run, off and on, for more than twenty years and ever after in reruns. "Just the facts," as Sergeant Friday liked to say: Gangster Johnny Rosselli was at least in part responsible for the most pro-police television program in history.

After shutting down in May, production restarted on July 21 for ten days of retakes and newly added material. Alfred Werker having moved on at the end of his contract, the new scenes were directed by Anthony Mann, a more artful and ambitious director, who collaborated with Alton on the film's most memorable sequence, the final hallucinatory chase in the underground drain tunnels. The production was readied for a scheduled premiere in Los Angeles in November. The initial intention was to have *He Walked by Night* follow the *Canon City* formula, with an introductory voice-over, a scripted interview with an authority figure, and a conclusive warning that crime was for suckers. The opening narration was kept, but other documentary trappings were downplayed, and narrative itself was reduced to an unusually minimalist construction. Counter to Hollywood tradition, the film refused to cross every T for the audience, withholding motive, never mentioning the (real-life) killer's background trauma, or the purpose of the strange goings-on in his garage, bringing to the film qualities more reminiscent of Kafka than the average Hollywood cops and robbers.

He Walked by Night was well received by reviewers across the country (*Variety* called it "a high tension crime thriller, supercharged with violence . . . sprung with finesse"), and in Europe—where the new wave of American film noir was beginning to achieve artistic recognition—it would win the first Prix du Policier at the Locarno International Festival in Switzerland. Like *Canon City* it was a box-office hit, with some theaters reporting near-record-breaking business. On a budget of $360,000 the film earned gross returns of $1,250,000, by Eagle-Lion standards a great success. The studio's producing partners saw multiple returns on their money within a year.

Johnny Rosselli was now, against all expectations, not only a movie producer but a successful movie producer. He had helped to make two films in a row that were original, popular, critically well received, cost-effective, and highly profitable. He'd extorted the industry, yes, embarrassed its most important people, was an ex-con on parole, all true—but Hollywood was a town that could forgive anyone (excepting perhaps communist screenwriters) if they knew how to make hit movies. Johnny was almost certainly looking at a rosy future, a legit future, money, career, respect—regeneration with a swimming pool thrown in—if only he had not found himself back behind bars.

7

A WARLOCK'S CARNIVAL

In August 1947 the government released Johnny Rosselli and the other Hollywood extortion-case convicts after the minimum time served on their sentences as allowed by law. Before the ink had dried on the parole board members' signatures, a chorus of disapproval echoed throughout Washington. The level of criticism broke along party lines, Republicans the most outraged by conduct linked to a Democratic administration, but misgivings grew on all sides, and as the press and public heard more about it the story became a headlined scandal. Why was the notorious criminal group given early parole? What government officials were involved in parole negotiations? Who had approved the dismissal of mail-fraud indictments against the gang that had allowed the parole considerations to proceed? Who had hired attorneys Maury Hughes, a close friend of Attorney General Tom Clark, and Paul Dillon, a close friend of the president of the United States? What was the truth behind the rumors of massive payoffs to various officials?

On September 8, 1947, *Chicago Tribune* reporter James Doherty wrote that "a congressional investigation of the parole last month of Chicago Capone gang bosses appeared probable today unless Attorney General Clark orders a full and open inquiry into the freeing by the federal parole board." The same reporter tracked down the parole board members for comment. As well-paid public servants they failed to impress. None of the three showed any interest in reexamining their decision, despite the widespread criticism. Ex-chairman T. Webber Wilson passed the responsibility to others: "If the Chicago city, state, and federal officials didn't report them to us as dangerous men to be at large, why should we treat them as such?" His former comrades on the board, Fred Rogers and B. J. Monkiewicz, felt the same. They were described as "amused" to hear that the prisoners belonged to such a thing as a "national crime syndicate."

Led by Rep. Fred Busbey of Illinois, Republican members of Congress kept up their demand that the attorney general open an investigation. With an unpopular President Truman about to enter an election year, the administration could not appear to be on the wrong side of a scandal. The attorney general agreed to investigate, sending the FBI on a hunt for the facts. The parolees were put under secret surveillance, and listening devices were placed on their telephones. Through that fall and winter agents conducted three hundred interviews nationwide, questioning everyone from T. Webber Wilson in tiny Coldwater, Mississippi (an attempt by agents to check his bank records for suspicious deposits was thwarted by Webber's friend, the bank manager), to mob boss Frank Costello in New York City. Most of those questioned had reasonable explanations for their involvement in the matter or else denied having anything to do with it at all. Costello remembered meeting John Rosselli many years ago, introduced by a Hollywood producer named Harry Cohn. Paul Ricca he might have met once at somebody's birthday party or someplace like that. The most provocative rumor attached to the case, that big money—the "million dollar bribes" as they were called in Congress—had gone to important people, maybe to AG Tom Clark and even to President Truman, seemed to evaporate under FBI scrutiny. Was it all just errant rumor after all? Even Warden Sanford of the Atlanta pen withdrew his written claims about money being paid to effect the transfers to Leavenworth, now saying it had only been prison-yard gossip.

Regarding the decision that had been made not to go forward with a prosecution of the mail-fraud indictments, which could have postponed a parole hearing, it had been a pragmatic move by Boris Kostelanetz; the prosecutor calculated that even if he were to win the mail-fraud case a judge was likely to impose a concurrent sentence on the already imprisoned gangsters, making the trial a needless and expensive waste of time. Certain that paroles for the convicts would be unlikely for years to come, he had inadvertently helped to make possible their release just a couple of months later.

Many other questions surrounding the case remained unanswered. The FBI was unable to determine the identity of the man calling himself "Mike Ryan," a mysterious "Chicago Italian" who had paid cash for the services of Paul Dillon and the other attorneys and then disappeared. If any of the people interviewed by federal agents had lied or withheld the truth about this or the many other unresolved matters, there was as yet no way to prove it. The work of Dillon and the others on behalf of their clients was, of course, protected by the law. Interrogations of the attorney general or of the president were not requested and were unlikely to have been granted. The FBI got what it could get, compiled a report such as it was, and submitted it to the AG.

Republicans in Congress had meanwhile opened their own investigation. That probe went on for months as well, with a hundred witnesses brought in for questioning. Like the Justice Department they had followed a trail of clues leading in many directions and ending up nowhere. Exasperation became outrage when Attorney General Clark refused to allow Congress access to the confidential FBI report. House Republicans demanded that President

Truman issue an executive order releasing the material to the investigating subcommittee. He refused. Truman's intransigence fueled further suspicions and anger. The hearsay was virulent. Never proved, never going away. Murray Humphreys paid five million dollars cash to the president's campaign fund. Paul Ricca personally guaranteed three Midwestern states for Truman on Election Day. The mob had the real Kansas City dirt on Harry if he didn't play ball. Like that.

Disgruntled, sore losers wanting something for their time and effort, the Republicans twisted arms at the parole board, did whatever it took, and in July 1948 the Justice Department responded. The paroles were revoked. Charging a boilerplate parole violation—"association with persons of bad reputation"—warrants were issued for the immediate arrest and return to prison of the "ex-Capone gangsters."

Federal marshals in Illinois picked up Paul Ricca, Charles Gioe, and Louis Campagna. Ricca's lawyer managed to get him released on bond pending a hearing on September 20, but Gioe and Little New York were rushed out of town and soon found themselves once more locked up in the Atlanta Federal Penitentiary.

The warrant sent to Los Angeles for Johnny Rosselli's arrest charged him with undesirable associations and in addition with "failure to register as a convicted felon in Los Angeles and Palm Springs as required by city ordinances in those places." On July 27, accompanied by his lawyers, Otto Christensen and Frank DeSimone, Johnny surrendered to U.S. Marshal Bob Clark at his offices downtown. The attorneys filed an application for a writ of habeas corpus, and a federal judge set a hearing for the following week. In the interim Rosselli would stay in the county jail. If he had held any hope of maintaining a low profile during this unexpected turn of events, they were dashed the following day when the local press reported his story in considerable detail. The *Los Angeles Times* gave it a half page, titled: "Rosselli, Film Extortion Figure Again in Custody." A photograph of Johnny and Christensen ran above the caption: IN TROUBLE AGAIN. Describing him as "a mysterious and apparently powerful figure in Hollywood in the palmy days . . . once the husband of actress June Lang," and as an "observer for the Chicago mob that ruled the unions for its own profit," the piece recapitulated the shakedown of millions from the motion picture moguls, the trial and conviction, and his present return to "motion picture connections," working at Eagle-Lion studios, where "he acquired a financial interest in at least one production on which he was technical adviser."

Otto Christensen was quoted declaring his client's behavior was "exemplary" and charged the revocation of parole to congressmen "searching for evidence of corruption and undue influence in the granting of the parole, but no such evidence was obtained." Johnny himself offered a single comment. He said: "It is all due to politics."

On September 7 Federal Judge Dave Ling denied the petition for habeas corpus, which would have kept the government from moving Johnny Rosselli to a federal prison. An appeal was filed, forcing the Feds to leave him in local custody until a district court made a decision.

He passed four months in the county jail. In November Christensen and DeSimone were finally able to get a hearing in Washington. The parole board seemed to take it as a chance to offer their congressional critics a middle-fingered salute. They offered no argument, and the charges were dropped, the parole revocation set aside. On November 15, 1948, in Los Angeles, Johnny came out of his jail cell, a free man again. The *Times* reported it, with an accompanying close-up photo. He was described as "an associate producer . . . and a technical adviser on a number of crime pictures." Rosselli, they wrote, "plans to return to his film work in Hollywood immediately."

Nine days later *He Walked by Night* had its world premiere in

Los Angeles. The film opened in New York early in the new year. It was a critical success, a box-office winner. The Foy-Rosselli production team had scored two for two.

Unfortunately Eagle-Lion did not have a similar rate of success. The studio was in serious trouble, swamped with debt payments, much past due. The first year of flops hung like a storm cloud over the company. And the promising relationship with the J. Arthur Rank company was a bust. The British studio's business was down, with many unsuccessful productions, and of the titles exported to Eagle-Lion for release in America, only *The Red Shoes* was a moneymaker. In regard to Eagle-Lion's homemade hits, due to the decision to share expenses with independent producers, the studio saw only a portion of the profits. By 1949 the studio was ready to roll "The End" in bright red ink. Rosselli and Foy's planned third film was to have been a World War II drama, from a story treatment by Joe Breen Jr., based on some of his own experiences at the time of the Normandy invasion. With Eagle-Lion sinking, Brynie went back to his old base at Warner Bros., taking the WWII project with him. After Johnny's arrest and months in jail, and the newspapers reminding Hollywood of his part in the Bioff-Browne crimes, Warner Bros. halted Foy's attempt to bring along his notorious associate. Jack Warner had just got done testifying in Washington about communist infiltration at his studio, and he was not about to go back and have to defend an infiltration by gangsters.

2

In the spring of 1948, Jack Dragna opened the books.

The Los Angeles Family had always been a small one compared with the cities in the East and Midwest. LA did not have the fertile bloodlines of New York or Philadelphia from which to recruit new members. Most of Dragna's gang had come to California from someplace else, few with noteworthy pedigrees. They were murderers and stickup men on the drift, ex-cons who knew somebody who knew somebody. For these and other reasons—Jack was cautious about most things—the Dragna family had never been overstocked with made guys.

But circumstances were changing in Los Angeles, upsetting the status quo. The sudden death of Bugsy Siegel. The rising ambition of Mickey Cohen. And as of April 6, a huge loss of income due to a crippling change in state law regarding the dissemination of horse-racing information across interstate utilities (Order, Public Utilities Commission of California, Decision #41415). In regard to the racing wire, which brought up-to-the-minute track results to thousands of local bookie joints across the country, organized crime had long profited from the federal government's generous reading of the commerce laws that said a company (Western Union, AT&T) selling private phone or wire services could not be held responsible for the illegal uses made of the information sent over said phones and wires. The Feds' reluctance to close this loophole had resulted—by 1948—in an estimated $45 billion changing hands in illegal off-track betting. Tired of waiting for Washington to do something, several states, including Florida, Pennsylvania, and California, began taking their own legislative or administrative action to prohibit utilities from enabling unlawful activities. All wire leases in those states would now be investigated and approved—or rejected—by the Public Utilities Commission. The racing wire in California was shut down.*

For the Dragna gang there appeared to be one way to make up for what they had lost, and to defend what they had left: Rival Mickey Cohen had to go. If they got rid of Cohen they could take

---

* In time the racketeers would devise a way to subvert the law, by bootlegging the wire results from border towns in neighboring Mexico, restoring much of the old service to California, but it was never as efficient or as popular.

his share of the rackets, the losses would be covered, order would be restored.

Jack and Johnny agreed that before such an undertaking they would need to upgrade the organization, recruit some new associates, and reward the allegiance of the long serving. In late April, at an Italian restaurant on Figueroa Street, the Los Angeles Family gathered for a ceremonial initiation of five men—Louis Merli (Sal Piscopo), Charles "Charlie Dip" Dippolito, Jack's nephew Louis Dragna, Jimmy Regace (Dominic Brooklier; a Cohen gang member who'd switched sides), and James Fratianno—to be made *soldati* in the honored ranks of Cosa Nostra. It was the largest induction in many years. Johnny had sponsored both Dago Louie and Fratianno. Johnny and Jimmy had bonded over the six months since they'd met. Even so, Jimmy knew Johnny was sticking his neck out vouching for him on such short acquaintance, and he'd made clear his gratitude. Johnny assured Jimmy that *his*— *Jimmy's*—own neck was stuck out even farther if he screwed up.

The ceremony observed the solemn rites from the west of Sicily, the incantatory words, the crossed dagger and gun, the pinprick of blood, the burning saint, the swearing of eternal loyalty: *We are one unto death.*

The pursuit of Mickey Cohen started slowly. Johnny was busy making movies in the spring, and Jack Dragna was reluctant to risk any unpleasantness until after his daughter's June wedding. (The lavish reception at the Biltmore Bowl would be attended by most of the Southern California underworld, *including* Mickey Cohen, who declared himself the guest of honor.) At last the calendar was clear. On August 18 (Johnny Rosselli was stuck in the county jail by now) a very loosely conceived assassination plan went into effect. On that day Jimmy Fratianno, accompanied by his wife and daughter, went to see Cohen at his haberdashery on the Sunset

Strip. Mickey had told Jimmy to drop by so he could gift him with some tickets to see Irving Berlin's *Annie Get Your Gun* at the Philharmonic. Jimmy alerted Dragna. The plan was to have a hit team wait near the store until Fratianno came back out and signaled to indicate Cohen was inside and off his guard. When Fratianno and his wife and daughter got there, Cohen was sitting around with three of his henchmen. Fratianno picked up the tickets. He wanted to get out of there so Jack's guys could come in and kill Mickey Cohen, but Cohen kept rhapsodizing about the fucking Irving Berlin show, how much Jimmy was going to love it. Jimmy tried to look interested, but all he could think about was the guys waiting to come in blasting, and that they might even come in early. At last he managed to leave the store, making for his car and hurrying his wife and child ahead of him. He gave the signal to point man Frank DeSimone (Johnny Rosselli's attorney). Frank Bompensiero (in signature Panama hat, sunglasses, a chewed-up Havana in the corner of his mouth) and two other shooters rushed the storefront, weapons raised, just as Hooky Rothman, Cohen's toughest henchman, stepped outside. Hooky reached to grab Bompensiero's shotgun by the barrel, and Bomp fired, blowing off Hooky's head. The Dragna gunmen charged inside, firing wildly, wounding the two other Cohen gang members, running through the rooms. But there was no sign of the boss. The germophobic Cohen, after reluctantly shaking hands with the departing Fratianno, had gone into the bathroom to wash. At the sound of the first shot he'd fled the building through the back door and gotten away.

The Dragna gang looked for another opportunity. In early '49 a plan was devised to gun Cohen down during a benefit show at the City of Hope Hospital. At the very last minute Dragna called it off, reason unstated but he probably realized that an assassination staged inside a charity hospital would not be good for public relations.

Next, they decided to blow him up. A bomb was improvised out of some piping, dynamite, and a fuse. This time they would avoid the public's censure and kill him in the privacy of his own home. Jimmy Fratianno and Jimmy Regace took the bomb to Mickey's house, slid it into an air vent, lit the fuse, and drove away. The fuse died, and the bomb never went off.

July 20, 1949, at 3:30 a.m. Closing time at Sherry's on Sunset Boulevard, a favorite stop for night owls like Mickey Cohen, who ended a long day schmoozing over coffee and cheesecake. Cohen and his entourage—gang members Frank Niccoli, Neddie Herbert, Jimmy "Muscles" Rist, and Eli "Roughie" Rubin, hulking Harry Cooper (a state trooper assigned to bodyguard Mickey by well-wisher Fred Napoleon Howser, the corrupt California attorney general), the Hollywood columnist Florabel Muir and her husband, and Dalonne "Dee" David (variously described by the papers as a bit actress, a doctor's assistant, and a blonde) were standing in a huddle outside the restaurant waiting for their cars to be brought around. Just as Mickey Cohen's sedan rolled up, blasts rang out from somewhere across the street. Groans, screams, bodies contorting. The big bodyguard hit twice in the gut. Neddie Herbert low in the back, the wrist. Dee David in the side. Florabel Muir in the ass. Mickey Cohen in the shoulder. Screaming and cursing. The wounded fallen, crawling. Soon—sirens, police, ambulances, bodies rushed to the hospital. Cops closed up the Strip, cop cars combed the neighborhood looking for the gunmen. Neddie Herbert, kidney and spleen punctured, would be dead a few days later. Mickey Cohen, with only a flesh wound, was giving interviews to the press before the sun rose.

One of the would-be killers claimed he'd had Cohen's head in his sight and pulled the trigger just when the gang leader moved to inspect a scratch on his car, evading his destiny again. The

Dragnas agonized over Cohen's astonishing good luck. It began to spook some of them. Jack Dragna, who was a superstitious man, decided they would forget about the ineradicable Mickey Cohen and go after his gang. At least those guys had the decency to die when you came to kill them.

Jack Dragna's brother Tom came up with a clever and cruel plan. Earlier in the year Mickey Cohen and the inner circle had gotten into a Damon Runyonesque adventure involving a poor old widow who'd been swindled by a vicious con man. Softhearted Mickey ordered his six top guys to beat the crap out of the con man. The six—Neddie Herbert, Happy Meltzer, Jimmy Rist, Frank Niccoli, Eli Lubin, Lou Schwartz, and Dave Ogul—beat him close to death. They got caught, arrested, and booked on an assortment of charges. Mickey felt obliged to guarantee bail for all six, which ran between twenty-five and fifty grand apiece, totaling a quarter million dollars, a serious figure even by Cohen's free-spending standards. Brother Dragna's idea was to pick off some of these men (excluding Neddie Herbert, already departed) while they were still out on bail, and hide the bodies, in this way depriving Cohen of his gang members and of his bail money, which would be forfeited when they failed to report for trial (being dead). This was the cause of Dave Ogul's permanent disappearance, and most likely that of the starlet Jean Spangler, the unfortunate young woman who was dating him, also never seen again.

Jimmy Fratianno recalled (to Ovid Demaris) his part in Frank Niccoli's demise. It happened on Labor Day, 1949. Fratianno lured Niccoli to his house in the Westchester neighborhood of Los Angeles. The two were friends from Cleveland, fellow stickup men back in the day. They talked about old times for a while until four of Jack Dragna's men showed up at the door. They grabbed Niccoli, tossed a looped rope around his neck, and then Jimmy and another guy pulled the ends from either side until he was dead (the "Italian rope trick," they called it). Fratianno saw that Niccoli had urinated on his new carpet. "Sometimes they shit," said the gangster on the other side of the loop. "Count yourself lucky."

To keep the missing-persons scheme in play, the Dragnas would now and then call the police or the sheriff's department with anonymous tips, saying they had just seen one or the other Cohen crony alive and well in Mexico or Las Vegas, when they knew very well the bodies were at that moment decomposing in somebody's back forty.

It was not until early in the new year that Dragna ordered another attempt on Mickey Cohen's life. Again they decided to blow him up. February 6, 1950, four fifteen in the morning. Two fuses this time. Cohen, his wife, and their maid were all asleep in their separate bedrooms. The bomb—making use of around twenty sticks of dynamite—was placed on the ground under the house. It lay below the area of Mickey's bedroom, but it was set directly beneath a large concrete-and-steel safe, which deflected the full impact of the explosion. It shook the area for miles around. One neighbor was fired out of bed like a torpedo, and another hit in the throat with a piece of flying glass. Cohen was unharmed.

The Dragna gang was dumbfounded. What the *fuck* was it going to take to murder this guy?

Help of a sort finally came. Cohen's publicity machine had been operating night and day, out of control. He got more press than Ava Gardner. People read about his bulletproof Cadillac Fleetwood, his fund-raiser for Israel, his custom-made suits and hats (after the explosion, alas, they became confetti). He appeared to be more partner than antagonist to the sheriff's department, operated his rackets with impunity, and he was rolling in ill-gotten dough. *Life* magazine printed a sympathetic piece with posed photos, and an article by Carey McWilliams compared him to Scott Fitzgerald's romantic gangster, Jay Gatsby. The federal government knew there would always be criminals, but when a criminal became a national celebrity it was too much: It gave people ideas, it was bad for business. Washington called in its own most reliable hit men: the Internal Revenue Service. It had worked against Al Capone and it was still magic. Agents began sifting every element of Cohen's operations, gathering data, interviewing associates, adding up numbers. On April 6, 1951, Mickey Cohen and his wife LaVonne were indicted for federal income tax evasion over a period of three years (charges against Mrs. Cohen were eventually dropped). The trial began on the third of June. A few weeks later: guilty on all counts. On July 9, the sentence: forty thousand dollars in fines, court costs, and five years in prison.

3

With the collapse of Eagle-Lion and Bryan Foy's departure for Warner Bros., Johnny Rosselli's career as a producer went on hold. Despite his estimable learning curve, and two successful pictures to his credit (if officially uncredited), he was reluctant to attempt another project without a more experienced collaborator or a studio sponsor. At the same time he was in need of legitimate employment. A requirement of parole was a regular, paying gig. It didn't matter how much money you had in the bank, or if your spouse was footing the bills. Keeping a salaried job was considered proof of your successful reentry into the society of law-abiding men. With the federal parole board under scrutiny for the initial release of the Capone gang, and now for having let them loose a second time, they were being careful to do everything by the book. Johnny had barely stepped outside the county jail when parole officers demanded he find a job soon or else.

He called on Harry Cohn. Their friendship had cooled after the trial and Johnny's years away in prison. But once they had been like brothers. They had done many favors for each other in the past, and maybe Johnny had done most of them. He was sure that Harry would do the right thing now that he needed his help.

He'd gone to the studio, and the Columbia boss welcomed him with a warm embrace. Cohn looked older and balder, but still fierce, predatory—now a grandfatherly vulture. At first it all seemed like old times.* They talked and drank, reminisced, and Johnny brought his old friend up to date. Harry sympathized with him for the years behind bars, congratulated him on his success with Foy and Eagle-Lion.

"I knew you could do it, didn't I?" Harry said.

"You were right," Johnny said. "I think I got a feeling for the picture business, Harry. I should have been in it from the beginning and not all that other shit."

"Goddam right. You're a helluva lot smarter than all these thieves and idiots I got working for me."

"Why I come to see you, Harry. I wanted to talk about a job."

"A job, Johnny?" said Cohn.

"Working for you, here at the studio."

"Working?" said Harry. "At Columbia?"

Johnny explained himself. About needing a job, a regular paycheck. It didn't matter how much, the money was no issue. The parole board was breathing down his neck. Put him wherever he could use him. Story department. Producer. A little B picture or something.

As Rosselli explained what he had in mind, Cohn's bonhomie withered and died.

"Johnny, you know I'd like to help you. It's not a good time now. I could never get away with it."

Cohn told him about Hollywood, 1949. Things were different.

---

* The meeting was recalled for me by reporter-biographer Bob Thomas, who got the story direct from Rosselli.

People sticking their nose in everybody else's business. These cock-suckers from Washington, Sacramento. Crime commissions. Un-American Activities Committees. FBI on all fours looking under the carpet for commies. You had to keep yourself squeaky clean. It just wasn't a good time.

Johnny listened, didn't take it well. His anger increased, and as it did his logic diminished. He blamed Harry for his conviction. If Harry'd done a better job in court, made them see how Johnny had protected him from Chicago, how he'd opposed Willie Bioff and saved Cohn's studio from that strike, if he'd showed some balls in that courtroom, Johnny might have gone free! Cohn protested. He hadn't done anything. It was the damn government had it in for him.

Harry tried to placate him with alternative possibilities. He could become an agent. Harry could set him up with some talent, send him some work. Johnny told Cohn he wasn't asking for hand-outs. He'd proved what he could do. He hadn't expected him to act like such a chickenshit. Johnny stomped out, driving off the lot with tires screaming, dress extras—cowboys, vestal virgins, Foreign Legionnaires—scattering for their lives.

It would be three years before he could enjoy a measure of revenge against his former friend. The event would be subject to mythifi-cation and fictional exaggeration in time to come, but contemporary witnesses to aspects of the story would confirm its basic truth. In the summer and fall of 1952, the great performer Frank Sinatra's career was in free fall. Desperate for a route back to the top, he coveted the role of the doomed Italian-American soldier Maggio in the upcoming film production of *From Here to Eternity*, cer-tain it would be the key to his comeback. But the producer of the film, Harry Cohn, for a mix of professional and personal reasons, refused to consider him. The singer asked almost anyone he knew

with a little juice to urge Cohn to give him the part. One of those
he begged for help was New York Mob boss Frank Costello—not
a friend per se, but like all Italian gangsters a man proud and protective of Frank Sinatra. Costello dispatched a lieutenant to the
West Coast to confer with Johnny Rosselli, who was happy to go
see Harry and convey to him Costello's casting advice: Give Frank
the part or else. For his performance as Maggio, Frank Sinatra
would win an Academy Award, and thereafter would rule the world.

Johnny looked for a way back into the movie business. He met with
old producer friends, people like George Burrows of Monogram,
who were willing to work with him, and meetings were set up with
various studio and independent outfits, but none of the considered
projects went anywhere. Everyone had their reasons; few were as
straightforward as Harry Cohn.

He had high hopes for one of Joe Breen Jr.'s screen stories, "The
End of the Santa Fe Trail," based on the diary kept by Sister of
Charity Blandina Segale, a Catholic missionary in the Wild West.
In June 1950, he went up the coast to Monterey, California, to discuss the project with Breen and visit with Brynie Foy, who were
there with cast and crew filming Joe's autobiographical war story,
Breakthrough. It was a gorgeous setting and a happy reunion for
the three Eagle-Lion veterans. Johnny joined them to view rushes
at the local movie theater, the trio sitting side by side, like in the
old days in the E-L screening room. Brynie threw a big weekend
party in his hotel suite, production assistants rounding up all the
loose women for miles around.

Foy introduced Johnny to Lewis Seiler, *Breakthrough*'s director.
Seiler was a solid professional, making pictures since the silent
days (he was the favorite director of Tony, Tom Mix's horse). John
and Lew hit it off right away. Seiler (as described by Paul Picerni,
whose first featured role was in *Breakthrough*) "was an ugly old guy,

short, fat and with a huge nose," with tastes similar to Johnny and to Brynie, a hard drinker and another Hollywood "swinger," on a constant lookout for available females (according to Picerni, Seiler would invite local girls up to his room to be interviewed for a part in the film and would greet them in the nude).

Seiler became interested in Johnny's Santa Fe Trail story. They discussed it in Monterey and continued the discussion in Los Angeles. Seiler knew of a wealthy rancher in northern Mexico who was looking to finance a movie, something that could be filmed on his own rangeland property. The two men drove down from Hollywood to Sonora to meet with him, but apparently the meeting was sidetracked, and the story of the saintly Catholic missionary was forgotten in favor of a casting session at the local brothel. Johnny talked up the project with other people from time to time. Nothing ever came of it.*

Eagle-Lion was looking like a fluke. Not to be repeated. The return to jail, the rehashed extortion story, his picture in the papers. He couldn't stay out of trouble was how it looked. Why would any legit movie company take the risk of working with such a man?

Like Harry said, things were different now. Los Angeles was becoming quite unfriendly to criminals. In November 1947, a Study Commission on Organized Crime in California had been appointed by Governor Earl Warren to investigate racketeering, gambling, narcotics, and bribery and corrupt practices of public officials. The first thing they found was that the state's attorney general was a crook. In Los Angeles the commission uncovered massive corruption throughout the branches of law enforcement. It was so well rooted you needed a deepwater drill to reach the bottom. The

---

* Rosselli's interest in courageous Catholics as film subjects continued; he would later develop a screen story about a northern priest in the Civil War South, and sought Jesuit college professor Albert Foley to write the script, Foley himself a hero of the civil rights movement who had battled the Ku Klux Klan in Mobile, Alabama.

mayor of the city in this period of mass malfeasance was Fletcher Bowron, the same Fletcher Bowron who had followed the venal Frank Shaw into office on a platform of righteous reform. Reformation had been easier said than done. Now it was time to find his old white hat and play the game again. Bowron and the police commission dealt a fresh hand. On August 8, 1950, the new chief of police took charge: grim, authoritarian, alcoholic William Parker. Chief Parker guaranteed clean cops and the return of law and order. His force would police Los Angeles as if it were an occupied enemy territory.

The crime commission in California would be the precursor to a similar federal probe out of Washington. Politicians in the capital had been hearing pleas for help from local governments, civic groups, business leaders. Crime and corruption, they cried, were overwhelming the rule of law. Congress did what it did best in the face of a national crisis: it formed a committee. Republicans had been garnering much publicity chasing communists, and now the Democrats hoped to do the same in pursuit of criminals. In May 1950, the U.S. Senate Special Committee to Investigate Crime in Interstate Commerce was established, a five-member group comprising a chairman, the first-term Democratic senator from Tennessee Carey Estes Kefauver, two more Democrats (Senators Lester Hunt and Herbert O'Conor), and two Republicans (Senators Alexander Wiley and Charles W. Tobey). The chief counsel, Rudolph Halley, would be assisted by an assortment of regional special counsels, including the redoubtable Boris Kostelanetz. A twenty-eight-person investigative staff was to be headed by Harold Robinson, who had served in that capacity on the California Crime Commission.

The committee prepared an ambitious schedule, with hearings to be held in fourteen cities over the course of a fifteen-month investigation. Based on public records and confidential information supplied by law enforcement officials in every area of interest, subpoenas were issued for hundreds of underworld figures across the country, a formidable list that included legendary Mob bosses, gambling kingpins, racketeers, henchmen, shady accountants, and gang molls. Meyer Lansky, Frank Costello, Murray Humphreys, Tony Accardo, Paul Ricca, Mickey Cohen, Jack Dragna, Frank Bompensiero, Virginia Hill, Louis Campagna, Jake Guzik, and Johnny Rosselli among them.

Not everybody subpoenaed wanted to submit to questioning. Some had gone into hiding, a few fleeing to Mexico or South America. Others tried evading an appearance with medical excuses, claiming to be ill, contagious, or dying (Al Capone's cousin Charles "Trigger Happy" Fischetti, in fact, craftily dropped dead of a heart attack nine days before he was to testify). Many of the mobsters who did appear at the hearings made clear their contempt for the prying politicians and would respond to questions with selective amnesia or wholesale invocation of their Fifth Amendment protection from self-incrimination.

As the committee moved around the country, setting up shop in city after city, press and public attention began to grow. At some stops the local television stations asked the chairman for permission to televise the hearings. Kefauver, who was already considering a run for the presidency in the next election, saw no reason to avoid a spotlight. Everywhere the hearings were broadcast, the ovaloid-screen exposure of the American underworld drew a huge audience. By the time the Kefauver show went on the air in New York in March 1951, carried live by five of the seven television stations, the response was unprecedented. Millions tuned in to the ashen-hued images, thrilling improvised melodramas like the combative interrogation of Syndicate boss Frank Costello, the camera (by agreement with the witness) focused on the gangster's hands only, which began to twist and knead in distress, a sequence worthy of a Hollywood noir. Even better: the bellicose, foulmouthed appearance of Mob strumpet and money mule Virginia Hill, who boasted to beet-red committeemen of her specific sexual prowess. The hearings became the most-talked-about television program in America. Senator Kefauver became a national celebrity, appearing on magazine covers and on TV game shows. Promoted as a rustic folk hero, he was fond of posing for photos in a Davy Crockett–style coonskin cap with tail (patently more American than the imported wool fedoras favored by gangsters). He *would* run for the presidency.

Johnny Rosselli accepted his summons without complaint. After nearly a half year confined in a local lockup—for nothing—with attendant unwanted publicity, the last thing he needed was another dispute with the law. The confrontational posture of some of his predecessors at the hearings had done them little good, several facing contempt charges and possible jail time. Johnny hoped to avoid such a result, and would present himself to the committee as a cooperative witness. Through attorney Otto Christensen, Johnny agreed in advance to answer all questions put to him and to make no use of the Fifth Amendment. According to his lawyer, Johnny would be only too happy to help, though in reality he had no intention of revealing anything not already known, or of implicating any of his associates.

It was a risky choice. Even the pretense of cooperation was frowned on by the nuance-free Mob bosses, who viewed the code of silence as inviolable; it was believed that the inconsequential but too chatty Kefauver appearance by New Jersey mobster Willie Moretti was the primary reason for his sudden death (shot in the face while dining at Joe's Elbow Room in Cliffside Park, New Jersey).

By negotiated arrangement (and the permission of his parole officer) Johnny would appear at the Chicago hearing rather than the one in Los Angeles, a matter of scheduling, maybe, or an attempt to minimize press attention in his hometown. On arrival he was taken to a Chicago hotel room where he was interrogated by the crime commission's chief counsel, Rudolph Halley, and a "special investigator," George White, loaned to the committee by the Federal Bureau of Narcotics—the same George White who had once accompanied Commissioner Harry Anslinger to Bryan Foy's office to demand they make a movie about narcs.

The executive session commenced on October 7, 1950, in room 267 of the U.S. Courthouse. Johnny Rosselli, accompanied by Otto Christensen, took his place before the celebrated chairman and his fellow committee members. Beside Senator Kefauver sat Chief Counsel Halley, and scattered about the room were an assortment of law associates, investigators, consultants, administrative assistants, Chicago Crime Commission members, and agents of the Internal Revenue Service. At nine thirty on that Saturday morning Johnny swore the oath of honesty, and then Kefauver requested the committee counsel to proceed.

"Mr. Rosselli," Halley began, "what is your present business?"

"Right now, nothing."

"Your full name and address?"

"John Rosselli, 1259 North Crescent Heights Boulevard, Hollywood, 46, California."

"You were convicted, were you not, in the so-called movie extortion case?"

"Yes, sir, I was."

"You served a sentence?"

"I did."

"When were you released from jail?"

"August 13, 1947."

"Were you ever convicted for any other crime?"

"None, only a misdemeanor, such as traffic violations, disturbing the peace—"

"Were you ever convicted of any Prohibition violations?"

"No, sir."

"Or gambling violations?"

"No sir."

"Were you ever arrested?"

"Yes. I have been arrested several times."

"For what?"

"Years ago. Suspicions of different natures on several occasions. That was during, I think, Prohibition, to the best of my knowledge . . ."

"Just for Prohibition violations?"

"Suspicions of other types of offenses."

"Since 1947 what have you been doing?"

"Since 1947 I have been in the picture business. . . . I was an associate producer of two pictures which I helped finance and produce."

"Since when have you been unemployed?"

"It is a little better than a year."

"What are the circumstances of your being unemployed? Are you retired?"

"The circumstance, I think, is that two years ago when my parole was revoked I was in the process of making these two pictures. . . . Since then I haven't been able to get any employment anywhere. . . ."

"Why was your parole revoked?"

"I don't know. I was never told officially. . . ."

"What was your occupation before you went to prison?"

"My occupation before I went to prison, I was with the Pat Casey Enterprise. Pat Casey is a labor relations man in the industry."

"What industry?"

"The motion picture industry."

"For how long were you with them?"

"Quite a number of years."

"Perhaps," said Halley, "we might do best by working up from the other end. When and where were you born?"

"I was born in Chicago in 1905. July 4, 1905."

"Where did you have your first employment?"

"Well, it's hard to say. I did almost anything. I sold newspapers, shined shoes. I went out to California at the age of fifteen or thereabouts, worked around as an extra in pictures and various jobs, odds and ends. I don't know just what you want to develop."

"Were you in the liquor business during Prohibition?"

"Well, in some manner, yes."

"Would you state what manner?"

"Very, very, very small."

"Where were you?"

"In Los Angeles."

"Prior to 1929, say, did you return to Chicago between the time you were 15?"

"I remember very distinctly I came back during the Dempsey-Tunney fight . . ."

"For the most part you were living back on the coast?"

"Oh yes, always."

"Between 1928 and 1933, up to the repeal of Prohibition, did you come back to Chicago often?"

"No, not too often. I was pretty sick those days. I had tuberculosis. I was confined in a sanitarium. . . ."

"You knew Al Capone?"

"I did know Al Capone."

"When did you first meet him?"

"During the Tunney-Dempsey fight."

"Who introduced you?"

"There must have been a thousand people in that place. . . ."

"You must have been in the Mob, so to speak, at that time, to have gotten there and gotten in to see the big man."

"No, I was just taken there."

"Let's not just brush this off quickly, Mr. Rosselli. It is all ancient history."

"Surely, I know. To the best of my recollection I will tell you about it."

"Let's try to take it a little slower and not give it a quick coat of varnish. It is old stuff. There is no reason not to be perfectly frank and open about it. . . . Here we are, you were a youngster of about 23—"

"Was I?"

"Well, that was 1928. It is simple arithmetic. You went to a party and met Al Capone, and made an impression to then visit him. . . . You must have been in the Mob. Let's be reasonable and get the story."

"I am sorry, sir; no, sir."

"How often would you say you visited the Hotel Lexington, headquarters of the Capone gang?"

"I remember once, maybe a couple of times. . . ."

"Would you say whenever you came to Chicago you stopped in there?"

"No."

"Did you see Capone whenever you came to Chicago?"

"No."

"You must have made a nice impression on him."

"I probably did, sir."

"Let's have the story. How did you fellows get to be friends? Here is the thing, Mr. Rosselli—"

"You either click with people or you don't. That is my impression."

"I am going to put my cards on the table and then you can put them on or not."

"I am going to give you everything to the best of my knowledge."

"Mr. Foy hasn't dumped you. He phoned me in a very nice way. He asked for no favors, but he told me he wanted me to know that in his opinion you were going straight, that you have had a lot of unnecessary trouble. He asked for nothing, but he felt he ought to give you that character backing."

"Thank you."

"I think it is up to you to tell this story so the story makes some sense. We all know you just don't meet these fellows and have a drink and then meet them some place else six years later."

"Let's put it this way, Mr. Halley: I was a young fellow with very little education. I am trying to sell whiskey, trying to do anything I possibly can to make a living. . . ."

Did he ever see Capone on the West Coast? Yes, sir. They were living at the Biltmore. Who else did he see there? Capone and Charlie Fischetti, several others. He didn't quite remember the others. He thought the police escorted them out of town. Was Jack Dragna there? No, sir. Momo Adamo? No, sir. When did he meet Dragna? Just around that time. Did he ever have a business dealing with Fischetti? Never that he could remember. He was pretty sure he never had.

The counsel asked about the race wire service in Los Angeles. How much business was there? Johnny didn't know. He got his percentage. What was his percentage? It varied. Month to month. Two percent. Six percent. It depended on the number of clients he found. How much went back to Chicago? He had no idea, he only dealt with the local owner, Normile. Who did he *think* the partners were? Well, said Johnny, he would hate to venture a guess. The others he really couldn't tell him. Who did they have to cut with in Chicago? He had no idea.

"How about Guy McAfee?"

"He may have had, I don't know."

"What was his relationship to the business?"

"I don't know. I never discussed it with him. . . ."

"Did you know Bugsy Siegel?"

"Yes, sir."

"How long did you know him before he was killed?"

"Oh, I don't remember, but I know it was a number of years. He used to come to California all the time."

"You would see him when he came?"

"Yes, sir. I think he lived there since maybe '35, '36, somewhere along there."

"What business was he in?"

"To tell you the truth, I never did know what his business was at that time. He seemed to get along all right. He had plenty of money. He went around with the best people."

"Who are the best people?"

"In that circle, the motion picture industry. You would always see him with very nice people."

"Who, for instance?"

"Oh, Countess DeGracio." (He meant Countess Dorothy di Frasso, the American-born wife of an Italian count and, for a time, Bugsy Siegel's lover.)

Halley waited for more. There wasn't any. The attorney had begun to perceive that Rosselli's responses were no more than affable evasions. He shook his head, harrumphed.

"I can just hear the wheels turning in there, Mr. Rosselli, trying to think, 'Who can I mention that I won't hurt—'"

"Not at all."

"'And not do any harm, and that will satisfy Halley.'"

"No. I would really like to mention the names, but I can't truthfully say that I saw him with such and such at a certain time because I can't truthfully answer that."

"I think you can. . . . In my opinion, and I am going to ask you to think it over, this investigation is far from finished. . . . I think you are trying to give this testimony of yours a quick brush over. If you are on our side of the fence—"

"I am on the truth's side, Mr. Halley."

"The truth's side is all the truth . . . we can distinguish between the people who come in here and sit there and try to find out how much we know and then admit it and the people who just say, 'Now here is the story.' There is no point in arguing it, Mr. Rosselli. . . . I don't think you are doing any more than trying to satisfy us. I think you are making an honest effort to try to give me enough . . . but are not making an honest effort to tell the truth. And the whole truth."

"The truth I will tell, but if you are going to get me to generalize and just think of what I saw at the time, I wouldn't be telling the truth. . . ."

"For you to sit here and say you don't know the score is just almost an insult, Mr. Rosselli."

"Mr. Halley, I am sorry—"

"It belies this 'reformation.'"

"I am sorry you feel that way. I am under oath and I am to answer what I know is positive facts."

Chairman Kefauver broke in, told the counsel to move it along. Halley, grim-faced, studied his notes. He asked the witness if he knew Joe Adonis? The witness couldn't say if he did. Little Augie Pisano? Yes. Johnnie King? Can't remember meeting him. Joe Massei? Yes. Tony Gizzo? Yes. Where did you meet him? In California. When? During the racing season at Santa Anita. With whom did you meet him? I think he had his wife, Johnny said, but it was so unimportant he didn't remember. Charlie Binaggio? No. Jim Balestere? No. Golf Bag Hunt? Possibly. Virginia Hill? No. Jack McGurn? Frank Nitti? Moe Sedway? Halley was like a fisherman who didn't know where they put the water.

Kefauver took over the questioning. He turned to a subject that continued to torment the politicians in Washington.

"Mr. Rosselli," he asked, "did you employ a lawyer to get a parole when you were in the penitentiary?"

"No, sir."

"Who represented you?"

"No one represented me."

"There has been something said about some lawyer in Texas representing the group of you."

"Well, he probably represented us, but I had nothing to do with it."

"Did you put up some money for a lawyer?"

"No."

"You just got out with the rest of them without any legal fee being put up?"

"Yes, sir. . . ."

"Mr. Rosselli," said Kefauver, "I think you could be very helpful to us."

"I would like to be."

"You look like a man who would like to be helpful, but I don't think you are telling us as much as you could tell us."

"I wish I could."

Another committeeman took his shot. There were more questions about the racing wire, which was now almost as dead as Al Capone. There was some talk about the movies Johnny had made. Mostly there were the endless name checks from some list of presumably dubious individuals. There was no work behind any of it. Did he know so and so? Yes or no? Any business with him? Yes or no? Little or no follow-up either way. John Stompanato, also known as Highpockets? Seen him but don't know him. Jimmie Rist? Do not know him. Mickey Cohen? A nodding acquaintance. Sebastiano Nani? Farmer Page? Bones Remmer? Mike Howard? The LaRocca Brothers? No. Yes. Business? No business. No. No. No.

"Maxie Weber?"

"Maxie Weber?"

"Yes, Mr. Rosselli."

"Maxie Weber? From New York?"

"Yes."

"No."

He seemed almost to be playing with the committee by this point, though his tone remained bland and respectful. Did he know Joe Sica? he was asked. Sica was a big-shot hoodlum who distributed narcotics in California, and was also the proprietor of a haberdashery, a health club, and some other businesses. The name, said the witness, did sound familiar. "Wait a minute now," Johnny said. "One time about two years ago I had a shirt maker by the name of Jackson who worked for the Savoy Shirt Company. They made six shirts for me. I later reordered some more because they made some good shirts. Mr. Foy ordered some too. Later I found out that Joe Sica *owned* the Savoy Shirt Company."

"You're saying you bought some shirts from him?"

"Yes, sir."

Funny stuff. But he kept a straight face.

"Did you know Tony Cornero?"

"Maybe bought a few cases of whiskey from him twenty years ago, sir."

"Have you ever been in the fishing business?"

"No."

"In any way, shape, or form?"

"No."

"Do you know Joe Profaci?"

"Profaci?"

"Profaci. P-r-o-f-a-c-i. With the Mama Mia Olive Oil Company."

"I may know him under another name."

"Sam Maceo?"

"Yes."

"Do you know Red Italiano in Tampa?"

"I do not know him."

"Have you ever been in the olive oil business?

"No."

It was like that quiz show on the radio, *Twenty Questions*, only this was funded by taxpayers.

They came to the end of their scheduled time. Counsel Halley again reprimanded Johnny for his calculating testimony, as if the meandering inquiry were all the fault of the witness. "Mr. Rosselli," he said, "I don't think you have done more than answer questions that you felt you had to answer."

"I wish I could be more helpful, Mr. Halley," Johnny said.

"I think you could."

"I would only be generalizing and not really be telling the truth, only rumors. I don't think you want that."

"I don't think you have crossed over the line from the defensive to the cooperative at all."

"I am sorry you feel that way."

The chairman said, "All right, thank you, gentlemen."

And Johnny Rosselli and Otto Christensen made for the exit as Kefauver called for the next witness.

4

The morning after the explosion, Moreno Avenue stank of smoke and the sweet aroma of dynamite. Mickey Cohen, in his striped bathrobe and pajamas, posed for the press photographers as he gazed upon the rubble. Crime-scene investigators sifted the area for evidence, and detectives roamed the block questioning the neighbors. But there seemed almost no need for an investigation. Everybody knew who sent the bomb.

Governor Warren's crime commission fingered Jack Dragna as the man responsible for the "terror tactics" in Brentwood, for the attempted murder of Mickey Cohen, and for several unsolved killings in the Los Angeles area, the result, they said, of a deadly squabble between two rivals for bookmaking operations, Cohen and "Dragna, an alien Italian." It was Dragna's side that was responsible for all the bloodletting, claimed the commission, describing Cohen as having "no appetite for a struggle with his rival." (Cohen, in fact, downplayed the gang war gossip and the supposed "rivalry," and was quoted as defending Jack: *He's one of my best friends. He's retired . . . and he don't bother nobody."*)

With encouragement from Sacramento, the police were directed to grab Dragna and anybody connected with him. Cops nabbed six men in the first roundup, including Jack's son, his brother, his brother's two sons (who were working at the family-owned grocery store when they were arrested), underboss Momo Adamo, and Moe Shaman (a bookie known to be seeking revenge for Mickey Cohen's killing of his brother, Max). But not Jack. Squad cars roared onto the front lawn of his home at 3927 Hubert Avenue. The man of the house was missing, but the cops rounded up his wife, Frances, and other family members and had them held in one room under armed guard while a half-dozen officers stormed through the house, pulling out drawers, upturning boxes and cases, and taking away every letter, contract, ledger, receipt, and cancelled check they found.

The jailed Dragna group was not charged and was released after three days. Jack came out of hiding. The police had been unable to find any evidence linking him to the bombing. Of course that didn't mean they thought he was innocent. By August "Whiskey Bill" Parker was in charge of the police, and the war on crime intensified, with the foremost goal of defeating gangsters with funny foreign names. Patrols were assigned to follow—and harass—Dragna twenty-four hours a day. Wherever he went, cops boxed him in, a prowl car trailing in back, another hugging his side or rolling ahead of him. When he went into the barbershop at the Beverly Wilshire for his weekly haircut, a cop followed him in a minute later, sitting nearby and thumbing a magazine until he left. His wife and son got much the same treatment. A cruiser parked all day in front of Frank Dragna's delicatessen, and the officers glared at the customers as they went in and out. Cops kept a close watch on all the known members of the Dragna gang. The assignment was referred to as "working the dagos."

Scrutiny grew even worse after Jack had his son Frank, the war hero, file a lawsuit against members of the police seeking $350,000 for false and illegal arrest. Cops could be thin-skinned about getting sued for doing their job, and now the whole force was ill-disposed toward the name Dragna.

A unit staked out the downtown warehouse of the Latin Import and Export Co., Jack's banana business. They photographed visitors from across the street and put a listening device inside. One day a visiting Joe Sica stormed out of the entrance holding the planted microphone and a trail of wires. He made like DiMaggio and swung the mike against a telephone pole until it split into pieces.

Jack was not used to this kind of attention. Unlike Mickey Cohen, he did not give interviews, pose for photos, host guided tours of his home, or get in powerful people's faces. He did bad things, but he didn't brag about them, didn't try to antagonize City Hall, paid graft to the big shots, and showed respect to the working cops (it was a well-known secret that any policeman in uniform was welcome to drop by the warehouse and take home a bunch of bananas for his family). He had kept a very low profile all these years. The average Angeleno had never even heard of him, even though for two decades he'd been the closest thing to "the Al Capone of Los Angeles." As a result he'd managed to stay out of prison, make a lot of money, take care of his wife and kids, and his gang, and his girlfriends—and take care of his enemies, too, and without having to pay the piper. Now it was all coming undone. Crime commissions, his name in the paper, the malevolent new police chief, the rousting of his innocent family members, the screwed-up results of the decision to (try to) kill Mickey Cohen.

Next—in late September '50—came a summons for Jack to appear before the Kefauver Committee. He found the prospect of an open-ended public exposure sickening. Evading the subpoena, he again disappeared. The police located him within the week. He'd been laying low with a beautiful young brunette woman. They'd gone shopping, had pulled to the curb in front of an apartment building at 7667 Hollywood Boulevard, and Jack and the woman were unloading bags of groceries when police cars appeared from nowhere and he was arrested. Dragna's appearance at the hearing in Chicago was an ordeal. His ragged attempts to steer clear of any unpleasant truths, denying any wrongdoing and remembering little, got him a contempt-of-Congress charge from the Senate. Now he was facing a possible year in a federal lockup.

The bad luck was just getting started. Police surveillance determined that Jack had set up his twenty-three-year-old mistress in a love shack on S. Mariposa Avenue. Late in January '51, the cops broke into the apartment and placed a bug in the bedroom, just behind the headboard. For two months policemen gathered at a basement listening post, monitoring Dragna's every conversation and every intimate encounter with the young brunette. A complaint was filed by police, and on April 10, Jack was arrested and hit with a misdemeanor morals rap, accused of committing "dissolute vagrancy and resorting" (that is, committing lewd sexual acts and occupying a home or other place for the purpose of lewdness or prostitution) and "associating with a known lewd person." He was booked at the city jail, paid the five-thousand-dollar bail, and went home.

On June 20 the case came to trial. It was the hottest show in town. The most salient of the two months' worth of police recordings involved some incriminating conversation and much incriminating moaning, gagging, and slurping. Dragna's *goomah* was heard to declare: *"The farther down my throat it goes the better it feels!"*

Elsewhere on the tapes, at the conclusion of another carnal encounter, Jack was recorded clamoring for a bottle of mouthwash, flustered when the mistress told him there wasn't any. *"It's all right,"* she said, laughing. *"It won't hurt you!"* The combination of dialogue and sound effects left little doubt that the old man and the young woman had committed acts of mutual "sodomy," illegal under the California Penal Code (and, as to his oral act upon her, seriously frowned on by dogmatic Sicilians). For Dragna, after so many years of maintaining a (relatively) discreet and dignified public image, it had come to this. Murder was one thing, but going to jail for getting a blowjob or licking a woman's *patonza* was just embarrassing.

He was found guilty on two counts, and sentenced to 180 days behind bars. Dragna's attorney filed a motion for appeal, and for the time being he remained free on bail.

But the heat continued. Now it was the turn of the Immigration and Naturalization Service. Dragna had first come to the United States as a child in 1898. He'd returned to Sicily later, then come back to America in March 1913. He'd made at least two attempts to obtain U.S. citizenship, and failed both times, the last shortly after the war ended. Without that citizenship paper, and *with* a bad character and a criminal conviction, Dragna was at serious risk for deportation back to his birthplace. Deporting an immigrant criminal could be very easy or very difficult, depending on how hard the subject fought the system. A man with the best legal team could tie up a case for many years before anybody bought him his boat ticket. Wanting to avoid such a situation, the INS spent months searching for a foolproof way to expel the Los Angeles crime king.

On December 8, 1952, Immigration agents appeared at 3927 Hubert Street with a warrant for Jack Dragna's arrest. He was taken into custody and transported to the INS headquarters on Spring Street. Charged with illegal entry to the United States, he was allowed bail, paid a thousand-dollar bond, and was released pending a federal inquiry.

The government's case centered around the discovery of decades-old Customs Service files. On July 24, 1932, Dragna had been processed by Customs and Immigration inspectors on two occasions, before departing by private aircraft from Lindbergh Field in San Diego, destined for Mexico, and on the same day crossing back into the United States by automobile. When interviewed by the Customs agent at the airport, said the INS, he had claimed to be an American citizen, born in New York. When he came back across the border by land he again stated that he was a citizen of the United States. This fraudulent claim of citizenship was a federal crime, and punishable by deportation to the person's country of origin. It was an unusual premise on which to hang the case, dependent on twenty-year-old hearsay and unsigned documents, but they believed it would get the job done. President Truman's new attorney general, James McGranery (Tom Clark, the Truman AG implicated in the Capone gang parole scandal, having by this time moved on to the Supreme Court) reviewed the evidence and signed off on the INS scheme.

The hearing began on January 6, 1953, before Special Inquiry Officer George Scallorn. The actual immigration inspector who had talked to Dragna at the airport in 1932 was there to testify, as were other inspectors claiming to have witnessed the interview or heard the name "Jack Dragna" under discussion that day. One of the men who had been working at San Ysidro recalled the time clearly, as he said he had been alerted by border officials to expect Dragna and to inspect his vehicle for firearms. As the hearing continued, evidence of other, similar "illegal" entries was introduced by the immigration attorneys. It was no doubt Jack's pro forma response to the question and had likely been given every time he crossed back from a visit to Mexico, without a thought that it could come back to haunt him decades later.

Dragna's legal defense had been a simple denial of the government's assertions. It would be in the long appeals process—if one was going to be required—that his lawyers would earn their fees.

The government closed its case on February 8. They awaited Scallorn's decision, expected within the week. As the hearing adjourned, the clerk, filling out forms, asked Jack Dragna, "Which country do you wish to specify in the event your deportation is ordered?"

Jack said nothing, smiling sadly.

A few days later Special Inquiry Officer Scallorn announced his decision. Jack Dragna was going home to Italy.

His attorneys promised to take the case to the Immigration Appeals Board, and if necessary to the U.S. District Court and to the U.S. Supreme Court. Jack Dragna was taken to the federal prison at Terminal Island.

In July, Frances Dragna, his wife of thirty-one years, became ill. She was rushed to St. Vincent's Hospital. Her condition worsened, and Jack was twice allowed to visit her in the hospital, accompanied by immigration officers. On the morning of July 23, Mrs. Dragna died.

Jack received the information in the detention center. He was devastated, inconsolable.

Within hours word came from the Department of Immigration in Washington authorizing the district director to give the detainee a compassionate release pending his forthcoming appeal. His attorney posted a fifteen-thousand-dollar bond, and Jack Dragna went home to bury his wife.

He remained free for the time being. Jack's loss seemed to cut him adrift. Business went on, but his interest waned. He spent more time with his two young grandchildren. He stayed at home and stared at the television. Wrestling from the Hollywood Legion.

I Love Lucy. Fucking *Dragnet.* On March 10, 1954, he was indicted by a federal grand jury on charges of income tax evasion. A trial date was set, then postponed, then postponed again when Dragna's doctor certified he was too sick to stand trial. His misdemeanor conviction remained unsettled, and the threat of deportation continued to impend.

In mid-1955, he left Los Angeles for an extended stay in San Diego, visiting with relatives and old friends.

On February 10, 1956, he checked into the Saharan Motor Hotel on Sunset Boulevard in Hollywood, registering under the name Jack Baker. The nondescript two-story lodging was one of his many in-and-out trysting spots, but this time he stayed for two weeks. On February 23, a Thursday, a maid entered the room—room 125—and found the guest lying in the bed in flamingo-pink pajamas. His limbs were rigid, and he did not appear to be breathing.

The medical examiner estimated the body had been lying like that for twenty-four hours. Police searched the room, gathering the dead man's belongings. On the nightstand where he'd left them cops found his wallet, containing cash in the amount of $986.71, bottles of heart medicine, and two sets of dentures. In the parking lot they found his Cadillac sedan. Within hours agents of the Internal Revenue Service had come, seized the car and the cash for payment of back taxes. They did not take the false teeth.

8

NEON BABYLON

The Kefauver Committee achieved a very mixed result in the way of legislative change when it returned to tribal Washington politics, but its social impact was enormous. The must-see TV show had revealed the spread of racketeering, gambling, and corruption in big and small communities nationwide. People learned of the startling scope and interconnectedness of organized crime, and many Americans for the first time heard about a secret society in their midst, a "Sicilian underworld syndicate" known as the Mafia. The Kefauver effect was further spread through the popular culture in "confidential" journalism, true-detective magazines, lurid paperbacks, and B movies. Numerous areas of the country touched by the committee's revelations demanded the law take action. Many a local racketeer was rousted, and gambling joints, betting parlors, and brothels that had operated for many years were shut down (a great many of the dispossessed gaming pros— and many of the prostitutes—resettled in Las Vegas). The determination to clean up and crack down was nowhere more evident than in Los Angeles, where state and city governments, a helpful

FBI and IRS, and a vigilant and oppressive new chief of police, made crime fighting into something of a holy crusade.

Mickey Cohen was sent to prison. Jack Dragna was harassed, prosecuted for acts performed in the privacy of his own sex pad, and was battling INS efforts to deport him. Some of Dragna's top men were taken down hard. Jimmy Fratianno bungled an extortion plot and earned a long stay in Folsom Prison. Frank Bompensiero, a loyal hit man, was caught running a liquor license scam and got three to thirty-two years in San Quentin (like Jack, Bomp lost his wife while in jail; he would attend the funeral in handcuffs).

Under Chief Parker the LAPD had reconstituted its intelligence operations, a West Coast version of the East German Stasi dedicated to spying, fact gathering, harassment. They compiled dossiers of would-be wrongdoers and staked out the airport and railroad station on watch for unwanted visitors. In January '53, Tony Accardo and entourage (traveling under assumed names) flew to Los Angeles from Chicago for an overnight visit en route to Las Vegas. Johnny Rosselli was host for a planned night on the town, sending the Outfit boss's group to his favorite fine-dining joint, Perino's. The gangsters took their places in the ethereal pink-and-peach dining room, and the waitstaff in their brocaded vests and blinding white aprons were making much of them, as instructed. The pleasant evening was interrupted. Cops arrived, surrounded the table. Everyone was made to stand up, produce IDs, submit to a frisk. The visitors were escorted out to the street, put into a police van, and taken back to the airport for the earliest flight to somewhere else. They were lucky. Some out-of-towners with the wrong résumés were picked up, beaten up, and tossed down a wooded LA canyon to entertain the coyotes.

Johnny Rosselli had evaded police attention in this period. It was a side effect of his (seeming) compliance with the rules of parole.

How could a man be up to no good if he was home every night for an early curfew? He made sure all Mob business was done with discretion. When conferring with the Dragna gang or other criminal associates, they would come together at the office of his attorneys or after dark in someone's home. If anybody needed Johnny's input on a more immediate matter he would meet the person in some unsung restaurant's bathroom or alleyway. It was a pain in the ass, all the sneaking around, but it did keep him off the authorities' radar.

To satisfy the parole board's requirement of steady employment, he continued looking for a legit job or business endeavor. He attempted another producing venture with two Hollywood pals, Monogram Pictures veterans George Burrows and Jack Dietz (Burrows a studio executive, Dietz a producer specializing in Bela Lugosi horrors and East Side Kids "comedies"), but the project went nowhere. The rest was wheel-spinning, a planned purchase of a drive-in movie theater in LA County, and an interest in a confectionery company called Tom Thumb Donuts. At least the law could see he was trying.

The obligations and deceptions were over in March 1954, when the term of his parole expired. Between arrest and trial, imprisonment, and parole, it had been eleven years of living with his freedom compromised. "He was so happy," Pat Breen, Joe Breen Jr.'s wife recalled. "It was like the chains had come off. He could hold his head up again." And his middle finger. He threw a party to celebrate the event—at Perino's, of course, where his custom was valued with or without the government's seal of approval. In attendance were friends like the Breens, columnist (and Mob devotee) Florabel Muir, a couple of film stars and producers, and a few underworld figures. The champagne flowed, and the police were nowhere in sight.

———

He could travel now. He could get away from California, call on long-unseen friends and associates. It was time to catch up or fall by the wayside. He was most eager to visit the new underworld wonderlands in Havana and Las Vegas.

In 1952 Cuba had been taken over in a military coup led by Gen. Fulgencio Batista. In the fervid Cold War world, the U.S. government cheered the anticommie strongman's return, the next American vice president, Richard Nixon, calling him "Cuba's Abraham Lincoln." Also pleased with Batista were assorted high-level members of the Syndicate. The island had long been a happy hunting ground for gringo gangsters, but now the relationship was up front, formalized, an outright partnership between a repressive dictator and mobster kings. The partners developed a literal criminal state in which the interests of government and gangsters were as one. While Batista's army and police maintained order on the island, the Mob ran nearly everything else, the gambling, entertainment, drug smuggling, high-end prostitution, state-of-the-art abortion clinics, and a growing array of financial, mercantile, and even agricultural activities.

In Havana, Johnny found a sybarite's capital ninety miles from the United States. A sultry Eden of sunshine and pleasure (if you overlooked the beggary and fear). Casinos, brothels, and grand hotels under one roof. Sex and daiquiris, warm sea breezes over the Malecón, mambo and nightclub voodoo, Eartha Kitt at the Parisien, Superman at the Shanghai. A guest could order cocaine from room service. Or two underage girls.

He called on old acquaintances: at the top, Meyer Lansky, Batista's best buddy, whose dream it had been of an open city in crooked Cuba, with holdings that included large parts of the Riviera casino resort and the legendary Hotel Nacional; and Santo Trafficante Jr., son of the *bolita* king of Tampa, Florida, who ran the Sans Souci, produced stag movies and dirty snapshots for sale to tourists, and was in charge of the heroin traffic that came through Cuba from France. Johnny entertained offers from both men to join their operations. He turned them down, with respect.

A good choice. Havana was a reverie not meant to last. Already the *insurgentes* were making known their dissatisfaction. There were violent protests, the occasional bomb exploding in the streets. The head of the secret police was assassinated in the crowded Montmartre nightclub. Tourists were not going to keep laying bets or laying *putas* if they always had to worry about being shot or blown up.

The smart money was on that other Mob paradise, the sparkling watering hole in the Nevada desert.

Though unheralded as such, Johnny Rosselli could be counted among the founding fathers of the reborn Las Vegas. In 1931 he and the Capone gang's Murray Humphreys had roamed Nevada doing what needed to be done to influence the passing of legislation in favor of open gambling. The Mob had big plans for the drowsy Mojave train stop at the state's southern tip, but the Depression had drained the pool of customers, and the completion of the Boulder Dam would see the departure of thousands of area residents, putting Vegas back in a coma until the 1940s. What gambling halls persisted were in the way of shit-kicking cowboy joints, floors covered in sawdust. The new age dawned with the coming of the Flamingo, opened in 1946. This was Bugsy Siegel's palace (after he'd wrested it away from Johnny Rosselli's friend Billy Wilkerson), set on unincorporated highway land beyond the city proper in Paradise Valley, built in a lavish style that mixed the glamour of Hollywood's nightclubs and the midcentury flair of Miami Beach resorts. After a bumpy first year, and Siegel's bloody dismissal, the running of the Flamingo was handed over to Syndicate-chosen gaming professionals, managed by veteran

Mob ally Gus Greenbaum, the gambling kingpin of Arizona. Revamped and under new management, it became a cash-spurting success.

Other casino hotels soon joined the Flamingo on the sandswept stretch of Highway 91 known as the Strip. The Desert Inn, the Sahara, the Sands, the Dunes, the Riviera. All followed and built upon the Flamingo's formula of gambling amid flashy opulence, full-service resorts with first-class accommodation, good food, and entertainment for the moments when visitors weren't losing their shirts at the tables. The new wave of casinos would almost all be backed by one or more faction of organized crime, with East Coasters Meyer Lansky and Frank Costello of the Syndicate and Moe Dalitz and partners of the Cleveland Mayfield Road Gang the heaviest early investors. Mob ownership of the casinos was disguised through the use of fronts or "shields," individuals pretending to own the properties or hold a ruling interest, businessmen and legit entrepreneurs (at least semilegit) who could obtain the necessary licensing from the state, sign the legal papers, and account to the government, receiving a few points for their service. People like the Desert Inn's Wilbur Clark, whose name appeared everywhere from the rooftop signage to the garbage cans, even though he had no more than a small share of the place.

Since most banks and other financial institutions considered the casino business unsavory and not a welcome association, the Mob used its own funds, painstakingly laundered. This was always a risk, as it left the real owners open to greater exposure to the law. Outside financing was desired most of all as evidence of a legitimate source for the casinos' bankroll. In time the casinos would find certain more idiosyncratic lenders willing to work with them, including the Bank of Las Vegas and the Teamsters Union.

The Nevada government watched the developments with enthusiasm and with trepidation. Gaming brought in unprecedented tax revenues, far more than any other industry, and no one wanted to give up that golden goose; but the presence of organized crime in booming Las Vegas was an open secret, and if the state didn't keep some hold on things the situation had the potential for going very wrong. A descent into overt lawlessness and corruption would mean intervention from Washington. And that could mean the end of legal gambling in Nevada (the Supremacy Clause of the U.S. Constitution allowed the federal government to preempt conflicting state law as necessary). The Nevada pols tried their best to have it both ways. The city went on booming, but the legislature made adjustments, meant to keep a closer hold on the casino industry, taking away the gaming authority from the county officials and giving it to the more imposing State Tax Commission, in '55 creating the Gambling Control Board to tighten the rules by which new applicants could be considered for licensing. (Those whose licensing predated the revisions were allowed to carry on without being reinvestigated, a crucial piece of good luck for the dubious Moe Dalitz, who had slipped through during less intrusive times.) The new rules sounded good in theory, but they could be applied only to the charade "fronts," not to the real owners who stayed in the shadows and went on with the business of counting the money.

Money: It flowed like a mighty river, washing across the casino tables, filling the drop boxes, filling the count rooms, filling the duffel bags and briefcases bound for the East Coast and Midwest cities, the official count and the unaccounted-for, tax-free daily mounds of cash that the secret investors lived for, known as "the skim." As word spread of the currency coming out of the new generation of casinos, the big gangs all over the country looked for a way in. For mobsters the rush was on, Las Vegas the new Klondike. The circumstances—start-up costs, the inside track, legal restrictions to be circumvented—precluded just any mob from building their own joint; they had to get in line and hope for a piece of a new project (a fourth, an eighth, a quarter of somebody else's fourth). But the money poured in for everybody.

Unlike Havana's disquieting meld of luxury and colonial decay, heaven with a social disease, Vegas was a purpose-built paradise, shiny and sanitary and safe (if you didn't count the cancerous particles from nearby atomic bomb tests). It was a neon wet dream, an Oz for swinging adults. Legal gambling, five-star coddling, six-foot showgirls, headliners for every taste: from Elvis Presley to Edith Piaf. Visitors were treated like VIPs, and for the "whales," the certified big spenders, Vegas rolled out an even thicker, redder red carpet; life for the high roller was nirvana—*moksha*—the ultimate release from karmic bondage.

In 1954–55, when Johnny Rosselli began making frequent visits following his parole's end, Vegas was like a gangsters' school reunion, with familiar faces everywhere. The casino managers were veteran mobsters or Mob associates, the pit bosses, dealers, box men, floor men also imported vets from "back home" often okayed for the jobs by the bosses themselves, who wanted vouched-for employees working around the money. Some of the people Johnny encountered in Las Vegas he had known in one town or another going back two or three decades.

His most important new friend was the current fair-haired boy in the Chicago Outfit: Sam "Momo" Giancana. Three years younger than Johnny, Giancana was a Sicilian American, native Chicagoan. A lifelong criminal, as a teen he'd belonged to the vicious Forty-Two gang, a kind of farm team where many a future grown-up gangster got his training. He'd first joined the Outfit as a young man in the thirties and worked as Machine Gun Jack McGurn's chauffeur. Giancana had been associated with every sort of wrongdoing, from murder to kidnapping to selling horsemeat as beef, and had done his share of time. An ambitious soldier, he'd made his mark with the Outfit by showing the way to take control of the African American–run "policy" game, a sort of half-assed lottery that was popular in the city's so-called "black belts"; the takeover would end up costing a few lives, but brought in millions per year to the Chicago Mob's coffers.

Giancana had lost his wife (it was a tragic season for Mob spouses, with the deaths of Mrs. Dragna and Mrs. Bompensiero) and was sowing his wild oats in Las Vegas. He was not an attractive man—in repose he resembled a giant house spider—but he was a dynamic and compelling personality; he came on to women like Errol Flynn, and had a similar rate of success with them. He could be temperamental, and had a known violent history, but some—family, neighbors, girlfriends—thought him warm, a good father, a considerate man; of course others were inclined to agree with the U.S. Army's assessment—at the time of his rejection for service—that Giancana was a "constitutional psychopath" and had an "inadequate personality manifested by strong anti-social trends." It was certainly better to stay on his good side whatever you thought of him. He and Johnny met for the first time on a golf course, introduced by a woman Johnny was going out with. Only that day she was going out with Sam. They played golf, then went for drinks, gambled a little, decided to all go to dinner. Johnny would say he "drummed up a friendship with him." Giancana was the right man to befriend at that point in time. But he found Sam an interesting person and loyal friend. They got along well. They made each other laugh.

Johnny's oldest friend in Vegas was that figure of legend in the annals of West Coast crime, his former boss and mentor, "king of the rumrunners," Tony Cornero.

Cornero had had an eventful and colorful time of it since his Prohibition heyday and the wild and woolly (and wet) adventures Johnny had shared with him in the 1920s. He had been the first person to build a modern resort in Las Vegas after the legalization of gambling in 1931. The Meadows (the English translation of *las vegas*), set along the road outside the old town, contained a casino, a hotel, a restaurant and cabaret, a predecessor by fifteen years to Bugsy Siegel's "unprecedented" Flamingo. After the Meadows burned down, Cornero went back to the Coast and for many years ran floating casinos, including the world's largest gambling ship, the SS *Rex*, which could carry up to two thousand guests. In more recent times he'd pursued a plan to bring Vegas-style casino gambling to bordertown Mexico, which ended after someone shot him in his Beverly Hills doorway. Now, in the 1950s, he was a late-middle-aged veteran of the life, slowed down in body but still filled with an adventurer's spirit. It was inevitable that he would be drawn back to a now-booming Las Vegas. Purchasing thirty-six acres of land on the northern side of the highway, he conceived of a super-size luxury casino and hotel (more than one thousand guest rooms), the largest gambling resort ever built.

The Stardust, as it came to be named, proved far more expensive and complicated than Cornero had planned. To keep the project going he had borrowed, and borrowed again, most of it from Moe Dalitz and his group of operators and investors. In the summer of 1955 he owed more than four million dollars, and the casino was far from finished.

By the time Johnny reunited with his old friend, Tony Cornero was in bad shape, his business problems taking a heavy toll. He feared his spectacular project was about to be seized by creditors or crumble under its own debts. He was distressed, drinking too much, gambling with other people's money. Johnny had promised to try to help, but it was too late for Tony. On July 31, 1955, after an acrimonious meeting at the Desert Inn with Moe Dalitz, he'd gone into the casino to let off steam. He was shooting dice, and sipping a seven and seven, when he fell out of his seat, dead of an apparent heart attack.

A rumor began to circulate that Tony Cornero had been murdered, his drink poisoned. The glass and its contents had disappeared. His body had been taken to someone's office and the police were not notified for two hours. The body was sent to a funeral home in California before a legal autopsy was performed. There was no hard proof of a murder but nobody said "That couldn't happen." Many knew that Tony Cornero was in debt to the Moe Dalitz team for millions, and long overdue to finish his project. *Everybody* knew about Bugsy Siegel, another casino builder who'd spent too much mobster money.

It was understood that Dalitz expected to collect what he was owed by taking possession of Cornero's half-finished casino (that was more or less how he had taken over the Desert Inn from Wilbur Clark). Instead, as the story was heard by Tony Zoppi, the publicity director at the Riviera casino for many years, Johnny Rosselli entered the picture and things went in a different direction. Right after Cornero's death Johnny met with Sam Giancana. He conveyed to him critical financial and legal information he'd been told by his late friend. Whatever that was, and whatever maneuvers then occurred, they resulted in Chicago moving in on the Stardust ahead of anybody else. The debts were paid off, and the Chicago Outfit became for the first time majority owner of a big casino on the Vegas Strip. Said Tony Zoppi: "Johnny was in on that. He got the property for Chicago. He told Sam Giancana what he had to do and Sam talked to the boys—and that deal *made* Giancana."

As this was happening, yet another Mob-backed casino opened for business. The Riviera was the first high-rise casino resort, designed in a modern "European" style, the largest and fanciest "carpet joint" to date. Most of it belonged to the New York syndicate, with smaller pieces spread around to other investors. The group chosen to run the casino at the Riv were either inept or crooked, as the opening weeks were terrible and things went downhill from there. It was an embarrassment for the owners. Smart-alecky magazine writers suggested the "Vegas boom" had "gone bust."

Desperate to turn it around, the powers-that-be got rid of the original management team and sought out Gus Greenbaum, whose magic touch as a casino operator had for many years made the Flamingo a great success. Exhaustion and an assortment of ailments including ulcers that cost him a chunk of his stomach, with a consequent addiction to painkillers, had led Greenbaum to take an early retirement. He moved back to his home in Phoenix, Arizona. With the Riviera failing fast, the owners went to Gus and asked him to come back to Vegas and run the casino for them. Gus begged off. He was retired, he had enough money, he wasn't interested. So they killed his sister-in-law. Gus reconsidered.

In Arizona there was a rising star politician named Barry Goldwater. In the midfifties a U.S. senator, one day he would be the Republican Party's nominee for president of the United States (losing by a landslide to Lyndon Johnson). Goldwater had jump-started his political career by attacking the sort of liberals and libertines who tolerated gambling and prostitution and other so-called vice crimes. But like a lot of politicians, he believed in the policy of "Do as I say, not as I do." And he did what he pleased. He liked Las Vegas very much, and many times he had gone there for a wild weekend as Gus Greenbaum's special guest.

Goldwater had another friend in Arizona, a man named Bill Nelson, who had come to serve as something of an unofficial adviser and sounding board for the senator as he made his way through the political jungle in his home state and in Washington. In the summer of '55, as Gus Greenbaum was getting ready to return to Vegas for his new assignment, and was looking to fill some key positions on his staff, Senator Goldwater recommended Bill Nelson for a job. Greenbaum, too, was impressed with Nelson's smarts and good ideas, and he took him on. Together the casino boss and his new assistant headed off to Nevada.

It was not long before certain people in Las Vegas came to realize that Bill Nelson, Senator Goldwater's good friend and Gus Greenbaum's new man at the Riv, was actually Willie Bioff, the former pimp, extortionist, union organizer. And squealer.

After their 1943 testimony in the trial of Rosselli, Ricca, and the rest of them, Willie Bioff and George Browne had been sent back to prison for a brief stay before being given an early release as payment for their crucial assistance in the gangsters' prosecution. The Justice Department sent them into hiding with new identities, new residences far from their old stomping grounds. Browne disappeared into his reassigned life in a small Iowa farm town, and was never heard from again. Bioff was settled in an upscale Phoenix suburb, posing as a wealthy semiretired businessman.*

As years went by "Bill Nelson" became a more visible member of the community, reasserting his talent as a self-promoter and befriending a number of prominent Arizonans. It had been more than twelve years since he had testified in that New York courtroom, and it was likely he believed that enough time had passed for him to be forgotten, if not forgiven, should he ever bump into anyone from the old days. In his favor was the fact that by 1955 most of the men he'd sent to prison were no longer alive. Frank Nitti, of course, had eaten a bullet before the trial began. Phil D'Andrea had died of assorted illnesses in 1952, at the age of sixty. Charlie Gioe and Francis Maritote (aka "Frank Diamond") had been troublesome figures in the years since their parole, talking too much and making problematic business deals of which the Outfit higher-ups did not approve. Gioe was executed in a friend's car in the summer of '54, and Maritote shotgunned a few days later as he was coming out of his garage. Louis Campagna died of a heart attack in May '55 after reeling in a grouper while fishing off

---

* Nick Circella, the other member of the Mob's three IATSE musketeers, served his full prison term without request for parole; when the government attempted to deport him to Italy, he voluntarily departed the United States, eventually settling in Mexico and, as far as is known, never coming back.

the coast of Miami; he was fifty-four. That left just Paul Ricca, Johnny Rosselli, and Louis Kaufman still living among the group Willie Bioff had betrayed, and the New Jersey–based Kaufman no longer kept up with his old associates. Willie must have thought the odds of escaping retribution were getting better every year. His arrogant thinking had reasserted itself. Why *not* take a cushy job in Las Vegas? Nobody there would recognize him.

Whether Johnny Rosselli was the man who fingered Willie the Rat, as some believe—perhaps too perfect a twist of fate—or if, as others say, it was someone else who spotted him is not certain. But word of the discovery was sent on to Chicago, and Paul Ricca and his colleagues pondered the news.

On November 4, 1955, Willie Bioff was home in Phoenix for a visit (having flown back from Vegas with Barry Goldwater in the senator's private plane). That morning he came out the door of his house on East Bethany Road, waved good-bye to his wife, and climbed into his pickup truck in the driveway. Some eight sticks of dynamite were wired to the truck's starter. When Willie turned the ignition the wire sparked, the truck exploded. An ear-splitting boom thundered through the valley, and windows for blocks around shattered in a symphony of broken glass. The pickup twisted in flame and frenzy and fired hunks of metal into the sky. Bioff's body was propelled through space in assorted pieces, crispy limbs landing in the drive and his torso and most of his head coming to rest in the shade of a grapefruit tree.

2

Jack Dragna was dead.

Gone in a cheap motel room, toothless in pink pajamas.

An autopsy was performed on the sixty-five-year-old criminal. He was found to have had heart and kidney disease, and was suffering from probable cerebral arteriosclerosis due to advanced hardening of the arteries in his brain. A rare conclusion for someone in Jack's line of work: death by natural causes.

For the West Coast it was the end of an era. Jack Dragna, the longest-reigning boss of organized crime in Los Angeles history, was no more. His legacy was still to be sorted out. As a gang leader he had not achieved the legendary status and recognition of others of his generation, the national headlines and silver-screen portrayals. He'd kept business—and risk—at a manageable size, never flying too high. He was no visionary to compare with Capone or Luciano, no empire builder. But Capone and Luciano had spent most of their good years in prison or twiddling their thumbs in exile. Dragna had ruled his piece of the country for a quarter of a century, challenged, at times sharing the spoils, but never defeated. The government had tried its best in the last years, but even that showdown had ended in a draw.

For Johnny Rosselli the death of Jack Dragna was the end of a friendship and a partnership of thirty years' duration. More than that. Since long ago cutting off direct contact with his own blood relations, the Dragnas—along with the Breens—were the closest thing he'd had to family. Jack was his big brother, not the wisest of men, too cautious in his last years, satisfied with booze and a woman and some cash, but loyal, strong, dependable to the end. Loved and now mourned.

Dragna dead and Tony Cornero cashing out just seven months earlier. For Johnny, midlife markers. The past turning to dust, the future growing smaller.

The Los Angeles Family needed a leader. They had been at a standstill for some time, disrupted by Dragna's legal problems, held up by the continuing police crackdown. There were several strong candidates for the job, but protocol favored Jack's brother Tom, or his longtime underboss, Momo Adamo. They were older, traditionalists, figures who would carry on in Jack's footsteps. The men of honor voted. The position went to a dark horse: Frank DeSimone, upper-world criminal attorney and sub rosa criminal, son of one-time LA don Rosario DeSimone. It was figured the majority wanted a fresh perspective for the job, someone younger, somebody with an education. DeSimone was forty-seven, American born (Pueblo, Colorado), a graduate of the University of Southern California Law School.

Then again, maybe he had stolen the job. There were immediate grumbles of dissatisfaction, muted complaints that DeSimone bought some votes or otherwise pulled a fast one. Both Jimmy Fratianno and Frank Bompensiero—both in prison at the time—would later charge that the lawyer falsely claimed to have had their backing.

DeSimone was known as a low-key character, circumspect and well-mannered. Maybe he had just been waiting for a chance to let his inner tyrant come out. Upon taking the leadership position he became abrasive and demanding. He was especially rough on the guys who had been the closest to Jack Dragna. Brother Tom decided to retire rather than deal with it. Momo Adamo did not get out so easy. He had expected to become boss and was hardest hit by what happened. He'd shown his dissatisfaction in one way or another, and DeSimone decided to exert his authority, teach a lesson. He demeaned him, demoted him. Adamo went back to San Diego with his tail between his legs. He was an old-school Sicilian, proud, emotional. His wife, Marie, was a flirtatious beauty. A rumor went around that Marie was cheating on Momo. If that was true, and with Momo already in his agitated state of mind, it might have been enough to explain what happened next. Back in San Diego, Adamo confronted his wife in their home and shot her through the head. Then he turned the gun around and killed himself.

Marie survived. She recovered, but she refused to recall her husband's last words or to offer a motive for his actions. Another rumor made the rounds. Momo Adamo had offended DeSimone, and it was decided that he had to be punished. The new boss had him brought in to LA with his wife. He was bound and gagged, held at gunpoint. He was made to kneel there and watch while Frank DeSimone himself assaulted and raped Marie Adamo. Unable to live with the humiliation, Momo had gone home with Marie and taken out his pistol.

The story, though persistent, seemed absurd on the face of it. Even with DeSimone's new tough-guy image it wasn't in his psyche to pull off such an act, and not even a boss got away with doing that to a made man's wife. There would be permanent consequences. Still, the story had legs, crazy sounding or not, which indicated that some people disliked the new leader so much that they repeated it knowing it wasn't true.

Johnny hadn't voted for anybody. Maybe he was still feeling the loss of Jack, didn't want to know. Now DeSimone was looking like a mistake. He had been a good-enough mouthpiece, back in the day. But running a mob was something else. Just being smart or showing you were tough was not enough. It took a certain presence, a strength of character, to be a leader of men.

He made a decision. No way could he work with an asshole like DeSimone. It was time to change his luck.

For a decade the Chicago Outfit had been jointly ruled by Paul Ricca and Tony "Joe Batters" Accardo, two shrewd, heavy-duty old crooks rooted in the original Capone gang in the Roaring Twenties. They ran things with sharp minds and iron fists, but kept their heads down while doing it, stuck to business and avoided public exposure. It had worked well for years but by the midfifties they were catching heat in the post-Kefauver stepped-up pursuit of organized crime. The government's usual battle plan: Accardo was being hounded for tax evasion, while Ricca was fighting the tax men and INS efforts to deport him to Italy. They needed to fade. Pretend to retire, give someone else the glory. Giancana had been

groomed for the job. He was commanding, ruthless, and full of
ideas. And if he fucked it up they would remove him in a heart-
beat.

Accardo had shown little interest in Las Vegas when the boom
started. It just looked too good to be true. How long could it last
before the G shut it all down? But Washington did not interfere.
Now Chicago was trying to make up for lost time. Giancana was
running things and unlike Joe Batters, Giancana couldn't get enough
of Vegas. He liked the lights, the noise, the celebs, the women, the
money. By '56 the Outfit was heavily invested in the Nevada oasis,
and everybody liked the money.

Las Vegas had been established as an "open city"—no one mob
could claim it. There were so many factions now holding big and
small pieces of the casinos that at some joints the skim had to be
divided twelve ways. Every gang worried about getting their fair
share. Each one sent their own man or two to keep an eye on things.
This meant twenty or thirty hoodlums in town, all working for different mobs, each wanting to make sure nothing got past him and
he didn't disappoint his boss back home. With so many hoods working for so many different interests, it was easy to imagine the place
degenerating into warring camps, going the way of Prohibition Chicago. (The Outfit's own "watchman" in Vegas, a sociopath named
Marshall Caifano, brought more havoc than order to the town; after
an argument over comps at the independently owned El Rancho
casino resort—a line of credit and free drinks denied—he set a fire
that burned the place to the ground.) There was too much at risk.
A referendum in Carson City or DC and the whole gold mine could
be closed. The major powers—the Outfit, Lansky, Costello,
Dalitz—imposed a peace plan for Las Vegas. A kinder, gentler Sin
City. The same rules for everybody. It remained open to all, anyone was welcome to invest. Anybody sending their soldiers to town
was responsible for their good behavior. The local law officers
were to be respected. Tourists and customers were sacrosanct. If

somebody had to be punished it was to be done with discretion. If somebody had to be clipped it was to be done out of town, preferably out of state. Any business disputes were to be settled by discussion and arbitration. There would be honor among thieves. It was never too late.

In the last months of '56 Johnny met several times with Sam Giancana. He talked about getting away from Los Angeles. Giancana showed interest in working with him. Giancana knew Johnny's history. He'd been a liaison with Chicago for thirty years and proved his worth long ago. Ricca had always sung his praises (Accardo's opinion was less positive, a resentment that went back to Al Capone days). Sam told him they were looking for somebody for Las Vegas. Somebody to oversee their interests. A troubleshooter. A mediator. Somebody who could keep people in line, keep people happy.

He went to see DeSimone.

"Frank, as of now, I'm putting it on record," Johnny said. "I want to transfer to Chicago."

"You checked this out with Giancana?" DeSimone said.

"Yeah," Johnny said. "I've talked to Sam."

DeSimone didn't know Giancana. Compared with Johnny's connections across the country, DeSimone didn't know anybody. It was never going to be easy getting out of Rosselli's shade. He would be glad to see the eminent gangster moving on.

Las Vegas in 1957 was at the top of its game. A neon kingdom visible from the moon. Money pouring down like rain. Big-budgeted expansion was ongoing along the once-barren highway beyond the city, the openings of the monumental Tropicana and Stardust casino resorts just ahead. That was the year the ultracorrupt James Riddle Hoffa was elected president of the International Brotherhood of Teamsters, the union of more than one million truck drivers and laborers, and the vast treasury of the Teamsters Central States Pension Fund opened wide to the Mob and to casino investments, ensuring endless underworld control and expansion in the gambling capital of the world.

Construction and business had doubled, then tripled in size since the start of the decade. Downtown was wall-to-wall gambling joints, and the Strip reached almost to the airport. It was an entertainment center to dwarf Broadway or the West End, road signage heralding the biggest names in showbiz. The Stardust would be the largest casino hotel in the world and the first to target the prosperous midcentury American middle class with its two-week vacations and disposable cash. The growing popularity of air travel and the beginning of the jet age now brought one million visitors a year to McCarran International Airport.

Johnny came back at the beginning of the new year, taking a junior suite (350 A/B) at the Desert Inn. The requirements of the Outfit job had been only vaguely defined. He was to do what needed doing. And better to do it carefully. There were inherent risks when you put yourself between mobsters and millions of dollars. A mistake in judgment could be fatal.

He was sent to oversee the team preparing the Tropicana casino resort for its scheduled April opening. The Trop was a no-expense-spared project fronted by Ben Jaffe of the Fontainebleau Miami Beach, backed by a veritable United Nations of secret Mob interests. Designed by the Miami architect M. Tony Sherman in a neon-festooned, tropic-modern style, it was a complex construction containing a sprawling casino, three hundred rooms and suites, a sixty-foot-high fountain, exotic landscaping, and an Olympic-size fan-shaped swimming pool with music piped underwater in stereo. There had been cost overruns and problems finding a casino manager acceptable to the State Gaming Control Board. As they approached the deadline there were additional last-minute delays, suspicions, and setbacks, including a shortage of available labor and equipment due to the renewed work on the still-not-completed Stardust (ill-fated Tony Cornero's dream venture) and several other constructions in progress. Johnny met with various factions, sorting through the confusion, solving problems, cooling heads. He filled a number of key positions on the casino staff, and brought in Monte Proser—the former operator of the Copacabana and La Vie en Rose nightclubs in New York—to produce the resort's live entertainment. He arranged to have his friend Alex Perino oversee the fine dining room (for a fee of three thousand dollars a month).* He made a similar arrangement for his Beverly Hills barber, Harry Drucker, who set up a men's salon on the hotel midway. Johnny moved into the hotel, sharing a suite with Monte Proser.

The Trop opened on April 4, 1957, to great excitement. The mayor of Las Vegas, the lieutenant governor of Nevada ("It Girl" Clara Bow's husband, Rex Bell), and numerous celebrities and Hollywood stars came to the ribbon-cutting ceremonies, and more than twelve thousand visitors passed through the mosaic-tiled entrance the first night (though actual owners, such as Frank Costello, Meyer Lansky, the Chicago Outfit, and New Orleans don Carlos Marcello, were nowhere in sight). The Red Norvo Trio performed in the Showcase Lounge, and in the Theatre-Restaurant (featuring "the world's largest nightclub stage") Monte Proser's quarter-million-dollar Tropicana Revue offered singing star Eddie Fisher, Nat Brandwynne and his Orchestra, scores of dancers and long-legged showgirls, outsize tropical scenery, and an original music score by Gordon Jenkins.

The press wrote breathless raves of the new resort, calling it "lavish," "fantastic," and "spectacularly beautiful," the *Vegas Sun* even

---

* Perino's Gourmet Room would offer "regal service and dining under the personal supervision of Alexander Perino and in a setting of continental charm and beauty [making] this richly appointed room one of the world's truly distinguished restaurants. Cocktails at 5. Dinners from 6."

heaping praise on the backstage facilities, dementedly declaring the dressing rooms "unsurpassed in the history of show business." The Tropicana was an immediate and great success, the huge take in the casino making for record-breaking profits on and off the books. The secret sharers in Chicago, New York, New Orleans, and the rest were very happy. For his efforts—having served in various capacities up to the successful launch—Johnny Rosselli was rewarded with the parking concession, the gift shop, a percentage of the entertainment budget, and a small taste of the skim. He reckoned his annual share would come to the mid-six figures.

There was one little bump in the road, after the Trop had been open about a month.

Tropicana partner Frank Costello, acting boss of the Luciano crime family, had been having a run of bad luck since his hand-jive performance and walkout during the televised Kefauver hearings. He'd done time on three convictions, one for contempt of Congress and two for tax evasion. With Luciano in permanent exile and Costello distracted, fighting the law, in and out of stir, capo and former Luciano underboss Vito Genovese decided the time had come for a change in leadership. He would take back his rightful place at the top. When Costello was released from prison in the spring of '57, Vito made his play.

On May 2, as the Mob leader crossed the lobby of his West Side apartment building in New York City a Genovese enforcer named Vinnie "the Chin" Gigante rushed him with a .38 revolver, shouting, "This is for you, Frank!" He shot Costello once in the head, then ran away, thinking he'd done the job.*

The bullet barely touched skin. Medics treated Costello for a

---

* Later a boss, Gigante was known as "the Oddfather," spending decades trying to evade criminal prosecution with a self-styled "crazy act," wander-

superficial wound behind his right ear. Police asked questions. Costello said he knew nothing about nothing. They grabbed his jacket and picked the pockets. In one they found a slip of paper with hand-scribbled notations marked *"Gross casino wins"* at the top, followed by dates, dollar amounts, names, initials. Costello claimed he'd never seen the thing before. Forensic investigators traced it to Las Vegas, followed the monetary figures to the Tropicana, and matched the handwriting to that of casino manager Lou Lederer. Agents descended on the casino, scrutinizing the books, cross-checking personnel files, and questioning staffers, rooting around for more evidence of gangland connections. The gaming board forced Lederer to resign, and others were forced to give up direct association with the property. Johnny was made to vacate his suite at the hotel. (He went back to the Desert Inn for a while, then leased apartment 106 at the Diplomat on Paradise Road, an enclosed two-story complex that catered to employees from the Strip, many of them dancers and showgirls sharing apartments.)

The Costello thing meant a lot of exposure and risk on account of some scribbled notes on a paper, and it showed on what kind of thin ice Las Vegas floated. Everybody took it as a lesson learned: You had to be extracareful. But the law did not uncover the Trop's deeper secrets. The Mob's business model held: the shields, the unwritten deals, the skim. The law backed off for now. The Tropicana went on its way, remaining a huge moneymaker for years to come.

After Johnny's good work on the launch, Chicago's support became wholehearted. They let it be known: This is our guy, with whom

---

ing the Manhattan streets in a bathrobe and slippers and jabbering to himself; it worked until it didn't, and he died in prison.

we are well pleased. New York was good with it. Johnny was liked and trusted by almost everybody who counted. It was a done deal.

His position in Vegas had no formal title. There had never been such a job. He was an adviser and problem solver. He put people together, put out fires, dispensed wisdom. If asked, he would describe himself as a "strategist" (the word went on his business cards). He earned a rep for fairness, for good judgment, for a judicious use of power. He didn't need a title, as things worked out. His name alone carried its own weight. In that time, the late fifties, early sixties, if you needed a favor, wanted to do business, had a complaint to be resolved, the maxim in Las Vegas was: "Go see Johnny."

His office as such was one or another of the Desert Inn's opulent public spaces, the golf club in the morning, on the course or at his table looking over the eighteenth green, afternoons by the hotel swimming pool, with iced vodka and a telephone, his shaded chaise angled for an unobstructed view of sunbathing females, evenings (according to Reid and Demaris) devoted to "twisting, romancing and drinking." In these agreeable settings he conducted much of his daily business, in sotto voce meetings, negotiations, phone calls to and from LA, New York, Chicago.

The casino owners didn't care how he spent his day as long as the money kept rolling in. It did, and with less stress than ever before. The locals were satisfied, the politicians were placated, and the Feds had been kept at bay. Everybody was happy. Including Johnny. For every piece of business that went through his hands— real estate, ice machines, parking lots, air-freighted lobsters, Jayne Mansfield (whose striptease revue, *House of Love*, he brought to the Trop in '58)—there were percentages, kickbacks, finders' fees. Through his secret ownership of Monte Proser Productions (the articles of incorporation were filed on September 5, 1957, with the directors listed as Monte Proser and the ever-handy Joseph I. Breen Jr.) he booked the showroom talent at several of the resorts and was in for a piece of every dollar (10 percent off the top) paid

to the performers. Under the corporate name of Nevada Concessions Inc., with official partners Lou Lederer and again Joe Breen,
he had a part of various large and small enterprises in business with
the Tropicana and other casinos. Over time he came to control a
reservations agency, a parking lot, several lobby concessions, and
supplied a brand of playing cards to the casinos (alas, the card faces
smudged to the touch and were quickly withdrawn). In addition to
these legit cash streams were the sizable piles he received from the
casino skim, first at the Tropicana, then the Stardust, and one or
two more at different periods of time, all completely tax free.

"I'm pulling fifteen, twenty grand under the table every month,"
he told his friend Jimmy Fratianno (according to Ovid Demaris's
The Last Mafioso). "They're skimming the shit out of [those]
joints. . . . I've never seen so much money. . . . The money's pouring in like there's no tomorrow. Like it's burning fucking holes in
the suckers' pockets.

"Everything nice and cool. Nothing flashy. I settle beefs but
everything's done in a gentlemanly manner. I tip good. I gamble
here and there, lose five, ten grand . . . spreading the good will
around, play lots of golf, eat good food, and see more cunts. . . .

"*I'm fucking all these broads*," he told Fratianno over gnocchi,
in a voice reserved for the most sacred matters. "Not chorus girls,
but the stars. You've never seen nothing like it. . . ."

Jimmy agreed, he had not. He beamed with admiration for his
friend.

"*You're on top of the world!*"

3

Jeanne (pronounced *Jeannie*) Carmen was a cotton-picking country
girl from Paragould, Arkansas, a beautiful, sexy, green-eyed brunette (later, a green-eyed platinum blonde) with a voluptuous shape

and "legs"—said a showbiz columnist—"from here to eternity." She'd run away from home as a young teenager, ending up in New York City, finding work in the chorus line of a Broadway musical starring Bert Lahr, then as a calendar pinup and a "cheesecake" model (working with the legendary Bettie Page) in magazines with titles like *Wink*, *Titter*, and *Beauty Parade*.

A modeling job for a television spot with the famous trick-shot golfer Jack Redmond led to the discovery of Jeanne's theretofore unknown talent for the game. She had an astonishing natural gift, could drive, pitch, and putt like a pro, and with a little coaching could pull off Jack's legendary trick shots, including his dangerous showstopper, driving a ball at full swing off a prostrate volunteer's lips. And she did it in high heels and a short skirt, something Jack Redmond had never even attempted.

Knowing a good thing when he saw one, Redmond signed her up as an added attraction for his Eastern Seaboard tour of country clubs and county fairs. Jeanne's new husband tagged along on the tour, a bad idea as Redmond fell in love with Jeanne and the two men did nothing but fight.

They'd been on the road for some time. They were driving late at night on this occasion. "Driving to our next gig in Florida," Jeanne Carmen remembered. "Jack Redmond, and my husband, and me. My husband sat in the back seat, smoking his cigars, shooting his mouth off, and making us crazy. We were all arguing, really getting into it. It went on and on. It was awful. All of a sudden Jack stopped the car. He pulled us both out of the car. He grabbed our bags and threw them out. They went into a ditch. And he drove away.

"It was the middle of nowhere. Pitch dark. My husband had to crawl into the ditch to get the bags back, and I sat by the road telling him how to do it. I sat there wondering what we were going to do next, and why did this happen to me? We'd been there a little while when a car came along. It slowed to a stop. I thought: What next? The driver got out and came around the front of the car. I could see him lit up in the headlights for a second. He looked like an angel, white hair, very dapper, wearing a beautiful white suit. He came over and looked at me and says, 'Do you need a ride?'

"My husband cuts in, says, 'Yeah, sure we need a ride, what do you think?'

"The man in the white suit says to my husband, 'I wasn't talking to you, pal.' He comes over and introduces himself to me. He says, 'My name's Johnny.' And he helps me up, opens the car door and sits me in the front seat with him while my husband got the bags and climbed into the backseat. And off we go.

"We'd been driving for a while when my husband said something very vulgar that he had to do. We finally saw some all-night diner up ahead and he shouted to stop the car so he could go into the restaurant and use the facilities. We pulled into the driveway. He ran inside while we just sat there in the car—Johnny and me— alone in the front seat. We could see my husband inside the place, he's running around, he runs in one direction, then he comes back, and he runs the other way.

"We watched this scene, and then Johnny looks at me and says, 'Are you going to stay with this guy?'

"I say, 'Not if I can help it.'

"He nodded. That was it. He hit the accelerator. And we were gone."

They drove all night, heading west.

"It didn't occur to me to be afraid of him. My life was pretty strange. I left home before I was fourteen. You learn to take care of yourself. I hitchhiked alone from St. Louis to New York. Maybe I was lucky. And I was ready for anything. I was strong and tough. I never took any BS from men.

"But Johnny was fine. He was a gentleman. Very impressive. Good-looking. His presence was a movie star presence. Confidence galore. You saw that more than anything. I had no idea he was a gangster or anything about that. Not yet. I just thought he was an interesting guy who picked me up on the road."

Johnny had played a lot of golf in his time and liked the game. He was amazed and amused by Jeanne's story of her newly discovered golfing mastery and her traveling trick-shot performances. She showed Johnny an article about herself in the newspaper. She told him how they'd put together the act, how Jack Redmond had rehearsed her to come out of the audience pretending she'd never touched a golf club, and then she would startle the crowd when she started to hit the balls around and make those crazy shots. Johnny laughed. That was a pretty good gag. He wanted to see for himself how she played, and somewhere along the way they found a golf course and Jeanne showed him what she could do. Johnny was delighted.

He worked it all out while they crossed the country. They were going to have fun, he told her. And they were going to make a lot of money.

When they reached Las Vegas, Johnny checked them into the Desert Inn.

"He took me to the best place for dinner," Jeanne remembered. "Then he took me back to the hotel. He said, 'Get your ass in bed. We've got a big game tomorrow.'"

On the resort grounds beyond the casino hotel was the DI's eighteen-hole golf club, one of the top courses in the country. It was the setting of the annual PGA Tournament of Champions. And it attracted some of the wealthiest bad golfers a con man could hope to meet.

"It worked like this: I would take a table inside or out in the sun where everybody could see me. Johnny would be at the bar.

He'd get into a conversation with this one or that one. He was completely prepared. He had people—caddies, bartenders, hotel people—tell him who was coming in, what they were worth, what kind of a golfer. He was looking for out of towners, rich country club types. He'd get talking with one of these guys, have a couple of drinks. Johnny would start needling the guy, he bet 'even a girl could beat him,' that kind of thing. And he'd point to me and say, 'I bet that girl over there reading a book . . . I saw her playing here. I bet even she's a better golfer than you.' He was so clever about it. They had no idea it was a setup. And they'd come over and introduce themselves. And the guy would say something like, 'She looks like she could kill me in bed, but she can't beat me at golf.' And I'd say, 'Okay mister, I'll give it a shot.' And they'd laugh and make a big bet. Lots of money. And sometimes there'd be other guys there and they wanted to bet too. And Johnny would say 'Sure. I'll take it. . . .' And he'd say to me, 'Gee, young lady, I hope you can play a little.'

"The first few holes I'd dump it. Like we planned. I'd hit it in the trees, in the water. The rich guys would try not to laugh. And Johnny would say, 'She's a little off her game. She's gonna be fine.' And they'd laugh some more and Johnny'd act annoyed and say, 'I have faith in this girl. Anybody want to double their bet just say so.' And the money went way up. And then, the next thing you know I started playing for real. I hit the ball straight down the middle. They'd hang their mouths open and I'd be so happy, tell them, 'My, this game is so easy!'

"We split everything fifty-fifty. I hadn't expected him to do that. Everything right down the middle. I thought that was pretty cool of him. Of course, I was doing the hard work and he couldn't have done it without me, but I couldn't have found these guys either. It was a good deal. And that's how it worked. We did it again the next day, and the next. There was no end to these suckers who thought no woman could ever beat them at golf. We'd start in the morning and go all day if we could. I was always ready. Sometimes the bets were huge. I'd never seen so much money.

"Johnny worried I'd feel bad about ripping them off. He said, 'Carmen, remember, we're never going to take a nice guy. Or somebody can't afford it.' He said, 'We never take the nice guys, only the bastards.' And I said, 'Whatever. I don't care. I'll take them all.'

"We had a lot of fun. We played golf in the day. And we went out every night. Everywhere we went they knew John. We got the best tables, the best service. Nobody ever gave him a check. But he'd leave a hundred-to-two-hundred-dollar tip. Sometimes one of his pals from Chicago or New York would come by and sit and chat. Sam Giancana, though he used another name. People like that. Nobody ever talked business. They were sweethearts to me. Giancana was a pussycat. Of course, maybe they went out and killed somebody later, but you wouldn't know it.

"We went to all the shows. Except for Liberace. Johnny wouldn't go near him. He said he'd never live it down. He had that macho man prejudice. I wanted to see Liberace and he just refused to consider it. But he loved Keely Smith and Louis Prima. We went to see them every night. And Frank Sinatra. He was playing at the Sands then. Johnny loved Frank Sinatra. To Johnny, Frank Sinatra was the greatest singer who ever opened his mouth. And they were friends. He wanted to introduce me. Okay, whatever. We went backstage and it was all hugs and kisses between the two of them. So much hugging, I don't know why he was afraid of Liberace! And Johnny introduced me. Frank's eyes went *boing*. I was pretty well-stacked in those days.

"After a while I think the golf thing dried up. Word started to get around maybe. One time a guy lost and he wouldn't pay off. He started yelling I was a shill. He'd been cheated. Johnny just shrugged. Told him to please lower his voice. Johnny was always cool, never got excited. But later he got the money. He had a couple of his boys take the guy up to the roof of the Desert Inn and told him they were going to throw him off if he didn't pay.

"That was about the time I left Las Vegas. Frank took me away. I was a pretty free spirit in those days. I got bored easily. And Frank said, 'Come on, baby, let's go to Hollywood.' And I said, 'Okay, Frank. Let's go to Hollywood.'

"And I didn't see Johnny again for quite some time."

4

In New York City, Vito Genovese's moment had come.

A rising star of the Syndicate in the 1930s, underboss to Lucky Luciano, he'd lost his place in the hierarchy when a murder charge forced him to escape from New York and flee to Italy. Years later, after the Allied invasion, he'd been captured by U.S. troops and repatriated to New York. He was to be prosecuted on the old homicide rap. But then one of the chief witnesses in the case died a mysterious death in his jail cell, of all places, then a second witness was shot to death in New Jersey, of all places, and the court had no choice but to drop the charges and release Mr. Genovese.

Vito's return to the American Mob was not a good fit. He disdained working under the "acting" leadership of Frank Costello, believing the position belonged to him. In the midfifties the Syndicate/Mafia families in New York became caught up in a growing rivalry between the "conservative" and "liberal" factions, and there was tension and uncertainty all about. Vito sensed the time was ripe for decisive action: He ordered the hit on Costello. The delegated assassin, Vinnie the Chin, blew it, his clumsy shot merely ruffling the man's scalp. But the inept attempt was enough. Frank surrendered, agreed to retire. He even forgave the apologetic Gigante.

Genovese lined up supporters for his power grab, including

Meyer Lansky and Carlo Gambino, underboss to Costello ally Albert Anastasia. Genovese wanted possible rival Anastasia gone, and Lansky also wanted Albert out of the way on account of the shit he was stirring in Havana. On October 25, 1957, Anastasia was being groomed at the Seventh Avenue Park Sheraton barber shop, swathed in hot towels, when gunmen charged in and shot him to death.* The bloody Anastasia rubout made the news from coast to coast. Now the whole national syndicate sat up and took notice: What the hell was happening in New York?

To answer this and a host of other pressing questions, Genovese called for a summit meeting, a national conference of Mob leaders. If all went well Vito hoped the get-together would serve as the perfect setting to announce his self-promotion, this one to the monarchic position Charlie Lucky had always disdained on principle: "the boss of the bosses."

Several locations had been considered for the big meeting—Genovese's coming-out party—but Buffalo, New York, crime boss Stefano Magaddino made a convincing case—seconded by Joe Bonanno—for the secluded, rambling estate of Northeast Mob boss "Joe the Barber" Barbera in upstate Apalachin, New York, near the Pennsylvania border. It was perfect. They could get together in the serene wooded landscape, relax, talk business, grill some meat. Barbera himself thought it a bad idea. He'd had a little feud with a local cop and was worried the guy would be keeping an eye out. Magaddino told him to sack up. The gathering was set for mid-November. Among those RSVPing were New Yorkers Vito Genovese, Carlo Gambino, Joe Bonanno, Bonanno underboss Carmine Galante, Gaetano Lucchese, Gambino underboss Joe Biondo, Gambino captain Paul "Big Paul" Castellano, Joe Profaci; Buffalino

---

* The barber chair was later bought by a collector for seven grand.

capos Dominick Alaimo, Dave Ostico, Ignatius Cannone, Buffalo soldier Salvatore "Vicious" Trivalino; Frank "the Cheeseman" Cucchiara from Boston; Philly boss Joe Ida and his underboss Dominick Olivetto; Pittsburgh's LaRocca Family captains Mike Genovese and Kelly Mannarino; Cleveland's big boss, John Scalish, and his consigliere John DeMarco; Chicago's Sam Giancana; Joe Zerilli of Detroit; Montreal's Louis Greco and Pep Cotroni; Denver, Colorado, boss Jim "Black Jim" Colletti; Florida's Santo Trafficante Jr.; Jimmy Civillo of Dallas; James "Jimmy the Hat" Lanza of San Francisco; from Los Angeles, Frank DeSimone. . . . And another eighty or so more from across the country, plus several from the motherland, representatives of Sicilian clans coming to discuss ways of improving the narcotics trade.

In mid-November the crime figures converged on the rural meeting place. It was not quite as secluded as they had thought. Locals noticed the number of gleaming new Cadillacs and Chryslers rolling through town, out-of-state license plates on many of them. State troopers traced the cars to the Barbera place, where they found a growing party in progress. The lawmen spent most of Wednesday, November 13, observing the goings-on and writing down plate numbers. On Thursday they were joined by backup from area police departments and a pair of Treasury agents. They set up roadblocks on McFall Road beyond the estate entrance. The soiree was in full swing, some of the gangsters outside in the yard and gathered around the barbecue pit. When they saw the cops coming the Mob men panicked. Some rushed to their cars, some jumped out of windows and ran for the trees. Most were still inside the house when the police got there. More than sixty of the visitors to Apalachin were arrested. The local lockup could not contain all of them. The jailed mobsters refused to cooperate with the cops and were charged with obstruction of justice.

Sam Giancana had been one of those who'd managed to escape, as he told Johnny Rosselli (overheard by Sam's daughter Antoinette, and recalled in her memoir), detailing the whole mortifying adventure. *"The cops start grabbing everyone,"* said the Outfit boss. "I took off like I was some sort of *gazelle* out the back door. I mean I ran like I was doing the hundred-yard dash in the Olympics! I made the woods in the back. When it was dark and safe I got the hell outta there. I *told* that jerk in Buffalo that we shouldn't have the meeting in that *goddam place!*" (Eavesdropping, Antoinette Giancana nearly burst out laughing as she listened, trying to picture her citified father in his gazelle-like sprint through the woods.)

The debacle was an embarrassing public exposure of the Mob elite, having their names printed in nationwide reports and many facing possible criminal prosecution. There was an angry backlash against the guys who'd pushed for Apalachin. Somebody tossed a hand grenade through the window of Stefano Magaddino's home outside Buffalo. Vito Genovese, who wanted the summit meeting to be about him, got his wish. Many held him to blame for what happened. The would-be boss of bosses saw his grand ambitions cut short. Just eight months after Appalachin the ambitious don was busted on drug-trafficking charges. Many believed he had been set up as a punishment by one or more of his peers. Genovese went to prison in 1959—attempting with only modest success to rule from his cell. He died there ten years later.

The law could not do much with those arrested at Apalachin once the gangsters' attorneys got to work, the charges either thrown out or the convictions overturned on appeal. But the consequences of the raid on the Mob's backwoods convention were nonetheless considerable, proving more ruinous to organized crime in America than all the prior government commissions and police crackdowns combined.

For decades J. Edgar Hoover had refused to credit the very existence of organized crime. In all the years of the national crime syndicate's maturation and the growing power of the American Mafia, even after the outright public exposure by the Kefauver hearings, the FBI chief had remained firm in his resolve, devoting few if any Bureau resources to tracking the Mob. Hoover's rationale was esoteric and inconsistent. He resisted the idea of using the FBI as a "national police force" (though his self-directed war on radical politics belied this; in the 1940s and 1950s there was a "Communist Affairs" section at every Bureau office). He was said to believe that racketeering and most other Mob crimes—even with evidence of interstate activity—were matters for local law enforcement alone. Some said he feared his agents' corruption by wealthy gangsters. Or that he considered gambling a victimless crime and personally loved to play the horses. And there was the most sensational of rumored reasons for his indulgent stance: that the director was subject to blackmail by one or another Syndicate big shot (Meyer Lansky in the most popular version of the story), the Mob having obtained hidden camera photos of Hoover in an oral-genital embrace with his associate director, Clyde Tolson. Whichever the actual motive, if any of these, the result was the same: Hoover's hands-off policy had helped to make life easier for organized crime for more than two decades.

The events at Apalachin were an embarrassment to the Bureau, exposing the lack of attention to organized crime in a single head-lined blow. How was it that more than one hundred major crime figures had come from across the country (and over the borders!) to a once-in-a-lifetime gangster convention and the FBI had known nothing about it? And what was worse, the credit for discovering this unholy summit had gone to a couple of rural state troopers.

Hoover's see-no-evil response to organized crime became I-see-the-light. Some said he was summoned for a private rebuke and a threat to his federal sinecure by President Eisenhower himself, told to do his job or get out. Within days of Apalachin, the FBI chief had reversed his policy in full. The Bureau began an immediate, high-priority, fully funded effort to research, monitor, and effect the prosecution of the major syndicate criminals. After so long looking the other way, the FBI would now turn upon the Mob a powerful, relentless glare.

The director's key strategy became a program to which he gave the name "Top Hoodlum." The program required agents in every field office and resident agency in the country to produce a list of active organized crime figures in their area, and for each name on the list they were to gather intelligence data and evidence of prosecutable offenses. Major names would merit extra manpower and increased resources. Whatever it took, up to and including illegal actions. Whatever it took to crush them and to put them away.

It was an intrepid plan on Hoover's part, a comprehensive response to racketeers not seen since the federal decision to take down Capone.

By Christmastime the Los Angeles office had its Top Hoodlum program up and running, with a list of significant area gangsters targeted for investigation and prosecution. At the top of the list was Johnny Rosselli.

9

THE SPY WHO CAME
IN FROM THE POOL

For organized crime in America the ignited interest of the Federal Bureau of Investigation meant an unprecedented level of scrutiny and peril. The Top Hoodlum program put hundreds of agents into a cooperative, nationwide operation. Targeted individuals would be kept under surveillance at all times and anywhere they went, with field office agents ready to engage with criminals in every part of the country. All information was cross-filed in Washington, growing the Bureau's big-picture database of criminal associates and organizational alliances. The Bureau, when required, could be an unwavering adversary. It could be ruthless. The world war and national self-interest had encouraged a lowering of legal and ethical standards in the FBI's search for enemy spies, saboteurs, fifth columnists. Agents then routinely violated the Fourth Amendment of the Constitution, and broke assorted other laws and protections without warrant or just cause. Director Hoover had erased many of the restrictions of his office, and the illegal actions were to be perpetuated in the subsequent Cold War and in the

pursuit of assorted domestic dissidents. Now it was the Mob's turn
to see the Bureau's unruly side.

The investigation of Johnny Rosselli began with the gathering
of biographical research, personal data, police, prison, and parole
records; continued with live sources, interviews of friends, neighbors, past and present associates; the cultivation of informants; and
the application of secret surveillance—telephone, microphone, and
human (also known as taps, bugs, and tails). Agents burned shoe
leather exploring the subject's home turf. They talked to the present and the former managers of Johnny's apartment house at 1251
North Crescent Heights. They talked to other residents (few
claimed to have any knowledge of him or even to have seen him
much in recent years), to his loyal cleaning lady, Mrs. Dillard Williams, who told the FBI agents to go away. Agents gained access to
Johnny's apartment (Apt. C) and planted a hidden microphone and
a phone tap. In the parking garage they placed a tracking device
on Johnny's Cadillac DeVille. The Feds were able to obtain use of
an apartment at nearby 1242 North Crescent Heights Blvd., and
from there agents were able to observe any persons entering or
leaving Johnny Rosselli's building.

With the cooperation of the local postmaster, the FBI put a
so-called cover on his mail, recording the names and return addresses of everything that was sent to him, and when something
was deemed of special interest, it was opened, read, resealed. At
his local bank the agents examined his account activity for the past
several years. At the travel agencies he used—Rand Fields in Beverly Hills and Fitzpatrick in West LA—they asked about his travel
activities, found that he flew at least two times a month between
Las Vegas and Los Angeles, and on occasion three or more times
a month.

Rosselli, the agents reported, dined out most nights when in Los
Angeles, favoring a select few expensive restaurants—Perino's,
Mike Romanoff's, the Marquis on Sunset, Charley Foy's Supper

Club—and at all of them was well known to the owners and staff and treated with deference. They had only good things to say about their customer, who was known to be friendly, remember everyone by name, and to tip with extreme generosity. Alex Perino stated that he knew very little of Mr. Rosselli's early life, except that he told him he was born in New York City. They talked of pleasant things, he explained, like sports and cars and Perino's food. Lately, Perino revealed, Mr. Rosselli was fond of the French lamb chops with the mustard-shallot sauce.

The agents investigated the subject's social life, gathering information regarding his female friends, old and new. Many had come and gone too fast for others to recall their names. Rosselli, an informant explained, was "sex crazy." Women played a big part in his life, and he was "always looking for women."

They talked to Johnny's ex June Lang, a former Twentieth Century–Fox movie star. She had retired from the acting profession many years ago, remarried, her second husband a businessman, a manufacturer of brassieres. The second marriage did not last either. She told agents she had not talked to Rosselli since her divorce in 1943. She said she knew nothing of his background except that he came from Chicago. She could not recall him ever speaking of his parents, any brothers or sisters, or his childhood.

Agents attempted to speak to Beatrice (Bernice) Frank (aka "Ann Corcoran"), the aspiring movie actress Johnny had been engaged to when he'd gone into the army, and then to prison. She'd married a wealthy man and had started a family. Her attorney brother spoke to the FBI. He explained that his sister had undergone several operations for cancer and was emotionally disturbed; in his opinion she would be upset by an interview concerning Rosselli. Anyway, she had not seen him but on one or two occasions for the past ten years.

The Feds spoke to a more recent romantic interest, Betsy Duncan, a pretty and vivacious entertainer ("the little lady with the big voice" the newspapers called her), based in Los Angeles. She didn't have a lot to say about Johnny to the FBI agents. Fifty years later, she would recall him with fondness, a lover who became a lifelong friend. They'd met while she was performing at El Rancho in Las Vegas. She was being harassed by the casino's ogreish owner, Beldon Katleman, and someone had sent her to Johnny Rosselli for help. Johnny went to Katleman, and there was no more trouble after that. Betsy began going out with him in Las Vegas, then in LA. She liked him. A bit of a character. But fun, interesting, and—whatever else he was up to—with her he was a gentleman. Getting to know each other they stumbled into an amusing coincidence. Betsy, whose real name was Zelma DeWar, was the granddaughter of Frank DeWar, the long-ago chief deputy sheriff of Los Angeles County. The same man who had caught Johnny for bootlegging when he was a kid, "He told me how my grandfather thought he was too young for prison and let him run away. Johnny said he never forgot my grandfather for doing that."

Betsy at first considered him to be something of a hypochondriac. He was always concerned about the state of his health, always complaining about his lungs, his gut (his years with tuberculosis and its lingering aftereffects were not yet known to her). But then some of his complaints proved to be justified. Not long after they began seeing each other he had to be rushed to the hospital and was operated on for an inflamed hernia. And all his concerns were not self-centered. On Mother's Day, 1958, in Los Angeles, he took Betsy and her mother to dinner at Perino's, and when her mother spoke of problems with her legs that wouldn't heal, Johnny made arrangements for her to be seen at the Sansum Clinic in Santa Barbara. Doctors discovered she had advancing diabetes. Betsy believed that Johnny's concern saved her mother's life.

The Feds found that Rosselli had made the Sansum something of a pet project. In addition to his annual three-day visits for a thorough examination and tune-up, he sent them regular charitable donations, and in 1958 used his influence to obtain for them a sizable grant from the Damon Runyon Cancer Research Foundation.

On January 13, 1958, agents went to speak with Monsignor Thomas O'Toole, of the St. Ambrose Catholic Church on Fairfax and Fountain. Johnny was a registered member, but the monsignor said Rosselli was not a regular attendant at services and that he had seen him no more than three or four times in as many years. O'Toole thought maybe the Jesuit priest Joseph M. Clark could tell them more.

The Feds went to see Father Clark, then in charge of the Jesuit Seminary Association office in Los Angeles. They were likely not expecting what the priest had to say. He knew of Johnny's reputation but he could not speak to that side of the man. The person he knew was someone else, a very kind person, one of the most generous people he had ever met. Clark could recall many quiet and mostly anonymous acts of compassion and philanthropy over the course of the twenty-five years he had known Johnny Rosselli. Johnny had never hesitated when his assistance was needed. He had given money to the Church and charitable causes whenever asked, though much of what he did was personal and on his own initiative. He had great sympathy for children in poor and neglected situations. Children without fathers, without hope. He had helped many kids get into the academy and in several cases practically acted as their guardian "from the time they were little fellows until they were adults and could enter the armed services." Johnny had once paid to build a swimming pool for an orphanage, and when the pool was near completion he had sent a sporting-goods salesman to fit everyone for a swimsuit. Twice, Johnny had given the priest dowries for young ladies who wanted to enter a convent. Another time there had been a young man who had been studying for the priesthood and had begun to lose his eyesight and had to leave the seminary. Johnny had taken him into his home to live for a time and had helped the man to find a new start in life.

The FBI investigation continued in Las Vegas. Agents talked with the local police and the Clark County sheriff's department. They talked with the chief security officer at the Desert Inn, and the pro golfer at the DI country club. They questioned waiters, valets, cocktail waitresses, dealers. The employees were only as forthcoming as necessary.

The Feds followed him around town, logged his daily/nightly routine. They monitored his meetings, kept a record of his visible contacts. They noted that Rosselli had many prominent and powerful associates, from politicians and business leaders to Hollywood celebrities. He was found to be a close acquaintance of top Vegas performers Frank Sinatra, Joe E. Lewis, and Louis Prima, among others. Agents reported that Rosselli and Prima socialized, and that the bandleader was known to use the swimming pool at the Diplomat Apartments where Rosselli lived, a gathering place for the resident showgirls.*

The Feds looked into Rosselli's business affairs. The particulars were hard to determine as his name seldom appeared on any legal or business documents, his participation hidden behind fronts and attorneys. But gossip and incidental evidence indicated that he had a wide array of investments and investment partners from all walks of life. He was said to own large and small pieces of various local start-ups and going concerns, among them a garbage collection business, an ice machine concession, part of a restaurant, a resort

---

* The federal file had multiple reports indicating that Prima was "connected" with the Chicago syndicate and was "partially owned" by them, and that Prima's wife and performing partner, Keely Smith, had become a "paramour" of Sam Giancana, that Prima was aware of the arrangement but "helpless to do anything about it."

under development at Lake Mead. His interest in the movie business continued, and from time to time he bought story ideas or funded screenplays. He had conceived and come very close to producing a film about Las Vegas, what would have been an "adults only" semidocumentary to be made in a style that anticipated the "mondo" exploitation movies of the 1960s, featuring uncensored footage of topless showgirls. (Rosselli brought bare-breasted entertainment to the Tropicana stage in the summer of '58, a trend that became omnipresent on the Strip; it was the cause of one of the rare arguments between Johnny and his dear friend Joe Breen Jr., a devout Catholic who was opposed to undressed artistes.) Johnny also had some interest in the music business: the Feds discovered in his tax papers a royalty payment from Capitol Records in 1959; FBI agents interviewed William Perrin, the record company's auditor, who could not explain what Johnny had done to earn it.[*]

For a time he was connected to a project being built on the north side of Vegas called the Carver House, the first luxury resort intended for a "Negro" clientele (Vegas was still racially segregated, and even headliners like Sammy Davis Jr. and Nat "King" Cole were not allowed to sleep or dine at the Strip hotels); for the Carver deal he partnered with a wealthy first-time investor who'd made his fortune importing monkeys for medical laboratories. The Feds suspected that at least some of Rosselli's business deals were elaborate "big cons" that slowly drained cash from suckers.

Many of those approached by the federal agents ran quickly to tell Johnny Rosselli about it, wanting to assure him they had said nothing of importance. He also learned that his apartment in Los Angeles had been visited without permission. Later he found out that the Feds had rented a room in a nearby apartment house from which they could keep Johnny's place under round-the-clock ob-

---

[*] I searched unsuccessfully for information regarding Rosselli's royalty income, in the hope of uncovering a hidden musical talent.

servation. He joked to the apartment manager that he should get a discount in his rent for providing the building with the extra security. He'd always tried to go about his business with caution, exercised discretion when talking on the telephone ("Phones are stool pigeons," he liked to say). Now he would proceed with even greater care. He often preferred to avoid the apartment when he was in town for a short visit, staying instead at the Beverly Hilton. Agents noted that Rosselli had become "extremely surveillance conscious."

Although many of his activities raised suspicions, the Feds could not get evidence of organized criminal activity, the sort that could lead to a major prosecution. Rosselli was too "conscious" to leave himself exposed. But the evidence they did find—rumors and gossip passed along—left them with no doubt that the man remained important in Mob affairs, his contributions valued at the highest levels. A story from a confidential source—he was given a code name in the Feds' report—with some access to the inner circles in Vegas, told of a recent fight between Rosselli and Carl Cohen, manager of the Sands Hotel casino and former associate of the Mayfield Road Gang (and the father of actor Corey Allen, James Dean's nemesis in *Rebel Without a Cause*). In the heat of an argument over the characteristics of personnel being sent from the East to fill jobs at the casinos, Cohen said things he shouldn't have said. Rosselli told him he had better shut his mouth, Cohen didn't, and Johnny said he was going to kill him. Cohen was summoned to New York, flown out, and brought before Doc Stacher, a Syndicate eminence grise and longtime partner of Meyer Lansky. Stacher told Cohen he was not a tough guy. Therefore he had to stop talking like a tough guy. He was to say "yes sir" and "no sir" to people of Johnny Rosselli's position. Stacher told Cohen he needed him now, and therefore he was not going to let Rosselli get out of line. But if Rosselli and Cohen quarreled again, he would let Rosselli kill him.

One intriguing story came to the Feds from Robert Notti, the assistant city manager of Las Vegas. Over a couple of years Notti had occasion to meet with Rosselli several times, matters of casino-related city business. Rosselli, said Notti, was a very closed-mouth individual and most people in town knew very little about him other than rumors. Around any state or city officials he was always guarded. The one exception, Notti recalled for the agents, was one evening in December 1958. Rosselli had seen Notti in the Tropicana Club and had rushed over to him to talk. It was a curious conversation. Rosselli said he wanted to tell Notti that the following morning at 5:00 a.m. he was going boating and fishing on Lake Mead with a Las Vegas attorney named Rosco Thomas. Rosselli said that they would be gone for four days and during that time he would be out of contact with anybody who wanted to reach him. Notti did not know what to make of it. Why was this man telling him this? Rosselli had never seen any reason to share his comings or goings with him before, and he didn't know why he had felt the need to do it now. The next day Notti got a call from the county sheriff. The sheriff told him that Gus Greenbaum, the manager of the Riviera casino, and his wife, had been found murdered in their home in Arizona. The house was not robbed; these were executions. Their throats had been cut with a butcher knife, Gus nearly decapitated. Notti thought about Johnny Rosselli and his strange declaration the night before. It had happened within hours of these savage murders. Notti told his story to the sheriff's department but was never asked any more about it. The Greenbaum murders were never solved.*

---

* As it has been told, Greenbaum was in declining health, addicted to drugs, leading a debauched private life, getting some local girls hooked on heroin; the casino started to lose money and—worst of all—Gus was robbing from the skim. It was decided that—most say Meyer Lansky sent the order—Greenbaum had to go. According to the authors Rappleye and Becker, when Johnny Rosselli was later asked by a Riviera employee if he knew what had happened to Gus, he became vehement. He shouted, "I would never be involved in something like that!" and hurried away.

The FBI's Top Hoodlum probe was costly and required considerable manpower. After two years the agency had not found enough evidence to charge Johnny Rosselli with a major crime, nothing to justify continuing the operation on such a scale. It was decided to suspend the Rosselli investigation and reopen it when or if circumstances changed. The agents involved moved on to other things. The abrupt shutdown meant that some discoveries in the case had not yet been given proper attention, odds and ends that had been accumulated and tossed into the file. For instance, there was the curious fact, uncovered by an agent in Chicago, Illinois, several years earlier, that Johnny Rosselli's only documented proof of birth appeared to be a forgery.

2

Las Vegas was ordinarily a ghost town in the first two months of the year. But the winter of 1960 was anything but ordinary. Late in January a motion picture company arrived from Hollywood to begin shooting *Ocean's Eleven*, the story of ex-army buddies heisting five Vegas casinos on a single night. The producers sought to heighten the authenticity with location filming and a cast that top-billed Frank Sinatra, Dean Martin, and Sammy Davis Jr., the ranking superstars of the Vegas Strip. An inspired Jack Entratter, the Sands Casino Hotel manager, enticed the three headliners to appear at his place after each day of filming, an assemblage heralded then as "the Summit at the Sands" and known forever after as the holy birthplace of the Rat Pack. The trio of stars, with the support of additional *Oceans's* actors Peter Lawford and Joey Bishop, and assorted guests plucked from the audience—Marilyn Monroe, Milton Berle—joined together on stage for a boozy, leering, anarchic wingding and a thrilling deconstruction of traditional nightclub entertainment. Audiences were ecstatic. The crowds converged on the tiny Copa Room like pilgrims to Mecca, the place filled with famous faces, Hollywood stars, sports heroes, and jet-set celebrities.

One night in early February the big name in the room—soon to be even bigger than Frank Sinatra—was the leading contender for the Democratic candidacy in the upcoming presidential election, Massachusetts senator John Fitzgerald Kennedy. "The brightest man in the political world," cried Sinatra from the stage, "in this country or any other country today . . . and I *personally feel"*—shifting to his favored Amos 'n' Andy–style minstrelsy—*"I'm goin'a visit him in da White House one day very soon—"*

"I'm gonna be in the *outhouse*," interjected an indifferent Dean Martin.

JFK stood and waved to general applause while Joey Bishop lifted up Sammy Davis Jr. (a recent convert to Judaism) and offered him to the candidate, saying, "You've got the Jewish vote!"

Sinatra and Kennedy had been pals for a while, a friendship spun from the entertainer's relationship with Peter Lawford and Lawford's wife, Jack's sister, Patricia. Frank was very enamored of the charismatic, ambitious brother. With the campaign on, he had pledged to help any way he could. Sinatra was Kennedy's host at the Sands on that glossy night, and the entertainer made sure the candidate had everything he needed. And by now Frank knew Jack's needs. The potential president of the United States was gifted with a young woman from the entertainer's retinue, a demure, well-bred, beautiful twenty-six-year-old brunette divorcee named Judith Campbell. Kennedy was pleased.

A small world. Judy Campbell was an old friend of Johnny Rosselli. She and her husband, movie and TV actor William Campbell (*The High and the Mighty, Cell 2455 Death Row, Love Me Tender*, with Elvis) were Crescent Heights neighbors in the '50s. When Johnny met her the first time she was just high school age, maybe seventeen. Bill Campbell had introduced the stunning young woman as the girl he was going to marry. Johnny told him, That's great, kid. Invite me to the wedding. Bill Campbell remembered those days on Crescent Heights. Many afternoons the three of them spent together out by the swimming pool (centerpiece of the U-shaped apartment house). Johnny was a great guy, generous spirit, sense of humor. They'd go for a meal some evenings. Barney's Beanery, the Formosa, or some Italian joint. Sometimes Johnny had a girl with him, but mostly it was just the three of them. One time he'd had them to his place and cooked a big dinner. And Johnny was a pretty good cook. Did he have an eye for Judy in those days? Well, it was hard to find anybody who wasn't attracted to Judy. She was gorgeous. Everybody thought she was in the movies, like her sister (Susan Morrow, star of *Macabre*, a film best remembered for providing ticketholders with a thousand-dollar life insurance policy in case of death by fright). Bill and Judy got divorced in '58. Her ex didn't know what to say about what happened later—JFK and all the rest of that crazy shit.

Johnny and Judy became close. It started after the divorce, or maybe a little before—why don't we say *after*. She was hard to resist. Her looks were unbelievable. More beautiful than Liz Taylor. A real sweet kid, he'd say, lots of class. They saw each other now and again. Never a big thing. He was in Las Vegas so often in those days, and she had things to do in LA. She collected $433.33 a month in alimony from Bill. For a time she had some sort of job at Jerry Lewis's production company. She became one of those young beauties on the swinging Hollywood/Malibu circuit, in with the in crowd, somewhere between a party girl and a trophy-wife-to-be. Not hookers, that was insulting, but sometimes somebody put some cash in a girl's purse, a gift for making the party more fun. She began seeing Frank Sinatra in '59. He took her with him to Hawaii and to his place in Palm Springs. After they'd been together a while he sometimes passed her on to other men, a display of his magnanimity, and of his crowded schedule (there were just so many of them—broads—and only one of him). According to Sinatra's valet, among the guests who enjoyed Judy's company was Joseph Kennedy, the father of the would-be president.

A very small world. Johnny was an old acquaintance of Joe's too, going back to Hollywood in the 1920s. The senior Kennedy was then a Boston tycoon, Wall Street investor, fingers in many pies.* He had come to the West Coast to invest in movie studios, and movie stars (silent-screen diva Gloria Swanson would be his mistress), and at the dawn of the talkies he helped create RKO Pictures. Johnny knew him from social gatherings and had played golf with him back in the day.

Now, in early 1960, with his boy having officially entered the presidential race on January 2, old man Kennedy had inserted himself into the campaign, determined to make this long-held dream come true. Though Jack's appeal was electric, and his support was strong, and his campaign manager–brother Bobby was steadfast and ruthless, victory—against his Democratic opponents, or in November against the likely Republican nominee, Vice President Richard Nixon—was no sure thing. Some Americans thought the senator too young for the job, or too Catholic, or too two-dimensional. In the primaries there were problematic areas of the country, leaning toward Dem rivals Hubert Humphrey and Lyndon Johnson. Nixon, though compared with Kennedy he had the star quality of a flophouse desk clerk, was a strong contender, rep-

---

* The oft-repeated story that Kennedy was a Prohibition bootlegger has been mostly discounted by researchers, labeled a confabulation of poor sourcing, anti-JFK rhetoric, mistaken identity (in Prohibition days there was a Canada-based distiller and distributor with the same name), and the fact that Kennedy was for a time—after repeal—a legal importer of several top-shelf brands. Papa Kennedy's questionable behavior in other, better-documented matters has no doubt helped to make the bootlegging accusation seem plausible.

resenting to many voters another four years of a placid, solvent Eisenhower administration.

Joe Kennedy was not ready to leave the election result to the whims of the ballot box. He was ready to do whatever it took, things he thought his children might not have the guts to do. Indeed, they may have had no idea what he'd gotten up to in pursuit of his son's victory. Running a kind of secret, dissident election campaign, Papa Kennedy's search for votes took him down the shadowy alleyways of power and politics. In a scheme that risked all if found out, he sought the assistance of certain criminal bosses and corrupt union leaders who controlled large and strategically invaluable voting blocs. Kennedy was particularly keen on getting the support of the Chicago Outfit and the Teamsters Union, two organizations he believed could just about guarantee his son primary and general election wins in Illinois and certain other key states. What they might have to do to secure those wins was up to them; Kennedy wanted only results.

There was one big hurdle in the way of luring Chicago and the Teamsters to the cause. His name was Robert Kennedy, Papa's puritanical third-born son, the candidate's close adviser and beloved brother. As the chief counsel for the McClellan Committee investigating labor racketeering and organized crime, Bobby had done a grandstanding job grilling mobsters and union leaders. In a much-criticized performance, Kennedy hurled unproved accusations, threats, and sneering insults at the witnesses, often making the hearings into a crass shouting match. He'd made his most violent attacks on the Outfit's Sam Giancana and on Jimmy Hoffa of the Teamsters, vowing not to give up till they were both behind bars. Now Joe Kennedy wanted the very same men to help Bobby's big brother get elected to the White House.

Joe's go-between with Sam Giancana would be their mutual friend Frank Sinatra. "You understand, Frank," Joe told him, "I can't go. I can't approach them but you can."

When Sinatra got together with Giancana for a game of golf, he whispered Papa Kennedy's request. In daughter Tina Sinatra's account, her father sounded more like the guy who'd crooned for brotherhood and tolerance in "The House I Live In," than somebody urging the boss of the Chicago Mob to help throw a national election. "I believe in this man," said Frank to Sam in this version. "And I think he's going to make us a good president. With your help, I think we can work this out."

Giancana rolled his eyes and took the request back home. The Outfit bosses could hardly believe the balls on old man Kennedy.

Late in February a meeting was held at Felix Young's Restaurant on Park Avenue in New York City. Giancana had come to hear what the old man had to say. The choice of venue showed Johnny Rosselli's fingerprints, Felix Young an old Sunset Strip crony, a degenerate gambler and former boss of the Trocadero and Mocambo nightclubs. The principals in attendance were Kennedy, Sam Giancana, Johnny, and an attorney named Mario Brod. Brod was there ostensibly to represent the interests of Jimmy Hoffa and the Teamsters, but was also—unknown to the rest—an underworld penetration of the CIA, a former OSS operative working on assignment for his mentor, the agency's paranoid schemer and master of the dark arts, James Jesus Angleton.

Kennedy arrived late, exacerbating what was already an uneasy atmosphere. They got down to it without further delay. Giancana conveyed the Outfit's mixed feelings. Kennedy waved them away. Do this, and the president would owe them. Who wouldn't want a friend in the White House? They had no problem with Jack, said Giancana, it was the other one, the troublemaker, the big mouth. (Bobby once told Sam to his face that he "giggled like a little girl.") The old man understood. He'd had his own wrangles with the boy. How he'd gotten to be such a prig nobody knew. He told them it was not going to be a problem. According to Mario Brod (interviewed by Kennedy historian Richard Mahoney) Papa Joe told them: "It's Jack who's running for president, not Bobby." And: "This is *business*, not *politics*."

Then Joseph Kennedy—busy man—was gone, leaving them to sit and ponder his few words. Had they heard right, did the old man promise to keep Bobby away from them when/if Jack got in? Considering that Bobby had vowed to lock them all up, it did not sound like a bad deal, if he could deliver. Johnny spoke, Brod would recall. They had to consider, Johnny said, that "it was Kennedy who came to them, and this was significant." He hadn't wasted their time with bullshit. Business not politics, he said. That meant a real deal, not pipe-dream promises. But they had to be careful if they did get involved. On a thing like this the whole country would be watching.

Giancana went back to Chicago. A vote was taken by the Outfit execs. Only Murray Humphreys, the fixer and the man who'd had the most experience with the fraudulence of politicians, voted against. The others couldn't resist the idea of the president being in their debt. Indeed, they could not contain themselves over it. The FBI, listening to a bugged conversation in Chicago, would hear Giancana boasting of the mob's new alliance with the Kennedys. He saw it as a personal victory (as in *Fuck Bobby—even his old man doesn't like him*). In Washington, J. Edgar Hoover pawed the surveillance transcript, put it away for another day. In Illinois and elsewhere the mobsters' machine was put to work. Orders given, favors called in, threats delivered. Murray Humphreys unleashed his politicos, ward heelers, union bosses. There were few holdouts. Teamster Jimmy Hoffa refused to cooperate, hated the brother too much, and in fact was doing all he could for Richard Nixon; Carlos Marcello, the Mafia boss of New Orleans, also not a Bobby fan, had pledged himself to Texas neighbor Lyndon Johnson.

Johnny liked Jack Kennedy. He was young, but sharp as a knife-point. Maybe some young blood and new ideas were what the country needed. He'd talked him up in front of the Breens. His approval was cause for grave consternation with Joe and Pat, who were staunch Republican conservatives and couldn't stand the senator. (Fifty years later Mrs. Breen was still deploring her friend's opinion.) He knew of Jack's vices through the Sinatra grapevine, and to Johnny they made him seem more sympathetic. He liked women. They had that in common. Even some of the same women. He also knew things about Papa Kennedy, and few of them good. Joe K's motive seemed clear enough here, but it was always wise to keep your guard up around people like him. He did whatever it took to get what he wanted, and in truth that went for the sons as well, though with Dad around they could keep their hands clean. That Sinatra: He was too far gone on this family, you had to beware his enthusiasm getting the better of him, getting his friends into trouble. Sam and others had begun to laugh at him for his hero worship. He was expecting to get a cabinet position, they said, or maybe made ambassador to the Vatican.

Anyway, they were all in it now, and Johnny would have to do his share. This would come to mean cleaning up the candidate's shit, shutting down scandal hawkers, paying off party girls, dissuading journalists, shutting up talkative sex partners or disgruntled husbands. There was, for example, the case of some Hollywood couple going through an untidy divorce. The husband wanted proof of his actress spouse's infidelities and had sent Hollywood ball breaker/private dick Fred Otash to get some dirt. It happened that one of the wife's extramarital flings was with the possible future president (others included Dean Martin and the ubiquitous Frank Sinatra). The double-dealing detective had planned to peddle the story to *Confidential* magazine when Johnny showed up at his door. After negotiations Otash took some cash to lose the evidence.

Johnny would be called on from time to time to babysit his old friend Judy Campbell, who had gone from JFK one-night stand to JFK mistress. She was now head over heels in love with him. ("*He was an amazing man,*" she gushed to author Seymour Hersh. "*When you talked to him you felt you were the only person on the planet.*") Kennedy was at least sweet on the young California beauty, though she was just one among a string of similar women he referred to as "the talent." He called her for long-distance pillow talk and found ways of seeing her as he campaigned around the country. The brief trysts inflamed her lovesick state when he went away again. She would become morose about the bumpy romance, and people worried about her saying the wrong thing to the wrong person. Johnny would show up, take her out to dinner, console her, let her cry on his shoulder. Once or twice—what the hell, sometimes she needed a lot of consoling—they would end up in bed. One day, home alone pining for Jack, she accepted an invite from Sinatra to come see him perform in Miami. There Frank introduced her to a homely but very confident man named Sam Flood. Mr. Flood was Sam Giancana incognito. Like everybody else, he was staggered by Judy Campbell's glowing beauty. And knowing she was sleeping with Jack Kennedy made her even more enticing. Sam was then in the midst of a love affair with Phyllis McGuire of the singing McGuire Sisters, and there were as well a couple of ladies he was seeing back in Chicago, but *Christ*, she was beautiful! He put on the charm. She was lonely, or whatever. Soon she was having an affair with both Kennedy *and* Giancana.

Judy Campbell distracted by a second boyfriend did free up some space on the candidate's crowded schedule. These were busy days. In addition to Judy, he was screwing starlets, friends' wives, campaign volunteers and interns, a famous flame-haired stripper, and perhaps here or there his wife, Jackie, all but the last potential scandals waiting to explode. It was a hell of a way to run for president.

Politics, showbiz, sex, crime, come together that season like dirty water clogging a drain, and Johnny wielding the plunger, trying not to get anything on his bespoke suit.

In July old comrade Jimmy Fratianno was granted parole. He'd been in the pen for most of the previous decade. Released to the outside world, he was sent to reside in a small town in Northern California, put to work washing dishes at a greasy spoon, then given a job with a small trucking company. He was under frequent surveillance by the local cops and visiting parole officers, and not supposed to go anywhere without permission, but he was eager to settle some business in LA and to see his old friend Johnny Rosselli, one of the only men in the world he trusted. Johnny, he knew, had pulled some strings to get him out of Folsom Prison and transferred to relatively civilized Soledad, and had come through again with a lawyer to help him with his parole. It was above and beyond what anybody else had done for him, and he would never forget it. As soon as he figured out how to sneak away, Fratianno drove the six hundred miles to Los Angeles. He and Johnny met for dinner, a happy reunion for both. It had been seven years since they had seen each other. For Jimmy a long time on the inside.

"Waddaya gonna do," said Fratianno. "It's one of them things."

They drank and dined. Jimmy talked about his seven-year stretch. The nightmare world of Folsom. Not even Hitler deserved that shit hole. He voiced his contempt for the new leaders of the LA Family. Jimmy told how DeSimone and his sidekicks had screwed him good, grabbed all his shylock money, a hundred grand, and then lied about it. They took care of his wife and kid for a few months after he went away and then cut them loose. His old lady had to get a job, for god's sake. Now that he was out, he'd tried to get them to square things and instead, he believed, they were trying to frame him, get him back in prison and out of their hair.

Fratianno worked himself up talking about it. "Look at the pieces of shit," he said (according to Ovid Demaris). "How could I've been so dumb. All they ever used me for was to kill people. . . ."

Johnny nodded his head in sympathy. "Today there's too much greed and jealousy," he said. "The greed and jealousy of little men. No vision, no imagination."

Johnny reached into his jacket and brought out an envelope, gave it to Jimmy, telling him it was something he and a couple of guys—Philly Alderisio, Tom Dragna—wanted him to have. The envelope was thick with cash.

Fratianno thanked him. Thanked him again.

Johnny snapped his fingers at a waiter and ordered another round.

The way he felt about the Los Angeles Family, and the way he felt about Johnny, it was no surprise that Jimmy Fratianno would want to follow in his friend's footsteps and transfer his allegiance to Chicago. The rules did not permit Johnny to get involved in that. You were not supposed to poach from another gang. So Jimmy had to make his own arrangement to exit LA and sell himself to Sam Giancana. It was awkward: As a guy on parole, with heat on him, he wouldn't be a big earner for a while to come. Giancana did approve the transfer, but—inevitably—there was a price to be paid for any kindness.

In the autumn of '59, the ABC television network premiered a period cops 'n' robbers drama, *The Untouchables*, produced by Desilu, the company owned by Desi Arnaz and Lucille Ball. The show was based on the unreliable book of the same name by Oscar Fraley and Eliot Ness, detailing Ness's supposed adventures as the head of a Bureau of Prohibition squad charged with destroying Al Capone's bootlegging empire. The show's violent, colorful mix of machine guns, speakeasies, police raids, flappers, and flamboyant gangsters made it a huge hit—with everybody but the many Italian Americans who resented the old stereotyped ethnic criminals. Mae Capone, Scarface's widow, was said to have been wounded by the vicious depiction of her late husband in the initial two-parter that aired on CBS, and was filing a lawsuit for defamation (she lost). And some of Al's old colleagues were outraged. The idea that millions of people were watching (as one veteran gangster described the program) "a bunch of Italian lunatics . . . slopping up spaghetti" made them sore enough to want more than money for this insult to their legacy.

In Chicago the Outfit bosses voted to kill the producer of *The Untouchables*. Desi Arnaz, the Cuban bandleader who had married the actress Lucille Ball and costarred with her in the television sitcom *I Love Lucy* (as, no stretch, Cuban bandleader "Ricky Ricardo"), was a very well-known man, who now ran Desilu (on the former RKO Pictures lot). Giancana assigned the Arnaz hit to their newest Family member, Jimmy Fratianno. Johnny delivered the order to him in person. Fratianno found it hard to believe they wanted to clip a Hollywood big shot over some stories on a television show. Who the fuck cared? Johnny assured him that the boys in Chicago cared. And he confessed to not being happy himself. Making Al Capone and Frank Nitti look like savage maniacs. It just wasn't right.

Jimmy knew he had to take the contract without complaint, owing a big one to Giancana, and not wanting to cause Johnny any trouble. But fuck. Killing another hoodlum was one thing, knocking off a celebrity was something else. The story would go straight to the headlines, and the cops would feel obligated to investigate. Jimmy teamed up with his old associate Frank Bompensiero, who had also just gotten out of prison. Bompensiero was a resentful crank at the best of times, and years in the joint had not made him any more cheerful. He hated DeSimone and his people as much as Fratianno did. He was nostalgic for the good old days when Jack

Dragna ran the Family and you always knew where you stood. Jimmy cut him off before the rheumy hit man started sobbing. And then they got back to the job, trying to figure out how they were going to murder "Ricky Ricardo" and get away with it.

But the hit didn't happen. Johnny Rosselli had stepped in and found another way. The story was recalled by Paul Picerni:

"I knew Johnny and Joe Breen Jr. since the time of making *Breakthrough*, and working with Bryan Foy. I was very good friends with Joe, and he was very close to Johnny, so I'd met him many times through the years, at parties and holidays at Joe's house. Johnny would be there, usually with a beautiful woman.

"*The Untouchables* had been on the air its first season, and a lot of Italians were up in arms, and the Mafia was up in arms, over all the Italian gangsters they had in this show. There were threats from the unions, boycotts against the advertisers. So Desi Arnaz decided he had to get ahead of this problem. And he agreed to meet with Frank Sinatra and Johnny Rosselli. They were representing all the angry Italians. They had a meeting . . . I think it was the Beverly Hills Hotel, in the Polo Lounge. And Desi says, 'Okay, you guys, this is getting crazy, what you want me to do? How can I make this work for you?' And they tell him he's got to stop every week with these terrible Italian mobsters . . . it's an insult to the good Italian people. I think Johnny had known most of these mobsters personally. And Desi tells him and Sinatra, 'Okay, okay. We'll change all the names. We'll call them Smith and Jones from now on.' And then Johnny says, 'And while you're at it, how about you make one of the good guys an Italian.' And Desi says, 'I already got an Italian Untouchable. His name's Rico.' But Johnny tells him, 'Not so fast. That actor's a Greek. You got to get an Italian actor.' And Desi Arnaz says, 'Who you want me to put in?' And Johnny says, 'Well, let me think a minute . . . there's a pal of mine, Paul

Johnny Rosselli, the Mob's man in Hollywood, 1948. (*Los Angeles Public Library Herald-Examiner Collection*)

Filippo Sacco, aka John Rosselli,
age ten.

Vincenzo Sacco, Johnny's father.

Maria Sacco, Johnny's mother.
(*Courtesy of David Nissen*)

Left to right: Albert Marco, Guy McAfee and Milton "Farmer" Page, vice kings of Los Angeles, leaders of the City Hall Gang aka The Combination, 1920s–30s. (*Los Angeles Public Library Herald-Examiner Collection*)

Producer Joseph Schenck (left), unidentified man (center), and Los Angeles Mayor George Cryer (right). (*Los Angeles Public Library Herald-Examiner Collection*)

Johnny Rosselli, police mug shot, age 20. (*Courtesy of David Nissen*)

Tony Cornero, the King of the Rumrunners. (*Los Angeles Public Library Herald-Examiner Collection*)

Al Capone (center), Chicago, 1930; attorney William Waugh on left. (*Chicago Daily News Collection, Chicago History Museum*)

Los Angeles Mob boss Jack Dragna, with lawyer.

Jack Dragna, amused.

Jean Harlow, Hollywood screen queen of the 1930s. (*Los Angeles Public Library Herald-Examiner Collection*)

Columbia Pictures boss Harry Cohn and wife, Joan. (*Los Angeles Public Library, Herald-Examiner Collection*)

Los Angeles Mayor Frank Shaw (right) and Police Chief James "Two Gun" Davis (center).

Joseph Shaw, the mayor's brother and bagman. (*Los Angeles Public Library, Herald-Examiner Collection*)

Johnny Rosselli, pulled in for police questioning, circa 1937. (*PhotoHistory Collection*)

Actress Lina Basquette,
"the Godless Girl."

Marge Champion with half sister
Lina Basquette. (*Los Angeles Public
Library, Herald-Examiner Collection*)

Benjamin "Bugsy" Siegel
(center). (*Los Angeles
Public Library, Herald-
Examiner Collection*)

June Lang.

Mr. and Mrs. Johnny Rosselli on their honeymoon, 1940. (*Corbis*)

George "Les" Bruneman, veteran racketeer, shot dead in 1937.

Clifford Clinton, restaurateur and racket buster.

Pete Pianezzi, "the Bum Rap Kid," wrongly convicted of murder. (*Los Angeles Public Library, Herald-Examiner Collection*)

Willie Bioff, panderer, union boss, racketeer. (*Los Angeles Public Library, Herald-Examiner Collection*)

Estelle Carey, Nick Circella's
girlfriend, the Outfit's victim.

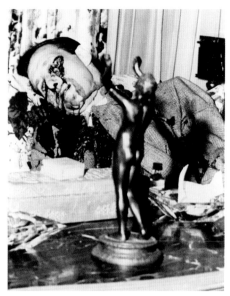

Bugsy Siegel, dead.

Johnny Rosselli in his U.S. Army uniform,
with lawyer Otto Christensen (left). (*Corbis*)

One of the prisoners recaptured after the real Canon City Prison escape.

Promotional event for the *Canon City* premiere, star Scott Brady (right), Warden Roy Best (center), and some models-as-prisoners.

Poster for *He Walked By Night*, co-produced by Johnny Rosselli.

Richard Basehart in *He Walked By Night*.

He Walked By Night, the climactic chase in the storm drain, lighting by John Alton. (*Courtesy of Alan K. Rode Archives*)

Johnny Rosselli (right) with attorney/mobster Frank DeSimone. (*PhotoHistory Collection*)

Jimmy "the Weasel" Fratianno.

Mickey Cohen and members of his
gang. (*Los Angeles Public Library
Herald-Examiner Collection*)

GIOVANNI ROSSELLI

World Traveller
International Lover . . . and Last of the Big Spenders

One of Johnny Rosselli's business cards,
circa 1950s. (*Courtesy of David Nissen*)

The Desert Inn, Las Vegas,
Johnny's home away from home.
(*Author's Collection*)

Jeanne Carmen, model, actress, trick shot golfer. (*Author's Collection*)

Johnny Rosselli in Las Vegas. (*PhotoHistory Collection*)

Las Vegas Strip, 1967, the Frontier casino in lower right. (*Los Angeles Public Library Herald-Examiner Collection*)

Santo Trafficante. (*Los Angeles Public Library Herald-Examiner Collection*)

Sam Giancana.

Johnny Rosselli in Washington, D.C., arriving to testify before a congressional committee. (*Corbis*)

Picerni, a good actor, he'd be great in there.' And, actually, I'd already done a small part on the show, the first episode. And next thing you know I'm doing the second lead on *The Untouchables*. Joe Breen told me the story. He knew about it before I got the call. And Johnny never said anything to me, like 'Hey, you owe me one.' I did that show for years. And that was it. There were no more protests and the Italians were happy again. I know I was."

3

In Cuba the reign of Fulgencio Batista had come to an end. For seven years the island despot had thrived on brutal security enforcement and an enriching partnership with foreign exploiters, mobsters, and corporate predators, abandoning the people of Cuba to lives of poverty, suppression, and debasement. A slow-growing resistance movement began with marches, demonstrations, moved on to random acts of violence, bombings, and assassinations. Rebel armies were formed, waging guerrilla war on Batista's forces. Foremost among the emerging *contra* leaders was a young lawyer named Fidel Castro, whose small group of hirsute warriors—*Los Barbudos*, the bearded ones—established a rebel stronghold in the mountains in southeastern Cuba.

Even as the conflict grew—bloody battles, kidnappings and murders, sabotage of sugar mills and oil refineries—business in the island's capital went on as usual. The casinos and hotels and nightclubs were full, and the American Mob continued to invest heavily in Havana's future. The rebellion in the mountains and the violence in the rural provinces seemed like things happening on another planet to those frolicking in the casinos, swimming pools, and brothels.

The regime's hold on power became more tenuous after the United States pulled back its support for the unpopular Batista, tilting in favor of the charismatic Castro, whose broadcast speeches from his mountain encampment promised to replace the dictatorship with a liberal democracy. The rebels moved forward slowly, steadily, then in a final rush to victory. In late 1958, when Batista learned of enemy forces at the outskirts of the capital, he abandoned all hope and fled the island, never to return. On New Year's Day 1959 the revolutionaries entered Havana.

The new government imposed sweeping changes, social and economic reforms that sought to dismantle every trace of the former oligarchy. The old Batista enforcers and enablers were relieved of their obligations (521 executed in the first three months of Castro's rule), most private and foreign-owned industries and businesses were nationalized, the press was controlled, the vice industry shut down. Untold millions of dollars in foreign investments were lost, several million by Meyer Lansky alone. Free enterprise became a crime against the state. The U.S. government, realizing they had backed the wrong horse, and had been double-crossed by Cuba's beatnik savior, seethed with anger, embarrassment, and fear: Ninety miles off the American shoreline there was now what appeared to be a communist tyranny and the newest client state of the Soviet Union.

By early 1960, after a year of revolutionary rule in Cuba, a year of wishful thinking in Washington, the American government had given up hope of Castro changing course. His defiant stance, his growing alliance with the Soviets, his stated intention of exporting revolution to other countries, were now to be considered serious, even existential, threats. To a country bilious with Cold War dread, Castro seemed a tipping point, the man who'd brought Red warriors to the country's doorstep. How soon before there were Soviet troops on the Malecón? Gunboats patroling off Miami Beach? President Eisenhower wanted something done. Something decisive. But something short of World War III.

———

One evening in Los Angeles, Johnny Rosselli and Betsy Duncan were out having drinks before dinner. As they sipped their cocktails, someone stepped up to the table and greeted them—it was Johnny's old friend George Raft, long-ago big-screen star of underworld epics like *Scarface, The Glass Key,* and *Each Dawn I Die.* The tough-guy actor had recently come back to the States from Cuba, and he had quite a story to tell. George had fallen on hard times lately, his career in pictures at a standstill and his movie-star money all gone (*"I spent a million dollars on hookers and horse races,"* he once said, *"and the rest I squandered"*). He told Johnny and Betsy how he'd taken an offer to work as the celebrity-in-residence at the (Mob-owned) Capri Hotel Casino in Havana, greeting the tourists and schmoozing with high rollers. On the night of New Year's Eve, having partied with the customers until several hours after midnight, Raft had retired to his penthouse suite at the Capri accompanied by a new friend, the lovely winner of a Miss Cuba beauty contest. The actor had climbed out of his silk tuxedo and was about to climb onto Miss Cuba when the sound of gunfire and explosions filled the predawn air. Looking out from his balcony, Raft saw the city streets becoming filled with people and honking vehicles. It appeared to be both a celebration and a battle. Some people cheered, while others screamed in panic, pistols and rifles cracking everywhere. It was a crazy scene, even for Havana. It was the revolution, and it had come to George Raft's doorstep. Hundreds of wild-eyed Cubans charged the front doors, racing through the casino, shooting their weapons, crying, "Viva Castro!" and "Death to the gangsters!" And George Raft, who'd faced similar threats in some of his pictures at Warner Bros. and never retreated no matter what it said in the script, got back into his tuxedo and bravely went back downstairs.

For most of a week George and a gaggle of American tourists were held captive in one wing of the hotel, subject to random threats and humiliations and, in Raft's case, the occasional request for an autograph, until Castro's regular army brought order to the neighborhood and the terrified gringos were escorted to the airport and sent home.

"We listened to George tell this story," Betsy Duncan recalled, "and John was very sarcastic. He couldn't believe these people had taken over down there, Castro and his gang with their beards. A bunch of amateurs. And he said, 'Just give me three or four guys and some machine guns and I'll kick them out of there.'"

In late summer 1960 Johnny Rosselli got a call from a man named Robert Maheu. The man had something important he needed to discuss, and they set a date for lunch at the Brown Derby in Beverly Hills. Johnny first met Maheu a few years before in Las Vegas. (Maheu was working for comedian Milton Berle, who wanted to break an expensive artist's contract he had with Louis Prima; Berle wanted to use the morals clause in the contract by "building a frame" on Prima, planting some narcotics in his dressing room and getting him busted.) He knew Maheu as a lawyer and high-end private eye, the man's biggest client the peculiar business tycoon Howard Hughes. But there were things Johnny didn't know. Maheu had been in the FBI in the 1940s, serving in Europe as a counterintelligence agent, a personal adviser to J. Edgar Hoover, and a liaison with the Central Intelligence Agency. Some years after the war he quit his government job and opened his own consulting and detective business, Robert A. Maheu Associates (known as RAMA). He divided his work between servicing wealthy private clients like Hughes (for whom on one occasion he'd done surveillance on Howard's sometime-girlfriend and Frank Sinatra's then-wife, the movie goddess Ava Gardner) and black-bag jobs for the Central Intelligence Agency (dirty tricks ops like the hidden-camera pornographic movie he'd produced starring a Russian stewardess and a lookalike for Indonesian President Sukarno).

A week before the call to Johnny Rosselli, Maheu had been visited in his Virginia home by two operatives from the CIA's Office of Security, Director of Security Col. Sheffield Edwards and Operational Support Chief James "Big Jim" O'Connell (the latter Maheu's regular case officer). The CIA had been tasked with getting rid of the deeply troubling leader of Cuba. With the Soviets breathing hard on their necks, the White House wanted it done without leaving any government fingerprints behind. The CIA was then at its imaginative zenith—these were the years of mind-control experiments, ultra-high-altitude spy planes, weaponized psychedelics—and the masters of weird science at the Technical Services Staff (TSS) had come up with many fascinating possibilities for eliminating Castro. But they had all been just a little too . . . fascinating. Then Edwards had come up with an exciting notion: Why not subcontract the Cuban job to the Mafia? He laid it out for his boss, Richard Bissell: The Mob hated Castro. The Mob killed people. The Mob could kill Castro. Maybe for money, maybe for the chance to get back all those casino properties Fidel had stolen from them after the revolution. Bissell agreed that there was a certain logic to it. With their own lethal habits and years of nefarious activity in Cuba, the gangsters were bound to have the ways and means for getting a job like this done. And they made an ideal buffer, concealing the government's involvement: If the Mob got found out in a plot to commit murder, no one would doubt it, no one would look for partners in crime. To further protect themselves, Edwards would put in place a second layer of separation from the hired killers, a "cut-out" handler with no official tie to the agency. That job was now offered to the adroit, unflappable Bob Maheu.

Maheu was reluctant. It sounded precarious, perhaps even preposterous, besides which Howard Hughes had been taking up more and more of his time. Edwards and O'Connell tightened the screws a little, let him remember how good they had been to him in recent years. Maheu took a day to consider the offer and the risks involved, sequestered in his den playing his favorite 101 Strings albums while he pondered. By evening he decided to tell the Office of Security boys he would do it.

Maheu had met a number of gangsters through the years and had made use of their special skills on a couple of occasions. None had been people he would ever want to be alone with in an elevator and a ten-dollar bill in his pocket. Johnny Rosselli was the exception. In Las Vegas, Maheu had first heard of him as the town's top fixer. He came to know him as something more than the typical hood. Maheu was no sucker. He had no doubt Rosselli did his share of bad things. But he had assessed him as a man of character and intelligence. He was certainly the only one of his underworld contacts Maheu would consider approaching with a delicate government project.

At the Brown Derby the two enjoyed their meeting. They ate lunch, chatted. They were having coffee when Robert—sotto voce, as the waiters, tourists, and Hollywood professionals passed nearby—finally explained to Johnny why they were there. Back in Virginia with Edwards and O'Connell he had been instructed to say to his criminal contact that he was working for some rich angry businessmen who had lost their investments in Cuba. Sitting across from Johnny Rosselli in the booth at the Brown Derby, he decided to tell him the truth. Rosselli was too smart, he would see right through a phony story, and it would mar their relationship to start off with a lie.

He was there on behalf of the government, Maheu said. The Central Intelligence Agency. He was there to ask for his help with a very important mission. A matter of national security. He was asking him, Maheu said, because he had gotten to know him over time, and he believed that whatever else he was he was a loyal, patriotic American.

"Help to do what?" said Johnny.

"To fight Communism 90 miles from Florida."

"Fight how?" said Johnny.

"Get rid of Castro."

"Get rid of him how?"

"Kill him," said Maheu.

Johnny sipped his coffee.

He looked at Maheu and laughed.

"Me?" he said. "You want me to get involved with Uncle Sam?"

Johnny told him the Feds had been trying to get something on him for years. The government wanted to throw him in jail. Was he sure he had the right guy?

Maheu told him this was a secret mission. Only a small handful of people would ever know of its existence. The people investigating Johnny, the FBI or whoever else, would never hear about it. And he—Maheu—would never discuss anything he heard or saw unrelated to the mission with anyone. There would be no public acknowledgment of John's service. If he—Maheu—were ever linked to the mission he would deny everything and never reveal anyone else's involvement. There would be no subsequent deals, no quid pro quo. It was a onetime request, and no one would ask anything more of him afterward. If he turned him down Maheu said they would never speak of the subject again. He had come to him because he held him in high regard and because he believed he and some of his friends would know how to put together such a mission. If he and they were to benefit from the results of it— Castro gone, free enterprise restored—that was their own business. He would pay him a fee of $150,000 for his time. But as far as Maheu was concerned, Johnny would be doing what needed doing for the good of his country.

They sat in silence for a time.

Then Johnny asked: When did they need this done?

Maheu said: Sooner, not later.

When did they need to know?

Now, Maheu said.

Johnny said to give him a day.

A cynic when it came to governments, politicians, upholders of the law—he'd seen them all with their hands out or their pants down—he was a sucker for God and country. However poorly his life reflected it, he counted himself a true believer and a patriot. "Maybe," he would joke, "it's because I was born on the Fourth of July." Hadn't he paid good money to get into the army during the war? He'd been eager to fight, ready to die for his country, but they'd thrown him in prison instead. If Maheu's story was legitimate, if America needed his help now—even if it was to put a bullet through Castro's skull—who was he to say no?

Johnny and Bob Maheu met again. Johnny said he'd thought it over. Whether to do it, and whether it could be done. "Okay," he told Maheu. "If this is on the up-and-up I'm ready to help."

He had two provisos: First, there was to be no payment; he would take the assignment as a call of duty. Second—remaining a cynic about people—he needed to meet Maheu's employers. He trusted Bob, but this wasn't the kind of thing that required trust alone. "I told him," Johnny would recall, "I would have to be satisfied that it was a government project, otherwise I wouldn't be interested."

It was an awkward request, as Maheu had gone against orders when he told Johnny the CIA was behind the Castro caper. Now he had to satisfy Johnny's requirement by arranging for him to meet Jim O'Connell in New York City, while somehow making O'Connell believe it was he who was coming to appraise Johnny. Maheu had O'Connell pose as an associate from his private-eye firm with an inside track on Cuba, and Johnny would pretend not to know

O'Connell was really from the CIA. Espionage was a complicated business.

The three men came to New York in the third week of September, all staying at the Plaza Hotel on Fifth Avenue (Johnny registered as "John Rawlston" from Oakland, California; O'Connell was "Jim Olds"). Preposterously they arrived at the same time as Fidel Castro, who had come to make a much-ballyhooed speech at the United Nations. While Johnny, Maheu, and O'Connell were in the Plaza suite brainstorming the assassination of the Cuban leader, the man himself was just blocks away, roaming Manhattan with his entourage, drawing crowds of supporters, protesters, reporters, and TV crews, plucking chickens and cooking them in his hotel room, tossing off incendiary bons mots, embracing Allen Ginsberg, and bear-hugging Soviet premier Nikita Khrushchev.

The plotters agreed that their base of operations would need to be in Florida, the heart of the Cuban exile community and of anti-Castro activities. They mapped out a tentative schedule for the next stage of the mission and then went their separate ways. O'Connell went back to Washington and reported to the agency that he'd met their man from "the Mafia" and the mission was a go.

Johnny left New York satisfied that Maheu's story was legit, the Castro job government-sanctioned. The next step was to share the news with Sam Giancana. This was first of all a matter of protocol. You didn't go to work for the CIA, or assassinate world leaders, and not tell the boss what was up. If Sam didn't like the idea, then it was over.

But Sam liked it. Another marker from the government. He was going to end up owning the thing. He liked it so much he counted himself in on the contract. This was a man with his hands already full, busy with an attempt to win Kennedy the presidential election, running an organized-crime Family in Chicago, overseeing Mob business in Las Vegas, dodging the constant surveillance of the FBI and various police forces, and trying to amuse several high-maintenance mistresses. But Castro had stolen a million dollars from him (casino points, nightclubs, a fleet of shrimp boats). Of course he wanted to help kill the fucker.

In a different year Giancana's impulsiveness would have been restrained by cooler heads. But the wise old men of the Outfit were otherwise engaged: Murray Humphreys, the fixer, working all-out on the Kennedy campaign, Tony Accardo in a war with the Internal Revenue Service, and Paul Ricca, having lost his own conflict with the IRS, now in prison doing a nine-year stretch for tax evasion. With no one looking over his shoulder, Giancana was free to do as he pleased.

Johnny sold Giancana to Maheu as a "backup man" if anything happened to him, a man who would "keep his mouth shut" and "had some contacts, too." Johnny wasn't sure Maheu's people would approve of Sam because he had "a pretty bad reputation." But Maheu said they were willing "to use the devil himself" to make this thing happen. (There are conflicting claims as to whether Maheu sought CIA approval for recruiting Sam Giancana, as Johnny said he did; at their first meeting with Giancana the agency liaison Jim O'Connell knew the gangster only as the pseudonymous "Sam Flood.")

In October the team of would-be assassins came together in Miami Beach. The sultry resort, sleek with midcentury glamour, dedicated to blissful escape, had lately seen the real world wash up on its pristine sands, the pollution of current events. The narrow beach town and the sprawling city to the west had become a home away from home to hordes of Cuban refugees. As many as two thousand persons a month continued to arrive, with or without permission, two years after the revolution. Their experiences of loss and violence and fear cast shadows over the sunlit Florida shores. Most were innocent victims of a wrenching social upheaval, but scattered among them were many who'd belonged to the Batista support system, who'd kept the poisonous regime running all those years, military officers, secret policemen, business owners, oligarchs, thugs. The exile neighborhoods were full of angry loyalists, plotters, backyard militias. Rumors of infiltration by Castro double agents stoked the paranoia. U.S. provocateurs prodded the daydream of a vengeful counterrevolution. *Newsweek* likened the new Miami to Casablanca, the Warner Bros. version, that is, filled with stateless persons, gunrunners, spies.

On October 11 Robert Maheu and Johnny Rosselli checked into a suite at the Kenilworth Hotel in Bal Harbour at the north end of the city, Johnny this time registering as "J. A. Rollins." Jim O'Connell arrived a few days later (his cover name again "Jim Olds"), staying at the more modest Florida Shores motel (due to a meager per diem from the CIA, he squawked) and joining his comrades at the Kenilworth. There Johnny introduced O'Connell and Maheu to the newest member of the team, "Sam Flood," who was described as the liaison with the Cubans, the man who knew the man who knew the man. The group talked strategy, what they had of one so far, then Johnny and Giancana/Flood went off to find that next link in the chain.

They sought a meeting with Santo Trafficante Jr., the ranking Mob leader in southern Florida. It was again a matter of good manners, to get approval before operating a caper like theirs in another leader's territory. Trafficante, a sober, evil-eyed Sicilian, second-generation Mob ruler, was an elusive character, perhaps the most mysterious and independent of the national syndicate bosses. Some of his rackets were unique to Florida, and though he worked deals with Meyer Lansky, the Outfit, and others, he also had criminal ties—like his drug trade with the Caribbean and South America—that were his alone. At the time of the Cuban revolution, Santo had been heavily invested in Havana and beyond, nurturing his goal of one day becoming the boss of bosses for the whole island. But things had gone another way, the bearded ones had taken it all from him, and he had even spent time in one of Fidel's prison cells. Yes, he told Johnny and Giancana when they first approached him, I will help you kill the fucker.

They all came together for another meeting at the Kenilworth. Giancana was accompanied by Trafficante, to be referred to as "Joe," or "Joe the Courier," offered up as a person with close connections in Cuba and among the anti-Castro community in Miami.

The five discussed the job at hand. They considered the possible methods of assassination and O'Connell suggested a gangland-style hit, of a sort he'd no doubt seen in the movies, sedan roaring up in front of Castro, window down, machine gun blasting. The real gangsters shook their heads. With Castro's public appearances well protected by soldiers and bodyguards, a hit from such close proximity could be thwarted and would be suicide for the gunman. They needed to shoot the Cuban boss from a greater distance, using a sniper, or else do him in with a slow-acting poison or a bomb that would allow the assassin an opportunity to get away. "Something nice and clean," said Johnny. O'Connell saw the wisdom there, and suggested he had a source for strong poisons if that was the method of choice. Trafficante agreed to find the right persons for the work and to put them in touch as soon as possible. He would require a down payment of ten thousand dollars to give the killer.

Meeting adjourned.

There was nothing to do but wait. After days of pretending that O'Connell was a Maheu employee named Olds and not a government agent, Johnny decided it was a nuisance and called him out. They were on the beach one morning playing cribbage. He stopped playing, said, "Look, Jim, I know who you are. You are not kidding me. You are with the Central Intelligence Agency." Maheu hadn't told him, Johnny said, he had just figured it out. He said, "I am not going to ask you to confirm it, you don't have to tell me. I understand your situation."

O'Connell was startled and impressed. "Rosselli," he'd say years later, "a very astute man . . . very sharp . . . he *knew*." But of course he had known all along.

Johnny told O'Connell he would not have been happy doing this job "for a client. But . . . as long as it is for the United States, it is the least I can do. . . . I owe this country a lot. . . . I owe it a lot."

Days passed, the conspirators cooled their heels. Johnny had become fond of O'Connell, and now that the CIA man was no longer trying to conceal his identity they could speak more freely. They had good conversations on the state of the world, Washington politics, and so on. One would not take them to be on opposite sides of the law. If he had any problem with "Big Jim" it was his hopelessly lackluster wardrobe. Every day he wore a bureaucrat's uniform of white shirt and black suit and tie. O'Connell saw nothing wrong with respectable attire. Johnny told him this was Miami, and he stuck out like a nun in a whorehouse. He might as well hang a police badge around his neck. One day they were walking downtown when Johnny stopped at a storefront and suggested they go inside. It was a haberdashery, expensive and with an emphasis on Latin tropical style. Johnny calculated the CIA agent's size and then picked out, purchased, and presented to him an extravagant patterned silk shirt worthy of a Havana gigolo.

With the killing of Castro on hold until Trafficante secured his Cuban contact, Sam Giancana got back to the more important business of his love life. One morning Johnny brought some news to Bob Maheu. Sam was leaving for Las Vegas. Las Vegas? said Maheu. What was he talking about? They couldn't leave Miami right now. Things were about to happen. This was a secret mission. They had to stay together. The CIA had been pushing Maheu for results.

A planned invasion of Cuba was well along, the refugee troops under U.S. supervision recruited and training in the jungles of Central America. Time was of the essence. Once ready to fight, the improvised army could be held together for just so long before it fell apart due to outside obligations, fear, boredom. The operation needed Castro dead—the island left without a leader—and on the double.

Johnny took Maheu to Sam to hear for himself. Giancana told him he was leaving, all right. He had heard a rumor that his girlfriend—one of them—was running around with another guy. He had to know if this broad—the love of his life—was cheating on him, and with some two-bit comedian, no less. Maheu sympathized but urged him to reconsider his departure for the good of the mission. Something could break at any time.

Maheu had an idea. They would put a bug in this man's Las Vegas hotel room. They would bug the room, tap the phone, record everything around the clock. He ran it past the CIA first, hoping they would do it. They gave no objection to the plan but wanted no direct involvement. Maheu told Giancana what they could do to solve his dilemma. He'd done this sort of thing before. They had the best people to do it, the listening equipment was the best, CIA approved. You could hear a pin drop (or a peignoir). In no time, he told the jealous gangster, the first intel from Vegas would be on its way.

"All right, hotshot," said Giancana. "Let's see what you can do."

The girlfriend was singer Phyllis McGuire, the comedian Dan Rowan, of Rowan & Martin, a comedy duo patterned after the disbanded Martin and Lewis. Maheu assigned the job to a Miami private eye whose work he knew and another man skilled in electronic eavesdropping. The two checked into the Riviera where Dan Rowan was staying. They secured access to his suite, filled it with listening devices, then returned to their own nearby room. The bugs worked fine, but there had not been much worth listening to in Rowan's rooms. One evening, after many hours of monitoring and the suite empty, they decided to go downstairs to the showroom and catch Rowan & Martin's act. A maid bringing fresh towels let herself into the duo's place, saw it filled with glowing electronic contraptions, headphones, crisscrossed wires, and called her supervisor, who called the cops. Bob Maheu's boys returned and were arrested. When the police looked at what was going on, and learned that the duo had been sent there from out of state, they called the FBI. Federal agents interrogated the two men and found out they were working for Robert Maheu, and then discovered from Bureau files that Maheu was among other things an ex-FBI man and a black-ops cut-out agent of the CIA. An alert was sent to Washington. A criminal investigation was opened, and the FBI went looking for Bob.

Johnny was appalled when he heard the story. He blew his top, ranted at Maheu. Their covers might be blown. The whole deal might be blown before it started. "I thought we had a highly sensitive mission," he said. "I believed in this thing."

He told Sam Giancana what had happened. Giancana started laughing. He couldn't stop. He laughed so hard that he nearly swallowed his cigar.

November 8 was Election Day. Jack Kennedy, his pregnant wife and his daughter, immediate family, relatives, close friends, and campaign staff had come together at the Kennedy patriarch's six-acre oceanfront compound at Hyannisport, Massachusetts. All day long and deep into the night they followed the reports from across the country, the rumors, indications, early results, in what became a long and grueling race to the finish.

On that same day in Forest Park, Illinois, a suburb of Chicago, a similar scene was taking place, though in circumstances less savory. At the Armory Lounge on West Roosevelt Avenue, a one-story former speakeasy that served as Sam Giancana's personal head-quarters, the Outfit boss and assorted minions were taking in the election news, air thick with smoke, a steady din of telephones ringing and the television volume way up. Johnny Rosselli had followed Sam from Florida, there to share in the glory or to en-dure the disappointment. He hung around the little tavern, roam-ing the main room, making small talk with the men and women who were tracking the contest, wandering back to Giancana's of-fice, bringing the latest numbers and shooting the breeze with Sam and whoever else had dropped by, ward bosses like Dave Yaras, Chuckie English. Now and again a call would come to Gian-cana from the West Coast—Frank Sinatra, checking on the Illi-nois vote.

The race against Richard Nixon came down to the wire. Kenne-dy's margin of victory was just 113,000 out of sixty-nine million votes cast, the closest result of the century, though through the contorted math of the electoral college this resulted in a three-to-two advantage.

To hear the wiretapped boasting, Giancana and his peers considered that their efforts had been crucial to the JFK win. Grandiosity aside, there were indications that the Chicago mob-sters *had* influenced the tally in areas where their presence was strong. In Chicago and Cook County, the margin for Kennedy was overwhelming, tipping the whole state of Illinois to the Demo-crats, a crucial win. Suspicions of voter fraud, tampering with the ballots, and so on, led to various postelection challenges, and inves-tigations and charges of illegal activity continued for months, though many of these carried the aroma of sour grapes. Rumors persisted that Nixon too had done his share of work outside the election laws, he just hadn't done as good a job of it.

With JFK's victory, Sam Giancana looked with enthusiasm to the good days ahead, sweet payback for the Outfit's efforts. A world without G-men everywhere he went. No more investigations, hearings, and loudmouthed prosecutors. And once they had taken care of Castro, who could say what gratitude would be forthcoming? Maybe an invite from Big Jack himself. A fancy dinner at the White House, with lots of sexy foreign dames from the embassies in attendance.

The bubble burst a few weeks later, when the president-elect announced he would be appointing his brother Robert to a cabinet position as the U.S. attorney general. Bobby Kennedy, rabid prosecutor of mobsters, the sworn enemy of organized crime, the man who Papa Joe Kennedy had promised would be marginalized in his son's administration, was to be the chief law enforcement officer for the nation.

"They fucked us," said Giancana. "The Kennedys fucked us good."

4

The Castro plot moved slowly, much to the distress of the CIA chiefs. The original plan had been for Fidel to be dead by late November or a Christmas gift to the free world at the latest, with the secret rebel invasion to follow soon afterward. But it was clear that they could keep to no real schedule for a mission like this, with people like this involved. Trafficante—Joe the Courier—had one excuse after another. One potential assassin had gone missing, another had gotten scared. Months went by. Johnny pursued other possibilities in the Cuban exile community. There was much big talk, but little ability. Meanwhile Giancana was back in Chicago distracted by other matters. Robert Maheu was in Washington to deal with the fallout from the wiretap mess in Las Vegas. (Questioned by the FBI, he would say only that he was involved in important secret government business and referred them to Sheffield Edwards at the Central Intelligence Agency.) Johnny Rosselli went back to his own affairs in Los Angeles and Las Vegas, ending 1960 wondering if this vital government mission was already muddled beyond repair, embarrassing to his self-image as a "strategist."

On the first day of the new year, Castro, looking alive and healthy, addressed his island nation from the Ciudad Libertad education center in Havana. The wide-ranging speech touched on many subjects, the most dramatic and unexpected being his claim that the United States was planning an imminent armed invasion. "Many have asked," said Castro, "if Eisenhower in his last days in power, that is, if imperialism before the change of administration, might not decide to clear us out of the way. Late in December we received information from a reliable source that the CIA, headed by Allen Dulles, had hatched a plan against our country, had hatched a plan to create a fictitious incident on our territory or near our shores, to invent an incident, propitiate it . . . to give a pretext for military intervention by imperialist forces. . . . We are sure the imperialists believe that intervention in Cuba will be a weekend affair. The imperialists believe that their work in Cuba will be a matter of hours and that the world will be presented with a fait accompli. We are sure that an incorrect estimate of the situation is being made by the imperialists. We have alerted the country and the world to danger facing Cuba. . . . We have taken steps to make the imperialists see that it will be no military weekend.

"Two years ago in the face of our advancing people, the servants of imperialism fled. Today we and the people, with a just cause, facing those who wrongly want to prevent us from having a life of peace and progress, are not here to flee. Those who are in the right never flee. They know how to die. What we have done is to gather here to say: Fatherland or Death! We will conquer!"

Two days later the U.S. government broke off diplomatic relations with Cuba. Uncle Sam was done with these Reds. A reckoning was coming. Down in Central America an invasion force of nearly two thousand Cuban exiles was trained and ready to go. Dozens of aircraft, bombers and surveillance planes, transport ships and landing vessels. Caches of weapons and ammunition piled up on the Caribbean coast, with backup resources ready for delivery from the Florida Keys.

The would-be invaders waited. They waited without explanation. What was the delay? The clock ticked on the Eisenhower administration (JFK would be sworn in on January 20). In discreet corridors of Washington it was said that Ike had decided to hold off on the Cuba surprise, pass the ball to his successor. He'd had his D-day, let the new guy handle this. Kennedy had been apprised of the invasion plan since the election but—even after taking office—he was unaware of the plot to kill the Cuban leader, and knew nothing about the mission collaboration with the Mob. At the CIA, meanwhile, those in the loop continued to believe in their unorthodox plan. Delayed, yes, but everything coming together. The mobsters had found their assassin, the deal was being finalized. Any day now the world would see the results of the CIA's invention and daring, even if the agency would not be permitted to take its rightful credit.

In March the members of the Castro assassination team came together again in Miami Beach. Trafficante had found them their killer. Santo took Johnny to meet the Havana connection, direct contact with the assassin-to-be. Trafficante served as translator as they went over the plan. The man was to deliver the client's deadly potion to an ally in the capital, a cook or servant, it was, with access to the dictator's food and drink. The fee was ten thousand in advance toward the full payment of a quarter million due upon Castro's demise.

Time was of the essence or surely the team would have gathered some week other than during the two biggest social events of the season, the heavyweight title fight between champion Floyd Patterson and Ingemar Johansson at the Convention Center on the thirteenth, and Frank Sinatra making an extended appearance at the La Ronde supper club in the Fontainebleau. The city was sold out, heaving with vacationers, gamblers, celebrities, press, police, thieves. Sam Giancana had been in town for weeks, making Miami his winter headquarters. He'd rented two large suites a floor below Sinatra's penthouse, enough room for everybody, visiting gangsters, spies, private detectives, bodyguards, drop-by pallies, girlfriends, hookers up from the Poodle Lounge, and a convoy of room service waiters; in addition there were two or three FBI agents downstairs in the lobby waiting for Giancana to make an appearance. It was a curious command post for a top-secret government mission.

Bob Maheu arrived with an associate, Joe Shimon, a fifty-four-year-old inspector in the Detective Bureau of the Washington, DC, Police Department. Shimon served as a special agent with the White House and other DC institutions, had run security for presidents and world leaders, and for many years moonlighted as a private investigator on various shadowy Maheu projects. He knew Johnny Rosselli, having met him in Las Vegas at the same time Maheu did, when they were working the Milton Berle/Louis Prima/marijuana case. Shimon thought he was going to Miami to relax and see the boxing match as Bob's guest, but in reality Maheu was grooming him to take Maheu's place should the ongoing Vegas wiretap mess go wrong. They went straight up to Giancana's suite, where Johnny Rosselli and Sam were finishing up a meeting with Vegas exec Lou Lederer, who'd stopped off en route to Jamaica, something to do with casinos in Montego Bay. Lederer left. Johnny fixed some drinks, everybody sat around on the overstuffed armchairs, facing the balcony windows with a view of the Atlantic that went all the way to Africa. A big plate of caviar with all the fixings sat on the coffee table. It was Sam's craze. He had it flown in every day and prepared it himself.

Giancana had a compact audio player beside him on the couch and was having trouble keeping the earphone in his ear. He was trying to listen to tapes his adoring friend Frank Sinatra had sent down from the penthouse. They were Frank's latest recordings. He'd send a tape down, then he'd call to see if Sam liked it. He'd send another, then call again.

"That Sinatra can be a pain in the ass," said Johnny.

After a time Johnny and Maheu started a furtive conversation. Shimon caught bits and pieces. Maheu got him alone in another room and told him what was happening. Shimon balked. You're talking about killing somebody? he said. I don't care who it is. I'm a cop, he said. I'm still wearing a pin [a badge]. Maheu said he didn't understand, this was an assignment from the U.S. government. All the way from the top. It was Johnny's contract, he said. Fully approved. Shimon gave this some thought. The president hiring Johnny Rosselli and Sam Giancana to kill Fidel Castro. That was . . . well, that was something. Then again, he'd been around Maheu and around the government and knew that anything was possible. The newspapers never learned half the stuff that went on. He had to admit that getting rid of Castro was not the worst idea in the world.

Shimon followed Maheu back to the living room. Johnny grinned and poured him another drink. They talked openly now, Johnny bringing the plot up to date. The package they were waiting for had finally arrived from Washington. A neurotoxin—there is some difference of opinion whether the toxin was in liquid or pill form—fresh from the CIA laboratory, the latest and deadliest formula (the creation of Cornelius Roosevelt, grandson of President Teddy). The assassin in Cuba would dose Castro's food or drink with the poison, and after ingesting even a drop or two Fidel would become ill and he would remain ill for two or three days, and then he would die. Nothing sudden. No trace of the toxin would remain in the body. No autopsy could show what killed him.

As they talked Giancana took out his earpiece and listened, nodding with vague approval. The telephone rang, and Johnny took the call. It was Sinatra wanting to talk to Sam. Giancana shook his head. Frank wanted to come down and visit. Giancana shook his head and cringed. Johnny told him they were busy just then, why didn't he make it later, hung up.

"Don't let that big-mouthed guinea in here!" Giancana said. "Don't open your mouth around him. You know, he blew off Lucky Luciano with that big mouth of his and if he gets any wind of this it will be all over because he'll brag about it everywhere."*

Disdain for Sinatra had increased since the election. He had given them no warning of the president's intention of making brother Robert the attorney general. There was no evidence that he'd known about it in advance, but Frank bragged about his access to Jack and his close ties with the whole family, and Giancana found him a satisfying whipping boy. Sinatra seemed oblivious to the mocking, remaining ardent before his outlaw idols. They were seeing him that evening. It was the singer's first night off in Miami, and he was taking a couple of dozen people out on the town, to dinner, then to see Jimmy Durante's show at the Deauville, then barhopping until dawn. Johnny found a hot date, some doctor's wife, and he decided he needed to borrow Sam's bejeweled ring

---

* In 1946 the exiled Lucky Luciano had left Italy and settled in Cuba, to be closer to business in the United States. Frank Sinatra had been invited to entertain during a Mob summit meeting, the so-called Havana Conference. Frank was so excited he was going to meet Luciano that he got him a present of an inscribed solid gold cigarette case—"From Frank to Lucky" it said— then showed it to everyone, with attendant details. According to Sam Giancana, Sinatra told everybody in New York he was going to meet Lucky in Cuba and it was his "big mouth" that alerted the Feds to Luciano's whereabouts. Under pressure from the U.S. government, the Cubans arrested Luciano and sent him back to Italy.

to impress her. "All right, go ahead," Sam said. "I guess I'll put on that goddamn ring Sinatra gave me." And this led to another jibe at Frank's expense, down in the dining room, as the singer made a beeline for Giancana's table, then stopped short, his face lighting up. "Oh! You finally wore the ring!" said Sinatra. "You finally put it on!" This elicited some eye-rolling, and Joe Shimon, with a few drinks in him, said, "Are you two queer for each other?" Which made Giancana burst out laughing. The singer waved them off and went back to his group at another table.

The poison was to be handed over to the courier late at night in the hotel. Johnny Rosselli and his band of Miami assassins were having a nightcap in the Boom Boom Room off the lobby. He didn't expect trouble, but he was handling a package of deadly poison and did not mind having the crew there keeping an eye out for him. The courier was a small, dark-skinned man in tattered clothes; he looked like any of the raggedy Cuban refugees and hustlers who now roamed the Miami streets. He was an unlikely figure to be playing a part in world events (though, to be fair, no less likely than said events occurring in someplace called the Boom Boom Room).

Johnny went out with the man, was gone for a while, came back. The poison was on its way to Havana, and that, for now, was that.

Later in the week Maheu called.

"John, did you read the paper?"

"No."

"He's sick."

"Yeah?"

"They don't know what's wrong with him."

"Yeah?"

"This is it. It won't be long now."

"Good."

Days passed. Castro recovered. The illness had been a coincidence. Or the poison had failed. Or the cook had been canned, or the agent had been caught, or Castro had found a new place to eat.

At CIA headquarters they were pacing the floors, tearing at their hair. They had invested forty million dollars in an invasion. Twelve hundred men stood ready. Stories about the "top-secret" rebel army were beginning to appear in newspapers. The element of surprise had all but slipped away. To postpone again was impossible.

Another plot was hatched, emphasis on urgency. This time the CIA suggested the man for the job. Juan Orta was a longtime Cuban politico and Castro supporter. In the new government he'd been appointed Fidel's personal secretary. He worked in the anteroom outside the leader's office, and saw him every day. It was believed Orta became disenchanted with Castro's ruthless style of governing and entered into covert dialogue with the United States. Talk got around to doing away with the brutal dictator, making room for a moderate, humane leader, someone like . . . Juan Orta. An arrangement was made. Again wanting to hide their fingerprints, the agency left the rest to Rosselli and Maheu. With a new deadly potion received, this time in the form of pills hidden inside a customized pencil, Johnny delivered the package to another Trafficante go-between. Days later he received word that the pills were in Juan Orta's hands.

They heard nothing more. By early April Johnny assumed Orta was scared or dead. In fact Castro had learned of his secretary's alienation, and Orta had gone underground, taking refuge in the Mexican Embassy, where he hid out for the next five years.

President Kennedy had been aware of the plan to invade Cuba—
code-named JMARC (known to the Pentagon as Operation
Zapata)—since before he took office. The CIA's Allen Dulles and
Richard Bissell had briefed him in full on November 18, 1960. Kennedy, according to Bissell, seemed "neither for nor against the operation." Months later, as the Cuban "D-day" approached, the
president remained undecided, weighing political concerns and
international consequences against the military realities of the
invasion itself. Kennedy wanted the appearance of an authentic,
Cuban-organized attack. He feared any overt sign of U.S. involvement. He feared triggering a Soviet quid pro quo takeover of West
Berlin. He feared the whole thing going very wrong. Demanding
a smaller footprint, a reduced "noise level," the president had the
mission planners change the landing point from the port of Trinidad, close by the mountains where the invaders could quickly find
cover, to a more secluded spot one hundred miles away known as
the Bahia de Cochinos, or Bay of Pigs, waters full of threatening
coral reefs and a beachhead separated from the mountains by many
miles of swamp. The changes to the invasion plan made the path
to victory more difficult, but the CIA's Bissell remained committed to action, optimistic in his reports to the president, afraid that
Kennedy would pull the plug if victory was less than certain. In
fact Kennedy was diffident throughout, giving piecemeal approval,
making dangerous adjustments to the end. The invasion had spun
out of control before the first shot was fired.

In the early hours of April 17, an armada of five aged freighters,
formerly used to transport bananas from Central America, now
carrying the 1,334 men of Brigada Asalto 2506, and two LCI ships of
World War II vintage, entered the Bay of Pigs on the southwestern

coast of Cuba, heading for the three contiguous beaches where the invasion would begin. There were disruptions at the start, problems with the landing craft coming toward shore, mechanical failures, and physical damage from the sharp-toothed reef. Bad luck abounded. Cuban military in a random security check spotted some landed *brigadistas* and radioed for help. Within an hour Castro himself was involved, rousted awake at the apartment of Celia Sánchez (known as the leading lady of the revolution), and by 3:00 a.m., his M1 rifle in hand, directing troop movements against the invaders. The brigade soldiers soon faced a large, fierce opposition. By dawn came vintage Hawker Sea Furies of the Cuban Air Force, firing rockets at the ships and landing craft, sinking one, badly damaging another, igniting the fuel reserves on another. Hundreds of the invading troops were thrown into deep water, struggled for their lives, losing their weapons and supplies, while those already landed were fighting and dying along the coastline. The support of the brigade aircraft (four of six in action shot down) and the landing of 170-some brigade paratroopers inland failed to have an impact on the direction of the conflict. The groundswell of anti-Castro resistance that an exile invasion was predicted to ignite among the rural population failed to materialize. On the beach the exiles made desperate radio calls for help, begged for air support. In Washington, President Kennedy monitored the situation. He dithered, pulled back, refused to authorize further American military involvement. Allen Dulles and Richard Bissell had been certain that (according to Dulles) "when the chips were down" the president would not accept defeat and would order a last-minute intervention. They were proved incorrect. The exile troops stuck on the beach fought bravely, outnumbered, blasted by 122 mm howitzers. The fight continued into a third day, but was now little more than a cleanup by the Castro forces. More than a hundred brigade soldiers had been killed. A few dozen escaped by sea, rescued by the remaining *contra* vessels and a U.S destroyer.

Hundreds fled into the dense swamp. More than twelve hundred *brigadistas* were captured, to be executed or thrown into prison.

With his CIA contacts lying low, Johnny Rosselli knew no more of what happened at the Bay of Pigs than anybody else. What you could learn from the newspapers was bad enough. Even without knowledge of the extent of U.S. involvement, the attempted invasion of Cuba was seen as an American defeat, a propaganda fiasco on the Cold War scorecard, and an embarrassing introduction to the new president's capability in a crisis. Beyond the public flaunting of their victory, the head men in Cuba themselves wondered what the *Yanquis* had been thinking. Why had they refused to seize the day?* The Kremlin was likewise perplexed—and pleased. Was the young president as weak as that? After a humiliating summit meeting with Khrushchev in June '61, Kennedy himself said the Soviet leader believed he "had no guts."

Johnny would wonder about his own contribution to the mess. Would Castro's assassination have meant a different outcome? It was difficult not to believe so. Fidel had shown his mastery as a leader, commanding his forces, directing a brilliant defense. The CIA had wanted him gone before the invasion, and they'd been right about that, if nothing else. Johnny had taken the assignment as an act of duty, any benefit—someday a small consideration from the government, perhaps—of collateral interest. His country needed a job done, and he was ready to do it. It had been his contract, his responsibility. And he had fucked it up, along with his band of eccentric secret agents. Once he permitted Sam Giancana to join the mission he'd opened the door to chaos. You couldn't blame that on Sam. It was the man's nature, like the scorpion in

---

* That summer at an OAS conference in Punta del Este, Uruguay, the White House aide Richard Goodwin bumped into Castro right-hand man Che Guevara; Che greeted him cheerily, saying, "Thank you for the Bay of Pigs— you made us stronger than ever!"

the fable. For a moment it had seemed to Giancana like it would be fun to kill Castro, before boredom set in. And when they'd recruited Trafficante—a more venomous scorpion—well . . . Johnny had come to believe Santo had done nothing but lie to them. That ten-grand deposit had probably gone directly into his pocket, and the botulin toxin too (he'd no doubt find some other good use for it). There were even rumors floating in the exile community that Trafficante was a Castro spy, had bartered his way out of prison with a promise to betray the Cuban exiles when he had the chance.

For all that, Trafficante and Giancana had been no more troublesome than Robert Maheu, the taciturn former law enforcer and experienced spy who should have known better. His disastrous Vegas eavesdropping plot had attracted the attention of the FBI, and his failure to hide his connection to the crime brought on high-level scrutiny.

The CIA's Sheffield Edwards attempted to stop the bleeding, running interference with J. Edgar Hoover, requesting he not pursue the wiretap prosecution on grounds of national security. But Hoover was not disposed to grant any fraternal favors. He had a particular disdain for his competitors at the CIA, with their flamboyance and their big budget and their preponderance of agents with Ivy League accents. What grounds? he asked Edwards. Was not Las Vegas still a part of the United States? The agency was not licensed for internal-security ops. In pursuit of Hoover's mercy, Edwards made things worse. He admitted that the agency had been collaborating with members of organized crime in a top-secret operation against the Cuban government. He also let slip that the attorney general was aware of it (an assertion he based on passing hearsay from Richard Bissell, who'd heard it from Allen Dulles). Hoover demanded Edwards give him a written statement to all he'd said, including the line about Robert Kennedy's complicity. Instead of getting the dogs called off, Edwards had thrown them red meat. Hoover had no love for Robert Kennedy, his new boss;

found him arrogant, conniving, disrespectful (he had perhaps heard about the AG's mocking references to his "confirmed bachelorhood"). Hoover had been keeping tabs on both Kennedys, shadowing them, filing away their every indiscretion. It was not material he intended to release, but it served as an insurance policy should he ever need it; for instance, to fight a White House request for him to retire. The problem was, Robert, unlike his brother, had too few secrets in his closet. Hoover had been looking for more dirt on the younger Kennedy. Evidence that the great gangbuster had been in cahoots with the Mafia was just the unclean data he needed for his collection.

The FBI delayed prosecution of Maheu, but the investigation went on, Hoover wanting to know much more about this CIA/gangster collaboration before the agency managed to make it all disappear.

One day in Beverly Hills—it was some weeks after the Bay of Pigs—Johnny Rosselli was going into Drucker's Hairdressers for Men on Wilshire for his weekly trim. Two men in suits entered the building just behind him. Neither of them seemed like customers. Both looked like they cut their own hair. One said they were from the FBI, but showed no identification. They did not want to flash their badges and embarrass him, he said. They wanted to ask some questions. Was that all right? How would it be if they told him some things and then asked him if those things were true or not?

Johnny said, "It's all right, as long as both of you tell me you're FBI agents. I guess I'll have to take your word for it."

The agent said, "Well, it's just something about Bob Maheu." He said, "It's something that occurred in Florida and Las Vegas. We would like to know if it was a favor. And other things you might know about this [wire]tap."

Of course. Maheu's fucking tap.

Johnny said, "Wherever you got the first part, you can get the rest of it."

The agent said, "Were you and Bob paying back a favor to Giancana? Or was it something else? We would like to talk to you about it."

He added, "We'd like to have you come have a drink with us or something."

Johnny said, "I do not have any time for that."

Baseball was on the television in the barbershop. He said, "If you want to talk about the ball game, fine. Otherwise . . ."

"Do you know Sam Giancana?" asked the agent.

"Let's discuss the weather," Johnny said. "I do not care to answer any more questions."

One thing for sure, his cover was blown. It had to be Bob Maheu. Under pressure, he'd squealed. When he reached him Maheu claimed it wasn't as simple as that. They'd gotten Johnny's name by tracking long-distance phone calls from their Miami hotel room charged to his credit card.

The first two agents went away, but there were more to come. Agents tailed him everywhere. It was like before but much worse. They followed him, took pictures, bugged his rooms. If he flew somewhere there were agents at the airport when he took off and at the airport when he landed. If he spent the night with a woman there was someone on the street waiting for him in the morning. It was all very disappointing. He had wanted to do something for his country, and this was what he got for it. Being a good guy was not all it was cracked up to be. He made calls to Jim O'Connell and Sheffield Edwards at the CIA, asking them to intercede, but after the muddle with Maheu it seemed no one wanted to go near J. Edgar Hoover. Forget about them being on the same side. It was like the rival gangs of Chicago in the old days, nobody trusted anybody farther than they could spit.

As time passed Johnny assumed that his term of service to the government was ended. Months went by with no word from the boys in Washington, only a birthday greeting from Big Jim O'Connell. The Kennedys were putting all the blame for the Bay of Pigs on the CIA leadership. At the top DCI Allen Dulles and DDP Richard Bissell were sacrificed, to be replaced by industrialist/government adviser John McCone and Dick Helms, a more cautious "team player." Everyone in the agency felt the humiliation, some of it deserved. Khrushchev meanwhile was baiting the president in his own backyard, sending Soviet troops and weaponry to help the Cubans defend themselves against any further American incursions (that same summer there was another Soviet-backed "defense" posture, the building of the Berlin Wall, aka "the Anti-Fascist Protective Wall"). Both Jack and Bobby were tormented and enraged by the post-Pigs situation, wanting revenge for the loss of face, and to be rid of their North American nuisance.

The Kennedys formed an intraagency committee, the Special Group Augmented (SGA), chaired by Robert and including the CIA director, the national security adviser, and members of the Defense Department, the State Department, and the Joint Chiefs of Staff. By November the committee had produced a plan. Operation Mongoose called for the overthrow of the Cuban government, the guidelines describing "maximum use of indigenous resources, internal and external"—and this time no dithering about U.S. involvement, the new plan recognizing that "the final success will require decisive U.S. military intervention." Appointed the operation's leader was Brig. Gen. Edward Lansdale, a roving anticommunist troubleshooter said to be the model for the murderous do-gooder title character in Graham Greene's novel *The Quiet*

American. The Kennedys designated Mongoose the *"top priority"* of the U.S. government. *"All else is secondary,"* RFK told his directorate on January 19, 1962, *"no time, money or effort is to be spared."*

The operation retained a top-secret component from the previous one: assassination.

5

The government was *not* done with him. It was after New Year's 1962 when he got the call from Jim O'Connell. They were back in business. A date was set for a reunion in Miami. Details to come. With luck these would be better than the last ones. Johnny's enthusiasm for an opportunity to prove his patriotism had dimmed since the first go-round, though he tried to show no sign of it to O'Connell. If they still needed him then he was ready. Loyalty was a discipline he had learned through the years with his other organizational associates. Maybe the second chance was a charm.

The meeting took place in the restaurant at the international airport. Big Jim arrived, accompanied by another man unknown to Johnny. He was a baleful, middle-aged man, disheveled, egg-shaped, with a ragged mustache and bulging eyeballs suggesting thyroid disease. He looked like a hungover Oliver Hardy. O'Connell introduced him, and Johnny shook hands with Bill Harvey, the spymaster some called—clearly not for his physical glamour—the American James Bond.

William King Harvey was a former FBI man who had migrated to the newly formed Central Intelligence Agency a couple of years after the war. Stationed in Europe, playing Cold War games with the Soviets and their minions, he soon became a star player in the clandestine service. He was imaginative, intuitive, ruthless. He was the classic maverick, not prone to following orders, best left to his own devices, abrasive. But damn good. It was Harvey who was first to suspect the Brit traitor/Soviet mole Kim Philby (by contrast, the vaunted counterintelligence oracle James Jesus Angleton defended Philby as the victim of a witch hunt). In charge of the volatile Berlin Operations Base (BOB) from 1952 to 1960, he'd commanded many a dangerous mission with lives at stake and sometimes lost. His most celebrated caper with the UK's SIS (Secret Intelligence Service) was the building of a hidden tunnel into East Berlin and the tapping of Soviet underground communication facilities, an extraordinary feat of engineering, among other things.* His adventures in espionage were the stuff of legend, as were his alcohol intake, his aversion to authority, and his reckless philandering.

Returned to the States in late '59, Harvey spent some thumb-twiddling time in the cryptological section at CIA headquarters before being plunged back into murky waters as the designated head of ZR/RIFLE, the agency's new, maximum-secret "standby" assassination program. Harvey's assignment was soon rolled into the expanding Operation Mongoose, the CIA's autonomous portion called Task Force W (named by Harvey after one of his heroes, William Walker, the American soldier of fortune who was briefly the ruler of Nicaragua, before being executed by a firing squad; some say Harvey chose the reference as a premonition of disaster). He worked out of the new CIA headquarters in Langley, Virginia, and at the growing agency base in Florida.

---

* The audaciousness of Harvey's tunnel plot was not diminished by the fact that the Soviets were aware of the tunnel almost from the start, thanks to an observant double agent.

In Miami the spy and the gangster faced off across a restaurant table, each assessing the other, neither enjoying what he saw. "Johnny did not like him at all," O'Connell remembered. He was not happy with a stranger joining them unannounced, even with Big Jim's endorsement. He trusted O'Connell well enough. But how sure could he be about any of these people? One way or the other, at the end of the day they were all cops.

Bill Harvey seemed no more comfortable in Johnny Rosselli's presence. He had been skeptical upon learning of the agency's alliance with the Mob. There had been too little security, too much chance of blowback. He had worked with professional criminals in the past—in Europe he'd used burglars, forgers, leg breakers, and worse—that was not a problem, but he had always found his own people for an operation and subjected those people to a long "period of assessment." And he just didn't like the idea of Bob Maheu's gangland buddies being dropped into his lap. (Harvey had known Maheu in their FBI days twenty years earlier and had never liked him.) Staring back across the table, Harvey made one of his signature moves, reaching inside his jacket and pulling out a .38 Detective Special from under his armpit. He laid it on the table next to a bottle of ketchup and waited for a reaction.

Johnny had been dealing with men pulling out guns for nearly half a century and was unmoved.

"Do you have a lot of need for that?" he asked.

"Not a lot," Harvey said. "But when I need it I need it in a hurry."

O'Connell gave Johnny the news. He was being transferred. He would go abroad in another month or so. Bill Harvey was taking his place. Bill was the best they had, Jim said. He had run things in Berlin for them for years. He had fucked the Reds up good. Big Jim said Washington was making an all-out push on Cuba, full support. Things would be better this time out. They were all on the same page, right up to the man at the top.

Harvey wanted to know more about the earlier venture. There were blank spots that needed filling in (his knowledge of the Maheu-Rosselli op was from recall by O'Connell and Sheff Edwards; there was no file kept). Johnny still looked doubtful, but answered as he could. Harvey's questions showed his great skill as an interrogator. They cut like a dagger, uncovering mistakes and weak links. Johnny found himself responsive to Harvey's command. A few rounds for everybody may have helped the mood. As the quiz continued, his answers grew thoughtful and detailed. The interrogation became a conversation. The give-and-take revealed character. It turned out they did not dislike each other after all.

Over the days and drinks ahead a friendship took root.

"They got real chummy," said O'Connell. "They fell in love."

Not quite, but close. It was one of those connections, kindred spirits, whatever you called it. Each man saw some reflection of himself in the other, for better or worse. Two bruised adventurers. Keepers of dirty secrets. Organization men who did not quite fit the organization. Maybe it *was* love. Johnny gave Harvey the flattering nickname "the Panther" for his stalking gait; in contrast his coworkers at the CIA called him "the Pear."

The new plan was the old plan: Make Castro dead and keep the U.S. government's name out of it. But this time it was going to be lean and mean. Harvey wanted the absolute fewest links, no loose threads. Rosselli was the man. Everyone else was cut loose. Maheu. Giancana. Trafficante. They'd done more harm than good. The only people who would know both ends of the operation after Big Jim's departure would be the two of them. Johnny agreed to the level of secrecy, though he knew that working behind Trafficante's back in Florida was dangerous. He had to hope that the ultimate result—Cuba returned to status quo ante—would make Santo forgive and forget.

They spent the next couple of days in Miami preparing for what was ahead. Harvey, according to friend and fellow agent Bayard Stockton, "gave Johnny a crash course in intelligence tradecraft . . . security, the use of the telephone, counter-surveillance, the use of cutouts, recruitment requirements and name checking." Stockton believed Bill also administered a polygraph test, to determine matters of loyalty and motivation. Friendship was one thing, but it was best for everybody to be a professional.

Harvey made it clear he was no cheerleader for the mission. Johnny couldn't look to him for "moral" support. He didn't hide his doubts about the ethics and legality of what they were doing. He called the governmental use of assassination "a confession of weakness." In the case of a serious and imminent threat to the United States, Harvey believed "no tool to remove that threat should be taken away from the President," but he was far from sure that Castro had come up to that standard. Either way, he wanted it known, a mission like this was not normal business for the agency. The two most-talked-about subjects in the CIA, he said, were "sex and assassination." But the latter, unlike the former, was very seldom attempted. "Executive Action" was something new and far from a codified policy. They were making it up as they went along. Harvey had taken charge of the program, he said, to keep it away from someone less responsible.

The émigré community was now—if possible—even more unhappy and restless than before, their hope of reclaiming Cuba drowned in the red waters of the Bahia de Cochinos. President Kennedy and the CIA had been added to the exiles' shitlist, though Castro retained his standing as the most hated man in Miami. Many were still prepared to lay down their lives to be rid of the tyrant. Persons willing to kill Castro were easy to find in this environment. It was finding someone with an ability and opportunity to do it that was the tricky part.

Manuel Antonio de Varona was the prime minister of Cuba from 1948 to 1950, and since going into exile in 1960 had become one of the most prominent of the anti-Castro activists, a big noise in the Cuban Revolutionary Council. He had been talking himself up as the best choice to rule Cuba once the current officeholder was removed, and Washington was vaguely keen on him for the job. Like many a would-be Cuban warlord in Miami, he had a small part-time private army, and down at the marina kept an armada of two power cruisers with which to launch a (small) invasion at a moment's notice. The word was that Varona had conspirators inside the current island government, and was cultivating one or another of them to depose their disappointing Marxist leader.

Johnny, again posing as the representative of angry businessmen, met with the former prime minister to discuss their mutual interest in a world without Castro. He found Varona to be a typical politician, full of himself and full of shit, but he made a convincing case for his having access to persons ready to kill Fidel. It would require expense money and a large cash payment when the deed was done. The assassin would prefer to remain alive afterward, and so it was decided that a delayed-action poisoning was the safest method of execution. For Johnny it had to feel, as a wise man once said, like déjà vu all over again.

Varona threw in a last-minute stipulation. He had a shopping list he needed filled: guns, ammo, grenades, radar, two-way radios. Whatever else happened, Varona wanted his private army looking good. The boss of JMWAVE, the CIA's growing Florida station, was Ted Shackley (aka "the Blond Ghost"), another of Bill Harvey's old Berlin buddies. He asked no questions, requisitioned the items himself, obtained a truck and U-Haul via multiple cutouts, drove the trove out of the JMWAVE compound, and handed it over to

Johnny and Big Jim O'Connell. It was a classic cloak-and-dagger evening. Johnny and Big Jim took the truck and trailer, drove to an empty unlit parking lot in South Miami, and left Varona's goodies to be picked up. They waited out of sight until another vehicle arrived, two men got out—"they *looked* like Cubans," recalled O'Connell—hooked up the trailer, and drove away.

A few days passed. Word came from Varona. The pills had made it to Havana. Now it was only a question of opportunity.

Weeks passed. Varona claimed that there were difficulties. Castro was never in the same place twice. A busy man. But soon he would be taking a long rest.

In late June Johnny went back to Florida. By now the preparations for the secret war on Cuba mandated by Operation Mongoose had become a covert extravaganza. The intrusion caused a real estate boom in southern Florida. The JMWAVE station in Miami alone occupied two thousand acres of land, headquartered among the abandoned buildings on the old Richmond Field dirigible base, disguised as an electronics company plant (Zenith Technical Enterprises), with other Mongoose-related properties hidden behind business fronts scattered all over the city. Farther south, in the sodden wilderness of the Everglades and obscure harbors of the Florida Keys, were dozens of new base camps, training grounds, docks, and airstrips, and thousands of Cuban exiles culled from the numerous anti-Castro action groups in Miami. The militias were being trained in guerrilla fighting, sabotage, intelligence gathering, training for the big invasion they were promised would be "the one." Small groups were sent out to Cuba on raiding parties, blowing things up, stirring up trouble however they could. There were regular shipments of weapons smuggled to the underground and a supply of anti-Castro Cubans, assigned to gather intel and incite rebellion across the island.

ZR/RIFLE had its own encampment at a secluded waterfront property on Key Largo. There were crudely thrown-together barracks, open mess, a shooting range cleared out of the mangroves, retrofitted powerboats at the floating dock. Human resources amounted to a handful of trusted agency personnel and a small number of Cubans coming and going, a half dozen or so at a time. The Cubans were drawn from the militia groups, selected for their good marksmanship, being trained as snipers (with a single target in mind). Paramilitary matters were handled by an experienced covert agent known as Dave M., a fierce Mexican-American operative, a veteran of the Bay of Pigs, now attached to Bill Harvey's program.

It was a kind of assassination summer camp, and Johnny Rosselli was the newest camp counselor. He kept an eye on things, stayed alert for Castro spies, and reported progress to Bill Harvey, who was more often than not in Washington battling with Bobby Kennedy and the Mongoose bureaucrats and considering potential assassins among his European sources. Though the Keys and adjacent lands were crowded with military and CIA special ops, ZR/RIFLE was meant to stay aloof and zipper tight. Few agency men involved with Mongoose matters ever claimed to have known anything about Harvey's most secret operation or its "Mafia" component, and the few who did, like Ted Shackley, were adamant that Johnny Rosselli had zero access to the JMWAVE offices and operations. Other reports and claims in later years, of Rosselli working openly in the Miami headquarters or among the other operations in the south, passing himself off as a U.S. military intelligence officer ("the Colonel"), seem unlikely, given Bill Harvey's fetish for secrecy and vest-pocket containment. Most Cold War historians agree with the assessment of Jack Colhoun: "[Harvey] kept the assassination operation separate and distinct from the task force . . . [and] kept his most trusted CIA aides in the dark." No files were created on the ZR/RIFLE op, and no notes taken.

Activity at the camp was circumscribed. Every day the same, only hotter and stickier than the one before. The Cubans practiced shooting with their long-range rifles and their telescopic sights. The Americans drank rum and beer, played cribbage, fought mosquitoes. Some days Johnny and a couple of others would go out fishing on the Atlantic. Every so often, on moonless nights, one of the V20 powerboats would roar off to Cuba with a team of newly qualified sharpshooters.

Not *every* day was the same. One morning Johnny was out exploring along the archipelago when he happened upon a view of unexpected activity just up from the shoreline. Forty or fifty people were huddled together under a halo of glaring reflected light. A movie was being made, a crew and cast of actors preparing to shoot. Boredom, or perhaps nostalgia for his picturemaking days, drew him to the scene. They were filming an adaptation of *PT-109*, the popular book by Robert J. Donovan recounting young navy lieutenant John F. Kennedy's experience in the Pacific during World War II, his command of a patrol torpedo boat sunk by the Japanese, and the harrowing, heroic story of survival that followed. The Florida Keys had been selected as an economical substitute for the Solomon Islands.

The laws of coincidence were showing off: The producer of the movie was Johnny's old pal and mentor Bryan Foy. They hadn't seen each other in years, their friendship having dissolved one day after some bitter dispute, and they'd never made up. Now there was delight—and no doubt some astonishment—at this unexpected reunion many miles from Hollywood. Foy was back working for his old boss Jack Warner, making a "prestige" picture on a frugal budget (Brynie remained the undisputed "King of the Bs"), and with an eye out to keeping the real JFK happy (Kennedy had already influenced the casting of a grave fortyish Cliff Robertson to portray his twenty-five-year-old self). It was not likely that Johnny said anything to Foy about his own JFK-approved project. They promised to meet again when they were both back home in California.

Another, more precarious break in the routine occurred one night when the latest batch of snipers was being taken by cruiser to Cuba. The camp was shorthanded, and Johnny volunteered to ride shotgun on one of the V20s. This was no Sunday drive. Task-force vessels had gone out, and some had never come back. The run to Cuba took hours at high speed in pitch-black night, hard against the powerful Gulf Stream chop. When at last the vague silhouette of land appeared in the darkness, the boats glided toward shore, all alert for Castro patrols, weapons loaded and ready. The snipers were sent off, and the V20s turned around toward Florida. The boat *was* spotted by the Cuban coast guard—years later he told Betsy Duncan and others this part of the story—spotted and strafed with automatic fire before they could get away, just barely outrunning the Cuban cutter and disappearing in the dark. Betsy kiddingly reminded him of the time he'd told George Raft he could take over that island with a few guys and some machine guns, but he did not find it funny.

Bill Harvey came down from Washington every week or so, stayed for a couple of days, and then went back to the capital. He was not a happy man. Harvey was no fan of the Kennedys to begin with. He was a small-town Hoosier who considered them arrogant and overprivileged brats. The attorney general—whose commandeering of the covert operation against Cuba was a position that was outside his appointed role and one for which many were finding him quite unqualified—was making life hell for his CIA subordinates, particularly William Harvey. Bobby demanded results in

Cuba *yesterday*, and by his pointed repeated reference so did his brother, whose name Bobby dropped like a club to stifle opposition. The intelligence professionals sought to explain the methods of their profession, the hard work and time that were required to prep a country for insurrection. Agency analysts warned that there was as yet no appetite for mass rebellion among the Cuban people. If the exile militias invaded now they would be wiped out unless America provided a large military backup—which, despite presidential declarations, and despite U.S. military rehearsals for a possible invasion, was looking to be as unlikely as it had proved to be at the Bay of Pigs—Kennedy still fearful of any direct action attributable to him. They wanted everything but the risk and the blame. While Bobby called for "boom and bang" operations and a dead Castro, he was planting a paper trail of false documents that would prove him innocent or disapproving of anything to do with assassination.

Kennedy saw it as the CIA not giving him what he wanted. He seemed to direct much of his venom at Bill Harvey. Bill wasn't taking it well. At meetings in Washington he was heard to call the president's brother an asshole and a faggot. He was drinking through the day. Worse, people were talking about him drinking through the day. Harvey had nursed a goal for the future, to be appointed head of the agency's Soviet operations. Now he was watching his career coming undone as a victim of what he saw as an unqualified bully and his half-assed Cuba policy.

In Florida, Johnny commiserated. There were things he could tell him about that Kennedy clan. He took Bill fishing. Out on the ocean they traded stories of Berlin and Las Vegas. Johnny watched Harvey trying to drink his problems away. He was going down the drain with Dulles, Bissell, Maheu. Johnny himself wanted out. The writing was on the wall. This Castro hit had a curse on it. The guy was harder to kill than Mickey Cohen.

———

The breakdown between Task Force W and the administration had gotten so bad during that summer that the White House at first refused to take seriously the clandestine reports of unusual Soviet shipping activity and evidence of advanced Soviet weapons arriving on the island. Subsequent U-2 spy plane photographs taken in mid-October convinced them of the shocking fact: The Soviets were deploying ballistic missiles to Cuba.

Khrushchev had seen it as a ballsy show of USSR power as well as a guarantor against an American attack on Cuba. "There's no other way to defend [Castro]," said the Soviet premier. "The Americans only understand force. . . . It's just to frighten them a bit." He had planned to keep the missiles a secret until they were fully operational sometime in November, then present them to the United States as a fait accompli. The Kremlin had negotiated a treaty with Castro, Che Guevara, and other heavies from the inner circle in Havana. Operation Anadyr, as it was called, went into effect by midsummer. The missiles began arriving in September, followed by nuclear warheads shipped via freighter from Murmansk. Khrushchev's weapons of mass destruction were expected to be fully operational by November.

The White House fell into a state of frenzy. On October 14, 1962, Kennedy gathered a roomful of advisers to assess the situation, members of the Joint Chiefs of Staff and National Security Council, assorted foreign policy experts, high-ranking military figures, and the head men at the CIA. Their advice covered the waterfront, from calls for a bombing strike on the missile sites, to a naval blockade, an invasion of Cuba, and direct retaliation against the Soviet Union. The group analyzed and argued the possibilities, the atmosphere in the room growing ever more tense, fraught with the collective realization that they were facing the prospect of nuclear war.

Bill Harvey was back in Langley with his people, strategizing round the clock. On October 16, Robert Kennedy called a meeting with the boys of Operation Mongoose. He told them to prepare for action. The covert invasion was about to begin. It was to be an all-out attack on the Cuban infrastructure, widespread sabotage, bombings, commando raids. Similar calls for readiness were delivered to the branches of the military.

The days ticked by, the crisis growing as the White House tried to determine a course of action and the Soviets held their place. President Kennedy ordered Defense Readiness Condition 2 (DEFCON 2), one level below the most severe state of combat readiness, the last step before a nuclear attack on the enemy. As the situation hovered near the breaking point, Kennedy ordered a blockade around Cuban waters, seeking to prevent any further weapons deliveries, and demanded that the Soviets remove all missiles from the island. The president revealed the crisis to the public in a speech on October 22. Fear spread worldwide. On October 24 U.S. warships enforced the blockade against a fleet of Soviet vessels. Military forces in Florida were made ready to move at an hour's notice. On October 26 Khrushchev sent a message to Kennedy: He would agree to remove the missiles from Cuba in exchange for the president's promise to never attempt to invade the island. Two days later Bobby Kennedy delivered the administration's official acceptance of terms. The Cuban missile crisis was over.

The two superpowers had managed to avoid wiping each other off the map. But the crisis had not been without casualties. Bill Harvey and Bobby Kennedy had continued their feuding right through the excruciating days and nights of October. In the course of Task Force W business, Harvey had dispatched nine covert operatives to Cuba. The attorney general, in the midst of secret, delicate maneuvering with the Soviets, demanded the operatives be recalled. Harvey had to deliver the bad news: It was too late, a recall was not possible. Kennedy was furious. Harvey had played by the rules this time, but no doubt his months of insubordinate behavior to the president's sibling had caught up with him. He was fired.

He didn't take it well. According to Bill's colleague Sam Halpern, he looked Kennedy in the eye and barked: "If you fuckers hadn't fucked up the Bay of Pigs, we wouldn't be in this fucking mess!"

Bill Harvey went down to Florida before the holidays to meet with Johnny Rosselli and tell him what had happened. He told Johnny the Cuban operation was being shut down. Everyone should forget it ever happened. It had looked for a time like Bill would be thrown out on his ass, but a few influential people had spoken up for him. Now he was killing time till he got his reassignment. Bill brought some expense money from Washington, and he and Johnny went around handing out Christmas cash bonuses to some of the Cubans who had gone above and beyond in those last six or so months.

They met up again in Florida the following April. It was a farewell get-together for the two friends, as Bill was on his way to a new post in Rome (his quirky friend Angleton arranged the assignment). It was a quiet place these days, and it was hoped Harvey could not do any harm there. From Miami, Bill and Johnny went down to Plantation Key, staying for a couple of days at the Yacht Harbor motel. They chartered a fishing boat and went out on the water both days. At night they dined on lobster and drank rum. Johnny had never taken a dime through this whole Alice in Wonderland adventure, but now Bill insisted on picking up the cost of the vacation, including Johnny's airfare home, first class. He would give the bill to the CIA. Fuck them.

The United States and the USSR had agreed to try and play nice. Operation Mongoose had been ended. ZR/RIFLE was shut down. There were going to be no problems with Cuba. That was the idea. But the Kennedy brothers' hatred for Fidel Castro didn't go away. They were still stirring that pot. Months after the missile crisis, the attorney general was said to be "freelancing" new plots with the Cuban exile leaders, who were eager as ever, even if it meant the end of the world.

Bill Harvey's replacement at Task Force W (soon to be known as SAS, Special Affairs Staff) was a man named Desmond FitzGerald, a wealthy, well-bred Bostonian who it was thought would get along much better with the Kennedys than Bill Harvey. In September '63, FitzGerald received a report regarding a man by the name of Rolando Cubela. Cubela was a hardened Cuban army major and a longtime friend of Fidel Castro. Ex-friend. He had gotten word to the CIA that he was fed up with Castro and ready to do away with him in support of a U.S.-aided coup d'état. Cubella was investigated, and his offer was passed along, finding its way to Bobby Kennedy. Despite the near-cataclysm in October, despite the signed agreement with the USSR, Kennedy liked what he heard and approved support for the Cuban major's offer. The assassination of Castro was back on the table.

FitzGerald and his colleagues pursued a deal with Cubela— given the code name AMLASH. The event was set to happen before the end of the year. In November, Cubela and his case officer met at a CIA safe house in Paris. The agent gave the Cuban the latest toy from the CIA's weird scientists, a silver ballpoint pen with a hidden spring-loaded syringe for the injection of poison. They sat down to go over the details of the op one last time. The meeting had just begun when it was interrupted by a phone call from Des FitzGerald in Washington. FitzGerald told the case officer to stop what he was doing. The deal with AMLASH was off. Everything was off. President Kennedy was dead.

10

A COFFIN FOR JOHNNY

Bobby Kennedy had made his national reputation as chief counsel to the McClellan Committee, confronting witnesses like Sam Giancana and Teamster boss Jimmy Hoffa with fearless, mad-dog interrogations. As attorney general he ranked the pursuit of organized crime and corrupt unions as his original signature cause. No one in Washington could remember an AG with such an aggressive agenda. He recruited an army of devoted young lawyers. He demanded greater cooperation among the various law enforcement entities (which often acted like independent and jealous fiefdoms), seeking to build one coordinated alliance of crime fighters. Kennedy used his position—and his righteous persona and his considerable connections—to influence the passage of new legislation that would strike at the Mob's revenue sources, at legal loopholes, constitutional protections. He sought to lower the restrictions on the use of wiretaps. He fought for tighter restrictions on communications facilities that sold their services to gambling operations. He established programs for the protection and relocation of witnesses in organized-crime cases. His prosecutors were encouraged to make full use of the laws against perjury, false statements, and obstruction of justice—minor prosecutions that might be used to coerce reluctant witnesses to talk. In regions of the country where federal attorneys were stifled or even corrupted by local influences, Kennedy would send one of his devout lawyers from Washington to run the grand juries and prosecute cases.

Kennedy and his legal brain trust devised a brilliant way of getting around the Fifth Amendment's defense against self-incrimination—the gangsters' favorite amendment—a special immunity statute for grand jury witnesses that disallowed the use of the Fifth and forced the witness to answer all questions or go to jail for contempt. Even more threatening to organized crime— aimed at deconstructing the legal means by which criminal organizations had thrived, and the bosses escaped punishment—Justice Department lawyers began to build the template for conspiracy charges, which would allow prosecution of not only those who committed a crime but those who ordered or in any way aided the commission of a crime (what would later become the federal law known as RICO—the Racketeer Influenced and Corrupt Organizations Act).

Organized crime went under a searing spotlight all over the country. In spring '61, the federal government began its first serious investigation of crime in Las Vegas. The gold mine in the desert had been left to expand unhindered, virtually impenetrable behind a wall of corruption and secrecy. Bobby's Justice Department determined to launch its attack from within. Disregarding legal restraints, the attorney general ordered J. Edgar Hoover to wiretap the Vegas gambling establishments. All of them. It was the largest electronic eavesdropping operation ever attempted. The goal was a microphone in every casino office and workroom. By November bugs had been placed in dozens of Strip and downtown locations (wires running from the FBI office to the main telephone exchange, to the select walls within the casinos), with more than a hundred persons monitoring live listening devices for sixteen to seventeen hours a day. For the first time the Feds were gaining an understanding of how things operated behind closed doors in the Mob's mecca. The enterprise put the lawmen literally at the table for meetings and conversations among the rulers of Vegas gambling.

At the top of Kennedy's personal hit list were his old enemies from the McClellan hearings, Sam Giancana and Jimmy Hoffa. The attorney general's pursuit of the labor leader was relentless. Bobby's boys had made thirty-four indictments of Teamsters officials, and thirty grand jury investigations of the union, each case uncovering more dirty secrets, each bringing them closer to their big target at the top.

Sam Giancana was proving to be a more slippery prey. The FBI had been stalking him for years now. With the bugs they had planted in his headquarters and hangouts, they'd gathered much evidence of illegal activity and hours of incriminating dialogue, but none of it was admissible in court due to the illegality of the listening devices. They were yet to find a "clean" case they could prosecute and win. In the meantime they did what they could: They made his life hell. The Feds began what they came to call "Operation Lockstep." Agents covered him like a second skin. Round-the-clock surveillance, repeated ID checks; they questioned his neighbors, family members, girlfriends, audited his taxes. It was meant to keep him on edge, get him to make a wrong move, blow his top. And it worked. There was the day Giancana spotted agents following his car home—he began speeding in traffic, a reckless, nearly lethal attempt to lose them; by the time he reached his house he was so worked up he crashed the car into his garage, and when he got out to inspect the damage the car rolled down the drive and into the street, hitting a passing vehicle. The agents got there in time to see it and had a good laugh. They had a lot of fun with him.

When he played golf, a team of government men would play right behind him, sometimes deliberately hitting golf balls at his head.

Giancana's boiling point was reached on July 12, 1961, as he and Phyllis McGuire departed American Airlines Flight 66 from Phoenix at O'Hare Airport in Chicago, en route to New York. A group of FBI agents were waiting and separated the couple so as to interview McGuire on her own. The gangster objected to the interference. He became, said the subsequent report, "obscene, abusive and sarcastic." The agents began throwing questions at him: What did he know about the wiretaps in Dan Rowan's hotel room? Was he acquainted with a man named Robert Maheu? Giancana shouted back at them: "Fuck off! Motherfuckers!" He told them to move away and leave him alone. The agents pointed out to him that he was in a public area and the agents had every right to be there. They assured him they were not detaining him, and in fact he was free to leave Chicago that very moment and never come back. Giancana seemed to lose all control at this point. He hurled accusations at fellow passengers from his flight, said they were all spying on him, then inquired of the FBI agents if they knew how many men he had killed. One of the agents asked if he could furnish them with information "in that regard." Giancana said that he could not, staring at the lead G-man, but, he said, he might be adding another killing to the list. The agent asked if that was a threat. "My sister-in-law told me all about you," said Giancana. "She told me that you said I had killed thirteen men." The agent indicated that he was misinformed. Giancana raced back onto his airplane, deciding to wait there for McGuire's return. When she did not appear he disembarked again, shouting that America had gotten just like Russia, "where a man is not free to escort a young lady where he pleases. Why don't you investigate these dope fiends?" The agent then asked him if he had any information to share relating to narcotics. Giancana screamed: *"Why aren't you investigating the Communists?"* He ranted on, about the Kennedys, about deals with

Fidel Castro. He declared that he was being persecuted because he was of Italian heritage. "I'm going to light a fire under you guys and don't forget that!" he roared. The agent asked if he would clarify that statement, and Giancana said, "I think I will kill myself. Why don't you give me a pistol so I can do this?" Giancana said he "had a cancer." Go ask his doctor, he said. He said, "Get away from me you *motherfuckers* and quit bothering me!" The conversation, according to the report, "was terminated upon the appearance of Miss McGuire. . . . Giancana accompanied by Miss McGuire then left the area."

Tony Accardo hauled him on the carpet. What the hell was he doing? Had he gone crazy? Losing his shit in public like that! As if things weren't bad enough. The increased scrutiny by the government law enforcers was having a terrible effect on Outfit enterprises. The Justice Department was coming at them on all sides. The rackets. The Unions. The skim in Las Vegas. The G was getting deeper and deeper inside their business. There was much unhappiness now. A lot of the guys were laying the blame on Sam. Wasn't he the one who pushed them to take the deal with the Kennedys? Wasn't he the man boasting how he had personally put Jack Kennedy in the White House?

Giancana tried to put it on Frank Sinatra. He was the guy, the big booster, the one who had brought them into this thing. He got them in the room with the lying old man Kennedy. Fucking Frank. You better straighten things out, Giancana told the singer. You have to talk to these pals of yours, they're killing us. Sinatra gave him repeated assurances. He claimed he put Sam's name on a paper and showed it to the president's brother. This is my buddy, Frank said. This is what I want you to know, Bob. But Giancana didn't believe him, and even if he had done it they still got nothing. He demanded Sinatra step up, deliver their grievances to his Mick friends. "Don't worry about it," Frank told him in Miami, in spring '61. He was headed for a visit to the Kennedy family compound in

Massachusetts and told Sam he would straighten it all out with Papa Joe. "If I can't talk to the old man," he said, "I'll talk to *the man.*"

That conversation had to wait. Jack was busy running the free world and by the end of the year Papa Joe had suffered a massive stroke, leaving him all but frozen in place, no longer able to exercise his shady influence, or to moderate his sons' noble aspirations. And it was not long after that when Frankie's chance of influencing the first family—in any way or with any one of them—came to a sudden end. In late March '62, the president was to visit the West Coast, and planned to follow his official appearances with a weekend of relaxation in Palm Springs. JFK would be the guest of good friend and supporter Frank Sinatra, and Frank spent a fortune making improvements to his desert compound, dreaming, if all went well, that Jack might consider it his official "Western White House."

But it did not go well. It did not go at all. At the last minute, the president cancelled his stay. In Palm Springs he would be bunking with Bing Crosby instead (not even a Democrat). The Brit brother-in-law, Peter Lawford, was delegated to break the news. He did not look forward to it. Falteringly, he made the call. *Ring-a-ding-ding* became a dirge. The Rat Pack padrone picked up. Peter tried to explain. A problem with security. Bloody nuisance, he said. Jack was very disappointed. Lawford listened to an awful silence. Can you hear me, Frank? Lawford white-knuckled the phone. Sangfroid began to puddle around his Bally loafers. Then the line went dead, and Frank Sinatra became a Republican.

The story behind Sinatra's dismissal from the Kennedy inner circle, the accepted narrative, had it that the FBI's J. Edgar Hoover met with the attorney general not long before the president's Palm Springs getaway and warned him to separate his brother from Sinatra, providing ample proof of the singer's close relationship with

Sam Giancana and assorted other gangsters. Shocked and alarmed, as the story goes, Bobby ran to Jack in the Oval Office and demanded he cease all contact with the man. The sequence of events seems essentially right, except for the quaint idea that Bobby—or anybody else who read a newspaper or gossip column over the previous twenty years—was unaware of Sinatra's fraternizing with the Mob. If Frank's fondness for gangsters had survived this long without making much trouble for the administration, why would it cause such an eruption now?

There was a variant of the story, and a more plausible—and altogether more personal—basis for Bobby's abrupt banishment of Sinatra from his brother Jack's life. This version was revealed—under oath—by Joe Shimon, the DC police detective who maintained close connections with the FBI and with Sam Giancana and Johnny Rosselli. As Shimon heard from his federal source, Hoover had come to Bobby Kennedy in March with some of the latest audio from Giancana's bugged telephones. Hoover played the selected tape and they listened to Giancana and Sinatra in private conversation. The gangster demanding the singer get them relief from the government. Sinatra telling Giancana he was working on it. The telling was blunt, ugly. Sinatra, the dialogue made clear, was having an affair with the president's sister, Pat Kennedy Lawford (Peter's wife). He was fucking the sister, Sinatra told Giancana, to get her to use her influence on the brothers. Sinatra made it sound like quite a sacrifice. He vowed he would *sleep with this goddamn bitch until I get something going.*

"The tapes were played to Bobby," said Shimon, "And Bobby went, 'WHOA. . . .' And overnight you saw Sinatra *out*. No more White House. No nothing. Shut him *off*."

With Joe Kennedy in limbo, and Frank Sinatra eighty-sixed, the Mob now saw no hope of cashing in on election favors granted. The government's crackdown on crime continued. Racketeers lost money, lost face, went to jail. Giancana seethed with paranoia and indignation. He couldn't do as Accardo ordered. He wouldn't keep his head down, his mouth shut. He said, If they wanted to fuck with him, he'd fuck them back. He'd use their own weapons. In June '63 Giancana went to court. He sued the FBI for harassment, invasion of privacy. The Feds refused to defend themselves, believing that the court did not have jurisdiction. Giancana won the case. The judge in Chicago granted an injunction limiting the amount and nature of FBI surveillance. They were allowed just one car to follow him, and the car could park no closer than one block from his family home. The ruling even specified the distance agents had to keep from the mobster's golf game. Giancana was jubilant. For as long as it lasted. The ruling came down from the U.S. Court of Appeals: The defendants were "not subject to direction by the courts as to how they shall perform the duties imposed by law upon them." The injunction was stayed, and a year later the original ruling was vacated. The Feds went back to the business of driving Giancana mad.

2

The FBI had been tailing Johnny Rosselli from the time Robert Maheu gave them his name. Pressure from the attorney general had forced Hoover to drop the Maheu prosecution, but the director refused to leave it alone. There was too much he didn't know. What exactly was the CIA up to with these people? More, he was sure, than the sneaky CIA, or the Kennedys, would ever tell him. Perhaps Rosselli would spill, if they could catch him at something, make a deal, make him talk.

They kept track of him, filed reports on his activities, his travels—to Chicago, Las Vegas, Miami. They would question informants for news. They would lose him, look for him. Find him again days later. They had been in his apartment on Crescent Heights, planting their listening devices. He later discovered a CAT (concealed automobile transmitter) in his new Thunderbird. (Re-authorization of the CAT was rejected after Bureau auditors real-ized the car had been monitored for a month while it sat idle in an airport parking lot.) Johnny considered having them all swept out. But how could he be sure he'd gotten everything, or that the Feds didn't come right back and place some more? He decided it was better to just assume they were listening and act accordingly. He tried to do a better job at his place in Vegas. He warned the man-ager of the Diplomat that if anybody went into his apartment he would know about it and hold him responsible. He installed expen-sive "burglar proof" five-pin tumbler locks on his front and back doors (later his landlord told him a good burglar could "pick" these too, so—what the hell).

When it was important that he do so, Johnny *could* shake them off, sometimes using tricks of the trade he'd gotten from his CIA friends, ways of detecting surveillance, losing a tail, altering your identity on the fly. Other times, when the stakes were low, he might make a joke of it. Make them look foolish. Once, driving around Beverly Hills, he told a friend to watch as he took an FBI tracker on a sudden merry car chase, squealing around corners, losing them, then pulling up behind them and blowing his horn, making the G-man jump out of his seat. Once he'd come out of a building and from the corner of his eye spotted an agent in a parked car trying to duck below the dash before he was seen. He walked over to the car and looked down at the agent curled up on the floor like a baby in the womb. He signaled him to roll down the window, gave him the address where he was going next, and told him to drive carefully.

The FBI showed as much interest in Johnny's love life as in any of his potentially unlawful endeavors. Agents filed their reports with the prurient enthusiasm of correspondents for *Whisper* magazine. "Rosselli," wrote one, was "keeping a young girl, twenty-one years of age, who has the most beautiful body he has ever seen." He was spending weekends with her and giving her money to pay her rent, this girl was in love with him and begged him to take her on trips with him, wrote the agent, but Rosselli was going to get rid of her, "kiss her off" as she 'knows too much."

Any female found in his company was identified, photographed, written up, a considerable labor as there were so many of them. Among those who rated more detailed mention in the reports were Vicki Lockwood (aka "Natalie Loughran," birth name Natalie Rosenstein), an occasional dancer in the line at the Desert Inn); Helen Grayco, singer and recording artist, widow of the bandleader Spike Jones; Nancy Czar, champion ice skater and movie actress, leading lady of the low-budget curio *Wild Guitar*; Dorothy Towne, interior designer, ex-starlet, ex-wife of *Dragnet's* Jack Webb (Towne was credited with finally getting Johnny to move from his Spartan digs on North Crescent to an expensive high-rise at 1333 South Beverly Glen, described in a *Los Angeles Times* advertisement as containing "some of the most beautiful and luxurious apartments in the nation"). None of the women in the reports was suspected of any wrongdoing, but nearly all were surveilled, some stopped and questioned on the street or visited in their homes.

"It was a real nuisance," Betsy Duncan remembered. "There was one guy from the FBI would keep coming to see me. I'd say to him, 'I don't know anything. And you should know that whatever you ask me, I'm going to tell John.' Well, finally, this FBI agent made a pass at me. He tried to kiss me. I was so mad at him, I hit him. I couldn't believe he had the nerve. Then later I was singing at a club and he came in with his wife. I went over to him and said, 'What the hell are you doing here?' I said, 'I'm getting sick and tired of looking at you. Stop following me and don't ever call me again.' And that was the end of it."

One woman suffered more lasting consequences for her friendship with Johnny Rosselli. Judith Campbell had been in Johnny's company on numerous occasions, and had stayed at his apartment in West Hollywood several times while he was out of town. The Feds eventually took notice. They photographed the pair coming out of Romanoff's. They found her name and background. Judith Immoor Campbell. The ex-wife of actor William Campbell. A friend of Frank Sinatra. Her circumstances were intriguing: Generally unemployed, her only steady income a modest alimony, but she made frequent flights around the country and always flew first class and stayed at the top hotels. The agents dug deeper. They pulled the records for the telephone in Rosselli's apartment and matched them to the dates she had stayed there. The records showed she had made repeated long-distance calls to two unlisted numbers. One of the numbers belonged to Chicago Mob boss Sam Giancana, and the other to the president of the United States.

Now Campbell herself became the center of attention. They followed her, questioned her, gathered details of her uncommon romantic life, compelling evidence of a secret friendship with the president, calls, visits to the White House, private encounters at various hotels and homes around the country and at a house she was renting in West Hollywood.

The FBI's evidence of the president having an ongoing affair with a close friend of mobsters Johnny Rosselli and Sam Giancana was now added to the growing pile of lurid intel, the renegade anti-Castro operation (whatever exactly that was); the tapes and transcripts of JFK's friend Sinatra revealing—among other sordid activities—his affair with the president's sister and attempt to seek influence on behalf of Giancana. Any of this information presented to the public would be the cause of scandal, national uproar, and maybe the end of the Kennedy presidency. But J. Edgar Hoover was not interested in the public. The info would serve a more personal purpose, proving to the administration his capability and the inadvisability of anyone trying to get rid of him. With the Campbell evidence accumulated, Hoover sent a memo to Bobby Kennedy and a copy to Ken O'Donnell, the president's special assistant: "*I thought you would be interested in learning of the following information which was developed in connection with the investigation of John Rosselli, West Coast hoodlum.*" Hoover's memo about Campbell conveyed just the right note of unctuousness with implied threat. The subtext was clear: Your brother has been sharing a mistress with the Mob. But do not worry. As long as I am in charge of the FBI no one will ever know. The president agreed to a meeting with Hoover on March 22, 1962, an awkward face-off from which the attorney general made himself conspicuously absent. After that day there would be no more talk about Hoover taking an early retirement.

Jack promised Bobby never again to see Judy Campbell, but the irrepressible president managed to sneak in a few more get-togethers with the woman before cutting her off for good in December '62. According to Campbell, sometime after that last embrace she discovered that she was pregnant with Kennedy's child. She was overwhelmed by events, depressed, drinking. Campbell said Sam Giancana found out about the pregnancy. Giancana told her he would marry her and claim the child as his own. Instead she had an abortion.

The FBI investigation of Johnny Rosselli had reawakened a dormant probe into the gangster's early life. Back in the 1950s a diligent agent with the INS in Chicago had combed through his natal paperwork. The examiner found a number of curious and outright suspicious items. The extant documents were all registered many years after the subject's date of birth. The signature of the subject had his surname spelled with a single letter *s* in some cases while other forms showed that he spelled it with two. The supporting affidavit of birth showed a signed and notarized statement by someone named Joseph Evangelista claiming to be a cousin of Rosselli, with "full knowledge that the facts contained in the Report of Birth are true and correct." But the INS investigators found that this Evangelista had no relatives by the name of Rosselli, and his signature on the document did not match other samples. The FBI was alerted at that time, but the report became lost in the mix, then forgotten. It remained unnoticed until the new probe, and Hoover's fired-up demands, brought it back into the light. Now they took a good look. The earlier alert had been correct. The documentation did not hold up. The investigators could find no evidence of anyone with his registered name and date of birth living in the Chicago area in that period, no evidence of the parents as named, no mother, no father, no family, no school or hospital records; they were certain that the person represented in the Chicago birth files as John Rosselli (or Roselli), did not exist as such, and the person going by that name today, a certain fifty-six-year-old silver-haired gangster, was not who he said he was.

So who was he? And what was the reason for disguising his past? The FBI was sure the answers to those questions would be incriminating. Was he wanted for some long-ago crime? Was he an escaped convict? A killer? A foreign spy? Of course, whoever he was, and whatever he had done or was still doing under another name, the charges had to be proved in a court of law. Even an immigration case—if he was believed to be an unregistered alien eligible for deportation—would require proof of his foreign origin or noncitizenship. The investigators had to keep digging. Find evidence of this other identity and hidden history. And then figure out what they could do with it.

Johnny had done a good job sealing off his other life. Only a handful of people, most of them family members, knew his real name or where he was born. But having the FBI poking around his origins and the prospect of being interrogated on the subject gave him cause for concern. With his Chicago papers—his "proof" of natural American citizenship—unquestioned (to his knowledge) for more than thirty years he had long ago stopped worrying about the past. Now he had to think: Would his story hold up?

While in Chicago on business he hoped to find time to gather some evidence of his fictitious bloodline, a little genealogical history he could throw at the Feds if they came to question him. Judy Campbell was also in the city at that time. She was under Sam Giancana's care, she wrote in her memoir, trying to sort her life out, reeling from the emotional roller coaster of her secret affair with Jack Kennedy. Sam had put her up in a hotel suite, and one morning while still in bed she received troubling news from California about her sister, who was having a difficult and dangerous pregnancy. When Giancana phoned her hotel room she was sobbing, unable to get up. Twenty minutes later there was a knock on her hotel door. A maid in the corridor unlocked the door, and two men stepped inside: Sam Giancana and Johnny Rosselli, come to the rescue. The pair got Judy up and out. They took her to headquarters at the Armory Club. The guys sat her between them in a booth, and the three proceeded to get plastered on martinis.

After a couple of hours of this, Johnny told Judy they were all going for some fresh air. They got into Sam's car and rode for a while, ending up at Queen of Heaven Cemetery out in suburban Hillside. Judy was disconcerted. Did somebody die? Sam said everybody there had died. They were looking for some of Johnny's ancestors, the boys explained. Arm in arm they wobbled into the graveyard, barely able to stay upright. The men left Judy on the pathway, and they went among the graves, examining the shrines and stone markers. The search, thanks to the many martinis, had less seriousness of purpose than Johnny had planned. They started shouting the names of the deceased at each other and exchanging rude quips. Embracing an old gray tombstone, Johnny lamented like Hamlet, "*Ah, look, here's Uncle Giuseppe! I knew him well! A prince he was . . . big man in olive oil and machine guns . . . died of lead poisoning.*" The two drunken gangsters laughed madly, and Judy—not sure what it was all about but enjoying the show—began to laugh along with them.

It was a fun day at the graveyard, and later she learned that her sister was doing okay.

3

In January 1961 the Friars Club of Beverly Hills opened its new home, a three-story space-age windowless yellow blimp of a building at 9900 Santa Monica Boulevard. The Friars had been established in New York at the turn of the century as a private social club for Broadway performers, high-end vaudevillians, and press agents. In 1947 the comedian Milton Berle, actor/producer George Jessel, and Columbia Pictures exec Jonie Taps conceived of a West Coast version, a place where fellow New York exiles could go to drink, dine, and kibitz. The club became a Hollywood institution in the fifties, hosting charity fund-raisers and the notorious "Friars Roasts" (inverse tributes at which guests of honor—Humphrey Bogart, Gary Cooper, George Raft, and the like—were subjected to slanderous comical abuse). The list of club members included many of the biggest names in Hollywood, superstars like Frank Sinatra and Bob Hope, though most of those were generally seen only at special events. The mainstays of the club, the ones for whom the Friars was the neighborhood hangout, were lower-wattage celebs, famous but faded performers (Phil Silvers, Tony Martin, a couple of Marx Brothers, one Ritz Brother), entertainment industry professionals, and wealthy local businessmen. The plush new digs at 9900 Santa Monica—and the bills engendered—

encouraged a wave of fresh applicants for membership. Johnny had many friends among the members, some of them fellows he had known since the 1930s, and in early '62 he applied to join them. His official sponsors were hard to top: Frank Sinatra, Dean Martin, and club cofounder George Jessel. Unwanted at many of the local country clubs and banned from visiting Hollywood Park Racetrack, he was given a warm welcome at the Friars. Dropping by the club became part of his daily routine when he was in Los Angeles. He would have a couple of drinks at cocktail time, have a few laughs, play some cribbage or gin rummy. It was a place where he could receive messages or make phone calls without the cops looking over his shoulder. It was a place where he could get away from all the commotion in his life then—presidential campaigns, assassination plots, FBI stalkers. On several occasions in the past Johnny had gone for weekends to the Jesuit's Manresa facility in Azusa, California, an old rancho in the San Gabriel Mountains that offered those in need a retreat from the material world. The Friars Club served for him much the same purpose, only with good liquor and a sauna.

One of Johnny's friends at the Friars, one of the non-Hollywood contingent, was a fellow named Maurice Friedman, a West Coast wheeler-dealer, millionaire real estate developer. He was a stocky, shortish, red-round-faced man in his midforties. Rough around the edges, convivial, sardonic, shifty. As a businessman he was known to some for unorthodox practices and ethical lapses (using fake stock certificates as collateral for loans, mortgaging properties he did not yet own, and so on). He'd put himself on the Las Vegas map in '55 when he and his partners bought the New Frontier casino hotel (formerly the Last Frontier) from Beldon Katleman and Jake Kozloff (contentious negotiations that included at least one fistfight). Friedman became—briefly, before shifting the property to others—the New Frontier's president and general manager.

It was around the time of the Frontier deal that Friedman asked barber Harry Drucker to favor him with an introduction to Johnny Rosselli. Friedman knew Rosselli's value as a friend. To stay in big business in Las Vegas you wanted to have connections and protection. Johnny had them both. Drucker was reluctant. He thought Friedman was not altogether trustworthy, and he said as much, but Johnny shrugged it off. He'd dealt with his share of hinky business guys. And Friedman had his own value, a millionaire developer who could invest openly in Nevada casinos. Whatever the guiding principles behind it, a friendship grew. Over the next few years the pair socialized, they talked business, they traveled together. Friedman found it very helpful to have Johnny Rosselli at his side when he went to meet potential investors. When Friedman brought him along, such men minded their manners. The sycophantic Friedman made it easy for Johnny to be his friend: He paid for everything when they were together, meals, hotels, plane tickets, women. And any time Johnny advised him or helped with a deal or a contact, Friedman handed over a generous commission.

At the Friars Club, Friedman was one of the gang of habitual cardplayers. For many members the card room was the most alluring part of the club. In there, at various sized and shaped tables, the men—there were no women members—played poker, gin rummy, cribbage, clobyosh. "Most of those guys played for relaxation," Tony Martin remembered. "Small stakes. A few hundred dollars. But there were some guys, Zeppo [Marx], Harry Karl—he was a shoe guy married to Debbie Reynolds—some others, they took it very seriously, you know. Somebody like Harry Karl was a degenerate gambler. That's a guy who plays till he wins or loses everything. And if he wins he goes on playing until he loses again."

It was legal to play card games in a private club like the Friars. But gambling was not legal. Which meant . . . it didn't mean anything, actually. It was an open secret that gambling went on inside the Friars Club. The police showed no interest, not even a friendly warning. There had been no complaints filed, and the Friars was a charitable nonprofit. What were they going to do, go in there and bust the place up, arrest some old comedians for having a little fun? Beverly Hills was an affluent, pampered community, and you didn't get far making trouble for its resident celebrities.

The thing was, the police likely had no idea how serious some of the fun had become: the all-night games, the stakes of twenty grand and more, and players who came to the club with a history of underworld connections.

It began in the summer of '62, like Hemingway's "dangerous summer" a season of fierce competition, not between two dashing rival matadors but between a pair of middle-aged gin rummy players, Maurice Friedman, the corpulent real estate developer, and Harry Karl, the flighty scion of Karl's Shoes.* Late in June, Friedman and Karl began playing head-to-head rummy. It was the start of what became an almost daily confrontation. The stakes grew larger and the play more heated, the opponents more belligerent. At first Harry Karl was winning. Some nights he took home as much as ten grand. Then he started to lose. He would win a game, but then he would lose and lose again. Karl was a vain man (he padded around the Friars in velvet slippers with his initials in gold thread

---

* From the It's a Small World Dept.: Karl was—briefly—married to Joan Cohn, immediately following the death of her husband, Columbia Pictures boss Harry Cohn. Previous to that, Karl had been married (twice) to voluptuous movie starlet Marie "the Body" McDonald, who was a onetime lover of Bugsy Siegel, and the former wife of Victor Orsatti, who was once married to Johnny Rosselli's ex, June Lang.

across the toes) and thought himself a great cardplayer. He was sure his good luck would return and he'd get everything back and more. He kept playing, and he kept raising the stakes. He'd win some and then lose much more. The money got so big and the games so intense that they started to draw onlookers. The other guys would crowd around and pull up chairs to watch.

That was the way it started, the way people remembered it, the way the card room went from a happy-go-lucky atmosphere to something more serious and much more expensive. In July the two-handed games switched to four-handed rummy. Karl and Friedman continued their rivalry, but now both of them had partners. Karl played with Theodore Briskin, a rich, retired manufacturer of camera equipment. Friedman teamed up with a longtime Friar, restaurateur Al Mathes, the co-owner of Lucy's on Melrose and the Luau on Rodeo Drive (with Steve Crane, Lana Turner's ex, father of Cheryl, who, with a knife, saved her mother from Mickey Cohen's best-looking thug, Johnny Stompanato). The quartet came together four or five times a week. It became like a tournament, going on for months. Karl and Briskin won sometimes. But not often. Their cumulative losses climbed to six figures and kept climbing. Briskin would write a check for his share, while Harry Karl (according to the reporter John Kobler) began paying off in cash, sometimes from a shopping bag stuffed with bills.

During this time, as Karl or Briskin were not always available, other Friars—drawn by the excitement and the big-money stakes—moved up to take their places: Phil Silvers, Zeppo Marx, Tony Martin, the agent Kurt Frings, this or that Beverly Hills car dealer or Cedars cardiac surgeon. Every one of them had good days/ nights, cashing out with eight, ten grand each. But the times they lost were much more frequent. After a while Friedman or Mathes needed some time off and they picked two other Friars to take their seats, Ben Teitelbaum, a businessman, and Ricky Jacobs,

an "investment counselor." Good luck, despite the change in players, continued to favor Friedman's team.

Johnny liked to play cards. But he was not a serious cardplayer.
Some said he wasn't a good player. At the Friars he would play a
few hands sometimes or sit in for somebody when they got called
away or wanted a break. Mostly he would watch others play. He
would sit with a vodka and a cigarette, enjoy the atmosphere, the
wisecracks and the caustic banter by the old comics. Johnny had
been away from Los Angeles during much of that summer. He'd
belatedly heard about the big-money games, learned of his friend
Friedman's winning streak. In time he got back to the club and got
to see for himself. He would pull up near the table and sip his vodka
and watch Maury Friedman and his partners play. He watched
them win. He watched with a growing interest. Johnny knew Friedman was a good cardplayer. But not all that good. He also knew
Friedman had a larcenous streak as wide as his belly.

The day came when Johnny had a talk with his friend.

"What's going on, Maury?" he said. "How does it work?"

His tone left no room for denial, only confession. If Friedman—
and any partners—had been running a scam under the nose of
Johnny Rosselli, without permission in what could be considered
the gangster's own territory—it was a very disrespectful thing to
have done. To lie to his face about it would have been even worse.
Friedman didn't try to argue or excuse himself. There was no excuse. It was simply his nature. So Friedman spilled. He told Johnny
the whole story.

Maurice Friedman didn't like Harry Karl. And he didn't like losing to him. Harry Karl was the kind of guy who smirked and gloated

when he took your money. Maury wanted to punch him in the mouth. Better yet, he wanted to beat him at the card table and take his money and then do it again. So there was ego involved in the beginning. And then the greed.

Friedman decided to cheat. Friedman was not the dexterous, sleight-of-hand, do-it-yourself type of cheat. As in his business deals, Maury preferred to go for broke. What he had in mind required certain conditions and collaborators and special skills. Friedman had run large-scale crooked games in the past, some in his own home, once at a hotel in Vegas, once at the Trinidad Club in Palm Springs. When setting up such an operation he turned to a small group of specialists—there were no more than half a dozen of these men in the country—whose method, taught to each by the person who invented it (Pete Gebhard), involved a complex integration of technological knowledge, mechanical skill, and physical endurance. These specialists, once they'd approved the circumstances, would study the setting—clubhouse, hotel, private home—and prepare the scene of play, then work with the client for the duration, taking a percentage of the winnings. To set up the Friars Club card room, Maurice Friedman hired a member of this expert group by the name of George Seach, a math genius and electronics wizard, who was currently out on appeal for a burglary conviction (when Seach went to prison for a time, he was replaced by Pete Gebhard himself).

The scheme would involve the use of what was known as a "peek"—an overhead view of the players' cards through an opening in the ceiling above the designated card table—and a method of electronic communication between the technician-accomplice above and the cheating players below. At the Friars Club, having bribed a low-level employee, the scammers were able to get access to the building after closing. At first the peek was set up in a large closet above the temporary card room on the second floor. It was then shifted to the crawl space above the permanent card room on the third floor. A small opening was cut out of the floor, and into it was placed an air vent sized to fit the hole. The lip of the vent held a telescopic lens aimed at the card table and virtually invisible from below. The technician in the crawl space viewed the players' cards in close-up through the lens and used a small short-wave radio to transmit signals to Friedman and his partners, who wore tiny receiving devices that were hidden under their shirts. The "peeker," crouched above the ceiling, would send coded electronic signals to the player that would be felt as silent vibrations, while the player would at times communicate information back by certain finger gestures or the position of a card. For example, Seach later explained, "Mr. Friedman placed an intended discard card on one end of his hand so I'd see it. I'd buzz once if his opponent needed that card. When the 'knock' area of the game was reached, Friedman would signal with his thumb, which meant 'Shall I knock?' and I would press the button, giving an impulse."

It was complicated, mentally and physically exhausting for all concerned. The players had to maintain intense concentration to keep track of their cards, the play, and the electronic signals, while the technician overhead had to do the same while remaining motionless for long periods (sequestered up to fourteen hours, the peeker had to pee into milk bottles and had nothing to drink and eat but water and candy bars). Some of the cheaters had difficulty maintaining their nerve, provoking suspicion, and there was an occasional close call. They spent much time privately debating what to do if anyone got caught (the consensus opinion: run like hell).

Despite their concerns, everyone involved seemed to agree that the winnings—sometimes eighteen to twenty thousand dollars a game—made it worthwhile.

Johnny was impressed. He was so impressed he said he was going to let Friedman make him a partner. He wasn't going to play. He might even stay away from the card room altogether just to keep from raising anyone else's suspicions. The group could continue as before. But from now on they would count him in for 20 percent of the take.

The cheating at the Friars Club continued.

Johnny had given much of his time in the first years of the decade to protracted and unpaid endeavors—the Kennedy election, CIA/government work, and frequent hand-holding and mess-cleaning duties for Sam Giancana and associates. He wanted the new year—1963—to be more about business and less about philanthropy. He was almost sixty years old. He needed to start thinking about future needs. A nest egg. A big score. There was plenty stashed away, and money coming in each month from various sources (including now a couple of grand a month from his piece of the Friars Club sting). Still, not enough to guarantee a comfortable retirement. He had made many small fortunes through the years, but he'd spent them too. Who thought about old age? The future? Gangsters lived for the moment.

The thing was, the old money trees were starting to dry up. Beset by the Bobby Kennedy–led crackdowns, the rackets everywhere were under siege. Las Vegas was in disarray. The Feds had crawled through the town like a secret invasion force planting land mines. They had tapped and bugged everybody, followed dollar trails, squeezed informants. They knew about the skim now, knew about many of the secret owners. It seemed only a matter of time before the whole town was raided. The government of Nevada, under pressure from Washington, was again attempting to scrub the state's image before the Feds did it for them. Among other maneuvers in Carson City, the State Gaming Control Board had instituted its "List of Excluded Persons" (aka "the Black Book"), which disallowed the listed individuals from entering any gambling establishment (Sam Giancana was among the first eleven in the Black Book, banned from ever setting foot in his own or anybody else's casino properties), with severe penalties and even the loss of gaming licenses if the owners/operators didn't cooperate. Meanwhile, Teamsters boss Jimmy Hoffa, provider of vast sums for Mob investment, and perhaps Bobby Kennedy's number-one target, was facing likely multiple indictments—the law was simply deciding where to hit him first. And then there was Sam. Giancana, for all his craziness, had been Johnny's greatest supporter, and had allowed him many opportunities to make money. Now his reliability was in question. To many he seemed to be out of control. Getting his name in the papers, flaunting his celebrity girlfriend, having temperamental clashes with the FBI. This was the year he would take the government to court for harassing him. He was accruing so much heat that people were outright refusing to do business with him. Even Jimmy Hoffa had turned him down for a loan. It was all making his bosses uneasy. The brain trust in Chicago had begun to wonder if he was still up to the job.

For Johnny these were all good reasons to look beyond the old alliances. Find some better and perhaps even respectable use for his talents. He had spoken at times longingly of going legit. But it was easier said than done. When you had lived the outlaw life as long as he had, a normal existence was hard to put in play. Many lines of work were simply not open to him because of his reputation. He looked into business ventures and investment ideas as they came up, but nothing seemed to click. Fitfully he continued his attempts to reenter the movies, funding story purchases and screenplays. These usually concerned religious themes and saintly and martyred Christians, subject matter that was Johnny's very *guilty* pleasure. His old businessman friend Herman Spitzel had put him in touch with a guy who'd written something about a Catholic priest during the Civil War. Johnny and his partner Joe Breen had attempted to interest Hollywood but without success (according to Paul Picerni, Breen had been essentially blackballed by the studios after an anti-Semitic rant during a meeting with some production executives a few years before). Another project evidently began with a Jesuit cardinal, one of whose minions had found his way to Johnny's door with three hundred thousand dollars to put toward filming a favored ecclesiastical tale. Johnny was enthused. He made plans to "story conference" with the minion in Las Vegas. If they could get a writer on it, Johnny told Joe, "and then take this guy's money, this Cardinal's money, and then take it to the studio and say go ahead and match this and make the picture, a guy could do some good." (However pious the project, the old urges *were* hard to kick: "Course," Johnny suggested, "if he can get 3 [hundred thousand] . . . he can get 5.")

The lack of good prospects left him more and more dependent on Maurice Friedman. Maury was a skilled big-money operator who could work deals in the light of day—how he had not befouled his own reputation by now was a miracle worthy of a religious picture—could talk to straight banks and investors, sign his own name on contracts. Friedman had interesting possibilities on the horizon, including a new Strip casino. If one of Maury's large ideas was to come to fruition, and Johnny could get a piece, he might possibly not have to worry about the future. The two men were now bosom buddies and seen together often.

Whatever Johnny's resolutions for the year, they were more easily conceived than accomplished. The FBI trackers found him doing not much more than marking time. On an average day in Los Angeles he played golf, went to the Friars Club in the afternoon, in the evening dined at a favorite restaurant (Perino's, the Villa Capri, Chasen's, later the new La Dolce Vita); in Las Vegas he played golf, palavered with various cronies in the coffee shops and at poolside in the day, in the cocktail lounges and restaurants at night.

At least his romantic life still seemed robust. His power and charm, and his bankroll, were still working magic on any number of women, many much less than half his age. In Vegas, for a time, he was often seen with a beautiful redhaired cocktail waitress in her twenties who worked the pit at the Desert Inn. In Los Angeles around the same period he showed much interest in Vicki Lockwood (Loughran, Rosenstein), another attractive female in her twenties. This one was a rambunctious relationship. Miss Lockwood had a propensity for the dramatic (according to a court-appointed psychiatrist) with a record of "suicidal gestures" like wrist-cutting and throwing herself out of a moving automobile. Johnny liked her. They made a lively couple, with lots of arguments and jealousy. Vicki gave as good as she got. There was one late night Rosselli showed up unannounced and inebriated, and Lockwood made her displeasure clear, enough so that he called to apologize the next day, ineptly stating his defense: "What do you care if I was drunk? I got to get up in the morning so I might as well let you wake me up." There were nights he drove by her residence just to confirm that she was at home and alone. He once, according to the FBI report, "bawled her out" for being on the phone when he tried to call, certain there was another man involved, telling her it was a known fact that "no one would be calling at midnight and talking for an hour unless he was sweet on her."

On the morning of July 18, Johnny and Friedman joined a party of around a dozen persons flown from Los Angeles to Reno, Nevada, via Western Airlines, all guests of Frank Sinatra, who was hosting a weekend at his Cal-Neva Lodge casino resort on Lake Tahoe. The recently and expensively renovated Cal-Neva lay across state lines at wooded Crystal Bay, about five hundred miles north of Las Vegas. Cal-Neva was Sinatra's baby, the first time he had his own joint and could run the whole thing "his way." The possibility, as some reported, that he may have been only a front and that the secret majority owner was Sam Giancana did not lessen his proprietary attitude one bit. By funding a junket of friends, important persons, and fellow celebrities for a splurge at the resort, Sinatra hoped to generate lots of word of mouth in all the right places.

But nothing was as easy as it used to be, not even a wild weekend. Phyllis McGuire (with her sisters) was entertaining in the showroom, and that meant boyfriend Sam Giancana came along, even though he was not supposed to visit any place in the state that had gambling. Knowing the mounting tension between Giancana and the guys in Chicago, Johnny hoped Sam would play it safe, keep his nose down. But what were the odds? Giancana got into a bloody fistfight with Phyllis's manager; someone must have called the cops, who reported to the FBI that Giancana had been spotted on the premises, which brought in the state gambling authorities. The weekend got word of mouth, all right. Johnny knew that Sam getting his name in the papers again would not go down well with the Outfit. But the incident did nothing good for Sinatra, either. In the Nevada capital the State Gaming Control Board tried to haul the entertainer on the carpet to explain himself. He refused to appear and cursed and threatened the head man at the Control Board (Sinatra: *"Don't fuck with me. Don't fuck with me. Just don't FUCK with me"*). The bad publicity (DID SINATRA HOST GANGSTER? was one headline) in the midst of a major corporate business deal with Warner Bros. forced Frank to give up his casino license and get rid of the resort. Which meant Sam Giancana giving up *his* resort. It caused a major rift between the two men. The whole incident was very upsetting for Sinatra, the terrible mistreatment by the state bureaucrats and by the press, the shocking claim that he had been socializing with a notorious Mob boss, of all things, the accusations of foul language, of threatening behavior. The world could be so cruel to the sensitive soul. *"He just hurt,"* wrote his daughter Nancy. *"There was more vulnerability in his life now, and a push closer to the line between skepticism and cynicism."*

Nearly as historic an event: In September a grizzled old veteran of the Genovese Family named Joseph Valachi, in prison for drug trafficking, became the first of his kind to openly, willingly testify about the inner workings of the American Mafia (the loose-lipped blips of Willie Moretti barely counted, though they *had* resulted in his execution by friends unknown). Broadcast on live television, Valachi, looking and sounding like Humphrey Bogart dragged out of a gravel pit, detailed the exotic mythology and vocabulary of the secret criminal society that he explained to the uninitiated was properly known as Cosa Nostra ("our thing"), introducing the public to such concepts as the "Godfather," the "family," the "made man," the "Commission," the ritual pledge of loyalty, the law of *omertà*. Valachi's testimony was the capstone to the series of organized crime exposés that had begun with the eye-opening Kefauver hearings and continued with the Apalachin fiasco and the combative McLellan Committee. Attorney General Robert Kennedy declared the Valachi confession "the biggest single intelligence breakthrough yet in combating organized crime and racketeering in the United States." That remained to be seen. But it couldn't *hurt*.

Johnny spent most of August in Los Angeles, leaving for Las Vegas at the end of the month. In the first weeks of September the Feds observed him nearly every afternoon at the Desert Inn Country Club, usually in the company of Maurice Friedman. They were heard to talk about development deals and other business projects. Johnny was considering building an apartment complex in the Las Vegas area. He later visited a few potential locations but soon lost interest (land in Vegas, he decided, had become over-priced).

In early October he was back in Los Angeles. The Feds now had an informant inside the Friars Club (this was likely movie ac-tor Michael O'Shea, later revealed to be an FBI spy). He was in-structed to tell them any time he ran into Brother Rosselli. It wasn't exactly top-grade intelligence. He reported one encounter with Johnny on October 8, around four in the afternoon. Johnny finished a phone call, came over to the informant, sighing, *"I can't even re-member that broad's last name."*

They chatted, the Friar/informant told Johnny he was back from a trip, and Johnny asked him where he'd been.

"On the east coast," said the informant.

Johnny said they were all "cheap hoods" on the East Coast. He told the guy he should be happy to be back in Beverly Hills "with the high-class hoodlums."

In mid-October he flew to Vegas to attend the three-day Western States Tavern Show at the Convention Center, where food and drink equipment businesses displayed their wares (Johnny contin-ued to control most of the ice business on the Strip). He arranged for the purchase of thirty-two Kold-Draft ice-cube-making machines. Another FBI informant recounted a conversation with the owner of a refrigeration company. The man said he'd heard that Rosselli would make a thousand dollars on each machine he bought. He said he could not understand why the hotels in Las Vegas bought ice machines from Rosselli when he charged them con-siderably more than they would pay others for the same machine. He said that if he offered to sell the same machines for fifty dollars each, the hotels would still buy them from Rosselli. He must be some salesman, the man said.

Johnny had been keeping an eye on Judy Campbell. It had been a difficult year for her. She continued to suffer from the breakup with Kennedy (it was difficult to forget about an ex-lover when you saw him in every newspaper, magazine, and nightly news report). Sam Giancana's interest had finally waned. She was lonely and despondent and increasingly frightened. She believed she was being followed and spied on. She was drinking too much and taking pills. She was in and out of the hospital, diagnosed with kidney problems. Someone, possibly her friend the singer Eddie Fisher, got her to see Max Jacobson, the notorious "Dr. Feelgood," with his amphetemine-laced vitamin shots (Jack and Jackie Kennedy had also enjoyed the good doctor's intravenous pick-me-ups). Most days now she was either high, craving, or hungover.

The surveillance increased by the summer. She was questioned by the FBI and the IRS. One time Judy was going to meet Johnny for a meal at the Brown Derby in Beverly Hills. She had driven away, then went back to retrieve a piece of jewelry. When she entered the apartment she found two men in the midst of searching the bedroom. They stopped her before she could scream and identified themselves as FBI agents, then took off without further explanation. Johnny put her in the care of his attorney, James Cantillon, who filed a complaint. Agents came to interview her in Cantillon's office. She was "emphatically informed" that her allegation of agents breaking into her residence was completely false, and that she would be held accountable for making such false allegations against the FBI. The FBI tried to serve her a subpoena to appear before a grand jury. She was terrified. What would they make her say? With Johnny's help she stayed out of sight, checking in and out of assorted hotel rooms. She spent days lying in bed and drinking herself to sleep. Late in November, Johnny had her move to the Beverly Crest, a small hotel where Maury Friedman kept an account.

Johnny and Friedman planned a trip to Arizona and Washington, DC, for the third week of November. It was going to be business mixed with a little pleasure, or maybe the other way around. Accompanying them were two young women. The FBI described them as call girls. They reported that one, Johnny's girl, was to receive two thousand dollars for going on the trip, and the other, Friedman's companion, would get a new car. On November 16, at 6:55 a.m., the four departed Los Angeles for Phoenix on American Airlines Flight 70. At 9:32 local time they checked into the Mountain Shadows Hotel in Scottsdale, taking a three-room suite. They stayed two days. The planned next leg to Washington, where they were to confer with an unnamed congressman about unknown business, was "postponed," the women were told. At 12:45 p.m. on the 18th all four went by limo to Sky Harbor Airport. The two women were ticketed for an afternoon flight to Los Angeles on American Airlines. Johnny Rosselli and Maurice Friedman bought tickets on Bonanza Air for a 1:50 flight to Las Vegas. They arrived at 2:00 local time. Johnny registered at the Desert Inn Hotel. He was seen again in the evening in conversation with Ruby Kolod, the DI's co-owner. The FBI records show no further account of his activities—or the report has gone missing—from November 20 to November 27.

4

On November 21st President and Mrs. Kennedy depart Washington for a two-day five-city tour of Texas. The tour is an attempt to mend fences and face up to his foes in a state that had voted heavily against him, a preemptive campaign stop for the next election. On the 22nd they fly to Dallas. At twenty-two minutes to noon Air Force One touches down at Love Field. The local morning paper features a red-baiting anti-Kennedy screed. "We are entering nut country," says the president.

The visitors from the White House greet an excited crowd at the runway's edge, then head to a waiting motorcade and the presidential parade limousine (the customized Lincoln Continental open-air this day, last-minute clear skies encouraging the removal of the steel and plastic bubble-top roof), taking their places on the pneumatically elevated backseat, the governor of Texas and his wife ahead of them on jump seats facing forward, a Secret Service driver at the wheel and the assistant agent in charge beside him in the front. Shortly before twelve the long motorcade departs on a planned forty-minute ride downtown en route to the Dallas Business and Trade Mart. More than 150,000 people line the way. President Kennedy is pleased and surprised to see so many happy faces. The wife of the governor looks back to tell him, "You can't say Dallas doesn't love you. . . ." At 12:30 the motorcade reaches Dealey Plaza on the western end of the district, turning deep, Houston to Elm, sunshine flashing on chrome, a sharp noise in the sky—

In Las Vegas, Johnny Rosselli is sleeping late. In his bedroom at the Desert Inn the curtains are drawn against the light. The only sound is the lulling hum of the air conditioner. Darkness and cool comfort all around. The morning passes.

The phone rings. This is how he will remember it. The phone rings and rings, bringing him up from a deep sleep. He answers, but he's hardly awake, he remembers. Someone at Columbia Pictures in Hollywood asks him to hold for Jonie Taps.

"Johnny?" says Taps. He is an old friend, a Columbia executive, onetime right-hand man to Harry Cohn. "Can you believe what's happened?" he says. "Can you believe this?"

Johnny doesn't know.

"You don't—" Taps says. "Oh baby, turn on your TV. He's been shot. Kennedy. Someone shot him."

Johnny doesn't follow. Still half asleep. The TV? No. Pal, talk slower. He makes Jonie Taps repeat it, tell him what's happening. He doesn't believe it. Taps tells him again, more details. The president has been shot. *Dead*. The governor of Texas has been shot too. Now, Johnny will remember, it starts to sound real. He feels shock.

"God almighty," he says.

He puts on the television, or maybe the radio. Years later he tries to remember what he and Taps say to each other.

"'The damn communists.' That was the first thing that came to my mind," he will say. He will say—years later—that he remembers thinking about Castro. There was some speech he'd read in the newspapers. A speech threatening the U.S. leaders. "It sounded just . . . like something he'd do . . . that was . . . my conversation with [Taps]. . . . How I would know anything like that coming out of a sound sleep is beyond me."

On the Strip some of the casinos shut down, for up to an hour.

Five days later.

The manager of the Beverly Crest let Johnny into Judy Campbell's hotel room. She had called him at the Desert Inn on the 23rd, in bad shape. Then she did not answer her phone for two days. He found her in a drunken stupor. The room reeked of spilled booze and vomit. She had been at it since the day. "The only way I could blot it out of my consciousness," she will remember. "Every time I woke up the shock was there, the horror repeated."

Johnny helped her to sober up, clean up. He made her leave the hotel. He put her in his Thunderbird. They drove to Palm Springs, joining Johnny's girlfriend, Dorothy Towne, for Thanksgiving. They stayed in the desert for a week, Johnny and Dorothy watching over her like worried parents as she sat in the sun and grieved. One night they went to dinner at the Canyon Country Club. Frank Sinatra arrived with a party. Sinatra saw them and moved on. Judy said Sinatra turned away when their eyes met. They never spoke again.

Johnny took her to Las Vegas for a New Year's party at the Desert Inn. Their host was Moe Dalitz, principal owner of the joint, one of the most powerful men in town. It was a noisy, drunken night, and Dalitz got the idea that Judy was a free agent and made several attempts to flirt with her. As they were walking away from the party—Judy, Johnny, Moe, and his female friend—Judy and Johnny bickered, she drifted away from him, and Dalitz made a move, kissed her. Judy hauled back and slapped him across the face as hard as she could. Dalitz reeled. Johnny stepped in and hurried her away.

"You know something," he told her. "You must be crazy."

The next morning Johnny came to her room. "You're really crazy," he barked. "Nobody smacks Moe Dalitz across the face! Haven't you learned anything? I thought I would have to start picking you up in pieces." Then Johnny started to laugh. He became doubled up laughing. "You nearly knocked him flat on his ass," Johnny said.

He continued to look out for her. It was not unappreciated. Judy would tell others of her "love and affection" for Johnny. But it was no good. Too much for him, or not enough for her. She remained in a tailspin, fueled by booze and prescription drugs. She went into hiding, a recluse at her parents' home. She attempted suicide with an overdose of pills. In January 1965 she learned that she was pregnant. She sought out Johnny, told him the baby was his. Johnny said he didn't believe her. She took it back, later said some Hollywood producer was the father, a one-night stand. In May she gave birth. Her life seemed a shambles. She could hardly take care of herself. Her child, a boy, was given up for adoption.

Johnny lost track of her after a time. She cut all ties to that period of her life and just disappeared. Johnny would recall her now and again, sometimes with sadness for how things had gone, always with reverence for her extraordinary loveliness. "You should have seen Judy Campbell," he would say to people. The girl who was more beautiful than Liz Taylor.

"Whatever happened to her?" his pal Jimmy Fratianno asked him one day.

"Sam ditched her," Johnny said, "Kennedy got killed, the feds were all over her. She fell head first into a bottle. And that's all she wrote."

"What a shame," said Jimmy.

5

In the immediate aftermath of the JFK slaying, and the murder of prime suspect Lee Harvey Oswald, which precluded a criminal trial, Lyndon Johnson (the thirty-sixth U.S. president as of 2:39 p.m. on the day of his predecessor's demise), ordered the formation of a commission to investigate the assassination in all its aspects and to issue a public report of its findings. The goal of the commission was to establish a historic record of the facts of Kennedy's murder, though (privately) implied in Johnson's directive was the need to make conclusive the "lone gunman" theory which had Oswald as the only shooter, entirely self-directed. Such a conclusion served not only the logic of the evidence as it was then known. LBJ wanted this national wound sewed up and forgotten, the "Kennedy legacy" removed to the basement. Proving that Oswald was a solo act gave the story a finish with no loose ends, no unanswered conspiracy theories to burden the current administration. The commission was made up of seven men—four politicians (Hale Boggs, Gerald Ford, Richard Russell, John Cooper); Allen Dulles, the former (fired) director of Central Intelligence; John McCloy, the president of the World Bank; and appointed chairman, Earl Warren, the chief justice of the United States. Within a year they took the testimony of over five hundred witnesses, examined more than three thousand documents, produced a nearly one-thousand-page report, plus numerous thick volumes of transcripts and raw data, and reached a unanimous conclusion: Oswald had done it, Oswald alone.

Time would reveal much in the commission's investigation to have been seriously compromised. From the beginning Chairman Warren had been under pressure from the White House to make a fast and perhaps preordained resolution. Warren seemed determined to steer the investigation away from conspiracy talk. There was no concern for the assassin's motive beyond personal grievance or self-aggrandizement. They had—perhaps unwittingly—left unexamined large areas of possible interest, for instance much about Oswald's trail of provocative connections, to Soviet Russia, Cuba, pro- and anti-Castro elements in the United States, the New Orleans Mafia, and the Cuban embassy in Mexico City. There was as well the pressure applied on the chairman not only by the current president but by the family of the previous one: The Kennedys, supposedly repelled by the possibility of public exploitation, suppressed the gruesome autopsy photographs and X-rays, allowing discrepancies in the pathology reports to remain unexplored. The commission was repeatedly led astray by government witnesses, receiving a considerable lack of cooperation from the FBI, the Secret Service, and the CIA. All chose to keep their own problematic behavior away from public scrutiny, even if it swept up relevant information in the process. There was no mention of the Bureau's private files on Judith Campbell—the lover of JFK and of at least two prominent gangsters—or the Mob influence in the 1960 election (J. Edgar Hoover was not going to be known as the man who ruined the martyred president's reputation), and no talk of preassassination threats to Kennedy by organized-crime figures, illegally recorded by FBI bugs. The Secret Service said nothing about its knowledge of numerous other threats against the president or the claims of one of its own men about a possible separate assassination plot uncovered in Chicago, with details similar to the event in Dallas. As to the CIA, John McCone, Dulles's replacement as director, had made himself the agency's sole spokesman at the commission hearings, and had deliberately offered only "selective assistance" (according to the September 2013 report in the CIA's classified in-house journal, *Studies in Intelligence*), steering the investigation wide of Company dirty laundry, including prior awareness and tracking of the restive Oswald, and the assassination attempts against Castro and that now-regretted alliance with organized crime. In this deception he was clearly abetted by one of the commissioners, as Allen Dulles had to know some of the same CIA secrets and made no attempt to reveal them. In retrospect, so much had been held back it was surprising that the commission was still able to find Oswald guilty, or Kennedy dead.

These evasions proved ill advised, the cover-up causing more damage than the truth. The Warren Commission would be scorned and dismissed. The intelligence services disgraced. Secrets, when they came to be exposed, would serve only to confuse and complicate. The more people knew, the less they believed. History had been thrown to the wolves.

6

The federal investigation into the facts of Johnny Rosselli's early life continued. Over many months they had turned up nothing, found only blank walls, dead ends. Their lack of success, the insolubility of the mystery, only encouraged the theory that this missing past held the key to the gangster's undoing. There was guilt there somewhere. But there was seemingly no way to uncover it. It was as if the man calling himself John Rosselli had simply stepped out of thin air, arrived from nowhere.

Salvatore Piscopo, aka "Louis Merli," aka "Dago Louie," had known Johnny longer and better than anybody in LA. From the Roaring Twenties to the present day, he had never been far from his side for long, as bodyguard, business associate, bagman, confidant, and friend. Louie had done things for Johnny, and Johnny had done many things for him. There were people who didn't like Dago Louie, and some—like the late Jack Dragna—who didn't trust him, but Johnny had always had his back. They were as good as brothers. They had a special bond, a loyalty that had lasted with no serious rift, no betrayal of trust, for nearly forty years.

Johnny had come a long way from the old days. Dago Louie not so much. He was still the street-corner gangster glowering in his black suits and loud shirts, his heavy Neapolitan accent murdering the English language. At this time he was running his own crew, though it was small in number and undistinguished (for the most part, according to the journalist John L. Smith, "a bunch of broken down transplants from New York or the Old Country"), with a steady if unremarkable income from bookmaking, loan-sharking, and shakedowns. He was a fixture around Hollywood, his office the bar at the celebrity-favored Villa Capri on Yucca Street, where he enjoyed standing cheek to cheek with the likes of Frank Sinatra and Robert Mitchum, not paying for his drinks, and stealing food from the kitchen. He was a small-time big shot, you could say. As regards Johnny Rosselli, anyway, never too big to do anything Johnny needed doing when his old friend called on him, and whether or not there was a dime in it. Like the time a few months back when (according to John L. Smith) Dean Martin's ex-wife had gotten conned out of fifteen grand and Dino asked Johnny if he could do something, and Johnny told Louie to take care of it for him, and Louie did just that. Louie never resented Johnny for the favors and errands he was asked to do, being treated as if he was a punk kid. They were like brothers, after all.

Dago Louie had been doing things the same way for so long that his defenses had gone down in recent times. Everyone in his world was paid off or paid up. He was not expecting any trouble. So it came as a big surprise late in '63 when the law came down on him like a big brick wall. Taking care of business at Santa Anita and Hollywood Park (where his on-site bookmaking allowed big-money bettors to avoid the tax man), Merli had attracted the attention of racetrack security officers. One way and another he was observed to be up to no good, and eventually some FBI agents came to have a look at him. They considered the veteran member of the Dragna gang no great catch, but with the FBI's war on the Mob at full speed they were not being picky. There was always the hope that an old-timer like Merli might help them catch a big shot. Utilizing the old reliable methods, the Feds put the IRS on to him. Dago Louie, it turned out, had never filed an income tax return.

The Feds told him he was going away for many years. Louie didn't want to go. The Feds said that was too damn bad. They tossed it around. What could he do? Louie asked them. The Feds said there was a chance he could stay out of prison if he was willing to help them out. Dago Louie looked at them and laughed mirthlessly. "You wanna me be a stool pigeon? You no wanna me go to jail, you wanna me be *dead*?"

Louie knew the laws of the Mob. To talk to the cops was unforgivable. If found out, even so paltry a bunch as the present Los Angeles Family would put a bullet in his mouth. But prison? He was getting old. His freedom and comfort meant a lot. The Feds worked on him, pressed their threats. After a while it began to seem like the only thing he could do. He tried to convince himself he could get away with it. He would give them things that didn't matter to anybody. Make up some bullshit. Throw them some crumbs. Nothing that would get him in trouble. He was a pretty smart guy, Dago Louie thought. He could do this.

And that was how it worked. Every week he would meet with the agents in some hideout apartment they had, and he would tell them some stories, most of them made up or things he remembered from the old days, former colleagues' crimes (it wasn't squealing on a guy if a guy was already dead). They listened, looked satisfied with him. After a while he almost forgot he was an FBI informant. He went back to running his rackets and not paying taxes the way he always did.

Getting close to the holiday season the time came to do one of those errands that Louie did for Johnny. For many years his friend had been sending money to his mother in Massachusetts. Twenty-five hundred in cash every year around Christmas. That Johnny had a family in the East was a well-guarded secret. Dago Louie, his oldest friend, thought he was likely the only man west of Boston who knew about his family, and he didn't know much. It was Dago Louie who each year took the envelope with the cash to Boston, by arrangement turning it over to local mobster Antonio Santaniello at his Paddock Café on Tremont Street, no questions asked; the envelope was then picked up by Albert Sacco, Johnny's forty-nine-year-old brother. When Santaniello sold the Paddock, Louis left it to Albert to arrange another drop-off, but Albert had trouble finding one.

The following year Albert came up with a new idea. Instead of Dago Louie coming to Boston, he, Albert, would go to Los Angeles. Albert was nearly fifty, his life was going by, and he made up his mind that a trip to sunny California for a few days was something he wanted to do. Before anybody could stop him he was on his way. Louie didn't say anything to Johnny. It was no big deal. For once he wouldn't have to go freeze his ass in Massachusetts.

The day came, and he picked the guy up at the LA airport and took him to his home.

The Feds had never said anything about spying on him being part of the agreement. He expected them to take him at his word. The agent who followed Dago Louie that day saw that he wasn't going to the track like he'd told them on the phone. The agent tailed Louie to the airport, followed him into the terminal, saw him meet a man there, take the man to his car, and drive away. The Feds went to the airline and were able to identify the man Dago Louie met, got his name and place of departure. Albert Sacco, coming in from Boston. Calls to the Boston office found nothing of interest: The guy was a school janitor, lived with his old Italian mother. Even so, Dago Louie had not wanted the Feds to know. That was enough.

They grabbed Louie for questioning. He was alarmed to learn that he'd been followed. He didn't have a story ready. When he talked he sounded like he was hiding something, all right. The agents reminded him of their deal, how it worked. One lie and it was off. They were going to take all his money and throw him in jail.

They said again: Who is Albert Sacco?

Dago Louie tried to think of something. But thinking had never been his strength.

Merda.

7

Early in '64 it seemed like Johnny's equivocal alliance with Maurice Friedman might finally pay off. The developer had put together the necessary preliminaries for the building of a new Las Vegas casino resort, a multimillion-dollar project. All he was lacking were the multimillions. For this he turned to his good and connected friend.

After nearly a decade of overseeing deals and distribution of wealth in Vegas, Johnny knew as much as anyone about the gambling capital's tangled web of hidden partnerships and percentages. He knew, too, those who were still looking for a piece of the action. The Mob in Detroit, Michigan, had missed out in the big Vegas land rush. As a Mob capital Detroit had never achieved the glorious notoriety of Chicago or New York, though not for want of trying. Indeed, Detroit had paved the way, with its own citywide gang rivalries and murderous beer wars long before Prohibition (liquor had been made illegal in Michigan nearly three years ahead of the Volstead Act), and for a time in the 1920s the Jewish-run Purple Gang had found a measure of recognition. But all that was a long time ago. The reigning Detroit Mafia remained, in a public relations sense, undervalued. To have big points in a new Vegas casino would mean a welcome increase in prestige. Enter Johnny Rosselli, the strategist: his feelers to Detroit got an immediate and positive response.

Representing the Motor City Mob were two second-generation Mafiosi, Anthony "Tony Z" Zerilli and Michael "Big Mike" Polizzi—the sons of boss Joe "Joe Uno" Zerilli (a member of the national Commission) and his former top associate, the late Angelo Polizzi. The two sons, both college educated, more businessmen than thugs (well, a little more), were seen as the modern face of the ferocious gang, and both were expected to step into positions of leadership in the very near future. Zerilli, Polizzi, Johnny Rosselli, and Maurice Friedman came together in Palm Springs on March 10. Johnny and Maury made a sales pitch, and the boys from Detroit ate it up. By the end of their Palm Springs weekend, Zerilli and Polizzi were in for 50 percent of everything.

Unfortunately the project ended before it began. Problems with Friedman's credentials may have been one reason—but the embarrassing situation was soon resolved. Maurice Friedman had been the co-owner of the New Frontier casino hotel for several years in the 1950s. Friedman and his partners had leased the resort to a series of management teams, and finally sold it in 1958 for $6,500,000 to an entrepreneur named Warren "Doc" Bayley. The new owner had a difficult time. There were periods when only the hotel portion was kept in operation, and other times when the whole property was shut down for reassessment. There were frequent changes of management, renovations, odd innovations (a season of large-breasted Japanese showgirls, a period when all card dealers sported mustaches, the addition of a health spa with the Strip's first "scientific colonics"). Nothing helped. There was a steady drop in business, unpaid taxes. In January 1965 the Bankers Life Insurance Company purchased the troubled property.

Bankers Life head John D. MacArthur (brother of Charles MacArthur, coauthor of *The Front Page*) kept the New Frontier closed while he looked for an acceptable tenant-manager. But by then the word was out that the Frontier was jinxed. If it wasn't jinxed—and in Las Vegas bad luck was as real as gravity—it was certainly old and out of date. The Frontier's cowpoke aesthetic seemed like somebody's grandfather's casino. No one was interested. The about-to-open Caesar's Palace was all anybody wanted to hear about, a sprawling theme-park casino intending to offer high rollers all the imperial glamour and sybaritic luxury of ancient Rome, or at least of one of the better Steve Reeves movies. Word of mouth had already generated more than forty million dollars in advance sales. With this in mind, MacArthur made an expensive decision. He would tear down the old Frontier and rebuild from scratch, put up a towering state-of-the-art gambling resort to compete in the new vision of a super-Vegas. To take charge of the project, MacArthur, a stranger in town, turned to an experienced local developer with his own connection to the Frontier's legacy: Maurice Friedman.

However much of a scoundrel, Friedman obviously knew his business and talked a good game. As partner and contractor he came away with six million dollars and a free hand to build and manage the massive project. Friedman went back to the boys from Detroit with the new deal. He would serve as front for the secret investors. Zerilli and Polizzi bought in. Johnny Rosselli took a near-six-figure commission and a guarantee of rights to the future Frontier's gift shop. It was good times for all.

Meanwhile, Sam Giancana's clash with the government continued. Although his nemesis, Bobby Kennedy, deeply traumatized by brother Jack's murder, had withdrawn from the war on organized crime—ultimately resigning as attorney general on September 3, 1964—his army of attorneys and investigators fought on. They had wiped away Giancana's harassment lawsuit and resumed their constant pursuit. Having come so close to a victory only to end where he began, Giancana now seemed doubly haunted. The Mob boss was seeing enemies everywhere. At the Armory Lounge, his Chicago headquarters, normally open to the public for food and drink, he now ordered the bouncers "to keep out everyone not invited" (they were to recommend that customers go to Maggio's Steak House instead). Giancana's suspicions even extended to the woman he loved, Phyllis McGuire. There were times he was sure the Feds had gotten to her. One day he stormed into the Armory, went to the jukebox, tore out every McGuire Sisters record, and broke them into pieces.

Sam turned to Johnny for help. Was there a spy inside the organization? He asked him to investigate, on the quiet of course. Johnny took the assignment, though reluctantly—it was not exactly wise to go snooping on Outfit members—and recruited Joe Shimon in Washington for the leg work. Shimon talked to some of his FBI sources, and installed some listening devices at Mob-friendly addresses; they found no smoking guns, but Sam's suspicions remained.

Giancana tried to elude the endless "harassment" at home with frequent trips around the country and overseas, to New York, Florida, Hawaii, Mexico, the Dominican Republic. The evasions were themselves a kind of victory for the Feds. As an FBI Top Hoodlum program report noted in October 1963, "Because of Giancana's constant traveling outside of Chicago . . . many decisions which are required to be made by Giancana have been left unmade and as a result underlings are receiving no direction as to their activity, rendering a somewhat chaotic state within the Chicago Organization." The Mob, said the report, was experiencing "a breakup into factions which were believed to be making the entire organization extremely vulnerable to Government investigations."

The Feds were sticking their noses in everywhere. For the Outfit it was embarrassing, so much heat in their own hometown. FBI and IRS incursions had closed down dozens of gambling joints, leaving a big overhead and hundreds out of work, in addition to the cost of lawyers, bonds, and fines. A raid on Sportsman's Park Racetrack in Cicero landed a multitude of Mob bookies in jail for six months each. Even humble policy racketeers and First Ward strip joints were set upon by federal agents and tax men. The situation had gotten so bad that judges could no longer be relied on to hand out suspended sentences.

"Because of the situation developing within the Outfit," a Bureau memo reported, "Anthony Accardo and Paul Ricca have recently assumed a more active role in the operations of the Chicago Organization." This was not good for Sam. Bad enough Giancana's spotlight forced Accardo and Ricca out from the shadows, but in fact Ricca was just returned from more than two years in prison for income tax evasion, was nearing seventy, and ready to let "Joe Batters" handle that active role for the both of them. And Sam

Giancana was Ricca's fair-haired boy, definitely not Accardo's. More and more the Feds began to pick up chatter about Giancana's lame-duck status and who would be chosen to replace him.

Fate stuck its foot out in the spring of 1965. The Outfit boss was subpoenaed to appear at a federal grand jury investigation of organized-crime activities in Chicago. Initially planning to make profligate use of the Fifth Amendment's protection from self-incrimination, Giancana found himself trapped by the immunity clause crafted by the former attorney general. Once immunity was imposed Giancana's only choice was to answer fully or be charged with contempt. His attorneys tried to work out a deal where the mobster would reply to a small number of predetermined questions, "self-incriminating," perhaps, but doing no broader damage. When the day of the hearing arrived, Giancana ignored the deal. He couldn't do it. He returned to Plan A, answered nothing. The court cited him. He went to prison.

Dago Louie, unable to face a prison term, had told the Feds Johnny's real name. He told them the city where Johnny grew up. He told them Johnny's mother's name, the names of other family members. It was painful to rat on an old friend. He regretted it the moment he did it. For one thing, maybe it would get him killed, though he hoped Johnny would be a bigger man about it and forgive him if he found out, being as they were very old friends. The G-men were excited, happy. But they wanted more. What about before Johnny got to California? Louie couldn't remember hearing much of anything. Johnny never talked about things like that. It was a long time ago. The agents would leave the room, come back. Start shouting at him again. He must have said something sometime! Was he on the lam? Did he kill somebody somewhere? Louie was getting a headache. He wanted to get up and walk out. He wanted to go down to his Cadillac and drive away. Forget this whole thing happened. Go over to Miceli's, order a big plate of Spaghetti Caruso, with the red wine and the chicken livers.

And then he remembered. . . . Wasn't there a pal of Johnny's knew him back East? Way back. A tough Italian Johnny ran with as a kid. The two of them came out of Boston, crossed the country together. Dago Louie'd met him once or twice in Los Angeles. That was a guy they should ask questions. If he was still alive. What's this guy's name? Louie couldn't remember. Was a very long time ago. He used a phony name, but most times Johnny called him by his real name. Louie said he couldn't recall it right now. The G-men barked in his ear. You better remember, Louie. You don't want to go down for *this*. Dago Louis closed his eyes. What the fuck was that wop's name?

It made his head ache worse, but finally he remembered.

Tancredi. *Si! Tancredi.*

Tancredi . . . Tortora.

With Johnny's real identity known to them, federal detectives moved forward. They found their way to the family's immigration records. They compiled a history of the Saccos, bloodlines, birthdays, places of residence, burial sites. And by means not clear, they obtained items of a personal nature, including old family photos and private papers. About the immigrant boy Filippo they found all that was recorded, including date and place of his departure from Italy, the date and place of his arrival in the United States, including his school record, his arrest record and other data up to the time of his disappearance from Boston. The efforts reached across seas, the FBI legat (legal attaché) at the U.S. Embassy in Rome sent to review public records for the town of Esperia, Filippo Sacco's place of birth, and to obtain a certified copy of his birth certificate. All agencies worked to maintain maximum discretion, hoping not to alert Mr. "Rosselli" to their interest.

The Feds were also trying to find Johnny's old friend. Tancredi Tortora was the sort of person who had traveled lightly through life, not leaving much of an imprint between encounters with the law. Luckily, his encounters with the law were many. The forensic manhunters painstakingly linked the name to scattered police reports, warrants for arrest, court cases, prison records, and at the end of the trail an order of deportation. The man they were looking for had been shipped to Italy in 1950 and never returned. Requests for help were made to the Italian authorities. It took them a month to find him. He was alive, and was living in the town of Acerra, twenty miles from Naples.

Tancredi lived with his brother, Parigi, who had retired to Italy after many years as an honest businessman in the states. Parigi's son, Carmine, was a lieutenant (JG) in the U.S. Navy and currently serving in the Mediterranean. Working through the ONI (Office of Naval Intelligence) the FBI requested Lieutenant Tortora's help in arranging a meeting with his uncle. On the afternoon of June 7, 1965, Carmine accompanied Parigi and Tancredi to the Naval Intelligence office in Naples.

They spoke in English, though Tancredi, having lost some of his fluency, frequently reverted to the Neapolitan dialect, allowing Parigi to translate. The legat showed them a photograph, a police mug shot dated 1926. The brothers both identified the individual in the photo as the man they had known (Parigi very briefly, at the tuberculosis clinic in Northern California), the one who now called himself John Rosselli, whose true name was Filippo Sacco.

The legat had questions, but Tancredi needed little prompting to talk. He recalled with enthusiasm his history with young Johnny, beginning at the time he had first seen him in the Charles Street jail in 1922 and going on to their last good-bye in Los Angeles seven years later. They were just kids, both in their teens when they met, said Tancredi, Johnny younger by a year or two. They struck up their friendship some time in January 1923. Johnny—Filippo—

lived with his mother and young brothers and sisters, Tancredi told the American. His father had died in the "plague" years before. The family was poor, said Tancredi, struggling. They lived on very little. Johnny had to bring home money so they could survive, said Tancredi. The two of them roamed the city looking for opportunities. They committed small crimes, and they worked at menial jobs. Life was hard, but they had fun, stealing, chasing girls. Rosselli, he said, was "single, quite handsome, and had a way with women." Tancredi recounted their life on the streets of Boston, then on the road, drifting across America in the Roaring Twenties, New York, Chicago, bootlegging in California. Exciting times. Gangsters and guns and girls (*le belle ragazze Americane*, raising his eyes to heaven). Though hazy on some names and dates, his memories were more often sharp and chronologically precise. The legat found him to be a credible witness. He had no ax to grind in any direction. He evidenced no animosity toward his old companion, nor any urge to bend the truth in his defense. The legat pressed for more. Tancredi said it was possible Rosselli had been involved in some crimes that he had gotten erased from the records when he gained power, but he did not know or could not remember any particulars. What of the Charlando murder in Chicago? the legat asked. This was something the Feds had pinned their hopes on, convinced that Rosselli was one of the unidentified suspects sought by police for a 1922 killing (and that this was the reason for his change of identity). But Tortora—a named suspect in the same crime—was adamant that the murder occurred before Johnny had ever left Boston, and that he—Tortora—had been falsely accused and later exonerated. Rosselli, he said, was not by nature a man of violence, unless there was no choice about it. If he had killed men—*if* he had—he was not the kind to take pride in it the way some men did. The legat asked why Rosselli had gone to such lengths to keep his real name and background a secret. Tancredi could not say. Was he trying to conceal that he was an illegal immigrant? Immigrant? No, Johnny was born in America, Tancredi said. In Boston. The problem was the birth records were destroyed in a fire. Johnny had told him this. The legat said that was not true, they had proof that Johnny was born in Italy. Tancredi was taken aback. "He would have had no reason to lie to me," he said. *"We were friends."*

Tancredi said he did not see or hear from Johnny again after he went to prison on a life sentence in '34, but had on occasion crossed paths with others who knew him. There were prisoners who brought news from outside, told him that Johnny had become a big shot in the Mob, that he practically ran Los Angeles, and later that he'd gotten into trouble in Hollywood and was in the pen himself for a long stretch. And he remembered one time, in 1951, shortly after he had arrived in Italy, when he'd met the great Charlie "Lucky" Luciano, and they had talked of their mutual acquaintance back in America. Lucky Luciano, said Tancredi, spoke with admiration of Johnny's success with women and asked him, Did he know that Rosselli had married a movie star?

When they were done the Rome legat thanked the three Tortoras for their cooperation. He assured them again what had been said was confidential, and their identities would be kept secret. Tancredi said he was too old and tired to worry about such things. They were his memories, to share or not as he preferred. It had been pleasing to talk of those times. A chance to recall the lost days of his youth, days of adventure.

All shook hands, and Tancredi and his brother went home.

It was another eleven months before the Feds were ready to make their move on Johnny Rosselli. The hoped-for evidence of a major crime connected to Rosselli's permanent change of identity had not been found. What they did have now was indisputable proof of the man's foreign birth and unlawful residency. With that evidence they believed they could put him behind bars and then throw him out of the country forever. Still, the FBI ached to make something more of this victory. The years of investigation had made it clear: Few persons in the underworld had Rosselli's intimate knowledge of nationwide organized crime at the executive level. There was no way to imagine the things he could tell them. If flipped he'd be a bigger prize than Valachi.

At midday on May 6, 1966, Harold Dodge and Wayne Hill, two FBI agents of the Los Angeles Division, stood a few shop windows away from the entrance to Drucker's Barber Shop in Beverly Hills. They were waiting for Johnny Rosselli to get his hair cut. At a minute or two past noon he emerged, stood for a moment in the late-spring sunshine, then set off on foot, heading up Brighton Way toward Rodeo Drive. The two agents followed, catching up with him as he paused at the next street corner. Dodge, station agent in charge of the Rosselli case in LA for many years now, said, "John. We need to talk to you."

The gangster flinched, quickly composed himself, started across the street. They followed, blocked his way on the other side. He told them if they had a problem, to talk to his attorney. Agent Hill warned him he would not want his attorney to know about this matter. He held out the manila envelope in his hand, but Johnny Rosselli refused to take it. The agent advised that the Bureau now knew who he was. He took out a business card, of a restaurant in the far-off suburbs, told him it was a spot where they could talk without being noticed. Johnny again told them to speak to his attorney and get a subpoena while they were at it. He went on his way. The two agents gave it up, hurried back to their car. They drove to the Glen Towers, a couple of minutes to the west, flashed their badges at the doorman, rode the elevator to the eighth floor, found apartment 803, and slid the envelope under Rosselli's door.

That afternoon Johnny's attorney, Jimmy Cantillon, called Harold Dodge at the FBI office in Los Angeles. What did they want to talk to his client about? Dodge asked about Johnny's reaction to the two photographs he and his partner had delivered. Cantillon said nothing. Dodge was equally guarded. There was a brief mention of the FBI's knowledge of Johnny's name, his place of birth, but Cantillon showed no awareness of this. Dodge said the talk would not necessarily concern Rosselli's identity. Cantillon said that he and Mr. Rosselli would be willing to meet with the agent, but the G-man insisted that Johnny Rosselli had to come by himself for "security reasons." There were things the FBI would mention only to Rosselli alone. Cantillon said Rosselli would be crazy to talk to them without an attorney present. They left it there.

Did they have him for something or didn't they? Why the hole-and-corner act? What did they mean by "security reasons"? Johnny's mind jumped to his job with the CIA. Was the FBI still looking for an inside track on the Cuba plot? According to what he had heard from Bill Harvey and Bob Maheu, Hoover was bitterly envious of the agency. Perhaps J. Edgar was still trying to get more dirt about the CIA's collaboration with mobsters (the FBI was aware that something had gone on regarding Cuba but remained ignorant of the details).

Johnny and Jimmy decided that direct communication was not a good idea. Whatever the FBI wanted to do with him, the best thing was to try to stop it before it started. The CIA had gotten Maheu off the hook with the Dan Rowan bugging business. Perhaps they would run interference for another of their "assets."

By the week's end he was in Washington. On the morning of May 12 he called Col. Sheffield Edwards, the former director of security at the CIA, and one of Johnny's handlers in the Castro plot; he was now heading his own consulting firm in the capital. Johnny said he needed five minutes of his time, and Edwards agreed to meet him the next day in the cocktail lounge at the Lawyers Club.

Edwards described the meeting to Sam Papich, the FBI's liaison with the agency, who retold it in a memorandum to Director Hoover. "Johnny arrived promptly at the agreed time," it read. "The Lounge at that hour is usually deserted except for the bar waiter. They ordered drinks. It is Colonel Edwards' impression that Johnny has aged a lot since he saw him last. Colonel Edwards got the distinct impression that although he was trying to put on a good front he looked worried and distraught. Colonel Edwards opened with some light conversation, but Johnny although friendly was anxious to get to the point of his visit. Colonel Edwards let him talk freely and asked only a few questions since he did not consider it wise to interrogate him."

Johnny told Edwards of his troubling May 6 encounter with the federal agents in Beverly Hills, the words spoken, the package slipped under the door. "He told Colonel Edwards that the FBI agents left a picture of a woman and of a child . . . that the child was himself at that age. Colonel Edwards tried to get more details concerning the woman but Rosselli was very touchy on this."

In phrasing to Edwards what the FBI agents said, he included the words spoken to Cantillon about "a matter of national security." Johnny of course hoped to imply their interest was centered around his collaboration with the CIA, the CIA's dirty secret. The agency was more likely to help him if they believed they were helping themselves. Asserting his loyalty, Johnny told Edwards if he did talk to the FBI, he was not going to tell them anything related to his work with Central Intelligence: "After Johnny had finished his tale, Colonel Edwards gave no advice and made no commitment."

The memo went on: "He feels Johnny is in some kind of bind personally . . . that Johnny believes that if he talks to the FBI alone Sam Giancana (now in jail in Chicago) or Sam's friends will believe he is talking [about them] and that will be fatal for Johnny. On the other hand, Colonel Edwards believes that Johnny wants to keep square with the Bureau. Johnny did not say so but Colonel Edwards is of the opinion that Johnny wanted the Agency to inform the

Bureau of these developments and is using this channel for the purpose.

"Colonel Edwards noted that Johnny barely finished one drink, which is unusual for him. He left saying he was meeting his attorney who was flying down from New York on the shuttle."

Next, accompanied by Cantillon and Joe Shimon, Johnny went to see Edward Pierpont Morgan. A distinguished and powerful Capitol Hill lawyer, Morgan in the 1940s had been the chief inspector with the FBI, in rank just two slots below J. Edgar Hoover, and since then had served in various advisory positions for the government, most notably as counsel to the Senate Foreign Relations subcommittee that helped to bring down the unsavory senator Joseph McCarthy. But Morgan was no Boy Scout, and his firm represented a number of dubious and unconventional clients, including Jimmy Hoffa. He was a longtime associate of both Robert Maheu and Johnny's friend Hank Greenspun, the crafty owner and editor of the *Las Vegas Sun*. If Johnny needed someone to stand up to the FBI for him, Edward Morgan was the man to see. He was tough, knew everyone at the Bureau, knew how to reach anyone of value in Washington.

Johnny told his story to the lawyer: the run-in with the FBI agents, the implied threat of deportation, the agent's demand to meet with him alone. He told Morgan of his meeting with Sheffield Edwards and his hope that the CIA would decide to come to his defense. This demanded explanation, and Johnny then gave Morgan an account of his government mission, the Castro caper, from his recruitment to the various attempts on Fidel's life, the approval for all of it by the White House, and the involvement of certain high-level members of the Kennedy administration. Johnny told Morgan it had been presented to him as something vitally important to the safety of the United States, conceived and administered by the top men in the government. He had done it as a service to his nation, had taken no money, asked for nothing. He told the attorney, "It's the one thing in my life that I'm really proud of."

Morgan listened with fascination. How such a story—involving so many prominent figures and such outrageous activities—had remained a virtual secret for this many years was remarkable. Johnny's account was so vivid and detailed with names and dates—including Morgan's own friend since their FBI days, Bob Maheu—he did not hesitate to believe him.

But there was more. One last twist, a coda unexpected and harrowing. As the attorney would recall it, what his client told him next—Johnny pausing and lowering his voice to a whisper—he said was something so secret that only a small number of people knew even a part of it. There had been a hit team, U.S.-trained, anti-Castro Cubans, sent in to do the job. They had been captured and tortured. They confessed everything. A highly placed source in Havana, a double agent for the Americans, had been at the scene. Castro was told of the White House plan to kill him. And Castro had exploded and said that he too could play that game. And then, as Morgan would remember it—then Johnny said Castro had ordered the captured hit men to be brainwashed . . . to be turned . . . *and sent back to do to Kennedy what they had been trained to do to Fidel.*

The shocking addendum came seemingly out of nowhere. It was the first known telling—but not the last—of the "turnaround" or "retaliation" story. Where had the story come from? What purpose did it serve to tell it? And did Johnny believe it? When questioned under oath years later, he claimed that anything he might have said on the subject was sheer speculation, just an idea or a rumor he had heard. Conspiracy speculators, when they began to appear en bloc in the 1970s, theorized that the turnaround story was part of a deliberate misinformation campaign, Johnny's *Manchurian*

Candidate plot intended to deflect attention away from the real assassins. The speculators, many not married to logic or the big picture, offered an array of suspects and masterminds who might have been pulling Rosselli's strings. Carlos Marcello. Santo Trafficante. Jimmy Hoffa. Texas oligarchs. The CIA's spooky James Jesus Angleton. But if Johnny Rosselli's story had a subversive purpose, most of these theories made little sense. Why would the CIA encourage him to tell a story that in part blamed them for what happened to Kennedy? As to Marcello and the other mobsters frequently accused of being behind the assassination (another question altogether), who would use a well-known mobster to float a story intended to deflect attention from the Mob? In the absence of evidence, the only logical rationale for Johnny's tale—though perhaps not logic's finest hour—was that he hoped by upping the ante on the "secrets" he was ready to spill, that the CIA, or any other government entity wanting him to keep his mouth shut, would come to his rescue with the FBI.

Morgan, when he could find his voice, said, "My God, Johnny. . . . Is this certain? Can we get proof of this?"

Johnny shook his head. He had to protect his source, he said. He had given his word and would never violate it. Who else knew? How many people? Johnny couldn't say. On this side, maybe a handful. In Cuba, who knew? He was telling Ed now because he would have the best idea what to do with it. "I'm figuring," Johnny said, "maybe it's my patriotic duty to tell what I know."

Morgan gathered his thoughts, not easy after such a story. He advised Johnny to keep quiet for now. The lawyer said it was possible that revealing government secrets could make Johnny liable for prosecution. At least let the statute of limitations run out, which Morgan calculated would happen late in the next year. What they did next depended on the CIA's response. If they spoke up for him he might be in the clear. It could blow away. If not, well, there were still people they could talk to before things went too far. Morgan thought the best idea at the moment was to speak to the agents in Los Angeles and find out what they wanted. The FBI's approach on the street had been unorthodox. Morgan suggested they had something in mind for him other than prosecution. Likely they wanted to make an offer, to bring him on their side. If he were willing to work with them, help take down one of the big fish—Sam Giancana, for instance—a good deal could be made—

Johnny told him to forget it. It wasn't a consideration.

There was one more thing he wanted from the well-connected attorney. He needed to know who gave the FBI his real name and place of birth.

Morgan said he would see what he could do.

Johnny's last stop was a visit to the Chevy Chase home of William Harvey. Bill was back working at CIA headquarters, recalled from Rome after three years. It had been an undistinguished and at times appalling three years. He'd been unhappy, causing problems, drinking heavily, had a heart attack. He was returned to the States, given nothing to do, and spent his days—according to his friend Bayard Stockton—"mouldering in disgrace." The agency was aware that Harvey had remained in contact with Rosselli (by phone and correspondence; the two had not seen each other since 1963). And the agency was not happy about it. He'd been told by his bosses to cut his ties with the gangster, but as a matter of stubborn independence and loyalty to a comrade, he had ignored them. When Harvey reported that he was having Rosselli to dinner at his home, the agency higher-ups began to wonder whose side he was on.

Johnny found Bill Harvey much changed since their last face-to-face. His fighting-bull spirit was diminished, and he showed the effects of alcoholism and high blood pressure. Their bond of friendship remained as before. Harvey listened with sympathy to Johnny's predicament but did not probe and offered no advice, feeling obligated to report whatever was said to his bosses at Langley. As he'd assured Sheffield Edwards, Johnny told Bill Harvey that he had no intention of revealing any CIA secrets. (Not yet, anyway.) Harvey later contacted Sam Papich and sounded him about the FBI's case on Rosselli, and their "prosecutorial intentions." He got nowhere.

Johnny returned to Los Angeles on May 13. On the seventeenth Jimmy Cantillon called FBI agent Harold Dodge and told him that his client John Rosselli had requested he arrange an interview. Rosselli would come alone, but there had to be only one agent present. On May 25 Johnny met Dodge at Du-Par's restaurant in Thousand Oaks. Dodge told him the FBI had done a painstaking investigation of his life and family, involving numerous records, and laid out some of the facts known to the FBI regarding his "true identity."

Furthermore, said Dodge, the FBI knew that he was "a member of an Italian association and has associated with numerous persons throughout the United States who are members of this organization." The FBI knew, said Dodge, "that he is knowledgeable of facts concerning many phases of gambling activities in Las Vegas, Nevada." The Bureau, said Dodge, was interested in receiving the type of information that he had and was "soliciting his cooperation."

Johnny said nothing while Dodge talked. When the agent was done Johnny asked him if he would repeat what he said in front of his attorney. The agent said he would not do that. Johnny asked him, if they did not make a deal, what the FBI would do next. Dodge said the next step would normally be an open investigation into his past, and that a federal grand jury would likely be used in such an investigation. A half hour had gone by, and Johnny asked if they were done. Dodge told him to think the matter over. They could meet again on the 27th.

On May 26 Jimmy Cantillon called Dodge. Cantillon said he'd had a long talk with Johnny Rosselli.

"Yes?" said the agent. "What did he say?"

"He will not be available," Cantillon said. And then, after some silence: "So . . . we'll be seeing you, I guess."

8

Fucking Dago Louie.

All the years. All he had done for him. In return a knife in the back.

Ed Morgan had come through. He had more contacts in the FBI than Hoover. Morgan didn't ask what Johnny was going to do with the information.

Johnny felt like killing the rat with his own hands. But reason took control. He would do everything "legal." He made his case to Chicago, and Chicago talked to Los Angeles. Dago Louie was one of theirs, so boss Frank DeSimone had to order the hit. Those were the rules. Good luck with that. Dago Louie was one of their few reliable money earners. And they needed every dime, even if it came from a snitch. The LA Family had reached a new low, ineffective, dwindling in number. DeSimone was a nervous wreck. In New York there was a gang war in progress. The Bonannos and Profacis had turned on the other Mafia families. A major power play, audacious but ultimately disastrous. There was a hit list of opposition bosses to be eliminated, and Joe Bonanno—who coveted Los Angeles—reached across the country to put DeSimone on the list. Frank lived in fear. He may even have worried himself to death. He expired of a heart attack the next year, in August 1967, at the age of fifty-eight. By then Johnny had more to worry about than getting Dago Louie clipped.

In November 1966 he got a call from Robert Maheu. Johnny and Bob had patched up their differences a while back. They made an agreement that neither would ever speak the word "Cuba" within earshot of the other. Johnny was a guest at Maheu's home the previous Christmas. Bob's kids adored him and called him "Uncle Johnny."

Maheu needed help again. This time no one had to be killed. But it was a very serious matter. He had to find rooms on the Strip for Howard Hughes. An entire penthouse floor and some or all of the rooms on the floor below. Johnny talked to Ruby Kolod at the Desert Inn—Moe Dalitz was away on one of his luxury vacations, which made things easier as Dalitz was a difficult prick while Kolod answered to the minority shareholders in Chicago. The deal was made: They could have the top of the DI for ten days beginning November 23.

Howard Hughes. The Texas billionaire, industrialist, businessman, inventor, investor, aviator, moviemaker, and playboy, had long been a familiar name in American life, a headline-making iconoclast hyped across decades in captivating accounts of record-breaking air flights, remarkable big-business deals, showdowns with motion picture censors and Washington investigators, and a glamorous, industrious love life that linked him to nearly every young actress in Hollywood. Always an exceedingly eccentric personality, by the midfifties Hughes had begun to show signs of serious mental illness, possibly the slow-growing aftereffects of head injuries he had sustained in multiple plane crashes, and enhanced by his daily abuse of pharmaceutical narcotics to treat chronic pain. Characteristics that had previously been visible as peculiarities and shortcomings—germ phobias, compulsions, racist animosities—

became aspects of a consuming obsessiveness, a crippling paranoia. Though somehow continuing to function and maintain his
reputation as perhaps the shrewdest businessman in America,
Hughes's mental disorder was growing worse each year. By the end
of the decade he had withdrawn from all public life. He became
his own jailer, allowing only the most functional, anonymous human
contact. For his domestic needs and for his personal protection he
maintained a cadre of young men, his own Swiss Guard recruited
for him by an agency of the Mormon Church in Utah. Even his
wife—the movie actress Jean Peters—could speak with him only
by telephone or through a closed door. In 1961 the richest man on
earth went into a bedroom in an isolated wing of his house in Bel
Air and did not come out of it for five years.

Robert Maheu had been working for Howard Hughes for more
than a decade by 1966. Hughes's reliance on Maheu had grown to
the point that the peripatetic lawyer and sometime secret agent was
now the chief executive for all of Hughes's private business interests, paid a half-million dollars a year, the top salary on the entire
Hughes payroll. Maheu relocated with his family from Washington to Los Angeles in order to be closer to his employer, yet the
two never once met in person. All of Hughes's constant communications with his right-hand man were by telephone or memo.

Early in '66, after a lengthy battle with shareholders over the
disposition of Trans World Airlines, fighting many attempts to bring
him into the glare of an open courtroom, Hughes sold his majority
ownership. To some his decision was read as a capitulation, but in
fact the Texas tycoon had once again outplayed his opponents. The
price for his stock shares—nearly seven million of them—had gone
through the roof, and Howard Hughes pocketed a half-billion dollars (current equivalent four billion), the largest cash payment to
an individual ever recorded. Alas, behind every silver lining a cloud.
Hughes's great windfall required him to pay out a large chunk of
his profit in capital gains and state income taxes (and Hughes hated

paying taxes even more than he hated communists and flat-chested women). To avoid this loss he had to make an immediate reinvestment of the money and move out of California fast.

Because the former pilot was now afraid of flying, Maheu had to arrange for Hughes to travel by train, leasing two executive Pullman cars originally built for William Randolph Hearst. After a traumatic departure from his bedroom, like a frightened child leaving home for his first day of school, the billionaire boarded a train in Pasadena and departed the Golden State. Days later he disembarked in Boston, Massachusetts, where he spent the next several months in seclusion at the Ritz-Carlton Hotel (Maheu believed he had come to consult with a favored medical researcher). In late November, just before dawn, Hughes was smuggled back to the train station, carried onto his private car, and by morning he was rolling west.

In the early hours of Wednesday, November 23, Thanksgiving Eve, Johnny Rosselli and Joe Breen Jr. drove out of Las Vegas. The night sky, lit by a cloud of neon glare, faded to black as they headed north. At a junction four miles on, they reached an abandoned depot, where, in darkness but for the lights of an idling sedan, was an assemblage of people and parked vehicles, among them a cargo van belonging to the Desert Inn.

Johnny knew Howard Hughes. They had first met in the early 1930s, in Los Angeles, when Hughes's foremost interests were making movies and dating actresses. He was preparing to produce a picture called *Scarface*, based on a novel of the same name, a fictionalized rendering of the Capone saga by one Armitage Trail (Maurice Coons). Big Al was not averse to motion picture glorification, but with that ugly title he had to worry about these Hollywood boys' point of view. Capone asked Johnny to have a word. Hughes could not have been more ingratiating. He assured him that the character in the movie would have nothing to do with the real Mr. Capone except for that lurid title, which was strictly to attract the yokels. He told Johnny in this picture the gangsters were going to be the "good guys." In Hollywood, working outside the big-studio system, Hughes saw himself as a maverick, antiestablishment (anti-Semitic, too), and likely identified more with the gangsters than the moguls. He cultivated Johnny's friendship for a time, the two played golf together, and he once offered him a job as his assistant. Hughes's movie did not turn out to be quite so innocent as he promised, making use of numerous incidents from Capone's life story, including the "controversial" St. Valentine's Day Massacre. As scripted by Ben Hecht and directed by Howard Hawks, *Scarface* was a hyperviolent melodrama that portrayed the title character as a bloodthirsty lowbrow, a savage with a perverse interest in his own sister. As it happened, Capone was on his way to the big house when the movie was ready for release, and the picture got more trouble from state censors around the country than from the Mob. It was outright banned in Chicago, a rare decision with which both the law and the gangsters agreed.*

Johnny hadn't seen Hughes in twenty-five years or so, though he had seen enough about him in the papers. He was a peculiar character, all right, but Johnny couldn't help admiring him—he cared nothing for the law, did as he pleased, and he had made more money than the entire Syndicate.

Just before 4:00 a.m. the train arrived. The two Pullman cars rolled to a stop by the old depot. Pat Breen, Joe's wife, heard the story from her husband later in the morning. They saw Hughes as he was carried out on a stretcher. He was visible only in the moment or two he passed through dim light, so they could hardly

---

* The Capone gang's Machine Gun Jack McGurn was passing through a town in the Midwest when he saw that the local movie theater was showing *Scarface*. He burned the theater down.

believe what they had seen. He appeared emaciated, unshaven, with long stringy hair, more like a derelict than a billionaire (a longer look would have revealed the missing teeth, the hollowed eyes, the coiling yellow nails). Hughes remembered both Johnny and Joe's father, Joseph I. Breen, former head censor of Hollywood, with whom the movie producer/director had had many a lively encounter over his violations of the Hays Code. He asked Johnny about his golf game, and Johnny suggested they play a round or two some morning. Hughes said no more. He was slid into the back of the van and was driven away.

The billionaire moved into a suite at the top of the Desert Inn. Per instructions, all windows had been covered with heavy black curtains so that day or night, neon or sunshine, no glimmer of external light would be visible inside. Hughes took over a bedroom and bathroom, and otherwise the rest of the suite and the rest of the floor were to remain unoccupied. His Swiss Guard—security staff, male secretaries, and servants—was billeted on the floor below. His personal necessities were carefully—sanitarily—unpacked: the boxes of Kleenex; the disposable towels; the personal sheets, pillows, blankets, the bottles of Poland Spring water; his medicines and "works" for self-administering grains of codeine; and a collection of sterilized containers for collecting his urine.

The Desert Inn's special guest remained in his room for the length of his stay. No one in the hotel ever saw him. No one other than his crew-cutted staff was allowed access to the top floor. No one knew what the hell he was doing up there. A vexed Ruby Kolod rolled his eyes, sighed, booked an hour with the in-house masseuse. Moe Dalitz returned to the city in time for Christmas Week and New Year's Eve, the biggest night of the year in Las Vegas. He was not happy with what Kolod told him. Fucking make sure he's gone before Christmas, said Dalitz. Those penthouses were all long-ago booked for the New Year's holiday, and by the DI's highest rollers. They were worth hundreds of thousands to the casino. But Hughes didn't go. The crazy man who never left his room and his aseptic stooges who never dropped so much as a nickel in the casino (Mormons did not gamble) refused to budge. Dalitz was ready to send up his own security guards to storm the billionaire's bedroom, and none of those guys were germ-free. Maheu intervened. Dalitz told him Hughes had to get the hell out. Maheu explained it to his boss. Hughes was intransigent. He wasn't leaving. Maheu pleaded: "They are ready to drag you out of the hotel and throw you on the street." And Hughes said, "Tell them I'll buy the place."

That is how Maheu said it happened, and how the tale would be told through the years: the random move to the Silver State, the hotel reservation run out, the ultimatum delivered and Hughes's startling, spontaneous response, a virtual whim that would come to alter the history of Las Vegas and of underworld rule in that city. But a closer examination of the circumstances, and later revelations, including notes in Hughes's own handwriting stolen from a safe in his Hollywood office, would tell a more complicated and far more calculated story. Hughes's interest in Nevada and Las Vegas as a potential base of operations had actually been developing over many months. Even as madness was devouring his daily life, Hughes continued to manifest his legendary foresight. He strategized for the future, plotted ways of achieving more power and absolute freedom (defining the latter as freedom from regulations, taxes, and collective responsibilities). For some years he had been considering a move out of California to a land more friendly to self-interest. Ultimately afraid of his vulnerability in a foreign country, he began to focus on a locale just hours east of Los Angeles. Nevada had a reputation for rugged individualism, anything-goes ethics, and easy corruptibility. It was a place that respected the power of money and did not hang itself up on Sunday-school morality. Hughes had known the area well in his old flying and girl-chasing days, the wide-open spaces and the flashy resorts, so many memories—he'd once crashed an airplane in Lake Mead and killed two people while Ava Gardner waited for him in a Vegas hotel suite—and he had always felt at home there. By the time the billionaire rolled into Nevada in late '66 he was invested heavily, having already bought thousands of acres of prime real estate, and numerous politicians.

As his dream of a desert Xanadu took form, it was only logical that Hughes would want for his portfolio what were the most significant and valuable properties in the whole state. *Not* to own a major casino in Vegas would be for Hughes like somebody going to Hollywood and not having a movie star for a mistress. But buying a Strip casino was easier imagined than done. Nearly all the valued ones belonged to a conglomeration of mostly secret shareholders, the assorted points and pieces of points never traded in the light of day. These were murky waters for deal-making, even with as sharp and ruthless a dealer as Howard Hughes. You could find yourself drowned without the right navigator.

This was where Johnny Rosselli came in.

In that year organized crime was experiencing something akin to a nervous breakdown. In New York the Five Families were waging a civil war. The Mob in Los Angeles had fallen to ruin. In Chicago, Sam Giancana came out of jail to face the same federal squeeze that put him away in the first place. They were not letting up till he talked. Ricca and Accardo gave him the bad news: He had to beat it. The man who'd led them to riches and glory was exiled to Mexico, and the Outfit would have to make do with an inadequate replacement. Jimmy Hoffa, the Mob's own loan officer, whose Teamsters Pension Fund provided the sweetheart financing for so much of the Vegas Strip, had been convicted of bribery, jury tampering, and fraud; out on appeal for not much longer, he was facing thirteen years in prison. The FBI, meanwhile, unable to use its wiretapped evidence against lawbreakers in court, had begun to selectively leak savory facts to sympathetic reporters. Now anyone with a dime for a newspaper could read about the Syndicate hold on Las Vegas, about the crooks and killers employed by the casinos, the cheating of customers (the Feds had information about "fixed" dice and electromagnetized game boards), the bribes to legislators and a former governor, the millions in untaxed profits known as the skim. There was great uneasiness over this exposure. The gangsters wondered, How much time did they have before the federal government swept in and closed down their empire of vice? Would it be like Havana all over again? They had waited too long then. Fortunes had been lost. Big players like Meyer Lansky and the boys in the Outfit did not want to be caught short in Vegas.

When Howard Hughes told Bob Maheu he wanted to buy a big casino, Maheu knew he needed to talk to Johnny Rosselli, the man he described as "a key to the city, the ultimate Mob fixer in the desert." And Johnny knew that selling a big casino was exactly what the Mob wanted to do. Johnny brought the prospect to Chicago, then to Johnny Scalish in Cleveland, and all other substantial investors. The stars were in alignment. Negotiations began, likely much earlier than most accounts have it. Ruby Kolod was under the Syndicate's thumb. If they told him they were going to sell the Desert Inn he could only say, "How high?" Dalitz wasn't convinced, but if the Mob wanted it done—along with Jimmy Hoffa, who was thrilled at the prospect of getting some of his Teamster pension money paid back with big interest and proving to the government they were not bad loans after all—it would get done, with Moe's cooperation or not.

Dalitz was not pleased that some people were negotiating

behind his back, sticking their noses in where they didn't belong. Just the loss of those penthouses for New Year's was enough to rile him, regardless of the bigger stakes.

Less than a week after Dalitz returned to Las Vegas, two days before New Year's Eve, he was sitting in a booth at the Desert Inn restaurant with Johnny and with Nick "Peanuts" Danolfo, a DI employee and associate of Sam Giancana. As they were finishing their business lunch a deputy from the sheriff's department approached the booth and called to Johnny to come outside, he needed to talk with him. The guys in the booth exchanged glances. On the Strip it was not considered proper etiquette for a cop to make such a direct approach to a big shot like Dalitz or an important insider like Rosselli. Just bad manners was all.

"Don't you see we're eating here, fella?" Johnny said. "Why don't you go out in the lobby. I'll come over when we're done."

The deputy weighed the suggestion and went away.

Dalitz shrugged. "Must be new," he said.

Ten minutes later there was another visitor. This time it was the Stetson-wearing, six-gun-toting, fire-breathing cowboy sheriff of Las Vegas, Ralph Lamb.

"Rosselli?" he said. "I hear you been giving my deputy a hard time. Now get yourself up and come with me."

Johnny sneered. "Sure. Just tell me what it's about?"

Saying only that he wasn't going to tell him to get up twice, Lamb reached forward, grabbing the gangster by the tie with both hands, yanking his head down and pulling him out of the booth. There was a scuffle. Peanuts Danolfo moved to aid his friend, but Dalitz held him back. Let Johnny handle it. Two deputies ran up, tackled him, grabbed him under the arms, and with Lamb readjusting his cowboy hat the four of them headed for the street. They threw Johnny into the caged backseat of a cruiser and drove him away.

The sheriff's stated reason for the roust: Rosselli had broken the local law requiring convicted felons to register with the department on arrival in Clark County. It was a law mostly meant to keep track of bad-guy drifters and troublemakers. Not Johnny, who'd been an off-and-on resident for a decade. Somebody with juice was behind this, somebody who could tell Ralph Lamb to teach the gangster a lesson. He was taken down, booked at the detention center, photographed and fingerprinted, stripped, and marched into the shower room, "deloused" with a spray of permethrin. He was locked up in the holding tank all day, then released.

Johnny had a good idea who had set him up—that vindictive shit Dalitz, wide-eyed in the booth like butter wouldn't melt—but there was a major deal with Hughes on the line now, and a lot of dangerous people wanted it to work out. Johnny would have to be a big boy and let it go.

The Desert Inn negotiations began shortly after the New Year. Johnny and Maheu brought in Ed Morgan from Washington to serve as legal adviser for the sale. Hughes alone slowed the process, poring over every detail up in his room, woozy on codeine, sending down endless niggling objections. Despite him the job got done. The agreed-upon price was $13.25 million (current equivalent $100 million), with additional payments of $1,115,000 per year until 1981, reduced to $940,000 thereafter, plus taxes and all operating expenses. For this Hughes did not actually acquire the physical property but only a fifty-six-year lease to control the hotel and casino. Ownership remained with Dalitz and the partners through a real estate entity called Desert Inn Associates. The deal was closed on April Fool's Day 1967. Ed Morgan received $150,000 for his services and kicked back fifty grand to Johnny Rosselli. Even more satisfying for Johnny—no one enjoys being deloused—Moe Dalitz agreed to pay him a finder's fee of $400,000, which he would split with Sam Giancana. It was the great strategist's biggest score.

———

Johnny's work was not done. On the day of the signing, Bob Maheu—as Howard Hughes's de facto representative on earth—took charge of the Desert Inn, gaming hall and all. The private-dick-turned-executive knew nothing about running such an institution, and he again went to Johnny Rosselli for help, though, years later when Maheu recorded his memoirs and his affection for his friend had cooled, the advice would be described as unwelcome interference.

"Right after the takeover," Maheu wrote, "Johnny asked to see me. It was a meeting I'll never forget. We ended up at a lounge in the Desert Inn. I was seeing a Johnny I'd never seen before. He looked me right in the eye and said, 'Now, I want to tell you who the casino manager is going to be here, and who your entertainment director is going to be.'" Maheu said he protested. Johnny insisted. He went on, naming his list of employees and the jobs they would hold.

"I couldn't believe this guy," Maheu wrote. "I said, 'Johnny, go to hell. If you want to remain a friend of mine, we'll never discuss this subject again.'"

Johnny told Maheu he was making a big mistake. "I'm just telling you."

In Maheu's recollection he responded with a declaration of his independence from Rosselli and the powers lurking behind him. And yet what Johnny "advised" was exactly what Maheu let happen. The core personnel of the new Hughes-Maheu casino operation would be most of the same people who had been around under Dalitz's rule. In the offices. On the casino floor. In the counting room. The same people. Had Johnny and his associates tricked Maheu into taking their preferred staff despite his objections? Had they threatened him? Or was he a willing partner in a spectacular scam? The skim at the Desert Inn continued as before, millions of Hughes's casino money siphoned off and sent out the back door without Hughes getting so much as a whiff of it. The billionaire himself, still up in his bedroom, blitzed on opioids, storing his urine, seemed to have little-to-no interest in what went on downstairs, busy with new schemes to peddle influence, change local ordinances and state laws in his favor, and buy, buy, buy before another dollar was lost to the infernal tax man. The huge tax saving that came with the purchase of the Desert Inn had him greedy for more of the same. The DI deal was barely done when he told Robert Maheu he was ready to buy another casino. Soon Johnny was back on the scene, "smoothing the way," putting Bob together with the guys at the Sands Hotel casino. Hughes bought it for $23 million. Johnny received $95,000.

"We roped Hughes into buying the DI," he told Jimmy Fratianno. "Now it looks like he wants to buy the whole town, if we let him."

They let him. Following the Sands, Hughes purchased the Castaways, the Silver Slipper, the unfinished Landmark, and the new New Frontier (Maurice Friedman's baby, sold for $23 million). Deals to buy the Stardust, followed by the Dunes and Caesar's Palace, were interrupted by Justice Department threats to prosecute the billionaire for violating antitrust laws if he didn't curtail his spree.

Howard Hughes was given a red-carpet welcome by the Nevada establishment. His takeover of the Strip was lauded by the press, politicos, and bureaucrats, much of the cheering impelled by campaign contributions, giant advertising buys, and outright bribes. In front-page editorials, the *Las Vegas Sun* publisher, Hank Greenspun, called Hughes a "genius" comparable to Isaac Newton, and a man devoted to the "betterment of mankind." The good people of Nevada were convinced. They sang his praises like a church choir. He was single-handedly rescuing them from the scourge of organized crime, saving their most famous city from its humiliating reputation as a haven for hoodlums and hookers, seeding the state with his benevolence, offering opportunities and improvements in recreation, tourism, medicine, industry, science, and property development. Hughes's influence on state legislators brought about a change in the casino management laws (before Hughes, all declared owners had to be personally vetted, finances investigated, and so on—a terrible inconvenience for the recluse), a change that eventually opened the city to major corporate ownership, and did in fact lead to the end of widespread underworld control. Across the state he was seen as a benevolent savior who was bringing forth a modern and honorable Nevada. Howard Hughes, the state's superhero: up on the ninth floor of the DI, naked, shooting opium alkaloids through his bloodstream, watching old B Westerns and crime movies on television till dawn, spending much of each day crumpled on the toilet fighting chronic constipation.

The Hughes era in Las Vegas lasted four years. In the end, the arrogant oligarch was shown to be not as smart as he thought. He had jumped into a viper pit with only a checkbook to defend himself, and he'd been bitten to pieces. By the end of his Vegas sojourn, late in 1970, after years of his casinos losing money, auditors concluded that, by one method or another, Hughes had been robbed of between fifty and one hundred million dollars in cash. According to one of his Washington influence peddlers, Hughes claimed to have discovered that Bob Maheu had been in collusion with big-time gangsters. "He's a no-good dishonest son-of-a-bitch," said the billionaire, "and he stole me blind."

On Thanksgiving Eve 1970, Howard Hughes left his Desert Inn bedroom for the first time since 1966. He departed as he had come, in the middle of the night, strapped to a stretcher, carried out through a fire exit to the parking lot, looking like a shriveled, constipated mummy being taken to his next crypt.

9

As much as President Lyndon Johnson hoped that the Warren Commission would have the last word on the assassination of John Kennedy, this was not to be. Questions, doubts, suspicions remained. Large portions of the American populace were left unsatisfied by the commission's judgment, regardless of the evidence at hand. To many of them a murder of such magnitude deserved a more impressive killer. Not that seedy little drifter in a T-shirt. Critics combed the report for mistakes, or worse, deliberate deceptions. Kennedy insiders began to break ranks, expressing a lack of confidence. There emerged provocative bits and pieces of overlooked or withheld information. It was like a gas tank with pinholes, dripping combustible material. By late '66 a Harris Poll survey showed that only 34 percent of Americans supported the Warren verdict. Even Lyndon Johnson, who had created the commission to end further speculation, and had nearly directed its finding, could not get past his own private uncertainties.

Early in 1967 the president became aware of two disquieting developments in the Kennedy quandary. From New Orleans news came of a district attorney named Jim Garrison, who had opened his own investigation into JFK's demise, the first official inquiry of any sort since the Warren Commission shut down. Garrison was a popular but erratic character, with a come-and-go impulse for reform and quixotic crusades. Like many others by that point, he no longer believed that Lee Harvey Oswald had acted alone. Since the time of the assassination, there had been rumors wafting around New Orleans, whispered stories about a locally based conspiracy responsible for JFK's killing. Garrison was determined to find out what there was to it. His mission, his provocative statements, began to attract attention outside Louisiana. Some said he was chasing headlines, raising his reputation in anticipation of a future Senate run. But others believed him and his cause, a man trying to find the hidden facts behind a great American tragedy. Perhaps both sides were correct.

Garrison seemed to base his case mostly on hearsay. His primary suspects—at least in the beginning—were a vaguely interconnected group of right-wing zealots and anti-Castro activists. On February 22, 1967, the investigation got a melodramatic boost in credibility when two of the DA's "persons of interest" died on the same day. David Ferrie was an airline pilot and a sometime-employee of New Orleans Mob boss Carlos Marcello (Ferrie was also a hypnotist, pederast, and completely hairless but for a home-made wig and pasted-on eyebrows) said to have known Lee Oswald as a young teenager; he probably died of an aneurism, though Garrison called it a suicide. Eladio del Valle was a Miami-based Cuban exile, former Batista enforcer, and an associate of Santo Trafficante; Garrison wanted him for questioning, apparently influenced by claims in a lurid newspaper article; the same day Ferrie expired, del Valle was savagely murdered in Florida. For some these two convenient deaths seemed to indicate Garrison was getting close to something big.

The second story President Johnson heard was communicated directly and behind closed doors. On January 16 he was visited by an ally in the media, Drew Pearson, a well-known muckraker and newspaper columnist ("Washington Merry-Go-Round" was the most popular political column in the country). Pearson had an astonishing tale to tell the president. It concerned an unnamed client of his friend DC attorney Edward Morgan. Six years earlier, said Pearson, Morgan's client—a man of some high standing in his own field—had been recruited by an agency of the United States to murder the dictator of Cuba. Under the man's direction a team with appropriate skills was gathered, and with the assistance of U.S. government personnel they attempted on several occasions to kill Fidel Castro. This was, said the journalist, done with the approval of the White House, and under the close supervision of that most trusted member of JFK's cabinet, Robert Kennedy. Shocking stuff (and indicative of Johnson's value in the Kennedy administration that he knew nothing about it). But Pearson's finale was still more explosive: The U.S.-backed assassination team had been captured in Cuba; they had been tortured and brainwashed and then sent back to America with a new mission: to kill President Kennedy.

"Lyndon listened carefully," Pearson wrote in his diary, "and made no comment. There wasn't much he could say."

There was more than enough in Pearson's story to render Johnson speechless. Here at last—if legitimate, and Johnson tended to trust Pearson's skills as a reporter—was the terrible "truth" behind the late president's death. It confirmed Johnson's own original belief in a conspiracy (though he had once thought it a revenge plot out of Southeast Asia). Pearson's revelations also contained dramatic implications for the future. Would the president now have to make a vengeful response against Cuba? Would the Soviet Union then come to the island's defense? Would it all end in war?

The story contained powerful political ramifications as well. There was much talk of Bobby Kennedy—Jack's pious brother, Johnson's perpetual burr in the saddle—considering a run against the incumbent president next year. If Bobby had in fact "supervised" a secret band of assassins, if the story was true, and if he had sent those killers to Cuba, with tragic, ironic consequences, didn't it make Bobby partly to blame for his brother's death? That would be a terrible, ugly thing for the public to learn about the boy. *Political dynamite*, that's what that was.

Johnson said nothing on the record, but kept an eye on the situation in the weeks ahead, conferring with his attorney general, Ramsey Clark, and a few trusted associates with ears to the ground. He ordered the FBI to follow developments in New Orleans, without interfering. But this whole thing got crazier by the day. Louisiana senator Hale Boggs—one of the members of the

Warren Commission—told the president that Garrison was now floating an idea that he—he, the president, Lyndon Johnson—might also have been involved in the assassination. Johnson was thunderstruck. He couldn't believe he was hearing something so insane. "[It's] just like you're tellin' me that Lady Bird [Mrs. Johnson] was taking *dope!*"

For a time, at least as far as the president and his confidants could assess it, the Pearson story and the Garrison story seemed only vaguely related. One had to do with Castro and the CIA and secret government missions. The other with a bunch of New Orleans screwballs and perverts (and—according to somebody—the president himself). Which meant that at least one of the two stories was bull, and that took away some credibility from both. Johnson remained intrigued, but there was nothing about either story he could address in public if he couldn't be sure of the facts, not even if it was going to put Bobby in the shit.

On the morning of March 2, Johnson received a call from John Connally (Texas governor, JFK's fellow passenger and gunshot victim on the fateful day in Dallas). A shaken Connally had rushed to tell him about an encounter with a New York reporter from the local all-news radio station. The reporter had told the governor off the record that he had a source with access to the files in DA Garrison's office.

These files, the reporter confided, contained material describing a plot to kill Castro, apparently overseen by President Kennedy's brother. "Garrison," Connally told the president, "has information that would prove there were *four assassination teams . . . assassins* in the United States. . . . One of the teams was composed of Lee Harvey Oswald; this fella Shaw [New Orleans businessman Clay Shaw, arrested by Garrison on March 1], and the dead man Ferrie [New Orleans weirdo David Ferrie, Garrison's first suspect, aneurism victim or possible suicide]; plus one other man. They were teams of four. . . . Some of 'em were captured and tortured, and Castro and his people—and I assume Che Guevara—heard the whole story. Then one of Castro's lieutenants, as a reprisal measure, sent four teams [to] the United States to assassinate President Kennedy. And Lee Harvey Oswald was a member of the team."

That was some goddamn story, Johnson agreed. But they had to hold their socks up and not let this thing get away from them till they knew more. He advised Connally not to tell anyone else what he'd heard, and not to be concerned. This man Garrison had a different story every day. He was probably just a nut, looking for attention. Connally nervously agreed. But in truth Johnson did not know what to think. He had always had his suspicions. The story was wild but contained a certain persuasiveness.

On February 28 an article in the New York–based Spanish-language newspaper *El Tiempo* referenced the Cuban retaliatory conspiracy against Kennedy. There was no more proof offered, no sourcing, but the story was certainly out there.

On March 3 the "Washington Merry-Go-Round" column appeared with the headline A RUMOR PERSISTS ABOUT ASSASSINATION. According to Drew Pearson, who was out of the country on a good-will tour of South America with Chief Justice Earl Warren at the time, his junior partner, Jack Anderson, wrote up the Cuba/JFK assassination story without authorization. But there it was. "President Johnson is sitting on a political H-bomb," the piece began, "an unconfirmed report that Sen. Robert Kennedy may have approved an assassination plot which then possibly backfired against his late brother. . . ."

Some major newspapers refused to run the column because its claims were so outrageous and so thinly sourced, and under the bombast no more than a rumor. Some saw it as anti-Bobby dirty tricks. It *was* an outrageous story—more a plot spun by Hollywood than anything real—except to those who were close to the historical events mentioned and knew that at least the first half of the story—the CIA working with the Mob—was quite accurate. Bobby Kennedy himself, who had long feared that his "wars" on Castro and organized crime may have played a role in Jack's death, was reportedly mortified by what he read.

Jack Anderson—enjoying the attention his March 3 column received—decided to go down to New Orleans to meet Jim Garrison. Anderson found the district attorney fascinating but strange. Garrison would tell him he had now concluded that the Kennedy assassination was the work of a CIA-backed homosexual cabal made up of David Ferrie, Clay Shaw, and Jack Ruby, with Lee Harvey Oswald their appointed patsy.

Meanwhile, in the White House, Lyndon Johnson decided he had to do something to avoid appearing like he was trailing behind the unfolding story. He ordered Hoover to send FBI agents to interview Ed Morgan and to come back with the name of his client. Morgan talked with the agents for two hours, telling them the whole story again as he knew it. He told them he had nothing to do with the Garrison investigation. When asked about his client, his source for these details, Morgan told them his client was not directly involved in the plot to kill Kennedy. He said his client was "a high type individual of the Catholic faith whose conscience bothered him." Morgan refused to further identify him unless they were offering complete immunity.

President Johnson called for full reports from the FBI and the CIA. Hoover, with enthusiasm, quickly delivered a memorandum revealing all he knew about the dreaded Central Intelligence Agency's collaboration with organized crime. The CIA, very reluctantly, compiled its report, and chief Richard Helms delivered it to Johnson verbally. Much of what they told the president confirmed and amplified aspects of the whistle-blower revelations coming from Pearson and associates. It may have tilted Johnson against his intelligence services when it came to the parts of the story with which the FBI and CIA claimed to be unfamiliar or disagreed. Helms, admitting the Castro assassination plot and the "Mafia" involvement, admitting that the CIA may have been less than forthcoming with the Warren Commission regarding Oswald and much else, pushed back on the business of a turnaround by Fidel and on any thought of Oswald's being part of a conspiracy. Oswald acted alone, Helms told the president. There was no credible evidence of anyone else involved, no direct Cuban connection to Oswald's act.

But it was too late to convince Johnson. He had suspected a conspiracy from the day of the shooting. The CIA was covering its tracks again. Perhaps they might even have some deeper involvement.

The president did not share his belief with the public, nor did he use the scandalous information against his rival Bobby Kennedy, but he was now sure that some version of this story was the truth, that this is what happened: The CIA had been running "a damned Murder Inc. in the Caribbean," and Castro had struck back. Events began to overwhelm Johnson in the months ahead, leaving him no time to deal with the past, only his crumbling present, the evident purposelessness of the war in Vietnam, growing social unrest, public disapproval, and a lack of support from his own party. In March '68 he announced he would not be running for a second presidential term of office. His feud with Robert Kennedy would come to a brutal end with Bobby's assassination in June. Johnson would go into retirement and a virtually permanent seclusion in Texas. He never again addressed the subject of JFK's assassination, except for one odd and unprovoked moment during a television interview with ABC reporter Howard K. Smith. Out of nowhere, off the record, Johnson mumbled, as though speaking to himself more than to the nearby newsman. "I'll tell you something that will *rock* you," the vanishing president said. *"Kennedy was trying to get Castro, but Castro got him first. . . ."*

10

More than a year had gone by since the FBI had rousted Johnny Rosselli on the sidewalk in Beverly Hills. He had done what he could to protect himself—talked to his connections in Washington, found the best lawyer to represent him—after which there was nothing left but to go about his business and wait for the other shoe to drop. The time passed and nothing happened. Maybe, without admitting to it, the CIA had done the right thing and gotten him off the hook.

Then it dropped. A crushing thick-soled hobnailed boot.

On July 20, 1967, acting on a tip, six agents of the Federal Bureau of Investigation raided the Friars Club on Santa Monica Boulevard. They uncovered evidence of the elaborate cheating operation set up in the area above the ceiling in the club's card room. The tip had come from Vegas hotel/casino owner Beldon Katleman, a longtime enemy of Maurice Friedman and a fellow high-stakes card cheat. Katleman got the story from George Seach, the wizard of "the peek" and the original man in the crawl space at the Friars. Soon the Feds had Seach confessing a blue streak. As the original electronics technician, as well as a participant and partner in the sting, Seach knew how it all worked, how much money had been made, and the names of everyone who collected a piece of the winnings. In August, Johnny was subpoenaed to appear before a grand jury in Los Angeles. In the courtroom he invoked his Fifth Amendment protection from self-incrimination. It didn't matter. U.S. Attorney David Nissen, chief, Special Prosecutions Division, had already gathered more than enough evidence to get an indictment. Defense attorneys attempted to wrest the case out of federal hands, arguing that the charges should be for grand theft and therefore should be tried in the local court. The Feds held on. They were not going to lose the chance to score against a top hoodlum, even if it was for card cheating.

While the first grand jury was in progress, Nissen was preparing writs for a second hearing. The government was at last going after Johnny on the immigration case. A doubleheader. This would be a far more personal prosecution: To prove his real identity the government would make good use of the FBI's multiyear investigation into Rosselli's early life and family connections. Subpoenas went out to Johnny's sisters, his brother, his eighty-two-year-old mother (attorneys would take the ailing Maria Sacco's deposition at her bedside in Boston). The family members attempted to stand firm under questioning, admit nothing damaging to Johnny's case, but the government was well prepared to refresh any faulty memories.

On October 21 the grand jury in the immigration hearing brought back a six-count indictment. The first charged him with failure to register as an alien; counts two through six charged violations of the law requiring aliens to report their address to the government once per year.

Just before Christmas the second grand jury returned indictments for Johnny and his five colleagues in the Friars cheating case, charging them with criminal commerce and racketeering. They were looking at the possibility of years in prison if convicted.

He tried to face the prospect of back-to-back trials with equanimity. Cool only counted if you kept it under difficult circumstances. In life sometimes you were the bug, and sometimes the windshield. As his pal Jimmy liked to say: It was just one of those things.

The law was no longer his only problem. He had seen it coming from the moment Sam Giancana had gone to jail, then into exile in Cuernavaca. Joe Batters/Tony Accardo was grumpily back in charge. He was no fan of Johnny's. It had been that way from the beginning, back to the days of Al Capone. Accardo was the glowering, no-nonsense mobster, with a family, a suburban home; Johnny was the Hollywood playboy, the suntanned adventurer. Who knew what it was about? A million fucking years ago, and he still had a hard-on. Italians and their grudges.

Giancana had lost his usefulness, forced to abdicate, and now Accardo cast a gimlet eye on Sam's boyfriend Rosselli. What difference if Johnny had just made them all millions and millions in Vegas? Joe Batters didn't like his haircut.

Soon after the Friars indictments, Accardo called Johnny to Chicago. A long time they had known each other. When they first met there were tin lizzies on the street and gunpowder in the air, and Big Al reigned supreme. Back then Accardo was a street thug crushing skulls with a baseball bat; now he ruled the roost. The two men were about the same age, but Joe Batters looked like somebody's grumpy old *nonno*, saggy and gray, jowls like two saddlebags. Tony told Johnny that this trouble he was in with the Feds was a shame. It meant they would have to make some changes. He was going to have to stay away from business until he got things straightened out. They were going to let Phil Ponto [Outfit made man] handle things for a while.

And that was that. His position was taken away, his Vegas share cut off.

While Johnny put up a good front, Maurice Friedman was another story. He had come unglued almost from the get-go, had half confessed the moment they arrested him. As the June date of the Friars Club trial grew near, his anxiety only grew worse. He was a sleazeball, not a gangster. He couldn't go to prison. He devoted much time to figuring out a way—legal, extralegal—to upset the prosecution's case. He bribed a court employee to obtain a copy of the secret grand jury transcripts (he and two of the defense lawyers would be caught with the stolen transcripts, and prosecuted). He determined that George Seach had been given immunity and would be the government's star witness (Pete Gebhard, who had substituted for Seach when he was in prison, refused to cooperate with the government and awaited a separate prosecution). Friedman turned to Johnny for help with the obvious solution to the problem. Johnny—a little wearily—agreed it had to be done. Friedman gave him some cash. Johnny called Jimmy Fratianno and arranged to see him.

Jimmy was not in the best of shape. He was fighting two federal indictments for fraud. Big penalties, five years in the joint if he lost in court. Jimmy had built up a trucking business. It had looked good for a while. Once more he thought he had it made, and once more he had ended up just a crook facing time. According to Ovid Demaris, he and Johnny met in James Cantillon's office in Beverly Hills.

They caught each other up on their various predicaments. What had they done to deserve such a fate? Johnny wondered.

They both grinned.

They talked. Jimmy asked about Sam Giancana. Sam had disappeared to Mexico. He lived for a time in Acapulco, in a fifteen-room penthouse at Club Nacional. He had a staff of a half dozen or so, maids, bodyguards, a cook brought in from Italy. When he got bored he went traveling. The Caribbean. Beirut. Majorca. He had a girl in every port.

They talked about the death of "that asshole" Frank DeSimone, and his replacement, Nick Licata, who neither of them thought was much of an improvement.

They talked about Chicago. About Accardo cutting Johnny off in Las Vegas. Jimmy expressed shock, disgust. What kind of people did they work for? Johnny had practically put that city on the map. This was how they thanked him.

Eventually Johnny got to his piece of business. He explained to Jimmy the situation they were facing in the Friars Club thing. This guy George Seach. The only man who could make the government's case against them. He could send them away for a long time. Johnny lowered his voice in the way one does when about to ask somebody to commit murder. Johnny said Jimmy would be doing him a very great favor if he could get rid of this Seach problem for them. "Bury the motherfucker."

Jimmy told him not to worry. It was done.

Johnny put an envelope with cash into Jimmy's coat pocket. He had been holding a lot in lately, and now he surrendered to a surge of emotion. He thanked Jimmy and put his arms around him in a long embrace.

George Seach lived in Las Vegas. Fratianno called Frank Bompensiero up from San Diego to help him, and they drove to Las Vegas, a length of rope and some .38s in the trunk. They staked Seach's apartment in town. It was supposed to be against the rules to clip a guy within the city limits, so the two men figured they would either kill him and whisk the body away to the desert or take him alive and do the job out there somewhere. The lights were not on in the apartment, and there was no sign of him. Johnny had a couple of trusted people keeping an eye open at the Stardust, Seach's favorite haunt. One of them called to say Seach was there, in the cocktail lounge with some people. Jimmy and Bomp rushed over. They saw him. They kept their distance, waited. They moved around, played the slots, not wanting to get noticed. When he moved again they would follow, waiting to get him alone, off the property. Seach and one of his pals got up suddenly and hurried away. Jimmy thought they were going to the can, but then he got worried. He called to Bomp and the two killers went to check. Gone. They'd lost him just like that. They went through the lobby and casino looking for him. They went out to the parking lot, but there was no trace. They got the guns and the rope out of the trunk and sped back to Seach's address. There was nobody home, but now the lights were on inside. Somebody had been there and left in a hurry. Jimmy and Bomp drove around a few times and then decided they better get away.

The next day Jimmy heard from Johnny: George Seach had been taken into protective custody. He would be out of reach until after the trial. Jimmy said he couldn't believe their fucking luck. The Feds must have snatched him right under their eyes.

They didn't know that Frank Bompensiero was now an FBI snitch. Earning Brownie points, he had likely phoned his federal handler with a heads-up, perhaps just minutes before Seach was whisked away.

The immigration violations trial got started on April 23, 1968. Johnny sat at the table in the courtroom, stony faced at all times—according to Dave Nissen—as the prosecution presented his biography from the witness stand. It was like an episode of that old television show, *This Is Your Life*, an array of figures from the past brought before him one by one, family members, long-ago neighbors, the "stepbrother" whose bedroom he shared and with whom he had once delivered the milk on cold Boston mornings, the Los

Angeles barber from the early thirties who identified a photo of Johnny's visiting brother, Vincent Sacco, introduced to him by Johnny as "Jimmy Rosselli."

There were as well the police spokesmen and government experts come to share incriminating data found in assorted arrest records, fingerprint files, affidavits, the recorded false and contradictory statements of birthplace (New York, Chicago), birth date (June, July, 1904, 1905), signature samples, real and forged documents, handwriting analysis with blow-ups projected on the wall and discrepancies described in numbing detail ("evidence of retouchings . . . a pen lift between the double L combination . . . recurves, a little eyelet at the top . . . the ending stroke of the letter R in line 27 similar to the ending stroke in line 26").

The government's case looked good. But Johnny had ceased to worry. His team had discovered what they needed. Everything, he was told, was going to be okay. They had dug through the family files, through the old immigration laws. There was a eureka moment. According to law at the time, when Johnny's widowed mother had remarried, and to a man who was a naturalized citizen, citizenship was conferred on her alien underage children. It was known as "derivative citizenship," from an 1855 statute not repealed until September 1922. Boston marriage records showed that Maria Sacco married Liberato Cianciulli in *February* 1922. Under this law Johnny, by any name, was a citizen of the United States and had been since he was sixteen years old.

The government was even better at research. They were able to provide to the court proof that Maria's "second husband," Cianciulli, already had a living wife at the time of their wedding. His marriage to Maria was therefore void. Further, even if it could be judged legal, there was no evidence that anyone had filed the necessary forms conveying the derivative change of status; additionally, the government showed proof that Johnny's mother had used the surname of her first husband without variation until the present day, and continued to file her residency condition as "alien non-citizen."

On May 24 the jury returned a verdict of guilty on all counts.

Johnny's attorney petitioned for his client's release on bail while they awaited an appeal hearing. Judge Pearson Hall consented to the release with an unusual and extrajudicial proviso: Johnny had to promise to "go home" and see his ailing mother, before it was too late.

He had three weeks before the scheduled start of the next trial. Taking Joe Shimon with him for moral support, Johnny flew to Boston. It was a family reunion forty years in the making. He was greeted with great warmth by his younger siblings and their spouses and children. There were nieces and nephews never before seen. And there was his mother, ill and worn with age, dying of cancer; Johnny sat beside her in the bedroom, both of them voiceless, overwhelmed.

The Friars trial began in June and went on almost to the end of the year. The government made a comprehensive presentation of its case. Federal agents recounted the raid on the club, exhibited the items they had found in the rafters, described photos of the vents and viewing devices that had been installed in the ceiling of the card room. Gaming experts described how all the card games at the Friars were played. Electronics experts explained how the transmitters and receivers worked. Hollywood celebrities called to the stand—Zeppo Marx, Tony Martin, Phil Silvers—testified to their victimhood with resignation and some humor. Asked how much he thought he had lost to the card cheats, television star Silvers said, "Let me put it this way, I'm hitchhiking home."

For the government, much was riding on the testimony of George Seach, the man whose technical and mathematical skills had served the gang so well for years. Now he was on the witness stand to rat them all out. Without much emotion and with remarkable recall he laid out the story, from Maurice Friedman's first call to him in Las Vegas, how the materials were gathered, installed, the amounts won and divided.

Before he saw him in the courtroom, Johnny had encountered Seach only once. The Friars Club sting had been going on for a while by that time. Good money was won month after month. The supply of suckers was never ending. George Seach worried that his fellow cheaters thought he was a sucker, too. He was supposed to have been paid his share of the enterprise even while he was away in jail, but he felt sure they had held out on him. He'd now come up with a way to reestablish his importance to the group. He told Maury Friedman that he'd invented a new technical device, and Friedman was eager to hear more. They agreed to meet at the bar of the Beverly Crest Hotel. Friedman introduced George to Johnny. Seach told them about the invention. It would revolutionize "the peek," he said, allowing the person in Seach's position to work safely off the premises, blocks away, even, no more human error, light reflections, or creaking floorboards to worry about.

Maury had gone off to the bathroom, and Johnny and George Seach continued to chat. Seach suddenly interrupted himself. There was something he had to say to Johnny while Maury was not there. Johnny told him to go on.

"Do not trust Friedman," Seach said. *"He will betray you."*

That was it.

"Yeah. You're probably right," Johnny said. "But, you know . . . I like him."

Later Johnny asked Maury about Seach. Wasn't there something odd about him? Oh sure, Maury said, he'd done his time in the nut ward at Vacaville. George was a psycho.

At the Friars trial the defense knew all about George's problems. They made a brutal attempt to undermine his testimony. A doctor from the psychiatric department in the prison hospital where Seach had been confined was brought in and grilled. They went over Seach's case history. The patient had been characterized as "schizophrenic, acute undifferentiated type, with paranoid features precipitated by homosexual panic." He experienced "auditory hallucinations . . . voices coming from the radio and from outer space."

The high point of the doctor's testimony came when he recollected his observation of Seach during an acute psychotic attack, giving the courtroom its most unexpected—and disturbing— moments as the doctor read aloud some of Seach's transcribed words, an excerpt of delirium poetry not unlike the deathbed rant of Dutch Schultz:

I told lies. Don't take my eyes out. I won't tell more.

My name is Charlie. I cheated, I stole. Saint Peter won't let me in heaven now.

I'll try to be good. Don't cut out my tongue.

Sometimes I think I am Howard Hughes. I am so damned rotten. I don't know what I am anymore.

My name is Charlie. I'm a Jew. Sometimes I think I'm Jesus. Don't want people to think I'm crazy. Can't trust anyone, not even God.

Only thing one can really believe in is math.

Maurice Friedman opted to take the stand in his own defense, trying to put across the interesting notion that it was not really a crime for rich people to cheat other rich people. His appearance was mostly an effort to clear Johnny Rosselli of any wrongdoing— out of friendship or fear, or both. There was, in fact, no proof Johnny had ever played in one of the dishonest games, and only Seach's statement that he had even been a member of the "team." "Mr. Rosselli was brought in at the eleventh hour," declared attorney Cantillon at one point, "to give this some kind of a national-organized-crime flavor for a bit of color and nothing more." But the government was not about to lose its headliner. The forensic accountants were able to track a check for ten thousand dollars from a Friars Club game in Beverly Hills that crossed the state line into Nevada and ended up as cash paid over to Johnny in Las Vegas.

The trial continued through the summer and the fall. Though Bill Harvey spoke up for him in Washington, the CIA made no official attempt to intervene. The appearance of the Pearson/ Anderson column—whose unnamed source the agency had to know—may have led them to wash their hands.

On December 2 the jury announced a guilty verdict against all defendants. Sentences, when they came, were tough. Maurice Friedman, as the ringleader, got the worst of it, six years' imprisonment and one hundred thousand dollars in fines. Johnny, as the most famous offender, came in second. "Mr. Rosselli," said the judge, "you were not the originator of this scheme. You didn't start it, but the Court is convinced, as was the jury, that you muscled into it when you found it in progress. If you receive the benefits, you must also accept the penalties."

Five years and fifty thousand dollars.

Sentencing for the immigration conviction, heard on February 4, 1969, brought him six months in prison for the first count of the indictment, and thirty days each for counts two through six, incarceration period to be followed by a deportation hearing.

He remained free, for the time being, while the lawyers sought to appeal the verdict.

The government was still hungry. They worked on a frantic Maurice Friedman. They put an offer of a reduced sentence on the table. They said: Convince us you're worth it. The Feds pushed him on a subject he knew well, hidden Mob ownership in Las Vegas. They put him before a grand jury. Friedman spilled all over the federal carpet. He told them the New Frontier story. He gave up his Detroit mafiosi partners. He gave up his friend Johnny Rosselli.

They brought Johnny in for grand jury questioning. He refused to answer questions, taking the Fifth Amendment. He was then given immunity, the government's clever subversion of the Fifth. Now he had to answer or surrender his bond and go to jail. The questions were tough, dangerous. He was skating on the thinnest ice, sharks just below waiting to rip him apart if he said the wrong thing. Nissen and team called him back for a second round of questions, then a third. It was clear to Johnny they knew too much about the situation at the Frontier. One day Johnny came out of another grand jury session at the courthouse and ran right into Detroit's Tony Zerilli, one of those hidden owners the law wanted to know all about. The face-to-face felt engineered. Felt like a setup. The law wanted Zerilli to see him there. Grand jury testimony was a guarded secret. No one knew who said what. "They're trying to make it look like I'm talking," Johnny told his attorney.

Maury had made a great snitch. Based on his grand jury testimony, the government got indictments against Zerilli, Mike Polizzi, Tony Giordano of St. Louis, and other partners, charged with racketeering, money laundering, fraud. At trial all were convicted, Zerilli and Polizzi getting four years.

With other options running out and imprisonment looming, Johnny, under the advice of Ed Morgan, decided to take his story to the press. It was a last throw of the dice before the cell doors swung shut. If there was any chance left to milk his government "service" for sympathy, it would not last much longer. Of course it would have to be done with some care. Anything he said for public consumption was bound to rub his Chicago associates the wrong way.

Morgan turned again to the nationally syndicated "Washington Merry-Go-Round" column. Drew Pearson having died in 1969, it was now written by Jack Anderson and Les Whitten. Anderson was already sympathetic to Johnny's story and was never averse to a scoop. "It was important that Johnny be able to say he had not spoken directly to any journalists," Les Whitten recalled. "We could not indicate that he ever said something *to us* or even that we were all together in the same room. So we came up with the idea that we would talk *through* Morgan, the attorney. When we asked a question, we asked Morgan. When Johnny said something he said it to Morgan, even though he was sitting right across from us. Johnny was somehow happy with this arrangement, and that was just how we did it."

It was more a monologue than an interview. Johnny was not about to open himself up to a wide-open inquiry. But even circumscribed, it was, Les Whitten recalled, "A helluva story."

Like the Ancient Mariner, holding them firmly in his grip, he spun his tale of CIA agents, gangsters, dictators, assassination plots, moonlit runs to the Cuban coast, everything but an albatross.

It was an impressive performance. "He was larger than life," said Les Whitten. "I remember thinking, here's the last of the buccaneers."

The "Merry-Go-Round" columns, when they appeared in January and February 1971, painted Johnny in vibrant colors. He was a leading-man type, "dapper . . . formerly married to a movie star. . . . Rosselli, a ruggedly handsome gambler with con-

tacts in both the American and Cuban underworld." Such a patriot, said the report, that his expenses were paid out of his own
pocket.

But Johnny was only the icing in the series of groundbreaking
columns that dug deep into the government's secret history, the
first well-sourced exposé of a renegade CIA, responsible not only
for the Castro caper (which Anderson again suggested may inadvertently have led to JFK's death) but—persistently rumored—
other assassination plots in the Kennedy era, the killing of Trujillo
in the Dominican Republic, Diem in Vietnam, Lumumba in the
Democratic Republic of the Congo. For most Americans, reading
the paper over the breakfast table or on the train to work, it was
the first time they had ever heard of such things. Even in an era of
cynical spy movies and bloody news from Southeast Asia, it was a
startling dose of reality. They were bombshell pieces that shook up
the country.

Anderson's portrait of a daring patriot was Johnny's best shot.
Now he would wait and see what happened. He had nothing better to do. By the time the last of the columns was printed, he was
in a frigid cell at the McNeil Island Federal Penitentiary in Washington State.

11

He returned to the world on October 5, 1973, paroled after three
years behind bars. He was sixty-eight years old.

The first months had been the worst, at the decayed old prison
on McNeil Island, where in winter the cold damp winds off Puget
Sound blew through his wounded lungs, nearly killing him. Sent
to the Feds' prison medical facility in Minnesota, he was treated
for pneumonia and digestive disorders. His lawyers and a few
friends with pull were eventually able to get him transferred to

the federal institution at Safford in southeastern Arizona. He was later moved to another facility at Lompoc, California.

His health had improved in the warmer climate. But his insides were a mess. His chest and gut were ravaged by disease. Emphysema, diverticulitis. Doctors had removed a large piece of his colon. His inoperable hiatus hernia made his stomach protrude deep into his esophagus.

He returned to Beverly Hills. He had given up his luxurious lodgings on South Beverly Glen. Money had gotten tight after years of attorneys' fees. It didn't seem worth it to pay rent for an empty apartment. He checked into the Hilton for the night. He walked to La Dolce Vita for dinner. The owner and the old waiters greeted him like a champion.

12

In November he went to Florida to visit his fifty-six-year-old sister Edith and her husband, Joe Daigle, an aeronautical engineer attached to NASA, the government aerospace agency. The Daigles lived in Plantation, a bedroom community in Broward County about thirty miles north of Miami. The Daigles were fine people, and Johnny very much enjoyed getting to know his sister. They lived in a modest-size two-bedroom house on a quiet street, and there was a swimming pool in the back. Johnny would sit by the pool, read, swim. At night they would all go out to dinner or stay in, take turns cooking, sit in the living room and watch television. He felt at home in a way he had never known before. Johnny was on parole. He was getting ready to fight his deportation. He couldn't afford to screw things up. He thought about Los Angeles, the risks and temptations before him there. When the day came to go back he asked Edith if she would mind him returning for another stay sometime. His sister told him she and Joe would love it. He could stay as long as he liked. Johnny told her he would have to see what his parole officer had to say.

13

Early in the morning of June 17, 1972, a gang of burglars was arrested at the Democratic National Committee office inside the Watergate building in Washington, DC. It was soon determined that the burglars were working indirectly for President Richard Nixon on a murky counterintelligence operation in aid of the president's reelection. There was much speculation as to the purpose of the DNC burglary. It was widely believed that the paranoid Nixon had been taking desperate measures to know what oppositional material the Democrats had ready to use on him. The aggressive denials of wrongdoing and criminal cover-up led to two years of uproar and chaos in the American government, culminating in the president's resignation on August 9, 1974, just ahead of impeachment and almost certain removal from office.

Six months before that, the unprecedented scandal and presidential poison known as Watergate had come knocking at Johnny Rosselli's door.

It was suspected by some members of the Senate investigating committee, possibly working from information supplied by former CIA chief Richard Helms, that Nixon's illegal actions had been motivated by his fear that the Democrats could link him to "dirty tricks" against Castro's Cuba—the early Eisenhower-era plans for invasion and assassination. The committee's need to learn more about these shadowy matters led them to Jack Anderson's groundbreaking 1971 columns that gave the first public exposure to stories that were still officially denied by the government. It was inevitable that they would want to talk to Anderson's "dapper patriot."

There was no getting out of it. With deportation hearings being scheduled Johnny could not afford to be seen as uncooperative. The committee interrogators met with him in a closed session, Johnny accompanied by a recommended capital attorney named Leslie Scherr. Considering the stakes on the table—the presidency, governmental crimes, international repercussions—the encounter was relatively bloodless. He responded as truthfully as possible, stuck to the facts that had already been told. The meeting was kept confidential, with no mention in the press.

Watergate had exposed corruption in the command post of American democracy. It would launch an era of doubt and anger, righteous indignation, demands for institutional housecleaning and comeuppance. In 1975 the U.S. Senate began an unprecedented look into covert and unauthorized activities in the intelligence services—the Select Committee to Study Governmental Operations with Respect to Intelligence Activities, chaired by Idaho senator Frank Church. The committee announced a broad range of targets, from the FBI to the then-little-known National Security Agency. By June they had turned their attention to the CIA and what had become its most exposed "secret operation," the one involving Cuba, Fidel Castro, and the Mob. With no qualms about revealing his predecessors' mistakes, agency director Richard Helms told the committee what he knew of the matter, supplying the names of the three mobsters involved: Johnny Rosselli, Sam Giancana, and Santo Trafficante.

Trafficante made himself scarce and avoided a subpoena, supposedly hiding in Central America.

Sam Giancana, the Outfit's Flying Dutchman, was back in Chicago after nearly ten years away. He had moved to a luxury estate in Cuernavaca in the late sixties and maintained his residence there while pursuing a jet-setter existence, sojourns in Paris, Madrid, Rio, a safari in East Africa. He'd backed a drug ring in the Mediterranean, a casino in Guatemala.

The fun came to an end in July 1974 when Mexican police took him into custody and placed him on a plane to San Antonio, Texas. Obviously someone important in Cuernavaca hadn't gotten paid. The FBI was waiting in San Antonio with a warrant and a grand jury subpoena. In Chicago he was questioned by police about the murder of an associate, Richard Cain. The grand jury hearings enforced a "use immunity": Answer or go to jail. He answered the attorneys' questions, doing what he could to avoid making any more trouble for himself. He appeared extremely docile during questioning. He called himself "an old broken-down man." He remained under subpoena until nearly the end of the year.

Giancana spoke of wanting to go away again as soon as possible, but then he had fallen ill. He had to have a gallbladder operation—to be performed by the celebrated Dr. Michael DeBakey in Houston, Texas—and it did not go well. He was bedridden for several weeks, then suffered a blood clot. The doctor had recommended Giancana remain at the hospital so he could keep an eye on him until he recovered, but the Houston police began showing up, standing in his room, questioning him at his bedside. He sneaked out one night in his hospital gown and returned to Chicago. He maintained a low profile back home, and many of his old associates didn't even know he was there. When the federal subpoena arrived from Washington, Giancana had no objection. He was getting used to these courtroom appearances. He had his act down pat. He knew how to say nothing a hundred different ways, until they ran out of questions. Besides, he'd barely been involved in that Cuba thing, he told friends. The G knew everything he knew by now.

On the evening of June 10, 1975, he was at his home in Oak Park. He had gone for a walk with his housekeeper, Joe DiPersio, who lived upstairs with his wife. They walked slowly, Sam still very weak from the operation. Around midnight, by himself, he decided to cook a late snack in the basement kitchen. The housekeeper came down to check on him and say good night. Giancana's body was stretched across the kitchen floor, faceup in a pool of blood. There were seven bullet holes in his head. Smoke swirled over the gas stove, where the small frying pan was burning a mix of spinach, beans, and Italian sausage.

14

Johnny grieved, agonized with rage. Why would they do it? Sam was sick, he couldn't hurt anybody. That motherfucking Batters and his new puppet, Joey Aiuppa. "May their souls burn in hell for a million eternities . . ."

Jimmy tried to calm him down. You couldn't talk like that. Somebody on top ordered the hit. Word was Sam had made millions overseas and refused to share. It would be bad if Johnny said anything about what happened to the wrong person. Jimmy told him he thought certain people didn't like that whole thing with Cuba, the CIA. He and Sam should have gotten permission for a thing like that. Now it was all over the papers. It wasn't good.

Jimmy was very concerned for his friend. He told him once more to be cool. Don't let the wrong people know how you feel.

Johnny went before the Church Committee on June 24. There was considerable tension in the air over Sam Giancana's murder. Many believed it was connected to their investigation. Were they too close to something big? This was uncharted territory for the senators. Gangsters, spies, killers. Even puffed-up politicians wondered if they had gotten in over their heads.

The opening session began at 10:15 a.m. in Room S-407, high in the Capitol Building. Present were Senators Church, Hart of Michigan, Mondale, Huddleston, Morgan, Hart of Colorado,

Tower, Baker, Goldwater, Mathias, and Schweiker. Staff members and chief counsel were also in the room. Johnny was accompanied by three attorneys, Leslie Scherr, Thomas Wadden, and James Cantillon. His handlers had gotten a few prerequisites approved: The witness was to be referred to as a businessman rather than a member of the Syndicate or similar terms; the Cuban agents he might mention would be referred to as Cuban #1, #2, and #3, and so on, and the person known to the committee as Santo Trafficante was to be referred to only as Mr. X. Johnny was sworn in, identified himself, and the show began.

Once again the Ancient Mariner told his tale, the patriotic mission to kill Castro. The senators lapped it up. His appearance, his self-assurance and charisma. He met them head-on, answered their questions without equivocation. If there had been any hostility in the room it seemed to evaporate. The questions were largely sympathetic. The questioners seldom challenged him, though a couple ranged far afield, sometimes cluelessly, one senator asking just out of curiosity if he had any involvement with the Watergate burglars, and another wondering how well he knew Fidel Castro and his brother. One tangent involved a question about Howard Hughes and whether Mr. Rosselli could be sure that the billionaire was not his real employer in the Cuba caper. Some of the committee members seemed to give less thought to their questions than a judge at a rigged beauty contest.

He was asked to return for a second round before the committee on September 22. It was a less happy experience. When they began to move into what he saw as gossip-column stuff, Johnny got his back up.

Senate staffer Andrew Postal asked if he knew the name Judith Campbell. Johnny said he did. Did he introduce her to Sam Giancana? He said he did not. Did he recall spending time with Judith

Campbell or being at a party with her in Los Angeles? Yes, Johnny said, I've taken Judith Campbell out many times. You have gone to her home or her apartment? Yes. In Los Angeles? Los Angeles. That would have been the period of '61? I would not know, Johnny said. I am not going to start guessing at times, about some young lady that does not even belong in this, or who did what to whom, or where. It is a little disgusting to me because I do not really like to talk about these things, Johnny said.

But the lawyer persisted. Did there come a time when Judith Campbell had made the acquaintance of John Kennedy?

I will not answer that question, Johnny said.

Did you ever have occasion to see Judith Campbell in the presence of John Kennedy?

I think I will stop, Johnny said.

A brief recess was taken. Johnny conferred with his attorneys. He was advised to keep calm, make an effort.

Now a Mr. Bushong asked: Was it common knowledge among people who knew Miss Campbell—

JOHNNY: In Hollywood and among the Jet Set it was common knowledge that she was friendly with the President, yes.

BUSHONG: Would you ever—if you were attempting to get in touch with Mr. Giancana and you were unable to get through to him, would you ever leave word with Judith Campbell for him to phone you?

JOHNNY: I do not think so.

BUSHONG: Did you ever give Judy a message for Sam?

JOHNNY: Did I give her a message for Sam?

BUSHONG: Yes?

JOHNNY: I would not give my mother a message for Sam.

A third, and final, trip to Washington was even less productive. The focus was on the Kennedy assassination. The questions related to his extraordinary story of the assassins turned back by Castro to kill the president. So many years later not even Johnny remembered how the story went, and he was likely its author. He told the committee it had been just a guess, a theory he'd had, or he'd heard, and perhaps repeated to somebody, somewhere, once upon a time.

15

Things were working out. The parole board in Los Angeles had approved his move to live with his sister and brother-in-law in Plantation. He was putting all his troubles behind him. The new set of Florida lawyers were doing a good job on his immigration case. With half of Latin America washing up on Miami Beach nowadays, they had plenty of experience in settling these matters, or in tying them up in the system for years to come. He did not expect to be kicked out of the country any time soon.

Plantation was a cute little town. Inland, it was sheltered from the tourist hustle along the coast. The sun shone every day unless it poured rain. It was the tropics, whatever the map said. The air was thick and warm, not much good for his lungs, but then the air in Los Angeles had been no bargain.

He was a permanent houseguest, like the Man Who Came to Dinner. Joe and Edith had done everything to make him feel at home. Out of respect and for his added comfort they had given him the master bedroom and moved to the smaller one down the hall. He had a connecting bathroom and a private entrance to the patio and the swimming pool outside. He hadn't bothered to get a car yet, but his sister let him use her Chevy most days. He seldom went far, only to run some errands or to play golf at the local course. They ate dinner out some nights, sometimes with the Daigles' grown kids who lived in other parts of the state. Sometimes they went down to Miami and ate somewhere fancy. He played golf, swam, read, sat in the sun. One day was pretty much like the one before, or the one to follow. He was leading a quiet life at last, just another law-abiding sucker trying to get along.

The calls to testify in Washington had caused some stress in the household. Despite Johnny's assurances, it sounded like trouble was still stalking him. But then he had gone and come back, and then the second time, and it seemed to be all right. Johnny himself had been a little worried, too. He didn't need to be dragged back into the news, connected to whatever it was they were looking for. But he had given up worrying after he'd gone there. The committee did not have a clue. Even when one of their witnesses was murdered days before he was to give testimony, they did nothing more than fret. They would end up causing some problems for the CIA, and for what remained of the Warren Commission's reputation, but those entities had done most of the work themselves.

He was on parole and did not want any trouble. He had to keep his hands clean, watch who he was seen with, not attract any police attention, which could quickly escalate into FBI attention, and parole office problems. He knew if he went back to prison again he would die there. But he did have to bend the rules a little in regard to an important neighbor, the local don, Santo Trafficante. It was Trafficante's territory Johnny lived in, and it was important to pay his respects, no matter the risks.

They had known each other for years—before and after the CIA caper—and gotten along well but were never close. To Johnny's surprise, in Florida Santo now cultivated his friendship. They got together for lunch or dinner on several occasions. They had long conversations, mostly about the news, world events, though now and then they would talk of more secret matters about which Santo wanted Johnny's opinion. Santo played host not only to Johnny but to his sister and brother-in-law. He took them out for cordial nights on the town, and to the races at Hialeah Park.

Trafficante offered Johnny job opportunities, supervisory positions at one or another of his businesses in the area, easy work and good money. Johnny figured it might be his way of bringing him into the organization for real; it might also have been a way to keep an eye on him. Johnny politely declined. It was too risky, for now anyway.

In the spring of 1976 Johnny returned to the West Coast. He was going for his annual check-up at the Sansum Clinic in Santa Barbara. He had done it most years for the past three decades. He always came away feeling years younger, and at age seventy he needed every year he could get.

While he was at the Sansum, Joe Breen came to visit, accompanied by Paul Picerni and the actor-comedian Dick Wesson. "Joe wanted us to surprise him," Picerni remembered. "And we drove up there and he was very pleased to see us. We went out and played golf. He looked good, getting older, but in good shape. He was enjoying Florida. A little boring, he said, but he was happy. We went out to dinner in Santa Barbara. It was a great night. Dick Wesson—who was a hysterically funny guy—and I had put together a nightclub act, a comedy act, and we were taking it around. We were talking about some of the bits we did, and Dick mentioned that we did a great parody of *The Godfather*, with Brando, which had been out a couple of years by then. When he mentioned it, I shrunk down. I thought, Jeez, don't mention that in front of Johnny, it's probably a sore spot. And then Johnny says, very serious, 'Go on. Let's see it. Let's see your Godfather skit.' He sounded like he was already miffed. So we start acting out the little skit. I played the consigliere, I guess, and Dick played the Godfather, imitating

Marlon, and the Godfather tells me I've betrayed him, I'm going to sleep with the fishes and all this gangster stuff, and then he grabs me to give me the *Bacio della Morte*—the Mafia 'Kiss of Death.' And he kisses me on the lips. And Dick rolls his eyes, and licks his lips and says, '*Hey, that's not bad . . . give me another!*' And we start making out. And I look at Johnny and he's laughing like hell."

He stopped in Los Angeles for a few days on his way back to Florida. He made the rounds of his old haunts, checked in with a few old friends. It was a visit tinged with nostalgia. His head filled with memories of a fifty-year-long relationship with the city. He drove high up into the hills where you could look down at the sprawling metropolis, high enough that he could reimagine the landscape as it had been long ago, before the buildings and the highways and the orange-and-gray cloud that hung over everything like a tattered, dirty blanket.

One night he went to dinner at Trader Vic's restaurant with Jimmy Fratianno and a couple of other old pals. Jimmy had looked anxious all evening, and when they were finally alone on a stroll outside the restaurant he began to explain. There was a rumor going around that Johnny was in trouble, Jimmy said. This was serious, Jimmy insisted. He might be on a hit list. Fratianno had heard it as more than a rumor, but he couldn't make himself say it for fear that his source—another old friend—would be found out and they would all end up getting clipped. Johnny laughed it off. There was always gossip like that, people starting rumors. There was no one needed to get rid of him now. He was old and retired. And Santo Trafficante was keeping an eye on him.

But Johnny had heard things, too. Tony Zerilli had done years in prison on the Frontier charges, and he was not happy. On account of being locked up for so long he had lost his position as the designated new leader of the Detroit Family. He had planned to be the boss of Detroit for the rest of his life, and he had lost his chance. Some were saying Zerilli held Johnny Rosselli responsible for what happened to him. Johnny had brought him in on the Vegas Frontier deal. And Johnny—he believed—had sold him out to the grand jury. Zerilli had pleaded his case for revenge to Chicago. That was something somebody said. It didn't have to be true. People talked shit like that all the time. Some said Trafficante was another unhappy man. He did not like all this publicity. All these Washington hearings. His name in the paper. But Johnny had seen Trafficante up close. He held no grudge. You could see that when you looked at a man up close, couldn't you?

Back in Florida Johnny returned to his new normal life—sunny and humid, slow, dull.

On July 16 Santo invited him to dinner. Johnny and the Daigles and Johnny's visiting nephew joined Trafficante and his wife at the Landings Restaurant in Fort Lauderdale. It was a very pleasant night, Trafficante again an affable and generous host.

On July 28 Johnny had a late breakfast in the kitchen with his sister. Outside, bright and warm, summer clouds in the sky. He sat by the pool reading the newspaper for a while, then came in and got dressed. At about ten minutes to one in the afternoon his sister heard him go out, heard her Chevy Impala go down the drive and away.

Edith thought she had told her brother to be back in the afternoon so she could go to her doctor's appointment. He had still not returned by sundown. Her husband, Joe, was working up at Cape Canaveral. She sat alone in the house all evening, her concern deepening. She was awake for most of the night. In the morning her husband came home, and the couple began phoning any of Johnny's friends they knew, calling around town, the pro shop, calls to Los Angeles, Las Vegas, Washington, hoping someone might have heard from him since he disappeared. The Daigles didn't begin to know the possibilities of Johnny's unusual life, but they thought it was possible he had responded to some emergency and gone away without explanation. Some situation, and he'd had to rush away, take a flight somewhere. Joe Daigle and his son-in-law drove out to the local airport and looked around the parking lot. They drove down to Miami International and did the same thing there. And there it was, Edith's '75 silver Impala. They opened the trunk and saw Johnny's golf clubs.

So maybe it had been an emergency. Gone out to the airport, caught a plane somewhere.

August 7: That morning three young men were fishing in the shallow, muddy waters of Dumfoundling Bay near Sunny Isles Beach in Miami-Dade County. One of the men caught sight of a large steel drum coming up along a sand bar, shifting in the water and the soft sand, bound in heavy chains. Curiosity brought the fisherman closer. The drum was weighted down. Openings gave glimpses of its contents, pink cloth and something bleached and swollen. There was a terrible smell. One of the young men called the police. The responding police officer inspected the barrel in the sandy water and looked close at what was visible of its contents and phoned in a homicide.

Lt. Gary Minium, chief of the Dade homicide squad, took charge of the scene. A marine patrol boat towed the steel drum to shore, and a tow truck lifted it up on land. Lieutenant Minium and the tow truck operators pried open the top of the oil drum and looked inside. A thickly swollen body, a pale and rubbery blob, was inflated against the steel enclosure and giving off a powerful stink of putrefaction. A stained and torn pink sports shirt clung to the bone-white flesh. Stuffed in against the sides of the bloated center portion were two severed legs.

16

It was a fifty-five-gallon oil drum, thirty-six inches high and twenty-two in diameter. Large holes had been punched through the steel to let water flow inside and sink it; chains were wrapped around to weigh it down. It was suspected that changes in the waterway and gases released from the decomposing body were responsible for the oil drum's rising to the surface instead of remaining at the bottom of the bay as intended.

Damage from water and decomposition made postmortem analysis problematic. The hands were so distorted that only one partial fingerprint could be obtained to make a positive identification. Reports from the Dade coroner's office indicated asphyxiation as the probable cause of death. An arm on the windpipe, a hand over the mouth and nose. A washcloth had been balled and stuffed in the mouth and taped over. A deep gouge in the stomach was likely caused by a tow hook piercing and tearing the flesh as it was used to raise the body off the ground and place it inside the drum. The legs were sawn off to enable the whole body to fit inside the three-foot-high container. While the murder and the disposal of the corpse were probably performed by two or more persons, the suggested circumstances made it possible that a single assailant could have done the job.

Initial police investigations turned up no witnesses. No one could be found who recalled seeing the deceased on the day of his disappearance once he had left home, nor had anyone seen any suspicious activity in Plantation or on or near the waterway. No suspect fingerprints were found on the oil drum or on Mrs. Daigle's abandoned Chevrolet, only an unidentifiable greasy smudge mark on one window.

Dade police began an investigation that took Florida detectives across the country looking for clues, questioning figures from the victim's wide spectrum of acquaintances, show-business stars, Mafia bosses, Washington lobbyists and attorneys, private eyes and secret agents. There were theories and suggestions from many corners, and some were pursued, but none led anywhere.

The murder of John Rosselli made headlines throughout the United States, understandable for a figure whose career seemed to inhabit so much of twentieth-century American history and culture, from the birth of organized crime to golden-age Hollywood, the rise of Las Vegas, the era of multinational enterprise, the years of the Kennedys and Cold War intrigue. Even so, the attention drawn by Rosselli's death was infinitely amplified by his unsettling collision with current events and the ongoing governmental attempts to uncover America's dark secrets. Who could believe in a mere intramural Mob killing when the murder victim was a man called to reveal those secrets? In such circumstances, logic or the facts were the least of anyone's concerns. *The Washington Post* editorialized about "monstrous interconnections." Senator Gary Hart of the Church Committee was dispatched to Florida to scrutinize the police investigation for overlooked links. CIA director William Colby went on television to declare that the agency was innocent of the Rosselli and Giancana killings, while members of the Senate Select Committee on Intelligence demanded that the Justice Department use its full power to solve the mystery surrounding the deaths of two federal witnesses. Only the FBI showed no interest in exploring the supposed ramifications of the murders, a matter, said the director, for local jurisdiction alone. Johnny would have been pleased to have the FBI off his back at last.

He was released to his newfound family on August 10. His body was cremated, and a small service was held at the Lithgow Funeral Home in Miami.

Jimmy Fratianno had known it was coming. He tried to warn him. Not hard enough. Cowardice. Self-preservation. He didn't like feeling guilt. It ate you up. Better to eat them. Someday.

There were those saying Johnny had talked too much. Jimmy knew that was bullshit. It was Joe Batters let it happen. If somebody else had made the request, it was still Accardo who'd approved it. With Sam out of the way he had decided to have his revenge. Some slight from a million years ago. Johnny didn't want to know. Maybe he'd just had enough. Johnny knew these people better than anybody. Jimmy's mind wandered through the past, all that had gone wrong, all that might have been. If Johnny had been made boss after Jack Dragna died, Jimmy thought. He would have taken them to the moon. Look what he did in Las Vegas. They'd all have been kings.

It was not long after they found Johnny that Jimmy had to go to Chicago to see Joey Aiuppa about something. He was the new guy, Sam's replacement. Accardo's boy. He was a joke, Jimmy thought. From Al Capone and Frank Nitti and Sam Giancana to this. They settled their business. Jimmy was eager to get out of there, but Aiuppa stopped him. He wanted to ask him something. He wanted to know if Jimmy'd heard about that guy they found down in Florida. What was that guy's name? Johnny Rosselli. Weren't you two friends or something? It wasn't a question. It was a dare. We were friends, Jimmy said. Wasn't that a shame what happened? said Aiuppa. They cut his legs off and stuck him in a barrel. Sank him in the ocean. Hey Jimmy, what do you think about somebody doing a thing like that?

Jimmy said he didn't think nothing. What're you gonna do? he said. It was just one of them fucking things.

ACKNOWLEDGMENTS

I thank the many people who helped me during the research and writing of this book. In some cases these associations go back more than twenty years, when I first began gathering stories of Johnny Rosselli and the Los Angeles underworld, long before I had any idea what to do with them.

Thank you to the following for interviews and conversations: James Bacon, Patricia Breen, John Bright, Sam Butera, William Campbell, Jeanne Carmen, Marge Champion, Lee Dearholt Chase, Betsy Duncan, Dean Elson, former Las Vegas mayor Oscar Goodman, Shecky Greene, Larry Cortez Hamm, Edward Hayes, Brandon James, Arnold Laven, Marc Lawrence, Robert Maheu, Tony Martin, David Nissen, Milton C. Page, Don Rickles, Mark Rodney, Budd Schulberg, Corinne Entratter Sidney, Bob Thomas, Sue Tom, Ed Walters, Les Whitten, Anthony Zerilli, Tony Zoppi; additionally, a small number of persons who agreed to talk with me but preferred to remain off the record and unnamed. A special thanks to Maj. Gary Minium, formerly of the Miami-Dade Police Department, for the interview with which the book begins.

For their aid, assistance, wisdom along the way, thanks to: Jim Gladstone, Jeremy Handel, Arlene Hellerman, L. P. Kane, Dan Peterson SJ, Cindy Putnam, Alan Rode, Dean Server, David Stenn, Lary Wallace, Tom Weaver; and a great many others who have helped me complete this project.

Thanks to these institutions, locations, and online sites: Chicago History Museum; Denver Public Library Western History Department; Larry Edmunds Bookshop, Hollywood; Christina Rice, Senior Librarian, Los Angeles Public Library; Margaret Herrick Library; *Miami Herald*; the National Archives, Laguna-Niguel; the National Archives, New York City; Palm Springs Library, Palm Springs, California; University of California, Los Angeles; University of Nevada, Las Vegas; University of Southern California; Wisconsin Center for Film and Theater Research, Wisconsin University–Madison; Fontainebleau Hotel, Miami Beach; Holiday Inn, Key Largo, Florida; Boston Historical Society, Boston, Mass.; Massachusetts Historical Society, Boston, Mass.; International Spy Museum, Washington, DC; the Mary Ferrell Foundation; Federal Bureau of Investigation; CIA.gov; Caesar's Palace, Las Vegas; El Cortez, Las Vegas; the Biltmore, Los Angeles; Musso and Frank's, Hollywood; La Dolce Vita, Beverly Hills; Gornik and Drucker Barber Shop, Beverly Hills.

My great thanks to Michael Bourret for all his gracious support and advice; to Lauren Abramo, Kieryn Ziegler, and everyone at Dystel, Goderich and Bourret.

To my valued and longtime editor, Elizabeth Beier, much thanks and appreciation for her steady hand, patience, and enthusiasm. To Sally Richardson for her help and encouragement. Thanks also to Jennifer Donovan, Michelle Richter, Susan Llewellyn, and the rest of the crew at St. Martin's Press.

And for everything else, and more, love and gratitude to Terri Hardin.

Lee.Server@aol.com

BIBLIOGRAPHY

BOOKS

Adler, Tim. *Hollywood and the Mob: Movies, Mafia, Sex, and Death.* London: Bloomsbury Books, 2007.

Asbury, Herbert. *The Gangs of Chicago: An Informal History of the Chicago Underworld*, 1940. Reprint, New York: Thunder's Mouth Press, 1986.

Bartlett, Donald, and James B. Steele. *Empire.* New York: W. W. Norton, 1979.

Basquette, Lina. *Lina: DeMille's Godless Girl.* Fairfax, VA: Denlinger's Publishers, 1990.

Berman, Susan. *Easy Street: The True Story of a Mob Family.* New York: Dial Press, 1981.

———. *Lady Las Vegas: The Inside Story Behind America's Neon Oasis.* New York: A&E TV and TV Books, 1996.

Broderick, Michael. *Vegas . . . The Mob and the Dead Pig on the Dance Floor.* Charleston, SC: BookSurge, 2003.

Brown, Peter Harry, and Pat H. Broeske. *Howard Hughes: The Untold Story.* New York: Signet, 1996.

Bugliosi, Vincent. *Reclaiming History.* New York: W. W. Norton, 2007.

Buntin, John. *L.A. Noir: The Struggle for the Soul of America's Most Seductive City.* New York: Three Rivers Press, 2009.

Capeci, Jerry. *The Complete Idiot's Guide to the Mafia.* 2nd ed. New York: Penguin, 2004.

Cirules, Enriques. *The Mafia in Havana: A Caribbean Mob Story.* New York: Ocean Press, 2004.

Cohen, Mickey. As told to John Peer Nugent. *Mickey Cohen: In My Own Words.* Englewood Cliffs, NJ: Prentice-Hall, 1975.

Cohen, Rich. *Tough Jews: Fathers, Sons, and Gangster Dreams.* New York: Simon & Schuster, 1998.

Dark, Tony. *The FBI's Files on Sam Giancana.* HoseHead Productions, 2004.

Davis, John H. *Mafia Kingfish: Carlos Marcello and the Assassination of John F. Kennedy.* New York: Signet, 1989.

Deitche, Scott M. *The Silent Don: The Criminal Underworld of Santo Trafficante Jr.* Fort Lee, NJ: Barricade, 2009.

Demaris, Ovid. *The Last Mafioso: "Jimmy the Weasel" Fratianno.* New York: Bantam, 1981.

Denton, Sally, and Roger Morris. *The Money and the Power: The Making of Las Vegas and Its Hold on America.* New York: Vintage Books, 2001.

Didion, Joan. *Miami.* New York: Vintage Books, 1987.

Doherty, Thomas. *Hollywood's Censor: Joseph I. Breen & the Production Code Administration.* New York: Columbia University Press, 2007.

Drosnin, Michael. *Citizen Hughes.* New York: Bantam, 1985.

Dunn, William. *The Gangs of Los Angeles.* New York: iUniverse, Inc., 2007.

Eghigan, Mars, Jr. *After Capone: The Life and World of Chicago Mob Boss Frank "the Enforcer" Nitti.* Nashville, TN: Cumberland House, 2006.

Eig, Jonathan. *Get Capone: The Secret Plot That Captured America's Most Wanted Gangster.* New York: Simon & Schuster, 2010.

English, T. J. *Havana Nocturne: How the Mob Owned Cuba . . . and Then Lost It to the Revolution.* New York: William Morrow, 2008.

Estrada, William David. With a foreword by Devra Weber. *The Los Angeles Plaza: Sacred and Contested Space.* Austin: University of Texas Press, 2008.

Farrell, Ronald A., and Carole Case. *The Black Book and the Mob: The Untold Story of the Control of Nevada's Casinos.* Madison: University of Wisconsin Press, 1995.

Fetzer, James H. *Murder in Dealey Plaza: What We Know Now That We Didn't Know Then About the Death of JFK.* Chicago: Catfeet Press, 2000.

Fischer, Steve. *When the Mob Ran Vegas: Stories of Money, Mayhem and Murder.* Omaha, NE: Berkline Press, 2005.

Fox, Stephen. *Blood and Power: Organized Crime in Twentieth-Century America*. New York: Penguin, 1989.

Gehman, Richard. *Sinatra and His Rat Pack*. New York: Belmont Books, 1961.

Gentry, Curt. *J. Edgar Hoover: The Man and the Secrets*. New York: W. W. Norton, 1991.

Gertner, Davis. *U.S. Supreme Court Records and Briefs, 1832–1978, John Rosselli, Petitioner, v. Joseph W. Sanford, Warden, United States Penitentiary, Atlanta, Georgia, U.S. Supreme Court Transcript of Record with Supporting Pleadings*. Farmington Hills, MI: Gale MOML Print Editions, 1946.

Giancana, Antoinette, and Thomas C. Renner. *Mafia Princess: Growing Up in Sam Giancana's Family*. New York: William Morrow, 1984.

Giancana, Antoinette, John R. Hughes; D. M. Oxon, M.D., Ph.D.; and Thomas H. Jobe, M.D. *JFK and Sam: The Connection Between the Giancana and Kennedy Assassinations*. Nashville, TN: Cumberland House, 2005.

Giancana, Sam, and Chuck Giancana. *Double Cross: The Explosive Inside Story of the Mobster Who Controlled America*. New York: Warner Books, 1992.

Goldfarb, Ronald. *Perfect Villains, Imperfect Heroes: Robert Kennedy's War Against Organized Crime*. Sterling, VA: Capital Books, 1995.

Gosch, Martin A., and Richard Hammer. *The Last Testament of Lucky Luciano*. Boston: Little, Brown, 1974.

Grieveson, Lee, Esther Sonnet, and Peter Stanfield, eds. *Mob Culture: Hidden History of the American Gangster Film*. New Brunswick, NJ: Rutgers University Press, 2005.

Groden, Robert J., and Harrison Edward Livingstone. *High Treason: The Assassination of President Kennedy and the New Evidence of Conspiracy*. New York: Berkley Books, 1990.

Headley, Lake, with William Hoffman. *Vegas P.I.: The Life and Times of America's Greatest Detective*. New York: Thunder's Mouth Press, 1993.

Hersh, Seymour M. *The Dark Side of Camelot*. New York: Little, Brown, 1997.

Hill, Jeff. *Defining Moments: Prohibition*. Detroit: Omnigraphics, Inc., 2004.

Hiss, Alan. *Viva Las Vegas: After Hours Architecture*. San Francisco: Chronicle Books, 1993.

Holland, Max. *The Kennedy Assassination Tapes*. New York: Knopf, 2004.

Horne, Gerald. *Class Struggle in Hollywood 1930–1950: Moguls, Mobsters, Stars, Reds, & Trade Unions*. Austin: University of Texas Press, 2001.

Jacobs, George, and William Stadiem. *Mr. S: My Life with Frank Sinatra*. New York: HarperEntertainment, 2003.

Jennings, Dean. *We Only Kill Each Other: The Life and Bad Times of Bugsy Siegel*. Englewood Cliffs, NJ: Prentice-Hall, 1967.

Kaplan, James. *Sinatra: The Chairman*. New York: Doubleday, 2015.

Kobler, John. *Capone: The Life and World of Al Capone*. New York: G. P. Putnam's Sons, 1971.

———. *Ardent Spirits: The Rise and Fall of Prohibition*. New York: Da Capo Press, 1973.

Kurtz, Michael L. *The JFK Assassination Debates: Lone Gunman versus Conspiracy*. Lawrence: University of Kansas Press, 2006.

Lacey, Robert. *Little Man: Meyer Lansky and the Gangster Life*. Boston: Little, Brown, 1991.

Lawford, Patricia Seaton, with Ted Schwarz. *The Peter Lawford Story: Life with the Kennedys, Monroe, and the Rat Pack*. New York: Carroll & Graf, 1988.

Lewis, Brad. *Hollywood's Celebrity Gangster: The Incredible Life and Times of Mickey Cohen*. New York: Enigma Books, 2007.

Lifton, David S. *Best Evidence: Disguise and Deception in the Assassination of John F. Kennedy*. New York: Dell, 1980.

Lowinger, Rosa, and Ofelia Fox. *Tropicana Nights: The Life and Times of the Legendary Cuban Nightclub*. Orlando, FL: Harcourt, 2005.

Maheu, Robert, with Robert Hack. *Next to Hughes*. New York: Harper Paperbacks, 1992.

Mailer, Norman. *Oswald's Tale: An American Mystery*. New York: Ballantine Books, 1995.

Mannion, James. *Mafia: Legendary Figures, Infamous Families, Chilling Crimes* (formerly *The Everything Mafia Book*). New York: Fall River Press, 2009.

Marquez, Ernest. *Noir Afloat: Tony Cornero and the Notorious Gambling Ships of Southern California*. Los Angeles: Angel City Press, 2011.

Martin, David. *Wilderness of Mirrors: Intrigue, Deception, and the Secrets That Destroyed Two of the Cold War's Most Important Agents*. Guilford, CT: Lyons Press (Globe Pequot), 1980.

Marx, Samuel, and Joyce Vanderveen. *Deadly Illusions: Jean Harlow and the Murder of Paul Bern*. New York: Random House, 1990.

Matusow, Allen J. *The Unraveling of America: History of Liberalism in the 1960s*. New York: Harper & Row, 1984.

McWilliams, Carey. *Southern California: An Island on the Land.* 1946. Reprint, Salt Lake City, UT: Gibbs Smith, 1973.

Messick, Hank. *The Beauties & the Beasts.* New York: David McKay, 1973.

———. *Lansky.* New York: Berkley Medallion, 1971.

———, with Joseph L. Nellis. *The Private Lives of Public Enemies.* New York: Dell, 1973.

Moldea, Dan E. *Dark Victory: Ronald Reagan, MCA, and the Mob.* New York: Viking, 1986.

———. *The Hoffa Wars: Teamsters, Rebels, Politicians, and the Mob.* New York: Paddington Press, 1978.

Moore, Judith. *A Bad, Bad Boy.* San Diego: Reader Books, 2009.

Morgan, John. *Prince of Crime.* New York: Stein & Day, 1985.

Moruzzi, Peter. *Havana Before Castro: When Cuba Was a Tropical Playground.* Salt Lake City, UT: Gibbs Smith, 2008.

Newton, Michael. *Mr. Mob: The Life and Crimes of Moe Dalitz.* Jefferson, NC: McFarland, 2007.

Nielsen, Mike, and Gene Mailes. *Hollywood's Other Blacklist: Union Struggle in the Studio System.* London: British Film Institute, 1995.

North, Sterling, and Carl Kroch. *So Red the Rose.* New York: Farrar & Rinehart, 1935.

Odessky, Dick. *Fly on the Wall: Recollections of Las Vegas' Good Old, Bad Old Days.* Las Vegas, NV: Huntington Press, 1999.

Olsen, Richard. *Hollywood Noir: Featuring Ronald Reagan.* Bloomington, IN: Xlibris Corporation, 2001.

Pearl, Ralph. *Las Vegas Is My Beat: A Fascinating Insider's Look at the Winners and Losers, Boozers and Lovers in the Fun Capital of the World.* Secaucus, NJ: Citadel Press, 1973.

Pianezzi, Pete. *The Bum Rap Kid.* Virginia City, NV: Silver Dollar Books, 1985.

Picerni, Paul, and Tom Weaver. *Steps to Stardom: My Story.* Albany, GA: BearManor Media, 1985.

Puleo, Stephen. *The Boston Italians.* Boston: Beacon Press, 2007.

Ragano, Frank, and Selwyn Raab. With a foreword by Nicholas Pileggi. *Mob Lawyer: Including the Inside Account of Who Killed Jimmy Hoffa and JFK.* New York: Charles Scribner's Sons, 1994.

Reid, Ed, and Ovid Demaris. *The Green Felt Jungle.* New York: Pocket Books, 1963.

Roemer, William F., Jr. *Accardo: The Genuine Godfather.* New York: Ivy Books, 1995.

———. *Man Against the Mob: The Inside Story of How the FBI Cracked the Chicago Mob by the Agent Who Led the Attack.* New York: Ivy Books, 1989.

———. *War of the Godfathers: The Bloody Confrontation Between the Chicago and New York Families for Control of Las Vegas.* New York: Ivy Books, 1990.

Rosow, Eugene. *Born to Lose: The Gangster Film in America.* New York: Oxford University Press, 1978.

Russo, Gus. *Supermob: How Sidney Korshak and his Criminal Associates Became America's Hidden Power Brokers.* New York: Bloomsbury, 2006.

Ruth, David E. *Inventing the Public Enemy: The Gangster in American Culture 1918–1934.* Chicago: University of Chicago Press, 1996.

Sartorio, Enrico C. With a new foreword by Francesco Cordasco. *Social and Religious Life of Italians in America.* 1918. Reprint, Clifton, NJ: Augustus M. Kelley, Publishers, 1974.

Scheim, David E. *Contract on America: The Mafia Murder of President John F. Kennedy.* New York: Zebra Books, 1988.

Schlesinger, Arthur M., Jr. *Robert Kennedy and His Times.* Boston: Houghton Mifflin, 1978.

Schwartz, Nancy Lynn, completed by Sheila Schwartz. *The Hollywood Writers' Wars.* New York: McGraw-Hill, 1982.

Schwarz, Ted. *Hollywood Confidential: How the Studios Beat the Mob at Their Own Game.* Lanham, MD: Taylor Trade Publishing, 2007.

Scott, Cathy. *Murder of a Mafia Daughter: The Life and Tragic Death of Susan Berman.* Fort Lee, NJ: Barricade Books, 2002.

Scott, Peter Dale. *Deep Politics and the Death of JFK.* Berkeley: University of California Press, 1993.

Silber, Arthur, Jr. *Sammy Davis Jr.: Me and My Shadow (A Biographical Memoir).* Valley Village, CA: Samart Enterprises, 2002.

Sinatra, Nancy. *Frank Sinatra: An American Legend.* Santa Monica, CA: General Publishing Group, 1995.

Sinatra, Tina, with Jeff Coplon. *My Father's Daughter.* New York: Simon & Schuster, 2000.

Smith, John L. *The Animal in Hollywood: Anthony Fiato's Life in the Mafia.* New York: Barricade Books, 1998.

———. *Sharks in the Desert: The Founding Fathers and Current Kings of Las Vegas.* Fort Lee, NJ: Barricade Books, 2005.

Spoto, Donald. *Marilyn Monroe: The Biography.* New York: Harper Paperbacks, 1993.

Stenn, David. *Bombshell: The Life and Death of Jean Harlow.* New York: Doubleday, 1993.

Stevens, Steve, and Craig Lockwood. *King of the Sunset Strip: Hangin' with Mickey Cohen and the Hollywood Mob.* Nashville, TN: Cumberland House, 2006.

Stockton, Bayard. *Flawed Patriot: The Rise and Fall of CIA Legend Bill Harvey.* Washington, DC: Potomac Books, 2006.

Stuart, Mark. *Gangster Number 2.* New York: Lyle Stuart, 1985.

Talese, Gay. *Honor Thy Father.* New York: World Publishing, 1971.

Tereba, Tere. *Mickey Cohen: The Life and Crimes of L.A.'s Notorious Mobster.* Toronto: ECW Press, 2012.

Terrett, Courtney. With a foreword by Morris L. Ernst. *Only Saps Work: A Ballyhoo for Racketeering.* New York: Vanguard Press, 1930.

Thomas, Bob. *King Cohn: The Life and Times of Hollywood Mogul Harry Cohn,* 1967. Rev. ed., Beverly Hills, CA: New Millennium Press, 2000.

Thomas, Evan. *The Very Best Men: Four Who Dared: The Early Years of the CIA.* New York: Touchstone, 1995.

Tronnes, Mike, ed. With an introduction by Nick Tosches. *Literary Las Vegas: The Writing About America's Most Fabulous City.* New York: Henry Holt, 1995.

U.S. Treasury Dept. Bureau of Narcotics. With a foreword by Sam Giancana. *Mafia.* New York: Collins, 2007.

Vanderwood, Paul J. *Satan's Playground: Mobsters and Movie Stars at America's Greatest Gaming Resort.* Durham, NC: Duke University Press, 2010.

Waldron, Lamar. *Watergate: The Hidden History.* Berkeley, CA: Counterpoint, 2012.

———, and Thom Hartmann. *Legacy of Secrecy: The Long Shadow of the JFK Assassination.* Berkeley, CA: Counterpoint, 2008.

———. *Ultimate Sacrifice: John and Robert Kennedy, the Plan for a Coup in Cuba, and the Murder of JFK.* New York: Carroll & Graf, 2005.

Watson, Bruce. *Sacco & Vanzetti: The Men, the Murders, and the Judgment of Mankind.* New York: Penguin, 2007.

Weisberg, Harold. *Case Open: The Omissions, Distortions and Falsifications of Case Closed.* New York: Carroll & Graf, 1994.

Whyte, William Foote. *Street Corner Society: The Social Structure of an Italian Slum.* Chicago: University of Chicago Press, 1943. Reprint, 1955.

Wilkerson, W. R., III. *The Man Who Invented Las Vegas.* Bellingham, WA: Ciro's Books, 2000.

Willis, Clint, ed. *Wise Guys: Stories of Mobsters from Jersey to Vegas.* New York: Thunder's Mouth Press, 2003.

Wolfe, Donald H. *The Black Dahlia Files: The Mob, the Mogul, and the Murder That Transfixed Los Angeles.* New York: Regan Books Harper-Collins, 2005.

Yablonsky, Lewis. *George Raft.* New York: New American Library, 1974.

Young, William, and David E. Kaiser. *Postmortem: New Evidence in the Case of Sacco and Vanzetti.* Amherst: University of Massachusetts Press, 1985.

Zuckerman, Michael J. *Vengeance Is Mine: Jimmy "The Weasel" Fratianno Tells How He Brought the Kiss of Death to the Mafia.* New York: Macmillan, 1987.

PERIODICALS

"4 Arrested for Gun Toting." *Los Angeles Times,* July 30, 1930.

"A Shadow over Camelot." *Newsweek,* Dec. 29, 1975.

"Actress June Lang, John Roselli Elope." *Los Angeles Examiner,* April 2, 1940.

"Actress' Former Husband Linked to Bioff Racket." *Los Angeles Times,* Nov. 10, 1943.

"America Put Under Italian Microscopes." *New York Times,* n.d.

"As Semenenko Seshes, Young Sez He Won't Sell." *Variety,* May 11, 1949.

"Beach Case Reopened." *Los Angeles Times,* Oct. 26, 1937.

"Bioff Murder Hunt Spreads Across Nation." *Los Angeles Times,* Nov. 6, 1955.

"Bryan Foy Dies." *Los Angeles Herald-Examiner,* April 21, 1977.

Schaad, Jacob, Jr. "Producer Foy Takes Dim View of Stars." *Paterson* (NJ) *News,* Jan. 31, 1961.

"Burbank Police Unearth Large Supply of Mash." *Los Angeles Times,* Aug. 27, 1925.

"Face Assault Charge, Cornero Accused of Trying to Kill Policeman." *Los Angeles Times,* June 3, 1924.

"Capone Aide Sought Here." *Los Angeles Times,* March 7, 1929.

"Capone Syndicate Links in Evidence." United Press, Oct. 7, 1950.

"Card Cheats Are Convicted in California." *Albuquerque Journal,* Dec. 3, 1968.

"Clean-Up Begun in Liquor Feuds." *Los Angeles Times,* April 13, 1926.

"Cohen and 21 Others Called to Face Senate Crime Quiz," n.p., n.d.

"Cohen Bombing Tie-Up Denied by Ex-Convict." *Los Angeles Times,* Feb. 18, 1950.

"Cohen-Dragna Gang War Charged by Crime Board." *Los Angeles Times*, Feb. 14, 1950.

"Costly Car of Cornero in Balance." *Los Angeles Times*, Jan. 23, 1927.

"Court Denies Rosselli Habeas Corpus Writ." *Los Angeles Times*, Sept. 8, 1948.

"Crime Report Showdown Demanded by Supervisors . . . Dragna Disappears." *Los Angeles Times*, Feb. 15, 1950.

"Crooks Warned to Leave City." *Los Angeles Times*, Aug. 6, 1925.

"Crooks Warned to Leave City." *Los Angeles Times*. Aug. 8, 1925.

"Deep Six." *Time*, Aug. 23, 1976.

"Dragna Found, Subpoenaed to Federal Crime Inquiry." *Los Angeles Times*, Sept. 29, 1950.

"Dragna Henchmen Rounded Up in Wake of Crime Expose." *Los Angeles Times*, Feb. 15, 1950.

"Dreadnoughts Best Means of Protecting Emigrants." *New York Times*, Jan. 12, 1913.

"Eagle Lion Film Corp. President Quits Post." *Los Angeles Times*, May 5, 1949.

"Eagle-Lion Resuming Prod'n." *Variety*, July 28, 1950.

"Eagle-Lion to Show a Profit for First Time in Its History." *Variety*, May 1, 1950.

"E-L Stays Clear of Prod. Though Renting to Indies." *Variety*, n.d. 1950.

"Ex-Felon Hunted in Gang Killing." *Los Angeles Times*, n.d. 1937.

"Exonerate Fox in Gang Deaths." *Los Angeles Times*, Aug. 7, 1926.

"Film Case Again Delayed." *New York Times*, Dec. 14, 1943.

"Film Man Rosselli Leaves Jail Again." *Los Angeles Times*, Nov. 16, 1948.

"Film Workers Beaten by Mob," n.p., n.d.

"Five in Film Extortion Case Paroled." *Los Angeles Times*, Aug. 14, 1947.

"Four Arrested for Gun Toting." *Los Angeles Times*, July 30, 1930.

"Four of Dragna Group Released After Roundup." *Los Angeles Times*, Feb. 16, 1950.

"Friars Figure Given 6-Month Prison Term." *Los Angeles Times*, Feb. 5, 1969.

"Friars Mystified over FBI Raid." *Variety*, July 25, 1967.

"Fun and Games." *Newsweek*, Sept. 18, 1967.

"Gangsters Invade Southland Cities." *Los Angeles Times*, May 11, 1953.

"Gifts Flaunted by June Lang, Says Morgan." *Los Angeles Examiner*, April 23, 1954.

"Girl, 5, Called Unmoved by Brassiere Modeling." Publication unknown, July 22, 1954. June Lang file, Margaret Herrick Library.

"Gunman Cool in Dual Killing." *Los Angeles Times*, Aug. 5, 1926.

"Harry Cohn Testifies Roselli Is a Good Friend." *Los Angeles Times*, Nov. 11, 1943.

"Hearst Lauds Film Folk and Hollywood Here While Unspeakably Reviling Them in East." *Los Angeles Times*, Feb. 26, 1922.

"Hesketh Death Goes Unsolved." *Los Angeles Times*, April, 7, 1926.

"High Gaming Chiefs Called in Inquiry." *Los Angeles Times*, Aug. 7, 1937.

"Hughes Linked to CIA." *Los Angeles Free Press*, n.d.

"Hundred Held by Night Court, Wholesale Arrests Made." *Los Angeles Times*, n.d. 1926.

"In '49 It's Eagle-Lion." Company promotional material, 1949.

"Inquiry into Roselli Slaying Requested of Justice Dept." *Los Angeles Times*, Aug. 11, 1976.

"Interim Report: Alleged Assassination Plots Involving Foreign Leaders." Church Committee, 1975.

"JFK and the Mobsters' Moll." *Time*, Dec. 29, 1975.

Davies, Reine. "Hollywood Parade." *Los Angeles Examiner*, June 1, 1937.

"John Rosselli Parole Hearing Set for Aug. 16." *Los Angeles Times*, Aug. 3, 1948.

"Journalistic Hypocrisy for Revenue Only," n.p., n.d.

"July Wither Love of June." *Detroit News*, July 15, 1937.

"June Lang and Spouse Divorce Contest Starts," n.p., n.d.

"June Lang Reported Wed." *Los Angeles Times*, April 2, 1940.

"June Lang Wedded to Vic Orsatti." *Los Angeles Examiner*, May 30, 1937.

"June Lang's Story Wins Cash, Decree." *Los Angeles Mirror*, April 23, 1954.

"Jury Indicts in Liquor-Running." *Los Angeles Times*, Dec. 23, 1926.

"Liquor Plot Suspects Hide." *Los Angeles Times*, Dec. 3, 1926.

"Looking at Hollywood." *Chicago Tribune*, Jan. 12, 1942.

"Los Angeles Bans Gangster." *Ogden Standard-Examiner*, Dec. 14, 1927.

"MacMillan Ends Doctor Chore at E-L Today." *Variety*, Sept. 15, 1949.

"Metropolitan." *Los Angeles Times*, Sept. 25, 1968.

"Mobster Roselli's Body Found in Bay at Miami." *Los Angeles Times*, Aug. 9, 1976.

"More Accused in Liquor Plot." *Los Angeles Times*, June 18, 1927.

"Mother-in-Law Angle Plea as Vic Orsatti Divorces June Lang." *Los Angeles Herald*, Aug. 5, 1937.

"Movie Trial Seen Opening New Drive." *New York Times*, Dec. 22, 1943.

"Mr. Capone Groans a Moan." *Los Angeles Times*, Dec. 17, 1927.

"New Rum Plot Angles Found." *Los Angeles Times*, June 19, 1927.

"Plummer Heads Dry Drive." *Los Angeles Times*, Aug. 12, 1926.

"Puzzling Angles in Mafia." *San Francisco Chronicle*, Feb. 14, 1976.

"Raid Gambling Boats; Police Seize Seven Off Long Beach, Cal." *New York Times*, Dec. 28, 1930.

"Raiders Seize Rum, Nab 4." *Los Angeles Times*, March 12, 1925.

"Remands Ordered for Capone Aides." *New York Times*, July 24, 1948.

"Rioting Marks Film Strike." *Los Angeles Times*, Oct. 2, 1946.

"Roselli Loses Fight on Parole; to Appeal." *Los Angeles Examiner*, Sept. 8, 1948.

"Roselli Move Again Delayed." *Los Angeles Examiner*, Sept. 26, 1948.

"Rosselli Holds Flashy Police History Here." *Los Angeles Times*, March 20, 1943.

"Rosselli Lawyers Hit Parole Violation Case." *Los Angeles Times*, Sept. 26, 1948.

"Rosselli Loses Fight on Parole; to Appeal." *Los Angeles Examiner*, Sept. 8, 1948.

"Rosselli Move Again Delayed." *Los Angeles Examiner*, Aug. 26, 1948.

"Rosselli Must Stay Here Pending Parole Decision." *Los Angeles Times*, Sept. 9, 1948.

"Rosselli Plea Put Forward to Next Week." *Los Angeles Times*, Aug. 17, 1948.

"Rosselli, Film Extortion Figure Again in Custody." *Los Angeles Times*, July 28, 1948.

"Rosselli, of Bioff Fame Faces Return Trip to Prison." *Los Angeles Daily News*, Sept. 8, 1948.

"Rumor Hounds Are Deadly to Cupid . . . Real Lovers Fear to be Seen Together." *Denver Post*, April 25, 1937.

"Scarface Al in City? Police Can't Find Him." *Los Angeles Times*, April 17, 1930.

"'Scarface Al'—Came to Play, Now Look—He's Gone Away!" *Los Angeles Times*, Dec. 14, 1927.

"Sea Gaming Plan Fought." *Los Angeles Times*, May 2, 1938.

"Search Is Pressed for Capone Aides." *New York Times*, March 21, 1943.

"Seven Held in War on Crime." *Los Angeles Times*, Aug. 9, 1925.

"Seven Taken in Hi-Jack Expose." *Los Angeles Times*, Feb. 21, 1926.

"Sica Dope Ring Case Suspect Stabbed." *Los Angeles Times*, Mar. 26, 1950.

"Six Indicted in Huge Rum Plot." *Los Angeles Times*, June 17, 1927.

"Slaying Lead Told." *Los Angeles Times*, April 10, 1977.

"Suspect Pair Surrender in Hesketh Death Case." *Los Angeles Times*, April 4, 1926.

"Talks to Determine Eagle-Lion's Future." *Citizen News*, May 6, 1949.

"The Girl with the First Modernistic Figure." New York *Daily News*, July 30, 1936.

"The Nation." *Los Angeles Times*, Aug. 10, 1976.

"The Nation." *Los Angeles Times*, June 26, 1977.

"There's Always Fun at the Friars," n.d., n.p.

"Trials Set for Four Held in Police Net." *Los Angeles Times*, May 6, 1926.

"Two More Called in Crime Inquiry." *Los Angeles Times*, Sept. 30, 1950.

"Union Extortion Leader Kills Self." AP, March 19, 1943.

"US Investigating Reports of Crooked Friars Club Games." *Los Angeles Times*, July 25, 1967.

"US Rests Its Case After Two Months of Friars Club Trial." *Los Angeles Times*, Aug. 14, 1968.

"Warren Says State Needs Strict Slot Machine Law." *Los Angeles Times*, Feb. 15, 1950.

"Who Killed Estelle Carey?" *Harper's*, June 1940.

Abrams, Malcolm. "JFK Murder Hatched in Ruby's Club—Oswald Was There," n.d.

Abramson, Rudy. "Grotesqueries Mar Inquiry on Kennedy." *Los Angeles Times*, Sept. 29, 1978.

An, Perry G. "Helping the Poor Emerge from Urban Barbarism to Civic Civilization." *Journal of Biology and Medicine* 77, 2004.

Anastasia, George. "Did the Mafia Really Manage JFK's Assassination?" *Baltimore Sun*, May 30, 1999.

Anderson, Jack. "Castro Stalker Worked for the CIA." *Washington Post*, Feb. 23, 1972.

———. "John Roselli Execution Was Grisly Torture." *Albuquerque Journal*, Aug. 29, 1976.

———. "Mob May Have Hired JFK's Assassin," n.p., n.d.

Anderson, Jack, and Les Whitten. "Smudge Only Clue in Rosselli Case." *Washington Post*, Aug. 27, 1976.

Bacon, James. "Some Sexy Muscle-Gals." *Los Angeles Mirror-News*, Aug. 1, 1957.

Bardach, Ann Louise. "The Spy Who Loved Castro." *Vanity Fair*, Nov. 1993.

Belcher, Jerry, and Bill Hazlett. "Mafia Chief Bompensiero Slain in San Diego Alley." *Los Angeles Times*, Feb. 11, 1977.

———. "San Diego Mafia Chief, a Reputed Informer, Slain." *Los Angeles Times*, Feb. 12, 1977.

Blake, Gene. "Figure in Friars Case Asks Cut in Term as 'Hero.'" *Los Angeles Times*, July 7, 1971.

———. "Friars Club Card Cheating Trial Nearing Climax." *Los Angeles Times*, Oct 29, 1968.

———. "Friars Club Defendants Lose Acquittal, Evidence Rulings." *Los Angeles Times*, Aug. 21, 1968.

———. "Friars Club Figure Testifies in Secret." *Los Angeles Times*, May 2, 1970.

———. "Friedman Claims US Offered Him Deal." *Los Angeles Times*, Sept. 12, 1968.

———. "Prison Death Threat to US Witness Told." *Los Angeles Times*, July 10, 1971.

———. "Rosselli Receives Immunity in Quiz." *Los Angeles Times*, May 2, 1970.

———. "Trial Told of Peepholes at Beverly Hills Hotel." *Los Angeles Times*, July 2, 1968.

———. "US Hints It Has Evidence to Explode Card Trial Defense." *Los Angeles Times*, Sept. 14, 1968.

———. "Witness Describes Peepholes Rigged at Beverly Hills Hotel." *Los Angeles Times*, July 2, 1968.

———. "Witness Ordered to Testify on Skimming." *Los Angeles Times*, May 15, 1970.

Blake, Gene, and Howard Hertel. "Attorney Again Balks in Quiz on Friars Trial." *Los Angeles Times*, Feb. 7, 1969.

———. "Attorney Indicted over Friars Club Stolen Transcripts." *Los Angeles Times*, June 27, 1970.

———. "Defendant in Friars Club Trial Will Admit Cheating at Games." *Los Angeles Times*, Aug. 22, 1968.

———. "One Sentence in Friars Club Case Reduced." *Los Angeles Times*, June 22, 1971.

———. "$10,000 Bill Slipped My Mind, Karl Testifies." *Los Angeles Times*, July 4, 1968.

Brandenburg, B. "How to Keep Out Undesirable Immigrants." *Los Angeles Times*, July 3, 1904.

Buchanan, Edna. "FBI May Enter Roselli Murder." *Miami Herald*, Aug. 9, 1976.

———. "Roselli: From '20s Rum-Runner to Trying to Kill Fidel Castro." *Miami Herald*, Aug. 9, 1976.

Burnstein, Scott. "Failing to take over the failed Riviera, Detroit Mob went after Frontier and Aladdin instead in Las Vegas' Heyday." Gangster-report.com.

Cohen, Jerry. "Grand Jury Calls 2 Mafia Chieftains." *Los Angeles Times*, July 4, 1970.

Craig, John. "Foreshadows of JFK's Death." *Back Channels*, Fall 1992.

Crichton, Kyle. "King of the B's." *Colliers*, Jan. 7, 1939.

DiEugenio, Jim. "The Posthumous Assassination of John F. Kennedy." *Probe*, Sept.–Oct. 1997.

Eng, Frank. "Eagle-Lion's Ambitious Program." *Los Angeles Daily News*, March 13, 1947.

Foy, Bryan. "Putting the Picture on Film." Screen Producers Guild. Circa 1951.

Gage, Nicholas. "Rosselli Called a Victim of Mafia Because of His Senate Testimony." *New York Times*, n.d.

Goodman, Michael J. "Spilotro Seizes 'Mickey Mouse Mafia.'" *Los Angeles Times*, Feb. 25, 1983.

Hager, Steven. "Kerry Wendell Thornley." *Tin Whistle*, Feb. 19, 2017.

Hertel, Howard. "At Rosselli Inquiry." *Los Angeles Times*, Sept. 19, 1967.

———. "US Grand Jury Begins Probe of Roselli's Past." *Los Angeles Times*, Sept 8, 1967.

Hertel, Howard, and Gene Blake. "Friedman Admits He Rigged Friars Club's Peekhole." *Los Angeles Times*, Aug. 24, 1968.

———. "Friedman Tells of Friars Club Winnings, Splits." *Los Angeles Times*, Aug. 28, 1968.

———. "US Jury Here Sees 2 Chicago Leaders of Mafia." *Los Angeles Times*, n.d. 1970.

Hertel, Howard, and Dial Torgerson. "Friars Witness Balks on Name, Told to Talk." *Los Angeles Times*, Aug. 26, 1967.

———. "Phil Silvers Tells Jury of Heavy Losses at Friars Club." *Los Angeles Times*, n.d.

———. "US Investigating Reports of Crooked Friars Club Games." July 25, 1967.

Hunter, David. "June Lang." *ClassicImages*, March 2009.

Jackson, Robert L. "Killing Leads Cia Probe to Offer to Guard Witnesses." *Los Angeles Times*, June 24, 1975.

Jerauld, James M. "Eagle Lion Gets a Colorful Associate." *Box Office*, Nov. 20, 1948.

Kobler, John. "The Million Dollar Sting at the Friars Club." *New York*, July 21, 1975.

LaBrecque, Ron. "Can't Probe Roselli Case, FBI Says." *Miami Herald*, Aug. 12, 1976.

———. "Cuban Threat to Roselli Doubted." *Miami Herald*, n.d., 1976.

———. "Roselli Suspected Cuban Agents in JFK Death," *Miami Herald*, Aug. 23, 1976.

———. "Roselli's Life of Crime Began with Fire at 16." *Miami Herald*, n.d., 1976.

Lang, June. "June Lang Describes Exercises That Won Her Acclaim as American Venus." *Seattle Post-Intelligencer*, Aug. 10, 1936.

Mazroff, David. "Who Killed Johnny Roselli?" *Mike Shayne Mystery Magazine*, n.d.

Mead, Edwin. "Boston Memories of Fifty Years," n.p., n.d.

Michaels, Pat. "What's Happening Around Town." *Coasters Magazine*, May 23, 1994.

Nathan, Albert F. "Death, Sudden and Mysterious." *Los Angeles Times*, Aug. 15, 1926.

———. "How Whisky Smugglers Buy and Land Cargoes." *Los Angeles Times*, Aug. 8, 1926.

———. "Rousting System Earns Curses of Rum Runners." *Los Angeles Times*, Aug. 22, 1926.

Nelson, Bryce. "Authorities Ponder Possible Link Between Mobster Slayings, Plot to Kill Castro." *Los Angeles Times*, Aug. 9, 1976.

Oberdorfer, Don. "JFK Had Affair with D.C. Artist, Smoked Grass Paper Alleges." *Washington Post*, Feb. 23, 1976.

Parsons, Louella. "June Lang Secret Bride of Army Officer." Hearst Syndicate, Jan 17, 1944.

———. "Snapshots of Hollywood." Hearst Syndicate, Feb. 10, 1943.

Rasmussen, Cecilia. "Rampart Site Was Noir Landmark." *Los Angeles Times*, Sept. 26, 1999.

Reich, Ken. "FRIARS Oust 14 Members in Gambling Inquiry by Club." *Los Angeles Times*, n.d.

Robarge, David. "DCI John McCone and the Assassination of John F. Kennedy." *Studies in Intelligence*, Sept. 2013.

Roberts, Bruce. "The Gemstone Files." *Hustler*, Feb. 1979.

Scott, John L. "Betsy Duncan and Dick Contino." *Los Angeles Times*, n.d.

Scott, Peter Dale. "Case Closed or Oswald Framed?" *Prevailing Winds*, Premiere Issue, 1995.

Smith, Bryan. "How the CIA Enlisted the Chicago Mob to Put a Hit on Castro." *Chicago Magazine*, Nov. 2007.

Torgerson, Dial. "Members of Friars Club Called in Grand Jury Gambling Probe." *Los Angeles Times*, July 24, 1967.

Weiler, A. H. "By Way of Report." *New York Times*, Feb. 2, 1948.

West, Richard. "Hit Man Describes Session at La Costa." *Los Angeles Times*, Feb. 23, 1982.

Whyte, W. "A Slum Sex Code." *American Journal of Sociology*, July 1943.

Wilson, Earl. "Gal has new gimmick!" n.p., n.d.

DOCUMENTS, TRANSCRIPTS, ETC.

More than two thousand previously classified documents from the files of the U.S. Government, Justice Department, Federal Bureau of Investigation, Immigration and Naturalization Service, and Central Intelligence Agency, including correspondence, interoffice memos, agent reports, "fisur" (physical surveillance) transcripts.

Transcript: U.S. v Louis Campagna et al., 1943.

Transcript: Senate Special Committee to Investigate Organized Crime in Interstate Commerce, 1950.

Transcript: Hearings before the Select Committee on Improper Activities in the Labor or Management Field, 1959.

Report of the President's Commission on the Assassination of President John F. Kennedy. Washington, DC: U.S. Government Printing Office, 1964.

Transcript: U.S. v Filippo Sacco, aka John Rosselli.

U.S. v Sacco Probation Report.

Transcript: U.S. v Maurice Friedman et al. (Friars Case), 1968.

Transcript: Senate Select Committee to Study Governmental Operations with Respect to Intelligence Actvities, 1975–76.

INTERVIEWS

James Bacon, Patricia Breen, John Bright, Sam Butera, William Campbell, Jeanne Carmen, Marge Champion, Betsy Duncan, Dean Elson, Oscar Goodman, Shecky Greene, Edward Hayes, Brandon James, Arnold Laven, Marc Lawrence, Robert Maheu, Tony Martin, Gary Minium, David Nissen, Milton C. Page, Don Rickles, Budd Schulberg, Corinne Entratter Sidney, Keely Smith, Bob Thomas, Sue Tom, Carmine Tortora, Ed Walters, Les Whitten, Anthony Zerilli, and Tony Zoppi.

INDEX